D1011180

To
Gettysburg
and Beyond

TO GETTYSBURG AND BEYOND

THE PARALLEL LIVES

OF JOSHUA LAWRENCE CHAMBERLAIN

AND

EDWARD PORTER ALEXANDER

MICHAEL GOLAY

CROWN PUBLISHERS, INC.

NEW YORK

For Julie and the girls

Published by Crown Publishers, Inc., 201 East 50th Street, New York, New York 10022. Member of the Crown Publishing Group.

Random House, Inc. New York, Toronto, London, Sydney, Auckland

CROWN is a trademark of Crown Publishers, Inc.

Manufactured in the United States of America

Design by Lenny Henderson

Library of Congress Cataloging-in-Publication Data
Golay, Michael.
    To Gettysburg and beyond / by Michael Golay. —1st ed.
      p.   cm.
    Includes bibliographical references and index.
    1. United States—History—Civil War, 1861–1865—Biography. 2. Chamberlain, Joshua Lawrence, 1828–1914. 3. Alexander, Edward Porter, 1835–1910. 4. Soldiers—United States—Biography. 5. Gettysburg (Pa.), Battle of 1863. I. Title.
E467.G65 1994
973.7'3'092—dc20
[B]   94–20499
                                                                                       CIP

ISBN 0-517-59285-1

10 9 8 7 6 5 4 3 2 1

First Edition

Contents

PART III: CATACLYSM

PART IV: TOUCHED WITH FIRE

PREFACE

THIS IS A STORY OF TWO MEN, TWO societies, war, conquest, and a flawed reconciliation. Joshua Lawrence Chamberlain came out of an austere northern world of granite and ice. Edward Porter Alexander's people were southern slaveowning squires favored with wealth and ease. For three years the two men fought on opposite sides of the great battlefields of the American Civil War: Antietam and Fredericksburg, Gettysburg, Spotsylvania and Cold Harbor, Petersburg and Appomattox. Yet had they actually met, in the clammy aftermath of battle or at any postwar moment in their long lives, they might have found as much to bond as to divide them.

Chamberlain (1828–1914) prepared for the Congregational ministry, taught rhetoric and languages at Bowdoin College, and, approaching his middle years, overrode the objections of his wife, family, and colleagues to go off to war. He invoked the abstractions of duty, honor, and Union, but restlessness and a pent-up longing for action compelled him equally. When war came, Chamberlain could not resist its lure.

Alexander (1835–1910) trained as a soldier. He graduated from West Point, crossed the Great Plains with the Utah Expedition, and served in a frontier garrison in the Pacific Northwest. Like Chamberlain, he required a suitable idea to cover his truer motive, the desire for action and adventure; he ventured states' sovereignty as justification for rebellion and war, though never with much conviction. As for his Confederate allegiance, Alexander had a straightforward explanation. "We didn't go into our cause," he said; "we were born into it."

Viewed from a distance, there was a chilly remoteness about Chamberlain. "He always reminded me of a mathematics professor we had in college," one veteran wrote. A brooder, self-doubting, he habitually fell short of his own lofty expectations. Yet he proved to be a gifted amateur of war, one of the Army of the Potomac's finest combat commanders. He possessed unmatched leadership qualities and an instinctive grasp of tactics. In the chaos of battle, a former commanding officer said of him, "His mind worked as deliberately and quietly as it would in his own study." Contemporaries were struck by his absolute indifference to danger.

Confident, cheerful, boundlessly curious, Alexander was a brave and skillful professional, a master of the military art. Quick intelligence, excellent eyesight, a feel for terrain, and familiarity with the technical aspects of soldiering made him an outstanding staff officer. He had no peer in the Army of Northern Virginia as a frontline artillery commander. "He was sure of winning in everything he took up," a wartime colleague recalled, "and never did he open his guns on the enemy but that he knew he should maul him into smithereens." Alexander had an eccentric side too. He once sat for a formal photograph wearing a most irregular broad-striped shirt, a sort of jailbird's garment. His battlefield forays in search of spent lead were legendary. He cut up what he scavenged into buckshot and kept his mess table in game through the hungriest days of the Confederacy.

Chamberlain and Alexander were middle-rank commanders, an underrepresented group in Civil War literature. Chamberlain never formally commanded anything larger than a brigade in battle. Alexander rated his artillery battalion the rough equivalent of an infantry division, and he assumed larger responsibilities later in the war as Longstreet's chief of artillery. But both men exerted influence far beyond their nominal rank. Lee and Longstreet relied heavily on Alexander's technical expertise. During the Appomattox campaign, Chamberlain's superiors turned to him time and again in moments of crisis.

Both men performed superbly in the epic landscape of the Civil War, directly affecting the outcome of several battles: Chamberlain on Little Round Top at Gettysburg, Alexander at First Manassas, Fredericksburg, and Chancellorsville. Each found a fierce fulfillment in the swirl of combat. "If *I* had to make Pickett's Charge all by myself," Alexander wrote one of his sisters, "that would have been rough! But all together! With all my comrades! Why, it was only fun!" Chamberlain used more formal language to make essentially the same point. "There are pressure-points of experience at which the insupportably disagreeable becomes 'a jolly good time,' " he wrote.

War crowded the experiences of a lifetime into a few years of these parallel lives. Chamberlain was thirty-six at the time of Appomattox, Alexander a few weeks short of thirty. Though they lived a decade and more into our own century, the events of 1861–65 marked them indelibly. Each man knew a measure of postwar success, but neither ever discovered an adequate substitute for war, or for the sense of high purpose soldiering had given him. For each, his true vocation was war.

Battle held a deep, almost hypnotic fascination for Chamberlain and Alexander; they responded powerfully to its aesthetic. This is easier to accept than to explain. William Manchester has remarked Winston Churchill's ability to romanticize squalor. But there is something more. "It's true, it's a funny sort of spectacle to see people killing each other," Leo Tolstoy wrote home from the Crimea in 1854, "and yet every morning and evening I would get up onto my cart and spend hours at a time watching, and I wasn't the only one. The spectacle was truly beautiful, especially at night." Something in the spectacle seized Chamberlain and Alexander and never let go.

They found large postwar audiences for their retellings of wartime experience. Chamberlain lectured widely, and published colorful recol-lections of Fredericksburg and Gettysburg. His memoir of the Appomattox campaign, *The Passing of the Armies*, appeared the year after his death. Alexander, a calmer and more professional writer, produced accounts of practically every major campaign of the Virginia theater. His *Military Memoirs of a Confederate: A Narrative* (1907) is considered a classic of the genre.

For all their compulsive reworkings, neither man showed much social or political vision, or any real understanding of the war's essential meaning. The South won on the great question—"Who is the best man?"—but "lost the minor point" of separate government, Alexander wrote an army comrade in 1866. He may have been half joking—but only half. Chamberlain attempted a more thoughtful summing-up. He considered the war an inherited curse for the sin of slavery. "We had purged it away, with blood-offerings," he wrote. This was mere fancy. Blood had flowed, rivers of blood, but there had been no purge. The old sickness remained: racial bigotry, hatred, and mistrust. For one brief moment during Reconstruction it looked as though the building of an

interracial democracy could bring a true close to America's decades-long
civil war. But that light dimmed, then went out.

Here they are, Chamberlain and Alexander, men with something
approaching a genius for fighting and the later remembering of it; men
who never quite understood that the end of their war had not meant
the beginning of peace.

ACKNOWLEDGMENTS

ONTEMPORARY DIARIES, LETTERS, AND documents give life to such a book as this one. They are the essential stuff of biographical narrative. For Chamberlain material, I would like to thank archivists and staff at Bowdoin College, Brunswick, Maine; the Pejepscot Historical Society, Brunswick, the First Parish Church, Brunswick; the Maine Historical Society, Portland; the Brewer Public Library, Brewer, Maine: the University of Maine, Orono; the Maine State Archives, Augusta; the Schlesinger Library, Radcliffe College, Cambridge, Massachusetts, the Sterling Library, Yale University, New Haven, Connecticut; the Library of Congress; and the National Archives. For Alexander material, thanks are due the Southern Historical Collection, University of North Carolina at Chapel Hill; the Washington Library, Washington, Georgia; and the Library of Congress.

I would like to thank, too, the staffs of the Honnold Library, the Claremont colleges, Claremont, California; the Huntington Library, San Marino, California; the Wallace Library, Wheaton College, Norton, Massachusetts; and the Rockefeller and Hay libraries, Brown University, Providence, Rhode Island.

Part I

ALLEGIANCES

Say, is my kingdom lost?

—SHAKESPEARE, *RICHARD II*

CHAPTER 1

BEGINNINGS

———➤●◄———

CHAMBERLAIN
THE FOREST'S EDGE, 1828–48

WORK HAD FIRST CLAIM ON THE Chamberlain boy. Subsistence farming in 1830s Maine was like an indenture, and from the age of seven or eight he labored alongside his father on the family's hundred-acre homestead, helping to sow corn and wheat in the Penobscot bottomlands and cutting fodder for the livestock in the meadows upon the bluff. Mowing there was hard, hot work. The elder Chamberlain swung the scythe in wide arcs. The boy followed a few paces behind, dragging a heavy wooden rake, as long as he was tall, through the damp grass hour after hour until the sun dropped down behind Bangor's dark spires.

Joshua Lawrence Chamberlain was born in a one-story cottage near Brewer, Maine, on September 28, 1828, the first of five children of Joshua Chamberlain, Jr., and Sarah Brastow. Chamberlains migrating north from Massachusetts had settled in these frontier reaches of the Penobscot Valley in 1799. In the three decades since, the region's chief town, Bangor, had become a crowded, noisy, cosmopolitan port. Across the river, in the companion town of Brewer, shipyards, ropewalks, and a big, dusty brickworks operated at full speed. But this was raw country still, on the edge of a great wilderness. To the north, just over the horizon, the pine forest stretched on endlessly, harsh, empty, virgin land.

The Chamberlains, claiming ancient origins, celebrated as their founder one William, Count of Tankerville, said to have accompanied William the Conqueror to England. John de Tankerville, son of William, became lord chamberlain to King Henry I and took the occupational title as his English surname. The line continued unbroken down to William Chamberlain, born around 1620. He sailed for the New World sometime in the 1640s, settling first in Woburn, then in neighboring Billerica, Massachusetts. His existence there passed largely unrecorded, with two exceptions. William Chamberlain's name appeared on a petition to extend the town boundaries in 1654, and Billerica's Puritans accused his wife, Rebecca, of witchcraft in 1692. She died in a Cambridge jail in September of that year, the victim, evidently, of a casual association with a crone known as Auntie Toothaker, a harmless witch, but persecuted all the same during the great hysteria. William Chamberlain lived on until 1706, bequeathing an English coat of arms and a Latin motto, *Virtuti nihil invium:* Nothing is impenetrable to virtue.

In direct descent, Jacob followed William; another William followed Jacob; Ebenezer followed the second William. Like the founder of the family in the New World, they all lived the hard, anonymous life of the smallholder. Ebenezer established the Chamberlain tradition of soldiering. He served in the Indian and colonial wars and in the Revolution; two of his sons were veterans of the war for American independence. Ebenezer's sixth son, Joshua, born in 1770, carried the Chamberlain name into Maine.[1]

"Everybody was a farmer," Alice Farrington, a Chamberlain descendant, wrote of pioneer days along the Penobscot, "and everybody was a shipbuilder." An artisan of modest means, Joshua Chamberlain established a shipyard at Orrington and prospered there in the early years of the nineteenth century. He became a soldier like his father, and had charge of the militia garrison at Eastport when war with England broke out in 1812. He joined the Orrington Committee of Safety in May 1814, and commanded militia troops when British forces began their advance up the Penobscot four months later.[2]

The British squadron, carrying 2,500 soldiers and marines, seized money, goods, arms, and ammunition, and burned ships and shipyards. Some five hundred Maine militia ventured a counterattack at Hampden September 3, but broke and fled when the invaders returned a disciplined and accurate fire. Crossing the river to Orrington, Crown forces took up a related business they knew well. Stacking their arms, working methodically, they wrecked the village. In an afternoon of coolly efficient violence, the redcoats destroyed Joshua Chamberlain's livelihood.[3]

When the Treaty of Ghent ended the fighting early in 1815, the British withdrew, leaving the charred timbers of two ships on the stocks at the Chamberlain yard. Joshua Chamberlain failed to recoup. He finally abandoned the Orrington yard and moved his family six miles upriver to Brewer, where he and his sons cleared a farm and started a new shipbuilding enterprise. But the 203-ton brig *Levant,* completed in 1819, did not restore Chamberlain's prosperity. The *Levant* is the last Chamberlain-built vessel to appear in the Maine custom lists.[4]

Joshua and Ann Gould Chamberlain produced nine children, seven of whom reached adulthood. Their first surviving son, Joshua junior, born in Orrington September 24, 1800, had gone to work for his father in the shipyard by the time of the British invasion. With hard times, two younger sons joined the westward migration. (One, Elbridge Gerry Chamberlain, named for a signer of the Declaration of Independence, eventually represented Indiana in Congress.) Joshua junior studied trigonometry and taught himself land surveying, a hard-cash trade he intended to combine with small-scale farming.[5]

Quiet, even-tempered, hardworking, he showed no ambition to follow his brothers out of Brewer. By November 1827, Joshua junior was established securely enough to marry Sarah Dupee Brastow, twenty-four years old, a farmer's daughter from neighboring Holden. The genealogists could only go as far back as 1660 for Sally Brastow's family, tracing her descent, on her mother's side, from a French Protestant of strict principles named Jean Dupuis, who immigrated to the freer air of Boston in 1685. Sally Brastow's grandfather, Capt. Charles Dupee (a careless army clerk had anglicized the spelling of the family name), also fought in the Revolution.[6]

Joshua Chamberlain, Jr., had no fund of small talk, nor did displays of affection come naturally to him. When, in old age, he answered a soft "What, dear?" to a grandchild's questions, his daughter responded with surprised delight. "He never spoke so to us," she said. He became a dutiful churchman, even if the fires of religious revival that swept periodically through Brewer never singed him. His politics were more highly spiced. Conservative, with strong states' rights convictions, he held southern traditions in high esteem. The second Joshua Chamberlain followed his own father's custom of naming sons after men he admired. His choices were suggestive of his values. His firstborn went down in the family Bible as Lawrence Joshua, in honor of "Commodore Lawrence of the American navy," hero of the USS *Chesapeake.* (As a young man, Chamberlain reversed the order of his forenames and became, for the

permanent record, Joshua Lawrence.) And he named his third son after
John C. Calhoun, the South Carolina theorist of secession.[7]

"His parents were typical characters," wrote the anonymous author of
*Joshua Lawrence Chamberlain: A Sketch.** Sally Chamberlain, pious, hardworking, strong-willed, kept a spare house, though she occasionally indulged a well-modulated taste for decoration—a collection of shells on
the mantelpiece, say, set off by a few sprigs of evergreen. A rosebush
grew untrimmed alongside the cottage door; as an old man, Chamberlain recalled the scent of roses as one of his earliest sensations. Sally
permitted herself one small vanity: three neatly arranged tendrils of hair
depending from either side of her muslin cap.[8]

The cycle of the seasons determined the pattern of the Chamberlains'
lives. During the winter lull, Joshua junior built up his surveying and timber-
appraising business. He acted as agent for large landowners who sold their
timber rights—stumpage, in lumbermen's jargon—and owned shares in one
or more of the three dozen or so sawmills in the Bangor area. He became
a soldier in his turn, drilling with the local militia. He held various local
offices and served on the governing board of the Brewer Congregational
Church. From 1820 on, the Chamberlains owned a pew there, although the
head of the family did not actually become a member until 1844. Sally, inher-
iting her Huguenot ancestors' spiritual fire, had joined as far back as 1821.[9]

Brewer in the 1830s retained something of the ramshackle air of a
frontier settlement, even though timber interests and land speculators
were pushing the boundary steadily northward. In 1838, Henry David
Thoreau, ranging up to Old Town, a dozen miles above Bangor, found
logs jamming the river and sawmills humming. This represented either
progress or plunder, depending on one's point of view. "Two or three
mile up the river one beautiful country," an old Penobscot Indian told
Thoreau then. When he returned eight years later, he looked out over
a gray landscape of stumps and brambles. "The mission of the [timber]
men seems to be, like so many busy demons, to drive the forest all out
of the country, from every solitary beaver swamp and mountain-side,"
Thoreau wrote in *The Maine Woods.***

---

*Chamberlain himself may have written—certainly he heavily edited—the *Sketch*. It is similar in style
and content to a partial memoir of Chamberlain's, in typescript with notes in his hand, in the
Bowdoin College Library, Brunswick, Maine.

**Thoreau wrote up this first trip for the *Union Magazine* in 1848. *The Maine Woods*, with accounts
of that and two later journeys, appeared in 1864, two years after his death. It is "easy" Thoreau.
He said he wanted the book to be of use to campers.

The frontier gateway was the tough, worldly boomtown of Bangor. Founded in 1769, Bangor battened on lumber, land, and shipping. By 1840 the city had become the world's leading lumber port. There were two principal hotels and a thriving tenderloin district, Haymarket Square, with bordellos and numerous saloons selling rum at three cents a dipperful. Students at Bangor Theological Seminary worked up practice sermons denouncing the evils of Haymarket. The sharp aroma of pine rose from the vast lumberyards on the riverfront, mingling with the everyday stench of coal smoke, animal dung, and industrial by-products.

Supplies of white, Norway, pitch, and jack pine seemed inexhaustible. There were reports of cut logs 150 feet long. One woodsman claimed to have measured a stump six feet in diameter. In the spring, the lumbermen sent the winter's harvest riding down the freshets to feeder rivers and then into the Penobscot. The timber collected above Old Town at the Penobscot Boom, where the rafting men, balancing on logs, probing and sorting with long poles, floated it downriver to the mills—242 in Penobscot County, according to the 1840 census, forty-two in Bangor alone.[10]

Joshua Chamberlain, Jr., found ample work during these years. A timber "cruiser," he surveyed large wilderness tracts for logging interests and speculators. From 1828 to 1835 the state of Maine sold off more than two million acres of public lands at prices ranging from twenty cents to $1.50 an acre. Much of it was bought on margin for speculation, though some buyers retained title and sold the timber rights. Joshua junior also sold stumpage on Chamberlain land. In a typical transaction, he agreed to let one A. C. Smith cut spruce, pine, juniper, and cedar from family property in the Indian townships. Smith agreed to a price of one dollar per thousand board feet for spruce, two dollars per thousand board feet for pine, and one dollar per ton for juniper.[11]

Most speculators moved swiftly to resell. "Brokers' offices were . . . crowded from morning until night, and frequently far into the night, by buyers and sellers," ran one account. "All were jubilant, because all, whether buyers or sellers, were getting rich." Fortunes were there for the taking. "It is rumored that one evening last week, two paupers escaped from the Bangor almshouse, and though they were caught early the next morning, yet in the meantime, before they were secured, they had made $1,800 each, by speculating in timber lands," the *Niles Register* reported, perhaps seriously, on June 27, 1835.[12]

When the boom collapsed later in 1835, the paper profits of hundreds of investors vanished into the pine-scented air. Still, Bangor had been built on a solid economic base of the lumber trade. Shipping crowded the Penobscot during the ice-free months, as many as 250 sail at a time. The Penobscot may have been the busiest stretch of waterway in the country. Ships delivered cargoes of coal, cement, iron, salt, grain, and fish and carried away bricks, ice, and, above all, lumber products: planks and wideboards, fenceposts, ship timbers, masts and spars, box shooks for fruit, hemlock bark for tanning, friction matches. During the peak years of the 1840s, Bangor exported an average of 150 million board feet of cut lumber a year to American markets and to northern Europe, the Mediterranean, South America, and the West Indies.[13]

With demand for wood products of all kinds holding steady, Joshua junior prospered. He had a growing family to support. After Lawrence, Horace Beriah followed in 1834, Sarah Brastow in 1836, John Calhoun in 1838, and Thomas Davee in 1841. In 1834 the elder Chamberlain built a new, larger house, gabled with an unfinished upper story, on the outskirts of the village.* From this base his eldest child set out on his solitary voyages of exploration. In time, Lawrence became familiar with the wild, dark woods Thoreau described, with what European settlement had spared of the Penobscots and their way of life, and with the kaleidoscopic color and variety of the riverfront. In slack times he used to finish his farm chores early and escape to swim or play roundball. Spring and summer were ship-launching season on the Penobscot. Lawrence boasted that he made it a point to hang his cap on the main truck of each vessel launched on the Brewer side of the river.[14]

Strong and well formed, a little above the average in height, slender in build, he had a high forehead, thick hair, and regular, attractive features. His eyes, a deep blue, suggested a kind of poetry in him, a pastoral kind. "He early learned to know the voices of the trees," his nameless biographer recorded, ". . . each having its own voice and song and scale—whisper, moan or roar, in the stress of winds." Even in darkness, in an unfamiliar woods, "he would know by their song what trees were over him."[15]

In provincial America, Romantic attitudes characteristically found expression in a passion for natural history—safer, for conventionally devout Yankees, than Byron's or Shelley's subversive verse. The 1830s and 1840s saw a vogue in collecting, preserving, and displaying plant and animal

---

*Now numbered 80 Chamberlain Street, the house still stands.

life. In 1844 a touring Prussian nobleman, stopping in Bangor for several weeks, instructed Lawrence Chamberlain's friend, Manly Hardy, in the craft of taxidermy. Hardy passed the technique on to Lawrence, who shot, preserved, and mounted a collection of birds. He eventually came to dislike killing birds and game,* though to avoid awkward questions he made it a point to carry a gun whenever he went into the woods.[16]

Handy and practical, he built his own playthings: bows and arrows, wooden guns, sleds. He developed his musical inclinations by crafting a bass viol out of "a stout, square-faced corn stalk, duly notched for strings and stops of the scale." He used a smaller stalk for the bow. Later, when he acquired the actual instrument, he found he could play it. The bass viol (or viola da gamba), with its deep, sonorous, respectful tones, was the first instrument approved for liturgical use when New England Congregationalists began easing their immemorial ban on church music. Probably some bass violist at the Brewer church caught Lawrence's musical imagination. At any rate, his tastes did not run to the vulgar. When someone offered him a book of sailor songs, a collection of airs such as those that drifted up from the port on any summer evening, he turned it down.[17]

Novels were discouraged at home, possibly forbidden outright. On Saturday nights, Sally might read aloud from the Bible or *Pilgrim's Progress,* but she would not allow Lawrence a copy of James Fenimore Cooper's phenomenally popular *The Deerslayer*—an attitude toward "frivolous" literature that suggests the Chamberlains were more than usually conservative. Natural history might be encouraged; works of the Romantic imagination were strongly suspect.[18]

Farm demands anyway left little energy or leisure for such diversions. In later years, Chamberlain, a devoted gardener, idealized his hardscrabble boyhood. "To a thoughtful spirit," he wrote, "sowing is a solemn, caring, trustful service. It is a communion with all the forces of the universe." In fact, farming was unremitting toil. Maine's growing seasons were short. Most of the work still had to be done by muscle power. After a day in the fields, sunrise to sunset through the spring and summer, father and son turned homeward stupid with fatigue, fingers numb and swollen, arms aching, legs stiff, temples throbbing.[19]

---

*As did Ulysses S. Grant, an army subaltern on the Mexican frontier when Chamberlain was building up his bird collection. Describing an 1846 Texas hunt, Grant wrote that he "stood watching the turkeys to see where they flew—with my gun on my shoulder, and never once thought of levelling it at the birds."

Farm life taught one to keep at a job, however difficult, and to improvise. One hot afternoon the Chamberlain ox team drew the haywagon between two large stumps, where it stuck fast. "There were only three or four hundred pounds of hay on," Chamberlain recalled, "but the thing was a dead lock, front and rear." From behind, his father called out for him to get the team moving.

"Clear that wheel!"

"How am I going to do it?"

His father shouted again:

"Do it; that's how."

Lawrence grasped the hub and strained to lift one wheel clear, heaving with such force "that the cart-tongue knocked against the nose of the off ox." The startled animal lunged forward, and "the whole team was off in a jiffy." The elder Chamberlain got on with the job without further comment. His son remembered the simple command for the rest of his life.[20]

The end of haying brought a brief respite. The pace slowed again after the harvest, though the foundation of the house needed to be banked with seaweed and leaves, and firewood cut, hauled, split, and stacked (the Chamberlains burned as many as forty cords a year). These were Lawrence's chores. On winter afternoons, Sally taught him his first letters; she saw to it that he attended the village ABC school, at least for a few weeks a year.[21]

He used to escape the clamor of the farmhouse kitchen and run down to the Indian camp on the edge of the Chamberlain lands, where on long winter evenings the Penobscots told stories, sang, and played games. Lawrence knew them just as their oral traditions were beginning to die out. They told him about Katahdin, throne of the storm-god, inhabited by fairies and spirits, and about Pomolo, the evil spirit of the night air. He listened to their tales of the fabulous Glooskap, man-god, great warrior, devoted father, who made the winds, caused the water to move, and fashioned the first men from ash trees.[22]

Thoreau had found the tribes debased. Forced into segregated farming villages, most notoriously the "Indian Island" in the river above Old Town, the Penobscots by the 1830s had fallen into what looked like irreversible decline. Having thus disposed of the natives, settlers on either side of the ill-defined border between Maine and New Brunswick turned on each other. In the summer of 1838 a New Brunswick official named James MacLauchan, known as the "Warden of the Disputed Ter-

ritory," protested a Maine survey expedition in the valley of the Aroostook River. In return, Maine officials accused New Brunswick loggers of
claim-jumping on Maine land.[23]

The dispute simmered through the autumn and into the winter. In
January 1839, Maine inaugurated a new governor, John Fairfield, who
took up the border question as his first order of business, requesting
legislative approval to send an armed force north. On January 23 the
assembly authorized Rufus McIntire, the state land agent, and Maj. Has-
tings Strickland, the sheriff of Penobscot County, to lead an expedition
of two hundred men into the Aroostook Valley, seize the New Brunswick
loggers' ox teams and provisions, and break up their camps.

In Fredericton, New Brunswick, the Crown's representative, Sir James
Harvey, made ready to contest the invasion. In Washington City,
Congress authorized President Van Buren to call out the militia if British
forces moved into the borderlands. In early February, Maine authorities
arrested some twenty Canadian loggers, including Warden MacLauchan.
A party of fifty New Brunswick lumberjacks retaliated by ambushing
McIntire and two others and jailing them in Fredericton. On February
16, Fairfield proposed military action to free the McIntire party. Three
days later the state issued a call for a total of 10,343 officers and men
to confront the British Empire in the Aroostook Valley.

> Bring out the big gun made of brass,
> Which forges July thunder.
> Bring out the flag of Bennington,
> And strike the foe with wonder.

The column led out, flags snapping in the wintry wind, from Bangor,
Capt. Joshua Chamberlain, Jr., marching with the Second Regiment. Van
Buren, alarmed, ordered the army's senior soldier, Gen. Winfield Scott,
to Maine to negotiate a peaceful settlement. Hot-tempered, querulous,
petty in his dealings with rivals, Scott was nevertheless a skillful diplomat.
Proposing mutual withdrawal and a parley, he argued the case for compromise at a series of dinner parties in Augusta, the Maine capital. Scott's
wife may have found life with him humdrum ("a tallow candle, a game
of whist and General Scott" is said to have been her definition of ennui),
but he brought a whiff of cosmopolitanism to Augusta. Though Fairfield
thoroughly enjoyed these affairs, they seem to have sobered him, figura-
tively at least. Scott, who had seen a lot of combat, may have frightened

him with realistic accounts of war. At any rate, Fairfield became percepti-
bly less bellicose. He agreed to negotiate.[24]

Scott eventually persuaded both sides to withdraw from the disputed
valley, bringing the Aroostook War to a bloodless conclusion. The governor released the militia. Joshua Chamberlain, Jr., returned home in early
April, just as the ice was beginning to break up on the Penobscot. He
resigned his militia commission at the end of this low-comedy campaign,
but a taste of active service may have confirmed his ambition for a West
Point appointment for his eldest son. Sally had another notion, the ministry, and she campaigned quietly for it. Even so, Lawrence attended
Major Whiting's Military Academy in Ellsworth for a time in 1842–43,
where he picked up rudimentary drill, studied French and Latin, and
struggled with mathematics. He returned home after a few months at
Major Whiting's, not in deference to his mother's views but because his
father could no longer afford the tuition fees.[25]

The record suggests Joshua junior was careless in business matters. His
son put it around in later years that his openhandedness with loan-
seeking friends caused most of the trouble. More likely it was ill-advised
speculation. In any event, he seems to have lost all but the farm in 1843.
His account books show him to have been deeply involved in nearly
every aspect of the timber business, from surveying to milling to shipping. Whatever the cause, his fortunes—investments in sawmills, shares
in one or more of the Brewer-built merchant vessels—slumped badly.[26]

While Joshua junior struggled to reestablish himself, Lawrence went
to work for wages, first in a Brewer ropewalk, later in a brickyard. He
taught school for a time and, in the custom of the day in rural Maine,
had to thrash the strongest boy in the class to confirm his authority. He
sang in the choir of Brewer Congregational Church, and taught Sunday
school there. He formally joined the church on June 25, 1845, giving
the obligatory public "relation" of his crisis of faith. He sped through
the rite, probably in an effort to outrace the stammer that, in adoles-
cence, had become an embarrassing feature of his speech.[27]

Meanwhile, he considered the future. An expedition to Katahdin with
three ministers in September 1846 offered an opportunity to think things
through. He had better luck than Thoreau, who complained in *The Maine
Woods* of blackflies, mosquitoes, midges, clouds, and mist the day he reached
the summit. Lawrence and his companions, ascending on a fair day, were
rewarded with vistas stretching to the horizon in all directions.[28]

He kept a school in North Milford during the winter of 1846–47.

Woods enclosed the lonely little community on all sides. On a clear day, he wrote his cousin Sarah Shepard in February, he could see Katahdin beyond the bare treetops. The views were not compensation enough. Bored and homesick, he found his lodgings disagreeable too. "A continual swearing from an ill-tempered boy and scolding, and a grumbling, growling and tumbling, and all the noise you can imagine," he wrote Sarah. He complained of feeling restless and melancholy. "I sometimes wish myself a child always," he went on, "for then it is that sport is the most innocent and joy most unbeclouded." Still, he carried on with characteristic Chamberlain energy, teaching singing three nights a week in addition to his schoolroom duties.[29]

For years, his parents had muffled their disagreement. But Lawrence turned nineteen in the autumn of 1847, and a decision, soldiering or the ministry, could be postponed no longer. Joshua junior argued for West Point as "manly, honorable, chivalrous," his son recalled. Sally believed garrison life to be narrow and enervating. Lawrence seems to have felt little enthusiasm for either profession. Each "bound a man by rules and precedents and petty despotisms, and swamped his personality," he wrote later. The issue went Sally's way. He agreed to prepare for the ministry, though on his own terms. Manly Hardy spoke of going out to an overseas mission. Lawrence decided he would be a missionary, too, and help civilize "some really heathen country, like Africa or the Pacific Islands."[30]

He resolved to go to Bowdoin College, then to the Bangor Theological Seminary. His schooling had been sporadic, subject to the primary demands of the farm. He lacked some entrance requirements for Bowdoin; an intensive preparatory course would be necessary, especially in the classics. Professors from the Bangor seminary tutored him in Latin and Greek. He threw himself into the ancient languages, and in time could recite verbatim the entire Kuhner's unabridged Greek grammar.[31]

He studied in a garret that he finished off himself and fitted out with a wood-burning stove. He worked, sometimes for twelve hours at a sitting, with an overachiever's singlemindedness—the same concentrated attention he would apply, in 1862, to the study of tactics, weapons, and drill. He split and hauled up his own wood, a welcome break from Kuhner, and found diversion as well in roughhouse duels with his father. Armed with wooden broadswords, these descendants of the Norman knight de Tankerville used to shuffle back and forth across the floor in duels the filial Lawrence nearly always let his father win.[32]

In February 1848, William Hyde, the Latin tutor, delivered Lawrence to Bowdoin after a two-day sleigh trip over roads thickly drifted with snow. Childhood came belatedly to an end. He was nineteen years and four months old, a shy stammerer, studious, intense, and ambitious. Nothing is impenetrable to virtue: He believed wholly in the family motto, and in duty, honor, knightly glory. There was, too, a hard practical core to this awkward young romancer. He had not forgotten what he called his father's "order for life." Nothing is impossible: "Do it, that's how."

The Bowdoin examiners met in a dank room in the medical school building. There, amid specimen boxes and in the macabre company of a group of grinning skeletons, Lawrence passed into the college. He tested well, receiving a conditional grade only in one of Sallust's texts, and joined the freshman class at six o'clock the following morning. Glancing around him in the cold gloom of a winter dawn, he thought the students at their benches looked like galley slaves resting on their oars.[33]

Alexander
The Home Place, 1835–53

Sarah Alexander doted on the newborns. Pregnant for 108 months altogether during the years 1824–48, mother of ten surviving children, she nevertheless charted with undiminished interest the progress of each successive arrival. "He looks very sweet, and as plump as a partridge," she wrote her husband, Adam Leopold, of their second son and sixth child, then three months old. "Baby laughs aloud!" she added a few days later. In a six-month report, she noted that he "sits alone pretty smartly, and can *patty cake* after a fashion."[1]

Edward Porter Alexander, born May 26, 1835, at Fairfield plantation, Washington, Georgia, seemed different from the others—"quite a prodigy," his mother soon had cause to observe. He responded with bursts of energy to color, movement, action. "The poor little fellow pines so to ride whenever he sees horses or a carriage that I am really sorry to have no way to gratify him," she wrote Leopold in the child's second summer. A few months later she remarked on his developing "oddity of speech & manner"; she saw originality in him. Clever and inquisitive, Porter (the Alexanders customarily called the children by their second names) showed early promise as a storyteller. "He entertains every stranger he sees with marvellous accounts of his possessions & exploits ... indeed, I fear he exhibits a wonderful tendency to romancing," Sarah boasted.[2]

This eccentric boy belonged to one of Georgia's first families. Besides Fairfield, the home place, Adam Leopold Alexander owned part or all of two other plantations, and around one hundred slaves. As a child of the planter class, Porter had nurses and house servants to care for him, black playmates to fall in with his whims, blacksmiths, butchers, and other plantation workmen to satisfy his curiosity about things, tutors to instruct him. As he grew older, the habit of command formed in him. Even as a boy he had the power to direct affairs "on the lot," Fairfield's slave quarters.[3]

The Alexanders had risen to gentility over two or three generations. Sarah's father's people, the Gilberts, were of Scots origin, pioneers who came to Wilkes County from the Shenandoah Valley of Virginia in the mid-1780s. Felix Gilbert and his brother William made a small fortune in trade, and they operated the region's first cotton gin, thus helping to establish the Cotton Kingdom in upcountry Georgia. Felix married Sarah Hillhouse in 1802. Their first child died in infancy. Their second, born in 1805 and named Sarah after her mother, would survive to become the mistress of Fairfield.

Sarah Hillhouse Gilbert died in 1808. Felix buried her in the family graveyard in a grove near his new brick mansion and had as little as possible to do thereafter with either the house or his daughter. In poor health, Felix turned the business over to his brother and took up the nomadic life of the invalid, moving from one spa or residential hotel to the next. When he died, in 1813, he left Sarah $40,000 and a slave girl— only a small part of his estate because, he recorded, he did not want her to become the object of fortune hunters.

Sarah grew up in the house of her Massachusetts-born grandmother, Sarah Hillhouse. She and her husband, David Hillhouse of New Haven, Connecticut, had migrated to northeast Georgia before 1790. Hillhouse published a Wilkes County newspaper, *The Monitor*. When he died, in 1805, his widow succeeded him as editor and printer. Capable and shrewd, Sarah Hillhouse prospered. The sturdy political connections she built over the years yielded, among other benefits, a lucrative contract to print Georgia's legislative reports.

The widow Hillhouse could be close, some said miserly. Physically vigorous herself, she showed little sympathy for the pains and discomforts of others. When the winter wind blew hard out of the northwest and her granddaughter asked for a fire, she sent her outdoors to warm herself by racing up and down the garden paths. Still, Sarah Hillhouse tried her best for the orphan. She sent her north to school in New Haven, where in due course she met Adam Leopold Alexander of Sunbury, Liberty County, Georgia, a student at Yale College.

Leopold's father, also called Adam, born in Inverness, Scotland, raised by maiden aunts and trained as a physician at the University of Edinburgh, had immigrated to America in 1776. Grants of fertile Georgia land were his reward for war service as a surgeon with the Continental forces. In 1802, Adam Alexander married Louisa Frederika Schmidt, daughter of a German-born Savannah cotton broker. She gave birth to their only son the following year. By then Alexander had become a successful slaveholding planter, master of Hopewell in Liberty County, rice and sea-island cotton country south of Savannah.[4]

Acquaintances invariably remarked on the curly-haired Leopold's good looks, intelligence, and agreeable manners. Sarah Gilbert met him often in New Haven society. They were engaged during a summer excursion to Niagara. Sarah was two months short of her sixteenth birthday when, on August 9, 1821, he proposed, using the great falls as a dramatic backdrop. Married in Washington, Georgia, on April 28, 1823, they spent their first months at Hopewell with Leopold's mother, who had been left a widow in 1811. For a time, it looked as though the newlyweds would make Hopewell their home. But William Gilbert had fallen on hard times after his brother's death. Cash-poor, he offered the Washington mansion, Fairfield, to Sarah as part of her inheritance.[5]

The Alexanders settled by easy stages into the routines of planter life. As farmer, banker, and investor, Leopold showed an early aptitude for making and holding on to money. He developed strong religious convictions, no doubt under the influence of his devout wife. Family legend says he read a section of the New Testament daily in Greek (and so contrived to display his piety and learning at the same time). Still, there was none of the dour, self-denying churchman about him. He savored the planter privileges. The library at Fairfield contained the latest books, from Thiers's *History of the French Revolution* to Dickens's *Martin Chuzzlewit*. He subscribed to the leading London periodicals, stocked his cellar with good wine and brandy, and enjoyed tobacco and congenial company. Society in Washington, Augusta, and Savannah knew him as a clever conversationalist, a wit.

Leopold's gifts seemed to mark him for public life. Yet he had no taste for politics, and gratefully left the upcountry stage to his friend and Washington neighbor Robert Augustus Toombs, who served in the United States Congress and later the Senate, and would become Jefferson Davis's first secretary of state. Leopold interested himself in the affairs of the Georgia Presbyterians,* and held a seat on the governing board of the state university in Athens. He recruited New England tutors and governesses for his and neighboring planters' children. He took his turn, too, with the Wilkes County slave patrol.

Fairfield lay on the northern edge of Washington village, the fields and slave quarters beyond. Downhill from the mansion, a few shops and the courthouse were grouped around a square. Just beyond, on the main street, stood the Presbyterian church, a New England–style white clapboard building with a tall steeple. One-story cottages or four-room uprights were ranked along either side of the rutted red clay track that led out to the cotton fields. When Sarah and Leopold arrived, these dwellings were unpainted or stained a dull gray. The brilliant white mansions, with their Greek columns, would come a decade or so later, during the full flood of cotton prosperity.

The Alexanders' firstborn, Louisa Frederika, arrived in 1824, followed by Sarah Gilbert in 1826, Harriet Virginia in 1828, Mary Clifford in 1830, and William Felix in 1832. Between pregnancies and a strength-sapping succession of illnesses, Sarah oversaw the operation of Fairfield's complicated domestic machinery. She ran the plantation, too, in Leopold's frequent absences, overseeing the full range of activities from field work to hog-killing.[6]

Something drove this fragile, sickly woman, some outsized sense of duty or responsibility. "I often feel as if I was but of little value in my feebleness," Sarah would write in 1849, "but yet it seems as if my presence exercises some sort of harmonizing influence over the discordant elements which compose the household." As a young mistress, she liked to spend winter evenings by the fire, devouring Sir Walter Scott's "Waverly" novels. In common with many Southerners of her class, she found in Scott's sentimental feudalism a mirror of the South's own caste- and color-bound

*In 1827–28 he took into his home an orphan of good Presbyterian family named Alexander Stephens (born 1812), who would become vice president of the Confederate states.

system. But as her responsibilties increased, she came to consider reading romances such as Scott's a dissipation. "I am very sensible that [novel-reading] is a criminal indulgence," she finally confessed. In the future, she promised Leopold, she would read only such works as would better fit her for a mother's duties.[7]

The novels of Maria Edgeworth met this strict standard. Sarah allowed herself Edgeworth stories in all but the most self-denying moods. The spinster daughter of an Irish Ascendancy squire, Edgeworth dramatized the "Irish problem." Edgeworth women raised large families, just as Sarah was doing. They ran farms, as Sarah was doing. They gave religious instruction to their dependents, as Sarah was doing. They supervised maladroit servants, just as Sarah was doing. When doubts assailed her, when the sundry demands of plantation life threatened to overwhelm her, she could turn for reassurance to the example of Edgeworth's Christian heroines.*

An 1828 portrait of Sarah Alexander shows a large-eyed, handsome woman with a long, thin nose and a narrow oval face. When she felt well enough, she liked to preen. "Lou [daughter Louisa, then twenty-two years old] says her companions tell her I must be her stepmother," Sarah wrote. "Lou says she is making capital out of my good looks, so she cultivates my curls and adjusts my caps, etc., with the utmost care." Invalidism aside, she prided herself on retaining her beauty deep into middle age.[8]

The Alexanders were often apart. Banking and railroad interests took Leopold away for extended periods, and there were the distant family plantations to manage. Sarah traveled for pleasure, or to recuperate after an illness or childbirth. Generally taking along one or two of the younger children, she spent part of each summer in the cooler hill country at Madison Springs. For several weeks in the winter she stayed with Leopold's sister Louisa and her husband, Anthony Porter, in Savannah. She went north for extended visits in 1828, 1834, and 1839.

The mails were the Alexanders' lifeline. A rich correspondence, amounting to a portrait on a small canvas of antebellum life, passed between husband and wife. Leopold discussed business affairs, religious matters, the children's education. Sarah wrote of the children, household affairs, illnesses—the complete catalog of nineteenth-century maladies: toothaches and colds, sore throats, fevers, pleurisy, bilious attacks,

*Edgeworth wasn't all uplift. "Some people talk of morality, and some of religion," one of her characters said, "but give me a little snug property."

sick headaches, and derangements of the bowels. There were devotions and reassurances, too, the incantations of love. The letters, unreserved and ardent, show the Alexanders to have been an unusually adoring couple.

"I have had no bedfellows except a little mouse, who, compassioning my widowhood, came two nights to my bed," she wrote him during one long separation in 1833. Seven years later, as they approached their seventeenth wedding anniversary, Sarah still sounded like a lovestruck belle: "Last evening I went out a dozen times to look at the moon & think of you—wondering where you were, and if you were looking at it, & thinking of me." For many years she complained of night terrors when he was away.[9]

Leopold wrote with equal intensity. He could be lighthearted, too, and joke of coming apart under the stress of bachelorhood. He felt like a vagabond, he said once, alone, adrift, undisciplined: "I have a propensity to segars & liquor & wearing a hat on one side." To cheer her, he would promise treats from the Augusta or Savannah markets. "I found mother engaged in boxing up for you 200 oranges," he told her, "in which I put three fine beef tongues, knowing you to be fond of them." Sarah appreciated practical gifts as well. He returned from one long absence with a potato steamer for her.[10]

The Fairfield of Edward Porter Alexander's boyhood was self-sufficient, self-supporting, a miniature sovereign state. "Everybody was comfortable, and nobody was rich," he wrote late in life, casting a long glance back to antebellum Wilkes County. Some fifty slaves raised cotton, wheat, corn, and hogs on the more than seventeen hundred acres of Alexander lands. Cotton brought cash. In a normal year, Fairfield yielded twenty-five to thirty four-hundred-pound bales, about a quarter-bale per acre of increasingly exhausted soil. Leopold could expect a cash return of roughly $1,000 on the cotton crop. Prices slumped during the financial panic of 1837, and remained low through most of the 1840s. To make up some of the difference, Leopold introduced pecans as a second cash crop.[11]

Sarah's orchards and kitchen garden provided an abundance for home consumption. In two or three yearly plantings, the garden produced cucumbers, melons, summer squash, peas, beans, cabbages, turnips, and potatoes. There were pear, apricot, and almond trees, English and French grapevines, fig trees. Leopold planted two linden trees near the house. They reminded him of Yale. Sarah took pride in her ornamentals: straw-colored hyacinths, dahlias, azaleas, roses, English iris, lilies, verbena, myrtle, jasmine, and camellias. In season, she kept a vase of freshly cut flowers on her work table. Her children remembered her always trailing the scent of lavender when she passed through a room.

The Alexanders were careful of their human property, paternal and kind, given the nature of the relationship. The slaves "were all looked after as if they were children," Porter Alexander recalled. Historians have documented the relative inefficiency of slave labor; the Alexander letters offer plenty of supporting evidence. Fairfield slaves were accident-prone, careless, slack, light-fingered, often ill, sometimes alcoholic. The correspondence suggests there were strong bonds of affection between the Alexanders and some of their slaves, particularly the house servants. That would not have been out of the ordinary. Still, it is likely that some slaves' manifold shortcomings were a form of passive resistance to an unjust and exploitative system.[12]

"The cotton picking does not come on very fast," Sarah complained. "Thornton was taken sick yesterday & Charlotte scalded her feet and legs very badly last night."* The field hand Hector had "taken a drunken frolic the whole of the week." She caught Fielding stealing eggs and selling them in the town. "I regret it extremely as I have always trusted his honesty." Cora, one of the chambermaids, was "heedless and thoughtless" and could not be given responsible work.[13]

Cynthia Peters, the inevitable mammy, functioned as head housekeeper and, in Sarah's absence, as surrogate mother. She nursed all ten Alexander children. (After Porter in 1835 came Charles Atwood, 1838; James Hillhouse, 1840; Marion Brackett, 1842; and Alice Van Yeveren, 1848.) She tried teaching table manners, with indifferent results. "No, thank you, I don't eat okra," one of the boys once told her. "It looks too much like horse slobber." Cynthia could read and write, and some of her notes survive; in them, she addressed Leopold as friend as well as master. The Alexanders rarely returned from a journey without something for her—jet beads, earrings, a head kerchief, a dress. When she died in 1874 she left 135 dresses, thirty-seven shawls, forty bonnets, and a cache of jewelry.[14]

Sarah catechized the slave children in a Sabbath school in the Fairfield dining room.** Leopold conducted Sunday services. A number of Fair-

---

*The Alexanders rarely mentioned their slaves by full name. Like many Southerners, they used the euphemistic "servants" for the house slaves; field hands were "the negroes."

**In addition, of course, to her own children, who were given intensive religious instruction. "Father," their daughter Sarah said, "I am four years old today and I haven't yet triumphed over the fear of death."

field slaves were literate; Sarah or one of the girls taught any who wanted to learn. As a trafficker in human beings, Leopold seems to have made an effort to keep families together, though Sarah considered occasional sales an opportunity to reduce Fairfield's dependent population. In August 1841 she wrote to suggest that he sell a young woman named Margaret. "I think it would be as well," she said, "for I dislike to have another set of children on the lot. I think it will be too many servants any how." Leopold also acted out of self-interest, naturally. He once refused permission for one of his field hands to marry a neighbor's servant girl until he could determine what it would cost to buy her and bring her to Fairfield. He raised needed cash through sales and hirings-out of slaves.[15]

Cynthia inhabited a cottage in the yard near the main house. During Sarah's illnesses, one or two of the younger children would sleep with her there. The other slaves lived, each family to its own dwelling, on the lot. "The big woodpile was common to all," Hattie Alexander remembered. "The meat, salt, molasses, and such things were given out every month from the smokehouse and storeroom." The slaves had their own patches of garden; some raised cotton for cash, and others grew potatoes, peas, and cabbages to supplement their corn and bacon fare.[16]

In his memoirs, written late in life, Porter Alexander recalled lame Adam the shoemaker and superannuated Bob, who lived with his wife, Dilsey, "near the big poplar." These were pensioners. The youngest boy, Hillie (James Hillhouse), helped look after the enfeebled Adam, carrying water and wood to the old man's cabin. Harry tended Sarah's gardens. As foreman, Emmanuel supervised the field hands. The sons of Jack and Morots Ryans, William, Stephen, and Joel, were all carpenters like their father. James the driver, his pass carefully tucked into a boot, could be trusted to take the wagon to Augusta or Madison Springs. There were Tom the cook, the seamstress Mary Ann, Mary the washerwoman. One or another of the slave children always stood near the dining table at mealtimes, ready to chase away flies with a peacock brush.[17]

When Felix went north to Yale in 1850, some plantation responsibilities fell to Porter. He took a keen interest in life on the lot. Writing to Felix at the New Year, 1851, he reported on two weddings, minor illnesses, money disbursed ($123) to buy slaves' produce, and the Fairfield cotton crop—thirty bales that year. He had gone over the plantation and "given orders to the negroes," he went on proudly, then spent the rest of the day helping the hands clear a thicket and split fence rails.[18]

Porter's labor was voluntary, of course. The planter's son could quit when he became bored or fatigued. Another boy might have stood back and watched the slaves at work, tapping a doubled-over whip lightly against his boot top. Porter preferred to pitch in. Why not? Nothing could threaten his place. To him, Fairfield's world seemed imperishable. His mother knew better. Sarah Alexander corresponded with her Connecticut and Massachusetts kin and traveled widely in the North. Yankee attitudes toward slavery troubled her. Her own conscience troubled her still more. Its sting drove her, from the early 1840s on, to try to persuade Leopold to sell the Georgia holdings and resettle in New England, leaving the Peculiar Institution to its fate.

"I confess my mind often dwells with painful apprehension on the prospects of our southern section as a slave-holding country," she wrote him in 1841, "& I do believe that a speedy decline of value & ultimately perhaps total loss & destruction is in store for it." She did not fear so much for herself, she said, as for the children. The belief grew in her that Porter and the others would inherit a ruin.[19]

Sarah may have considered slavery doomed, but there is no evidence she judged it an absolute wrong; still less did the patriarchal Leopold. In both, ambivalence took the form of an unusual interest in the affairs of former slaves. Leopold lent money to ex-slaves and helped them find work or shelter. Sarah showed interest in the colonization movement, which, for a time, before opinion hardened in the North and the South, seemed to offer a way out of the slavery impasse. But she continued to campaign for the sale of Fairfield, and there were times when she thought she was making progress. Leopold had taken on the cashiership of the Washington bank, a more or less full-time job. The overseer, John Eidson, was proving unsatisfactory. (He would leave in 1850 to take a job tending bar in a backcountry tavern.) But King Cotton had the final say. By the late 1840s, prices for both cotton and slaves were on the rise. The richer Liberty County cotton lands produced an income of as much as $6,000 a year. Leopold turned down two offers for Fairfield in 1849. By year's end, he had resolved to resume direct supervision of the home place and coax as much cotton as he could out of the tired soil.[20]

"I dread and dislike it all exceedingly," Sarah wrote one of her daughters on New Year's Day 1850, "& have used all my influence to prevail upon him to sell negroes and all—but the high price of cotton is so tempting that he cannot resist the trial." The new decade indeed brought record prices, though crop yields in their aging fields were not high enough for the Alexanders to take full advantage of the boom. According to one historian, total agricultural income actually declined in Wilkes County during the period, while the percentage of slaves in the population increased.[21]

His mother's apprehensions cast no shadow across Porter's childhood. He grew up happily oblivious. Fairfield was a lively, noisy place, thickly settled with children, congested with the traffic of servants. Brackett the governess, Wright the tutor, and one kinsman or another were usually in residence. The high-spirited Alexander girls kept the house humming. Even the visit of so grim and unwelcome a figure as the doctor could inspire a burst of comic invention such as this one from sister Sarah:

> *You give me oil most every day*
> *You give me too much oil I say*
> *I do not like your starving plan*
> *You ugly great long-legged man*

Porter stood a little apart from this hive. Some of the oddity his mother had noticed came out in his friendship for two old men, neighbors Frank Colley and James Dyson, with whom he spent long hours hunting in the woods or fishing the Little River. His sisters used to chaff him about this preference for elderly companions. He responded to their ragging with a solemn smile. Mary Clifford, his favorite sister, described him as quiet, matter-of-fact, strong-willed. Visiting Porter in the sickroom one afternoon, Cliff asked him what he had been thinking about. "Thinking about God," he told her, "and how hard I could butt." He really detested milk, Cliff remembered; she thought the description of Paradise as a land of milk and honey robbed the afterlife of half its charm for him.[22]

He seems to have inherited his mother's remarkable mixture of hardiness and fragility. Sarah used to worry whether he would survive the bumps and bruises of boyhood. His return home with a bloody nose one January afternoon sent her into paroxysms of alarm. "He would turn almost purple in the face & then vomit repeatedly," she wrote Leopold. The doctor prescribed mustard baths. These were duly administered. "Next day he seemed quite well again," she went on. "But he will never do for any profession involving much hardship & exposure. What a strange compound of roughness & sensitiveness he is!"[23]

Porter would endure four years in the Army of Northern Virginia, a byword for hardship, without the slightest damage to his health. Still, Sarah's overprotectiveness may explain why Leopold discouraged his ambition to be a soldier. Porter had fixed his hopes on West Point by the age of eight or nine. His father flatly refused to consider it. But soldiering—and firearms, a soldier's tools—held an unshakable fascination for the boy.

He did not go in much for killing at first. "Mother, how miserable them poor birds is when the boys throws at them," he once lamented. "I'm so glad I can't hit 'em when I throws at 'em." Later, however, he became rather bloodthirsty. He returned from one hunt with a bag of seventeen squirrels. He took a leading part in a high point of Fairfield's winter routine, hog-killing. Two or three times a season, some thirty or forty hogs were slaughtered. "As the most humane way of killing them," he recalled, "I was usually allowed to stay at home & shoot them with a rifle."[24]

Porter's education reflected Fairfield privilege. The patriarch journeyed north for the children's teachers. Sarah Brackett came down from Easthampton, Massachusetts, in 1835 to instruct the girls in such ladylike pastimes as drawing and piano-playing. ("She draws for them, & they colour," Leopold quipped.) Miss Brackett later established a girls' school under Alexander patronage that attracted students from all over the South. Russell Wright, an Amherst College graduate, tutored the boys. As a subsidiary duty, he trained and trimmed Sarah's roses. Wright, too, eventually set up his own thriving school in Washington.[25]

Porter had an early passion for geography; he used to bore the servants with lectures on the prominent features shown on the large maps his father tacked to the sitting room wall. His earliest ambition was to be a fisherman, an engineer, a fireman, or a preacher. Whatever his fancy of the moment, Wright kept him hard at work. Porter would study dutifully for a time, attacking his lessons with an intensity that foreshadowed the drive for perfection he would show at West Point. Then he would ease up, neglecting his books to tend his traps, hunt with Dyson and the pointer Ponto (named for the rascally Alfred Jingle's dog in *The Pickwick Papers*), or go fishing with Colley.[26]

Sooner or later, Leopold felt bound to lay down the law. He might threaten to send Porter to Trenton, a boarding school of evil repute in the wilds in back of Lookout Mountain, Tennessee. Sometimes, rather than lecture, he would contrive to set a trap for his trapper son. One afternoon, when Porter had wandered in from the woods an hour or so later than usual, Leopold summoned him into his presence.

"Did you catch anything?"

"No, sir."

"Why, wasn't your trap down?"

"Yes, sir, it was down. But there wasn't anything in it but a Davies' Arithmetic."[27]

Old Mr. Colley initiated Porter's first lesson in the destructive power of political passion. Southerners were agitating for the spread of slavery into the vast territories the United States had won in war with Mexico. Northerners were mobilizing against expansion. Colley sketched in some of this background one afternoon in 1848 as the two walked home from the river.

"Mr. Colley told me that sucession was being talked of, & I remember well the spot in the road where we were, & the pang which the idea sent through me, & my thinking that I would rather lose my gun—my dearest possession on earth—than see it happen," Porter remembered.[28]

The upcountry communities were soon entangled in a fierce debate over the issue, splitting, generally, along class lines. The quality, including Leopold Alexander, Judge Garnett Andrews, and neighbor Toombs, a rising Whig, were strong for Union. "Every barkeeper and every rowdy in the town was a hot secessionist," Porter wrote later. Vigorous expression of his own pro-Union views provoked a quarrel with two older boys, the proto-fireaters Jim Hester and Ben Kappell. Porter heard the two had armed themselves and meant to attack him. He borrowed overseer Eidson's revolver and prepared to defend himself.

Porter and Hester met in the dusty street; Hester broke a stick over Porter's head and bloodied his nose. Porter stepped back, drew Eidson's pistol, aimed at his tormentor's chest, and pulled the trigger. The charge failed to detonate. Hester reached for his own weapon. Porter fired again; again the pistol failed him.

"Hester paused a moment," Porter recalled, "& made no motion to aim or fire at me. This made me pause in the very act of pulling the trigger for a third trial." He reckoned that his weapon would continue to misfire, while Hester's would likely go off. The interval gave several boys hovering at the edge of the fight a chance to rush the combatants and disarm them.

"Someone said to the boy who took mine, 'See if that pistol is loaded,'

He raised it over his head & pulled the trigger. This time it went off loud & clear."

Porter, dazed, turned up late for supper, a serious infraction in the Alexander household. The patriarch began firing angry questions at him. The boy's halting, half-coherent replies struck him speechless. Only merest mischance, Leopold saw at once, had prevented a killing. "He was most shocked at it," Porter wrote "so much so that I did not get the punishment I expected, & felt that I deserved." He and Jim Hester soon made up, and met thereafter as if nothing had happened. But he never forgot the incident. Politics were "too prolific of quarrels to one who, like myself, is liable to become reckless of consequences when in a passion," he decided. The lesson stayed with him, and he remained shy of politics throughout his life.[29]

Giving way without warning, Leopold withdrew his opposition to West Point later that summer. Porter was in the drawing room, drowsing on a sofa while his sisters took their discordant turns at the piano, when someone called for him from the piazza. He shuffled lazily out of doors. "Then I was told that father consented to my going to West Pt., provided I would promise to study hard enough to 'graduate in the engineers,' " he recalled. "I was wide awake in a moment & ready to promise anything."[30]

Sister Sarah had married a West Pointer (Alexander R. Lawton), and sister Louisa soon would marry another (Jeremy F. Gilmer). That may have influenced Leopold. At any rate, he had a word with Robert Toombs. In the House, Toombs voted consistently to cut spending for the army, but otherwise showed little interest in military affairs. Still, he promised to help the neighbor's boy. As it turned out, all of Georgia's places were filled. Toombs could not obtain an at-large presidential appointment, and Porter had to wait a full two years for an opening.[31]

The formal letter offering him a cadetship arrived during the third week of February 1853. The political compromise that had nearly cost Jim Hester his life seemed to be holding, though many northerners found one of its key provisions, the Fugitive Slave Law, repulsive. An obscure Yankee matron had published, not long before, a novel called *Uncle Tom's Cabin*. It was selling hugely, advancing the cause of abolition immeasurably. And in far-off Kansas, along the marches of freedom and slavery, the killings were about to begin.

The view from Fairfield remained unclouded. In April, Felix Alexander married Louisa Toombs in a glittering ceremony at the Toombs mansion in Washington village. Miss Louisa wore a white silk dress trimmed with Honiton lace at the neck and sleeves. "She reminded me of some of the romantic descriptions in novels of 'fair and fragile' brides," one of her attendants wrote. It was the upcountry social event of the decade. Porter had hardly recovered from its pleasures when the time came for him to set out for West Point.

CHAPTER 2

OVER THE HORIZON

CHAMBERLAIN
BRUNSWICK AND BANGOR, 1848–55

H IS CLASSMATES CALLED HIM JACK. THE nickname pleased him, for it showed the other freshmen liked him and had taken the trouble to penetrate his rather forbidding exterior. Chamberlain made it clear he had come to Bowdoin to work. He had started a term behind the class, and meant to close the distance. Taking his own private pledge, he vowed to stay out of the Androscoggin taverns; the Saturday prayer circle would be his only diversion. The others seemed to understand. They let him confront the second-term freshman's course without the distraction of hazing. He plunged into Smyth's algebra, Livy, the *Memorabilia* of Xenophon, weekly translations into Latin, and Greek prose composition.[1]

Bowdoin in 1848 consisted of four principal buildings and an unfinished Romanesque chapel. Tall, red-brick Massachusetts Hall, built in 1802, stood with its back to the village and the mills, tenements, stables, and woodyards grouped picturesquely down by the Androscoggin falls. Then, one after another, there were Winthrop and Maine halls, the twin-spired chapel, and Appleton Hall. These buildings looked westward over a sandy tract toward Maine Street, a wide, unpaved thoroughfare that led away into a wasteland of blueberry thickets and scrub pine.[2]

Bowdoin College had come into practical existence on September 3, 1802, with one instructor and eight students. The college governors were orthodox Congregationalists, the curriculum rigidly classical. Bowdoin grew slowly, carefully guarding its orthodoxy; the authorities continued to enforce the Puritan sabbath, which began at sundown Saturday, far into the nineteenth century. The college built a distinguished faculty over the years, and by the end of the 1820s it could claim an impressive number of graduates bound for distinction. In the class of 1825 alone were Franklin Pierce, a future president of the United States; Henry Wadsworth Longfellow, who would become a popular poet and professional man of letters; and Nathaniel Hawthorne, one day to be recognized as a literary artist of the first rank.

Hawthorne was an indifferent and insubordinate scholar, except in Latin and thematic composition. The college assessed him nearly twelve dollars in fines one year (about half the annual tuition fee) for, among other things, Saturday-night visits to Ward's Tavern. Classmates recalled that the solitary Hawthorne rarely had much to say during those convivial evenings. Oblivious of his surroundings, he would fall into a brown study, lost in contemplation of his ancestor John Hathorn, the Massachusetts magistrate who had condemned innocents like Rebecca Chamberlain during the witch hysteria in Salem 130 years before.[3]

Chronically hard up, Hawthorne was in no position, as a not-yet-distinguished alumnus, to help Bowdoin through the financial panic of 1837. The slump seriously depleted the college's resources. Leonard Woods, who became president in 1839, trimmed expenses and approached successful alumni such as Longfellow and Pierce for contributions. Woods had an ally in Professor Thomas Cogswell Upham, a scholar of high reputation with an unexpected talent for fund-raising. "He traveled far, he begged earnestly," a Bowdoin historian wrote of Upham. Between them, the president and the professor restored a modest prosperity to Bowdoin.[4]

By Chamberlain's time, Woods and eight faculty members superintended the intellectual and moral development of 105 undergraduates, all male. Woods, a bachelor, headed a long-service faculty. The senior man, Parker Cleaveland, had taught chemistry and mineralogy since 1805. Generations of students compiled a rich fund of anecdote about his twin terrors, dogs and lightning. Upham, tall, stooped, and shy, came to Bowdoin as professor of mental and moral philosophy in 1824. He impressed the governors with his critiques of Kantian thought, which conservatives judged subversive. William Smyth, the professor of mathematics, joined the faculty in 1828. By 1848 he had become a colossal, even alarming figure, with his hair, gray whiskers, and black coat all dusted with chalk (he is credited with inventing the blackboard), an abstract thinker, a rambling lecturer, a teacher with little liking for students.[5]

Bowdoin men, periodically in rebellion against their orthodox and teetotaling (if sometimes eccentric) faculty, cultivated a hard-drinking, roughhousing reputation. They snatched a partially dissected cadaver from the medical school and hung it from a tree. They burned asafoetida on a residence hall stove. They whitewashed one of Professor Smyth's blackboards. Chamberlain had neither time nor inclination for such pranks. Preoccupied with work, he remained aloof from most forms of undergraduate leisure. He did, however, make acquaintances among the men of the Saturday prayer circle—they sounded, Benjamin G. Snow,* a professor at the Bangor Theological Seminary, wrote him in March 1848, like "the right sort of fellows." When one of the new secret socities, the fraternity Alpha Delta Phi, rushed him, Chamberlain wondered how he ought to respond. Snow told him he knew of nothing in fraternity life that might offend his religious sensibilities, though he did acknowledge that on occasion "there may be an excess of hilarity & jocoseness at which an exceedingly scrupulous conscience might be a little troubled." There were the long-established Peucinian and Athenean societies too. The Atheneans were said to be indifferent scholars, and rackety. Chamberlain joined the Peucinians.[6]

He boasted to another clerical confidant, the Reverend Stephen Thurston, of how easily he managed to resist temptation. "I really think I have never been so faithful to myself and my duty as since I have been at the College," he wrote toward the end of his first term. The others knew better than to rap on his door when someone had smuggled a cask of wine into college. "My classmates seem to understand me now," he told Thurston. "If there is to be a class cut or *spree*: 'O! No! Chamberlain won't go into it.' They seem to understand my duty pretty well. I have found myself sometimes alone but all came out right."[7]

As his circle expanded, Chamberlain learned to let down his guard. He did not ask others to adopt his own rather priggish standards, and as a result his classmates came to like and respect him. He had reached his full height of five feet, ten inches. Slender, well built, graceful, he was an undeniably good-looking young man. Sometimes the strain of overwork showed in his tired, red-rimmed eyes. But he relaxed as the

*Snow became one of the first missionaries to the islands of Micronesia, sent there by the American Board of Missions in 1851.

winter advanced, and by the end of the term he had begun to allow himself an occasional mild jaunt.

Mischief at Bowdoin increased with the onset of spring, when even such a tame tradition as Class Tree Day became an occasion for the release of winter-numbed animal spirits. Chamberlain's class chartered a two-horse hayrick, loaded it with liquor, and juddered off toward upcountry Lisbon in search of a tree to transplant onto the college grounds. Most of the party returned insensible. Woods summoned Chamberlain the next day and demanded the offenders' names. He refused to supply them; the president threatened suspension. Chamberlain remained defiant. His friends rallied around him. "Boys, let's go down and own up to the cider. This sha'n't come on Jack." They got reprimands on top of their hangovers. Jack stayed in school.[8]

The 1840s were an evangelical time.* Writing long afterward, Chamberlain would make light of his profession of faith in Brewer in 1845, but he seems to have been caught up in a surge of religious intensity at Bowdoin. The 1848 revival struck Maine with irresistible force. Snow wrote Chamberlain to report scores of conversions in Bangor. When the troupe of traveling evangelists known as Bailey's Praying Band came to town, the Bangor churches rang up another fifty-two converts. At Bowdoin, twice-daily chapel services were mandatory. Extracurricular Thursday-night Bible study sessions and the Saturday-night prayer circle were well attended. "At the beginning of the term there were only two pious persons in the class," Chamberlain wrote Thurston late in his first year. "There are six now"—Chamberlain emphatically among them.[9]

He found time to spare for his classmates because he had prepared himself so thoroughly. "I am not obliged to study as hard as I did at home and the labor I there accomplished seems now almost impossible. I do not attempt to read much—my *Bible*, Greek text, & Upham's *Interior Life* are almost my only reading," he wrote Thurston. Math problems continued to perplex him. On one occasion, unsure of the material, he cut a recitation with the olympian Smyth. "I think you took the right course," Snow told him, "for if old Smyth had taken hold of you, there would not have been a greast spot left."[10]

Chamberlain fought off recurrent illnesses, minor but draining, during

*Millennial too. A prophet named Miller attracted a large following in Maine with his prediction that the world would end on April 3, 1843. His influence waned as spring shaded into summer that fateful year.

much of his first term, and it may have been on account of his health that he gave up his ambition to take a degree in two years. Snow gently endorsed the decision. "I am inclined to think that you will need the whole 4 yrs. of College life to rub off your greenness," he wrote. It was enough to have overcome his inadequate early schooling and to have caught up with the class. He went home to Brewer in August 1848 with, he reported proudly, "a clean sophomore ticket."[11]

He returned in September for the second-year course: more of *The Odyssey*, Horace's *Odes*, tutorials in geometry and French, weekly declamations in all classes. Afflicted with that embarrassing stammer, especially on initial *p*'s, *b*'s, and *t*'s, Chamberlain endured agonizing sessions with Alpheus Packard, the professor of ancient languages, until he learned to apply his father's "order for life" to master the impediment. He used to scout a text beforehand for difficult passages and rehearse a rhythmic chant—it came close to a form of singing—that would carry him over the rough spots. "The old Spartans used to sing their laws for after-dinner past-time," he explained later. "And Spartan laws were no laughing matter."[12]

Chamberlain worked hard through the winter and spring of 1849 at Demosthenes, Horace, and Terence, and Smyth's trigonometry. Not satisfied merely to draw even, he resolved to pull ahead of the class. He pushed so hard he nearly killed himself. At summer's end his health broke down, and he reached Brewer in August in a state of collapse. He spent his twenty-first birthday, September 28, 1849, in the sickroom. The illness, never diagnosed, baffled the village doctor. For several weeks he lay near death. Sally Chamberlain discharged the local man and consulted a homeopath. The patient began to rally. Though there is no record of whatever course of treatment the physician prescribed, Chamberlain credited him with restoring his health. He missed the entire academic year of 1849–50, but returned to Bowdoin in September 1850 at full strength.[13]

By then the echo of large issues could be heard, even in backwater Brunswick. Maine had scarcely been touched by the antislavery agitation of the 1830s and 1840s. The state normally voted Democratic, and its Yankee individualists, Joshua Chamberlain, Jr., among them, tended to hold strong states' rights views. The passionate, prophetic William Lloyd Garrison lectured in Maine, but failed to stir audiences there with his call for immediate abolition. Mainers preferred to allow slavery to wither gradually. Some offered tepid support for African colonization. The state's most powerful religious organization, the Congregational General Conference, declined to take up the crusade in any practical way.[14]

Still, pressures were mounting. The Fugitive Slave Law of 1850, which committed federal authorities to return runaways to their owners, converted many mild liberals into radical abolitionists. Chamberlain's mentor Thurston had been a gradualist content to lobby quietly among the Bangor seminarians. Now he became a firebrand, damning the fugitive provision as "worthy to be reckoned only in the code of Draco, whose laws were written in blood." Professor Smyth cast the only vote for the antislavery Liberty Party in Brunswick in 1840, served on antislavery committees, and exchanged polite letters with a slavery apologist from South Carolina. The 1850 law provoked him to direct action. Smyth helped operate an Underground Railroad station in Brunswick. "I remember the wales and scars on the backs of the poor creatures," one of his sons wrote in recollection of Smyth's seditious work.[15]

The fugitive law stoked the creative fires of one of the professor's Brunswick neighbors, Harriet Beecher Stowe, the matronly consort of the Collins Professor of Natural and Revealed Religion. She arrived in Brunswick from Ohio in the spring of 1850 after Calvin Stowe accepted the Collins professorship. The Stowes took the Parson Titcomb house on Federal Street, where Harriet painted and put up new wallpaper, negotiated with the landlord about the well and the sinks, and gave birth to another child, her seventh. There, too, she found her antislavery voice.

Inspiration visited Mrs. Stowe in the First Parish Church, Brunswick, on Communion Sunday in February 1851. The Reverend George Adams droned on from the pulpit that morning; his brown-eyed daughter Fannie sat drowsily at the organ; Lawrence Chamberlain listened from the choir, casting an occasional glance in the organist's direction. Back in Pew 23, Mrs. Stowe lapsed into a sort of trance, transfixed by a vision: a white-haired slave being savagely beaten by his master, praying for his tormentor's forgiveness as his life bled away. That afternoon, in her bedroom, she wrote down the vision on scraps of brown grocery paper. Mrs. Stowe called the old slave Uncle Tom. She called the master Simon Legree.

The first of forty episodes of *Uncle Tom's Cabin* appeared on June 5, 1851, in an antislavery journal called *The National Era*. She worked away at the weekly installments all through the autumn and winter of 1851. They were an immediate hit. Readers passed copies of *The National Era* from hand to hand. In many northern households the reading aloud of the latest episode became a Saturday-evening ritual: Eliza fleeing across the Ohio ice floes; Little Eva on her deathbed; St. Clare's accidental death; and Tom's sale to the sadistic Legree.[16]

Mrs. Stowe herself read to select weekly gatherings in her parlor or at Professor Smyth's house. Smyth and Thomas Upham were increasingly pessimistic about the future. Like more prominent New England intellectuals, they were fascinated with the idea of a blood purge that would atone for the nation's great sin.* "Not that they desired war, or would have carried willingly their agitation to such an extremity," wrote Newman Smyth, the professor's younger son, "but they [seemed] to think that . . . so great a wrong as slavery could not be settled without the shedding of blood."[17]

Chamberlain attended the readings at the Stowes', sometimes in company with Fannie Adams, the minister's daughter. No one dreamed then, he wrote later, that Mrs. Stowe's book would be so influential. Still, *Uncle Tom's Cabin* made little impression on him at the time. Mrs. Stowe's parlor was a convenient place to meet dark-haired Fannie. In any case, other matters claimed his attention. He led the First Parish Church choir in his junior and senior years. He was president of the Praying Circle, now grown to twenty-two members. He read his first fiction around this time, on assignment from Henry H. Boody, the professor of elocution and rhetoric: Hawthorne's *House of the Seven Gables,* published in 1851. The novel's action turned on an ancient curse that followed a family down the generations. Hawthorne's tale appealed to Chamberlain's Gothic tastes, and called his ancestor Rebecca to mind. The curse had been hurled by one of the accused witches at a Salem witch-trial judge: "God will give you blood to drink." Later, after the blood purge Smyth and Upham foretold had come to pass, Chamberlain had cause to remember the moral of Hawthorne's tale: "The wrongdoing of one generation lives into successive ones."[18]

Then there was Fannie. Frances Caroline Adams, born August 12, 1826, in Boston, came as a child into the home of her clergyman uncle George Adams and his wife, Ann. He formally adopted her, along with another child, Anna Davis. Fannie was not an orphan, however. It is not clear why she and her natural parents parted. Ashur and Amelia Wyllys Adams lived on in good health for many years. As a young woman, Fannie exchanged letters with them and sometimes visited their Boston home.[19]

*"It is plain, now, that our pilgrimage must lead through a Red Sea, wherein many a Pharaoh will go under and perish," Theodore Parker, the Boston abolitionist, wrote.

A handsome, lively girl, vain and willful, she had a taste for ornament that drove her adoptive father to deliver regular scoldings about her extravagant ways. Older people, women especially, judged Fannie lacking in the dignity proper in a minister's daughter. "Beads & furbelows & finery depend upon it are very unbecoming to one in your situation & your expectations," her spinster cousin Deborah Folsom admonished. "Your love for such things is a weak spot in your character & you ought to fight against it." Appearance and health figured large in Fannie's fitful correspondence with her cousin Deborah and other friends. She seems to have had a lot of trouble with her teeth.[20]

George Adams made little effort to conceal his misgivings about Fannie's growing intimacy with Lawrence Chamberlain. Pastor of the First Parish Church since 1829, Adams was a Brunswick eminence. Even the merchant princes were in awe of him, despite his abolitionism and a decided taste, freely indulged, for pastoral innovation. Adams introduced the organ to the First Parish Church; as late as 1840, traditionalists were still unreconciled to it. He scandalized the congregation one Sunday in 1841 when he invited a black clergyman to stand with him in the pulpit. Several outraged parishioners rose and walked out. Adams ignored the commotion and went on with his sermon.[21]

If Chamberlain had qualms about risking conflict with this powerful personality, they did not deflect him from his pursuit of Fannie. Adams left no record of the grounds for his disapproval, though they evidently had as much to do with the unquiet Fannie as with Chamberlain. On the face of things, it seemed a match of equals. Chamberlain lacked polish, but Fannie was two years older and, though pretty enough, despite her rickety teeth, had hardly been besieged by suitors. "Your father has not much faith in our relation—I cannot call it engagement, it seems something more—he does not expect that much will ever come of it, or that it will last very long," Chamberlain, full of resolve, wrote her. "I do not need to be told that—I see it plainly enough. I simply say he has mistaken his man."[22]

He began courting Fannie during a period of upheaval in the Adams household. Ann Folsom Adams had died in February 1850 after a long illness; the widower was hardly out of mourning before he found himself preparing for a new marriage. The first Mrs. Adams had been much loved in the parish, combining, as one admirer put it, "the wisdom of the serpent with the harmlessness of the dove." Her friends were chagrined that her place could be filled so easily—and so soon.[23]

Adams met Helen Root at a missions conference in Chicago in June 1851. In September he called on her at her father's North Redding, Massachusetts, home, where they walked out together, read Tennyson's "In Memoriam," and reached what he took to be an understanding. "I infer," he confided to his diary after puzzling out the first letter from Miss Root after his return home, "that we are to be considered now as definitely engaged." He was fifty; she was a few months older than Fannie. Adams was giddily happy. "Did not sleep last night," he wrote on December 28, 1851. "What a change this week will make in my condition! I expect to be married on Tuesday—& to such a woman!"[24]

They were wed December 30 in North Redding, with Fannie a reluctant witness. Emotions ran high in Adams's all-female household. Fannie and Anna disliked their young stepmother from the start. "Helen gets along nicely—don't she? How do people like her have to dress so much more than Mother ever did?" Anna wrote her sister in March. Fannie, Anna, and Deborah Folsom kept up the pressure. Adams worked patiently to bring all three around, especially Fannie. But by the summer of 1852 he had heard and seen enough. He decided to clear out the parsonage, inviting Fannie to spend the season elsewhere—in Bangor, if she liked, or with friends in Massachusetts. "Helen cannot stand it long as things have gone lately," he told her bluntly.[25]

In any event, Fannie set her own course. She decided to go south to teach, as so many young Yankee women had done before her. Chamberlain urged her to defy her father and stay home, boldly suggesting that Adams and his young bride decamp instead. Doubtful at first, he gradually came around to Fannie's scheme. "I see now the wisdom as well as the nobleness & independence of your present resolution and undertaking," he told her. Meanwhile, he had his own arrangements to make. Chamberlain's distinguished undergraduate career was drawing to a close. He had been special assistant his senior year to the venerable Professor Cleaveland. He had read Dante and Tasso in Italian. He had attended Calvin Stowe's lectures on Hebrew literature, and Smyth's on the steam engine. By year's end he had achieved first rank in Greek and French and, overcoming the stammer, won prizes in declamation. By dint of hard work he excelled in mathematics too.[26]

He raised the West Point issue again. College graduates not uncommonly went on to the military academy; Oliver Otis Howard of Bowdoin's class of 1850 was finishing his second year as a cadet there. But Sally Chamberlain had not forgotten the original agreement: Bowdoin, then the seminary. Sister Anna remembered too: "How do you and Chamberlain come on now? Is he still bent on going missionary?" she teased Fannie. In the spring of 1852, Chamberlain was in the last stages of decision. He talked the matter over with Fannie, who evidently had no wish to follow the drum. Still, he did not finally give up the idea of West Point until the summer.[27]

Bowdoin celebrated its fiftieth commencement on September 1, 1852, and the speakers' platform sagged under the weight of the dignitaries upon it. Franklin Pierce, who would be president-elect of the United States within two months, was there; Longfellow was there, looking sleek and prosperous; Hawthorne, dark, massive, solitary as ever, was there, too, but he arrived late, sat at the edge of the tented enclosure, and vanished when some orator spotted him in the audience and began to praise him. Chamberlain spoke and declaimed, but found the going hard on account of the celebrities. He reported a bad case of stage fright and a mortifying recurrence of the stammer—a failure, he said, that "lessened the pang of parting" from Bowdoin. Adams thought he did well, except for what he charitably described as a lapse of memory toward the end.[28]

The strains of the Germania band died away, Hawthorne made good his escape, and Chamberlain and Fannie boarded the train for Bangor. She stayed with cousins there, and paid calls on the Chamberlains in Brewer. He and Fannie both were anxious about the pending separation. Chamberlain consoled himself by recalling details of their courtship the year before, when they had been much alone. "We shall live over some of the olden days again," he promised her, "& the deep dark beauty of those summer nights will not be a shadow of memories but a life in resurrection." Sally and Joshua Chamberlain signaled their approval. He and Fannie were formally engaged that autumn.[29]

Marriage would, of course, have to be put off until Chamberlain could complete the three-year course at Bangor Theological Seminary and receive a minister's call. West Point, he could note with forced cheerfulness, would have taken four years. "Only think, honey-bee," he wrote Fannie, "it is like a dream—three years will go like a flash. In three little years we shall come *home* forever. What'll you bet I shan't be as old as you are, then? So you won't fuss about that any more." Slowed by "a lameness in her feet," Fannie put off her departure for several weeks. She finally left for Georgia December 22, her father accompanying her on the train as far as Freeport.[30]

From the first, Chamberlain tormented himself with doubts about

Fannie's constancy. "The sky is all overcast, and the rain is rushing down, & the wind is sighing and moaning, and my heart is overspread with loneliness and gloom," he wrote her during one of his recurrent periods of misery. He worked hard at Hebrew and Greek, biblical criticism, natural and revealed religion, the rights, duties, and responsibilities of pastoral office. There were courses in homiletics and instruction in the order of exercises in the Congregational service: prayer, scriptures, hymn, prayer, hymn, sermon, prayer, hymn, and benediction.[31]

It was a drab existence. "I finished Cicero's select orations today at 2½ o'clock P.M.," he noted in August 1853. "By examining my journal of sometime back I find that I commenced these orations on the 6th of June, making 2 mo. 12 da. which I have spent on them." He varied the academic routine by teaching a ladies' class in German language and literature, serving a term as Brewer supervisor of schools, and playing the organ in the Brewer church. Moonlight jobs kept him clear of debt, and a full schedule helped take his mind off Fannie.[32]

She had been seasick on the steamer ("I never held my head up but once," she complained), and found Milledgeville, the Georgia capital, uncomfortably chilly and damp that first winter, not at all like the spiced tropical place of her imagination. "I have a constant severe headache," Fannie wrote her natural sister, Charlotte Adams, "and such a cold on my lungs that I can scarcely speak a great deal of the time, and then there is such a tedious and painful oppression at my chest." Despite these maladies, she plunged into her work, teaching voice at the Milledgeville school, giving private piano lessons, and playing the organ at the Milledgeville church. From Bangor, Chamberlain struck off passionate letters to her, full of complaint about the infrequency of her replies. When she did write, she veered wildly from warmth to indifference, emotional swings that vexed and bewildered him.[33]

As Grant's biographer William McFeely has noted, the "eroticism of hesitation" was a convention of Victorian courtship. Fannie faithfully observed it during their long engagement. At times she could be sexually suggestive. "I'm afraid you are getting to be a naughty girl," Chamberlain, titillated, responded to one letter. Then she would turn distant and cold. Fannie once likened childbearing to prostitution, and decreed theirs would be a sexless, childless marriage. He could hardly believe it. "Let me beg of you not to pretend you have no passionate feelings," he shot back. "I do not like to contemplate you as a fossil remain." For the most part, though, dreading exposure, she wrote cautiously. She accused him of showing her letters, intimate passages included, to Cousin Deborah and even to his mother. Fannie continued to write with constraint long after they were married. "I cannot bear that the sacred expressions of affection should be bandied about and left lying about the house like a tailor's bill," she once told him.[34]

Fannie soon adjusted to Southern ways. Though raised in an antislavery household, the reality of slavery did not distress her. Southerners were charming. Their black dependents were well cared for, happy, and loyal. She could see no reason for New England and the South to quarrel. President-elect Pierce, of New Hampshire and Bowdoin, was shortly to promise, in his inaugural address, a rigorous enforcement of the Fugitive Slave Law. Georgians, Fannie felt, would be equally reasonable. "I just glanced up to the mantelpiece in this room," she wrote Charlotte, "and what book do you suppose I saw there? No other than *Uncle Tom's Cabin* in two volumes, well-thumbed, too!"[35]

In ice-shackled Bangor, Chamberlain plodded through the second- and third-year courses at the theological seminary: church history, systematic theology, sacred rhetoric. Uncertain about the future, he considered emigrating to California, where gold strikes were sustaining an unprecedented economic boom. He thought of starting a college there. Fannie took the scheme seriously enough to mention it to Deborah Folsom in Brunswick. "There is a man here from that land of gold wanting five or six to go back with him," Deborah wrote helpfully. Chamberlain let the opportunity pass.[36]

Fannie was restless too. By 1854, Milledgeville had begun to pall. She left off talking about the celibate life. She wanted to be married, and the sooner the better. "Keep up a strong heart," Cousin Deborah advised, "Chamberlain will soon finish his studies." Fannie, impatient, job-hunted in Georgia on his behalf, urging him to apply for an opening at the state university in Athens. When he replied that he lacked the qualifications for a professorship, she proposed an alternative—a teaching position in a girls' school. "Now if I can get the situation for you still, are you willing to enlist for one year?" Fannie asked. She reminded him, too, that she had shown herself capable of making a living. "I can always lend a helping hand in this matter of our '*support,*' whatever turns up," she offered. "I'm not afraid!"[37]

Her exile, as she had begun to call it, ended in the midsummer of 1855. By mid-August she was home in Brunswick. Chamberlain took his degree at Bangor and delivered the master's oration at Bowdoin at the end of the month. He lobbied hard for a job, though without much success. George Adams had little to suggest, beyond fill-in preaching. The oration, titled "Law and Liberty," left a good impression. "Everybody here, high and low, praises your commencement performance," Fannie wrote him. As a consequence, Bowdoin offered him a junior instructorship in religion. His practice sermons yielded calls from two Maine churches. Chamberlain turned both down. "I am more of a scholar than preacher," he told Fannie, who anyway had little desire for a half-share in a country parson's life.[38]

George Adams had defended the Gothic design of the new First Parish Church from accusations of popery. The furor gradually died down, and parishioners grew accustomed to the arches and ornaments of their board-and-batten church, painted gray to give the effect of stone. Quelling his doubts, Adams married his adopted daughter and Lawrence Chamberlain in the nave there on the sunny, cold afternoon of December 7, 1855. "I feel sadly about poor Fanny," Adams wrote that night, "fearing greatly she will not make herself happy." The newlywed couple found rented quarters near Bowdoin early in the new year. As though born to it, Chamberlain began to live the secure, ordered, and predictable life of a country college professor.[39]

Alexander
West Point, 1853–57

The West Point setting struck Leopold Alexander with awe. "There is no place like it this side of heaven," he wrote of his first view of the fortress on a clifftop plateau 180 feet above the Hudson River. His son would experience loneliness there, long stretches of boredom, near-despair. But Cadet Alexander saw the green heights and the shining river at their most majestic in June 1853, the novelty of new surroundings and the shock of immersion in cadet life postponing the inevitable attacks of homesickness, doubt, and distaste for the pettiness of military ways.[1]

He arrived June 12 after a three-and-a-half-day railroad journey, a brief stopover in New York City, where he stayed in the fashionable Astor House, and a visit with Hillhouse cousins in Troy, New York. At the entrance examination, he measured five feet, nine and a half inches and weighed 150 pounds. He had nothing else to say about the exam, for which he had been more than adequately tutored. In any case, a young man had to make an effort to fail the admissions exam at 1850s West Point. One candidate told his father the board questioned him on simple fractions, then asked him to read an extract from Blair's *Rhetoric* and write out a sentence. "This I done and was sent to my seat," he went on. "This closed the examination."[2]

Alexander entered just as James McNeill Whistler was leaving, dismissed after two years for a long list of deficiencies.* Drawing had been Whistler's best subject, though he showed little deference to his instructor, Robert W. Weir, a painter of conventional ability and a popular teacher. Philip Sheridan, John Bell Hood, and James B. McPherson had just graduated. J. E. B. Stuart and Oliver O. Howard were first-class cadets. Fitzhugh Lee had advanced to the third class. His uncle Robert E. Lee was superintendent.[3]

West Point had survived a series of attacks in the 1830s and 1840s with its reputation enhanced. Academy graduates distinguished themselves in the Mexican War, and West Pointers on the frontier were given credit for pacifying the native peoples and policing the emigrant trails. Jacksonian Democrats had charged the academy with elitism. In fact, West Point drew from a wide range of backgrounds. Cadets from small-town, middle-class families outnumbered southern patricians like Alexander. The academy trained soldiers and engineers. In common with such secular institutions as Chamberlain's Bowdoin, it also aimed to turn out an accepted Victorian type of gentleman, upright, honorbound, Christian.[4]

Cadet Alexander outfitted himself with the required "articles of clothing and necessaries," some thirty-three items, from a greatcoat to candlesticks, prescribed in academy regulations. In warm weather he wore a gray double-breasted coatee (with three rows of bell buttons and a stiff collar) and white duck trousers. Shod in clumsy ankle boots, he practiced the toe-and-ball step that gave cadets their peculiar gait. His headgear, a seven-inch-high black leather cap with a bell crown, an eight-inch black plume, and a polished leather visor, weighed fully five pounds. It gave some cadets headaches.[5]

After a few days in barracks the new fourth classmen—the plebes—went into summer encampment. This gave Alexander his first taste of practical soldiering. That first summer was mostly drill. A typical day opened with reveille at five o'clock, then drill until six-thirty. Breakfast

---

*"Had silicon been a gas," Whistler wrote many years later, "I would have been a major general."

followed at seven, then parade till eight, with more drill at nine. The plebes attended dancing class from 3:00 to 4:00 P.M. and returned to the parade ground for more drill at 5:30. Evening parade and inspection followed at seven, with dinner at eight and taps at nine o'clock.[6]

Growing up in a large family had accustomed Aleck, as the cadets began to call him, to a fair amount of rough-and-tumble. He could hardly have been unprepared to face West Point hazing. It was mostly coarse jibes and silly pranks, such as the time a gang of upperclassmen pulled a sleeping cadet, Alexander's Georgia friend Tom Berry, from his tent by the heels. Forgetting his manners, Berry damned their souls; the hazing went on anyway. Alexander, quick-tempered and proud, despised the practice. Teasing from your older brother and sisters was one thing. Manhandling by some loutish third classman from Michigan or Ohio was quite another.

He complained privately, but kept his anger in check in public. His newlywed brother Felix, visiting West Point in July, noted his self-command with approval. He bore "patiently all the little indignities the older cadets at times impose on the younger," Felix wrote their father. Leopold responded sympathetically to Aleck's laments. "When I read your complaints, & the story of the shameful conduct of the older cadets, I almost regret that you ever went there," he wrote. The third classmen eased up as the summer advanced. A first classman, James Deshler of Alabama, took an interest in Alexander and helped him through the worst of it. By the end of July he could write his sister Cliff that his chief vexation was the tendency of his shirt collars to rise.[7]

His brother's visit further revived him—"A gladder man to see anyone you never saw," Felix reported—and he found life under canvas exhilarating. For the time being, at least, his mother could stop fretting about his health. "He is looking very well, and I think his cadet's uniform becomes him," Felix went on. "His bearing too is quite erect, and all the change that I see in him is for the better."[8]

The cadets broke camp in September and returned to barracks. Alexander, assigned to Company D, shared a room with Lawrence Kip, son of the Episcopal bishop of California. Their quarters were spartan. Regulations permitted one looking glass, one washstand, one washbasin, one pitcher, one pail, one broom, and one scrub brush per room. Alexander and Kip each had one iron bedstead with mattress, a straight-backed chair, a table, and a lamp. Fairfield seemed impossibly far away.[9]

He had vowed to "graduate in the engineers," but there were only four or five openings a year in the army's elite corps, so he would need to finish near the top of the class—to place "in the fives." The entrance exam might have been a farce, but West Point's curriculum was demanding. Reforming Superintendent Sylvanus Thayer laid it down in the 1820s that each cadet would be drilled in every subject, every day. For an ambitious cadet, that meant devoting nearly every free hour to work.[10]

During the first year he studied algebra, geometry, trigonometry, English grammar, and French. Math, heavily emphasized in the West Point system, came easily to Alexander—fortunately so, for William H. C. Bartlett, the mathematics professor, had a reputation as a poor instructor. Nervous, dyspeptic (he could not digest meat), he sped through complex problems, leaving the duller cadets to puzzle out solutions later, on their own.[11]

Alexander's desire to rise to the top drove him to work at a furious pace. He was soon complaining of aching eyes and blurred vision. His mother sent him an eyeshade. When it failed to arrive, she accused Superintendent Lee of intercepting it. She urged him to confront Lee about the missing article. Sarah scolded him about his irregular methods of study, especially his habit of rising in the middle of the night to work.[12]

"This is the very *worst* way in which you could do it," she wrote. "The exposure of rising from the warm bed at midnight, & the transition from total darkness & repose, to lamplight & study, is too severe—& both your health & your eyes will be greatly endangered." She went on to remind him that she and his father cared more for his well-being than for academic achievement, and to caution him about his ambitions. "You must not feel that we expect so much from you that you must overtax yourself. Perhaps you covet distinction too earnestly as an *end*, & this is not right for a Christian. Try to think less of your competitors, & do your duty without reference to them."[13]

Alexander might have replied that, if nothing else, hard work at least helped pass the time. West Point routines were monochromatic and repetitive. Outside the section room, cadets rode, fenced, and drilled interminably. Little else happened, apart from an occasional brawl or drunken frolic. There were few extracurricular activities. Alexander lamented the lack of opportunities for worship; his upcountry Presbyterianism remained strong. ("I long to know if there is *really* no church organization at W. Point," his mother asked.) The academy library contained mostly military studies and engineering texts. In any case, novel-reading was against the regulations. So were drinking, smoking and card-playing.[14]

He survived mental and physical exertion, cold and dimly lit quarters, execrable food. The colicky Professor Bartlett might be offered the tend-erest part of a chicken; cadets got boiled meat, boiled potatoes, and boiled pudding. (Fare in the chronically underfed Army of Northern Virginia would be little worse.) Daydreaming hungrily of hog-killing sea-son at Fairfield, he complained the beef was so tough he couldn't drive a fork into it.

Alexander enjoyed a second short respite from the numbing grind of academy life in October, when his sister Louisa and her husband, Jeremy Gilmer, an 1839 graduate and a career army engineer, stopped at West Point for several days. Lee spoke highly of Cadet Alexander to Captain Gilmer. The instructors validated Lee's assessment. Aleck had fallen be-hind socially, though, and he resisted the Gilmers' invitation to accom-pany them in a call on the Lees. Gilmer thought the young man could learn something of the social arts from the superintendent's wife, Mary Custis Lee. "She would do much to give him confidence in himself when in the society of ladies," Gilmer wrote Fairfield.[15]

The sorry state of his clothes may have explained Alexander's stand-offishness. Used to having his wants supplied, he had difficulty adjusting to the academy's strict sumptuary laws. By midterm his coat and trousers were falling apart. A cadet's modest pay (thirty dollars a month) went entirely for necessities at the post commissary. Alexander never saw a penny of his earnings. His father schemed to get cash into his hands, but the authorities were vigilant.* When a packet from Sarah containing five shirts disappeared, Alexander found himself in a crisis. Lee, hewing to the regulations, refused to let the elder Alexander deposit money in the commissary account for shirts, trousers, and a greatcoat. "The object is to teach economy," Gilmer wrote the patriarch in an effort to explain why the boy should be kept in rags. "But I much fear he will look like a beggar before the first of January."[16]

In spite of such irritations, he placed fourth in the examinations of January 1854. His parents were delighted. Sarah, though, scolded him about his developing southern chauvinism. She had lectured on ambi-

---

*"My remittances at any one time will be small, since you have no safe place to keep your funds, and West Point (unlike Heaven) is a place where thieves do break in and steal," Leopold wrote him, enclosing five dollars.

tion; now she lectured on bigotry. Sectional tensions, growing out of the slavery dispute and on the rise since the close of the Mexican War, were reflected in the West Point cadet corps. Fights had broken out between Northerners and Southerners. Some cadets found themselves ostracized for holding supposedly abolitionist views.[17]

Alexander developed friendships with northern cadets (one of his West Point intimates, New Yorker Guilford Bailey, would be killed commanding federal artillery at Seven Pines in 1862), but did not allow his regard for individuals to soften his general condemnation of Yankees. The chip on his shoulder exasperated his mother. "These extreme prejudices are unworthy of liberal & enlightened minds & are especially unbecoming one who has pledged to serve the country as a *whole*," she wrote him. "You must bear in mind that there are many good people at the north, however they may be led to embrace mistaken views & opinions concerning the South and its affairs."[18]

One of the Alexanders' New England connections took it upon himself to enlighten his fellow Yankees. Nehemiah Adams, a Boston Presbyterian clergyman, had held mild antislavery views, akin to those of Bowdoin's Professor Smyth. He signed a petition opposing the extension of slavery into the Kansas and Nebraska territories, and contributed to a fund to help a freed slave buy his wife and children out of bondage. But when the frail, ailing Adams spent a restorative winter at Fairfield in 1853–54, the scales fell from his eyes.[19]

Adams conceived *A South-Side View of Slavery*, which he published in 1854, as a counterblast to Harriet Beecher Stowe's *Uncle Tom's Cabin*. He shows healthy, happy Negroes whistling at their not particularly taxing work. "The lifting of one leg in laughing," he wrote, "seemed as natural as a Frenchman's shrug." Slaves on cotton plantations worked no harder than northern agricultural laborers. Their dwelling places might look like hovels, but in fact they were snug and comfortable, cool in summer and warm in winter. There were no paupers under the slave system. "I feel," Adams went on, "like one who has visited a friend who is sick and reported to be destitute and extremely miserable, but has found him comfortable and happy."[20]

Adams's unabashed apology for slavery left no impression on the political debate (though, Alexander wrote later, "it caused him some trouble with some of his friends at home"). Still, it gratified Sarah; she could apply it as a sort of salve to her sore conscience. Her health had continued to deteriorate. Leopold took her for long winter stretches to the milder coastal climate of Hopewell, the Alexander plantation near Sunbury in Liberty County. Sunbury was an abandoned settlement, and the old house at Hopewell where they had spent the first months of their married life had fallen into decay. The patriarch built a smaller place nearby that became a sort of hospice during his wife's last years.[21]

She seems to have viewed Hopewell and its surroundings as a metaphor for her own failing condition. Wandering among the ruins, she lost herself in reverie. "Of the scenes where we met and walked and rode and were merry together, not a vestige remains. Of our old dwelling ... only a few broken bricks can be seen," she wrote dreamily to Cliff. "Even the old trees, the old houses, the streets are gone, and cornfields occupy the place of the streets, the gardens, the houses." Sarah looked into the future too, and saw her own end. "I thought how youth had passed away, and friends and relatives and companions had also gone, and I felt that I too am passing away, and must soon be numbered among those whose places shall know them no more on earth."[22]

By the winter of 1854 she was bedfast. Leopold fretted that she had begun to lose interest in the life around her. That may have been the effect of morphine. The dosage had been gradually increased over the years. Morphine and other opium derivatives were widely prescribed for a vast range of nineteenth-century ailments. For the relief it gave, Sarah might have agreed with the novelist Wilkie Collins, who said, "Who was the man who invented laudanum? I thank him from the bottom of my heart." But the treatment carried a high price. She had become an addict.[23]

When she rallied in the early spring of 1854, Leopold decided to go ahead with a planned trip north. Specialists could be consulted, a visit paid to Porter at West Point. They sailed for Philadelphia June 7 in the new steamer *Keystone State*. For all her frailty, Sarah was a good sailor. She drank in the fresh breezes and spent hours looking out upon the sea. Leopold, seasick, remained in their stateroom for most of the voyage.[24]

The Philadelphia specialist, a homeopath, ordered an immediate reduction in Sarah's morphine intake. Within a few days she had cut the dosage in half. Withdrawal left her pale, nervous, and weak. "Her system is undergoing a severe trial," wrote Leopold. "I think she had better let it remain [at one-half] for a little while until her system recovers from the shock." He left her in Philadelphia in early July while he traveled up to West Point. He found his son in flourishing condition, invigorated by his second summer encampment. "He is a fine looking fellow now though he is as brown as a nut," Leopold wrote Fairfield.[25]

Sarah longed to see him, and felt well enough later in the month to attempt the journey. She relapsed shortly after reaching West Point. Alexander visited his parents' rooms in Roe's Hotel, near the post, as often as he could. These were grim weeks. Sarah could not shake the addiction, and the effort was dealing a final blow to her enfeebled constitution. For weeks she lay too ill to be moved. Leopold finally decided to risk the return trip to Philadelphia. By then she had wasted away to seventy-nine pounds, a skeleton covered by a gauze of flesh. She refused to allow her son to come to Roe's that last morning to say good-bye.[26]

Sarah Alexander's flickering existence came to an end at Fairfield on February 28, 1855. The victim, probably, of tuberculosis, she had taken the morphine to alleviate, among other symptoms, a racking cough. Leopold and their daughters took turns by the bedside through her final hours. They buried her a few days later in the family graveyard. Her end haunted Cadet Alexander. "I have spent many evenings lately on the plain in front of the hotel looking at the little window of the room where I last saw my dear mother," he wrote more than a year afterward. At first, Leopold seemed unable to accept his loss. "I am still drinking the bitter cup, but it has no remorseful dregs in it," he said. "I think of her with unmingled pleasure." It was as though she were away in Savannah or Madison Springs.[27]

Alexander did not apply for a compassionate leave of absence. In any case, Robert Lee almost certainly would have denied him; he rarely approved such requests.* Alexander could take Lee or leave him alone. He expressed no regrets when the superintendent's tour of duty ended in late March 1855, reporting his departure as a routine incident of the trooping season. "Lt. Nelson's regiment is ordered against the Sioux Indians, & we hope to get rid of him also," he wrote with a cadet's unshakable conviction that one officer was as good (or bad) as another. As it happened, he found Lee's successor, Maj. Jonathan G. Barnard, even more difficult to deal with, especially in the matter of erasing what he considered an undeserved set of demerits from his record. (A cadet officer had accused him of failing to keep his platoon's rear rank closed with the front on a march to parade, a charge he vehemently denied.)

*Though in 1853 Lee did give Whistler permission to go to New York to meet his soon-to-be-immortalized mother.

"Maj. Barnard is more obstinate than Col. Lee, & deaf as a post besides," he complained.[28]

By June, Alexander had advanced one place, to third in the class. A few days after the examinations, he headed south to Fairfield for his summer furlough, the only interval in West Point's four-year ordeal. He visited Cliff and her husband (she had married George C. Hull, a civil engineer, in 1854) in Athens and did the circuit of the Georgia hill spas. There he put to use such social skills as he had been able to acquire from Mary Custis Lee, practicing the arts of seduction on a friend's sister, one Annie Church. She did not respond. "I never saw her again," Alexander wrote later, adding rather heartlessly, "She married a Whitner and died in Anderson, S.C., leaving a large family."[29]

He returned to West Point at the end of August. A photograph made at about this time shows a cool-eyed, smooth-shaven, stiffly dignified young man some little way short of handsome. He looks certain of himself, impatient of obstacles. The family agreed it was a fair representation. "We think it somewhat like you," the patriarch wrote, "but the nose is exaggerated." He could not resist an aphorism. "Remember you were nursed at the heart, not by sucking a cartridge," Leopold added, thinking perhaps of the severe, imperious expression the camera had captured.[30]

As his response to the demerits suggests, Alexander reacted forcefully when he believed he had been wronged. He chafed under petty injustices, those everyday unfairnesses that seemed to be built into the West Point system as part of a soldier's training. "My French teacher, Prof. Agnel, aggravates me almost as much, now, as my reports have done," he wrote his father. "He treats me shamefully in marking me, so that the whole section has noticed it, & he has put me in marks fully five files below where I ought to be." Alexander protested; Agnel continued to mark him down.[31]

Leopold periodically renewed his warnings against overexertion. When Alexander, in a temporary slump late in 1855, reported that his studies had become "tasteless and burdensome," the patriarch expressed alarm: "I fear your mind has been overtaken & is beginning to break down under the burden it has carried. I have known striking cases of this kind before, & the person from being one of the best of scholars became an imbecile." The specter of mental collapse failed to deter him. "There will be a very close race this year for the four standings after 2nd between Robert, Strong, Baylor & myself," he wrote home in May 1856, adding that he expected to trail Henry Robert in philosophy but to finish ahead of him in drawing.[32]

Loneliness and boredom could be as enfeebling as intense study. Alexander wrote wistfully in December 1855 of having to miss the Fairfield Christmas celebrations. "Instead of being 'merry,' it is with me the dullest time of the year," he confessed. The half-starved cadets were given oysters on Christmas Eve, turkey on Christmas Day. Cadet excesses nearly spoiled the treat for Alexander. "I can look now out my window & see them coming back from 'Benny's' (Benny Havens's famous tavern) where they have been to eat breakfast," he wrote on Christmas Day. "About one-third of them have to be led back by someone, & in many cases it looks like the blind leading the blind." He did not say whether he had declined an invitation to Benny's, or had not been asked.[33]

Alexander accepted his responsibilities as orderly sergeant of Company D as though born to them. As a mere cadet, he could be dismissive of regulations he found pointless, and withering about officers he considered dim. ("If he had two grains less sense he would be a jabbering idiot," he said of one witless lieutenant.) In authority himself, he proved to be a strict enforcer of the rules. Overcoming initial doubts about the exercise of power, he went on the offensive in hunting out delinquencies. In fact, he seems to have been something of a martinet.[34]

"There are stormy signs in my company but no open hostilities, though Berry comes to me once in a while to let me in on a plot to get me broken or in a scrape which some who don't relish being under strict discipline are concocting," he wrote Fairfield early in 1856. "But by being certain first of being right, & *then* being strict & firm with them, I think I am in no danger." A cadet could be arraigned for an astonishing range and variety of offenses. Standard crimes were talking or whistling on parade, fighting, smoking or eating in one's room, and cutting class or chapel. One cadet admitted to publishing a letter in *The New York Times* over the signature of an officer of the West Point garrison. A plebe, arrested for drunkenness, tried to save his appointment by persuading his entire class to take the pledge. "But it is a large class, & they have four years to stay, & refused to do it," Alexander reported.[35]

He and Berry snuffed out the suspected mutiny, and by early spring company afffairs were running smoothly again. The same could not be said for the cadet corps as a whole. A new political coalition, the Republican party, was preparing to nominate an antislavery soldier, John C. Frémont, to run for president in 1856. In May, Alexander wrote his brother James Hillhouse that his class had split more or less down the middle. The two factions "have nothing to do with each other, northern & southern," he went on, and there had been fighting. Alexander brawled publicly with at least one Yankee, Vermont free-soiler George Strong, one of his rivals for a place in the fives.[36]

The new commandant of cadets, the officer responsible for academy discipline, made little effort to moderate sectional and political disputes. William J. Hardee arrived at West Point in May 1856 with a high reputation as a scholar of military science. The army used his *Tactics* as a standard text. A Georgian, Hardee expressed his southern sympathies openly. He spoke of the inevitability of secession, and left no doubt that when the time came he would quit the army to follow his section.[37]

Still, Alexander's second class year ended agreeably enough. He received his first extended exposure to artillery theory and practice during the summer of 1856, and so could indulge his lifetime fascination with firearms on a grand scale. He fired siege guns, field batteries, mortars. "The place is rather noisy when the soft notes of the mortars are heard at the same time with the pleasant little voices of the field battery," he wrote home with manifest delight.[38]

His father came north to West Point in August. A bittersweet reunion, it recalled the pain of those seven anxious weeks he had spent at Roe's Hotel with his dying wife. Leopold was in flourishing health, but Sarah's passing had created a void in his life. He told Porter he often found himself staring for long stretches at her portrait in the sitting room at Fairfield, where she had joined a gallery of the dead: Felix's frail young bride Louisa Toombs, who had died in 1855, a cousin, an uncle, his grandmother, Sarah's kin.[39]

Alexander entered the first-class year as captain of Company D, a position that carried both an increase in authority—he really liked being in charge—and unwanted distractions. He roomed with Thomas Baylor of Virginia, now his closest friend at the academy. With only nine more months of cadet life to endure, he and Baylor could begin seriously to plot their future courses. Alexander dreamed of far-off places. "I have always had an *intense* desire to visit unknown and unexplored regions," he wrote. And he craved action. A minor dispute with Britain in the Caribbean stirred him into a frenzy of anticipation. "You cannot imagine what excitement & hopes were raised by the prospects of a war with England," he wrote his father. "Everyone saw promotion and glory ahead."[40]

A few final months of drudgery remained. Aleck conceded first rank in the class to John C. Palfrey. The son of a Massachusetts clergyman-historian, Palfrey had taken a degree from Harvard before entering West Point, where he found much of the curriculum to be familiar territory. He turned out to be a military paragon too, his deportment beyond reproach. Second, third, and fourth places were competitive. "I am willing to do anything possible for the place in the Engineer Corps which I covet so," Alexander swore. "I will graduate *third I think,* if not, certainly fourth." Still, there were scares. The philosophy instructor, he complained, examined him on the one question he had not prepared for. He had copied out and studied a list of fifty subjects assigned to previous classes; the fifty-first appeared on his exam. Even so, he managed a sixth—high enough to maintain his place.[41]

A series of experiments in projectile design relieved the monotony of Alexander's last months at the academy. Exercising the talent for experimentation and improvisation he would demonstrate over and again in Confederate service, he designed a keel-shaped rifle ball that he believed would effectively double the one-thousand-yard range of the minié. In an unusual response in the prewar army, senior ordnance officers backed his experiments and cooperated fully in the project.[42]

To the last, he found West Point discipline nettlesome. One of the garrison officers acquired a pair of india-rubber shoes to wear on inspections of cadet barracks, assuring tactical surprise. "On tiptoe at unexpected times [he] hived nearly all the barracks doing something," Alexander wrote in disgust. "He even got Palfrey for 8 demerits for visiting & he collected a bag full of pipes of all sorts & sizes, from fifteen dollar meerschaums to one cent clay pipes." Alexander was one of the few cadets to escape one charge or another.[43]

Police duties left academy officials little time for military history and theory. Alexander had been schooled in mathematics and French, in horsemanship and dancing; he had learned to sight and fire a mortar and to supervise the building of earthworks, using Professor Dennis Hart Mahan's *Complete Treatise on Field Fortification* (1836) as a guide. His practical mind responded to the problems of artillery deflection and the throwing up of temporary bridges. He left no record, however, of his views on the theory of warfare, perhaps because these subjects were rarely discussed at West Point. The academy did not offer a course on the nature of war during Alexander's time there. Mahan included a mere week's worth of such material in his course "Engineering and the

Science of War." Practical battlefield problems were dealt with during the summer encampment, out of Hardee's *Tactics.*[44]

What Alexander called his long agony ended on June 8, 1857, after six grueling days of examination in engineering, ethics, and geology, and in artillery, infantry, and cavalry tactics. He sent the patriarch a hurried note to say he had graduated third out of the thirty-eight members of his class. Palfrey was, of course, first. (He would fight an unremarkable Civil War in backwater posts as a Union staff officer and engineer.) Virginian Richard K. Meade ranked second. (Meade would join the Confederate service and die of fever in Petersburg in July 1862.) Robert and Strong, Alexander's other chief academic rivals, stood fourth and fifth. (Strong would be mortally wounded while leading a Union assault against Fort Wagner, South Carolina, in July 1863. His brigade contained a regiment of freed blacks and emancipated slaves, the famous 54th Massachusetts.) In the test of loyalty to come, Alexander's Virginian friend Baylor would choose the old flag. (In 1864, he would march with Sherman's army from Atlanta to the sea.)[45]

For now, they all were free to disperse for their three-month post-graduation furlough. "I left West Point without a tear in the one o'clock boat on Tuesday the 16th in company with nearly the whole class, and a merrier boat never floated down the Hudson," Alexander wrote at the outset of his homeward journey. Benny Havens himself came down to the jetty to see the 1857 graduates off, waving a red handerchief with one hand and a flattened beaver hat with the other. A poor sailor like his father, Alexander was seasick for most of the three-day passage from New York to Savannah. He idled the summer away at Fairfield and in the hill towns, where, with his crisp military manner and a newly grown mustache, he cut a dashing figure. His first posting was to the West Point garrison. He headed north in September, and, on the last day of the month, took up his duties as a sapper officer and assistant instructor of practical military engineering.[46]

CHAPTER 3

PRELUDES

————∙❖∙————

CHAMBERLAIN
BRUNSWICK TO THE POTOMAC, 1855–62

MARRIAGE MAY HAVE WORKED A REVO-
lution in Chamberlain's manner of living, but new routines he found at
Bowdoin unaltered. For his Greek class, he used the same Kuhner's grammar he had memorized to prepare for the entrance exam seven years
earlier. Circumstances of near poverty were all too familiar as well. His
instructor's earnings were a modest fifty dollars a month, so he and Fannie
were chronically short of money. His father helped occasionally with small
cash grants; in return, Chamberlain looked out for his younger brothers
Horace and John, both undergraduates at Bowdoin. The newlyweds played
piano and bass viol duets when the brothers came to call. An airtight stove
warmed their little sitting room, and left the smell of hot iron in the air.[1]

George Adams had warned him not to count on a permanent position
at Bowdoin. As late as November 1855, when a dozen of his students
signed a note warmly wishing him well, it seemed unlikely he would
return for the winter term. Chamberlain was well regarded, however,
and President Woods laid hands on the money to retain him. A half-
year later, Woods promoted him to professor of rhetoric, a permanent
position with an annual salary of $800. This made things easier, but only
temporarily. In October 1856, Fannie gave birth to the couple's first
child, a daughter. With this new responsibility Chamberlain cast about
for extra income. He agreed in January to take German recitations for
an additional $100. Then brother John came to board with the Chamber-
lains, paying prevailing student rates.[2]

Fannie spent several weeks that winter with the elder Chamberlains in Brewer, returned briefly to Brunswick, then continued on to Boston to shop for furnishings for their rooms. She stayed on with her Massachusetts kin for an extended period, the first in what would prove to be a regular series of sabbaticals from domestic life. Her husband missed her; she seemed reluctant to come home. When she wrote to say she meant to prolong the holiday, he replied plaintively, "How can I let you stay away from me another long, long dreary week?" His letters, in which he referred to himself as her "Nonny," were ardent. In reply Fannie, still a great *malade imaginaire,* complained about her health. Chamberlain suggested she try Clarke's female pills, and offered to send her a bottle by post.[3]

Fannie could be careless, and Chamberlain sometimes had to remind her of the limits to their income. For the moment, he could think of no new way to raise money. "Everything is flat," he wrote her. "Even the College is pretty hard up for funds." He worried he would fall ill and be unable to support her and the baby, whom they had begun to call Daisy. (The couple waited several months to name the child, eventually settling on Grace Dupee.) "At the best I can hardly keep up with our expenses," he went on. "You ought not to have married a poor boy like Nonny." In August, Bowdoin renewed his faculty appointment, with a $100 increase in salary.[4]

The Chamberlains were content that summer and autumn. Fannie began to enjoy being a faculty wife. Chamberlain liked his job, and bucked tradition by seeking extra work: Spanish classes, a course in Old Norse, a series of lectures on Anglo-Saxon and early English literature. He had begun to take on the pallid hues of his profession. A photograph of the period shows an earnest, bespectacled young man in a frock coat, silk tie, and high stiff collar, his narrow face clean-shaven except for bushy sidewhiskers. So professorial is the effect that one might mistake the discoloration around the photo's edges for chalk smudge. Chamberlain claimed he corrected some twelve hundred themes a year, a circumstance that could explain the expression in the photo, and the spectacles too.[5]

Fannie delivered a son in November 1857, a "six months child" who lived only a few hours. She soon became pregnant again; Harold Wyllys, born in October 1858, survived to join Daisy in the nursery. Chamberlain began to look around for larger quarters. In the spring of 1859 he moved the family into a Cape Cod cottage on Potter Street, near the campus.

Small, distempered a dingy brown, forty years old, the house had attractive Federal-style architectural features and a garden and barn out back. Longfellow, now a literary lion, had lived in rooms there in the 1830s. Chamberlain warmed to the idea of owning a house a celebrity had once inhabited.[6]

Recalling the bills that came due after Fannie's Boston excursion, he consulted his mother about furnishing Potter Street. "Can you find remnants for making comforters?" he asked Sarah Chamberlain. "Can you get feathers cheaper than 55 cts. a pound—*first quality*?" (Sixty pounds of feathers were needed to stuff a bed.) "Shall we want featherbeds, or will mattresses do? What can you get blankets for? *Carpets*. We shall want 2 new ones before winter."[7]

To pay for these necessities, Chamberlain forced himself to dun the parents of students who had fallen behind with their tutoring fees. From one father he sought payment of thirty dollars for German lessons, along with the return of a five-dollar loan. "Even so small a sum as this would be a great service," he admitted. Then an angel appeared in the form of one of Brunswick's bankers. An early riser himself, he had observed the young professor up and hard at work in his garden before breakfast. Impressed by such dedication, he offered to lend Chamberlain as much as needed to buy the Potter Street house. In July 1860 the college raised his salary to $1,100 year.[8]

He tended the garden in season, and went sailing in Middle Bay, sometimes with Fannie, more often with students. He sang bass in the First Parish Church choir. George Adams continued to agitate the congregation with his innovations. Adams oversaw the first observance of Christmas as a religious festival in 1859,* and on March 31, 1861, his son-in-law offered the closing prayer at the first observance of Easter on record there.[9]

Chamberlain continued to manufacture work for himself. Old Norse may not have been the most popular course in the catalog, but he at least made an effort to expand the range of instruction at Bowdoin. The college remained conservative by circumstance and conviction. For decades, Professors Upham and Smyth had been vigilant for orthodoxy against liberal Unitarianism, Kantian philosophy, and romantic Transcendentalism. The philosophy department's narrow-mindedness surprised even Professor Smyth's son Newman, who ought to have known

---

*By 1862, Adams had introduced a Christmas tree to the church vestry, and Santa Claus paid a visit to the parish children.

better when he entered Bowdoin as a freshman in 1859. "I found myself
lost in a maze of questionings which my professor seemed to shun as
forbidden ground," the younger Smyth wrote.[10]

Such an atmosphere could be deadly. Chamberlain's colleagues expected him to lecture and supervise recitations. Those tasks accomplished, he was free to go home and root around in the garden. In a
long letter in October 1859 to his colleague Nehemiah Cleaveland (a
son of Bowdoin's longtime professor of mineralogy), he poured out his
ideas about teaching and scholarship—and his frustrations with college
authorities.

"My idea of a college course is that it should afford a *liberal education*,
not a special or professional one, nor in any way one-sided," Chamberlain wrote, suggesting that Bowdoin should be something more than a
training school for the Congregational clergy. The department of rhetoric, he went on, should offer intellectual fare more stimulating than
warmed-over literary criticism. It should draw out "what every man most
cherishes & most sensitively regards, that is *the expression of himself*—the
outward manifestation of the thoughts and feelings which are most real,
most characteristic, most sacred to him."

His friends, he told Cleaveland, either congratulated him for having
so little to do or else pitied him his life of drudgery. He decided to
reform the department on his own. Under the old system, themes were
written, corrected, returned, and dropped into the fire. "Without materi-
ally altering the face of things—for that would not do—I have virtually
superseded that course by adopting a regular system of *rewriting;* for the
sake of 'getting at' the student's mind (& heart too, for he has one),"
he wrote. He proposed taking the process a step further, adding a third-
year course in which he would meet regularly with the students, discuss
their "themes," comment on draft versions, and oversee the rewriting
until they had "actually carried a point once for all."[11]

The Bowdoin authorities raised no objection. After all, Chamberlain
taught literature and languages, not philosophy; he could do little harm.
They were willing to leave him alone to work out his own approaches.
In any case, personal matters now began to overshadow professional
ones. Recurrent attacks of neuralgia laid Fannie low. A scarlet fever epi-
demic swept through Brunswick in the autumn and winter of 1859–60.
"The town is all in mourning," he wrote John Chamberlain. Fannie
gave birth to a daughter in May 1860; the baby, named Emily, died
in September.[12]

He complained, uncharacteristically, about his own health. "I was never more plagued by pains & sleeplessness," he wrote his mother at the end of January. "Rheumatism or some such sort of thing has got a fast hold of me, & has of late struck into my head in such a way as to make me incapable of doing anything which requires attention or mental effort. I am hoping the powerful remedy I am using will give me some peace soon." The remedy was doubtless an opiate. Regular doses would have increased his moodiness and lethargy. There is no doubt about Chamberlain's general physical soundness. (He would prove indestructible during 1862–65.) His complaints suggest a psychological explanation: lassitude, nervousness, depression growing out of a compound of grief for the lost child, frustration about his work, and boredom.[13]

He may have been lonely, too. Though he had many acquaintances, he seems to have had few intimates in Brunswick. Horace, his closest friend, graduated in 1857, established a law practice in Bangor, married, and, in 1860, was sickening for his last illness. John graduated in 1859 and went on to Bangor Theological Seminary. College politics continued to be an irritant. "We have our usual diplomacy this term—plotting and counterplotting," he wrote his mother. The liberals stepped up their campaign to secularize Bowdoin. Conservatives pressured Chamberlain to accept the chair of modern languages, evidently counting him an ally—or at worst a neutral—in the battle for orthodoxy. He put them off. Amid the dreariness, in the brown fogs of a Brunswick winter, he tried to remain hopeful. "How little can we judge by the present moment of what our life is on the whole," he wrote his sister Sarah (Sae, to the family) a few weeks later.[14]

In the background, America drifted toward disunion. Business continued as usual at Bowdoin. In August 1858, a few weeks after Abraham Lincoln's "house divided" speech to the Illinois legislature, Bowdoin's governors granted an honorary degree to Mississippi senator Jefferson Davis, by then the chief spokesman for a rebellious, increasingly hostile South.

Davis had come to Maine to recuperate from an illness. Bowdoin received him cordially, though he made no effort to conceal his immoderate views on slavery and secession.* He moved on from Maine to Boston, where, in a speech at Faneuil Hall, he offered a blunt and unapologetic defense of the Peculiar Institution. Who, Davis asked on October 11,

---

*As though to show evenhandedness, the governors also gave an honorary doctorate to Maine's antislavery Republican senator, William Pitt Fessenden.

gave abolitionists the right to call slavery a sin? "By what standard do they measure it? Not the Constitution; the Constitution recognizes property in many forms; not the Bible; that justifies it. Is it in the cause of Christianity? It cannot be, for servitude is the only agency through which Christianity has reached the Negro race." Two weeks later, William Seward delivered his "irrepressible conflict" speech, laying it down that the United States, sooner or later, would be all slave or all free.[15]

Lincoln, not Seward, led the Republican party into the presidential election of 1860. Chamberlain set down his views on Lincoln only in retrospect. No record survives of his thoughts on Lincoln, slavery, and secession in the autumn of 1860. The evidence, such as it is, suggests he held firm convictions about preserving the Union, and that the question of slavery meant little to him. "In no wise did we take the field to assume the right to abolish slavery, but to abolish those who dared strike at the old flag, and what it stood for," he wrote shortly after the war.* His father-in-law's abolitionist convictions remained strong. Adams voted for Lincoln on November 6, 1860, even though he, like many abolitionists, had supported Seward for the nomination. "Went out before breakfast to learn of the great (possible) triumph of the Republican Party," he wrote the day after the election. "God grant that it be a triumph, rather, of truth and justice."[16]

But it was secession that triumphed. South Carolina left the Union on December 17, 1860. The other Deep South states soon followed. Seven states allied as the Confederacy in February 1861 and chose Jefferson Davis as president. On March 4, Lincoln took the oath as the sixteenth president of the United States. Chamberlain's preoccupations were personal that day. He wrote to ask his brother Tom, a clerk in a Bangor store, to order a keg of a special brand of ale for his peaked wife. "I want to see if I can't put a little flesh onto Fanny's cheeks; she is thin as a shadow," he told Tom.[17]

Confederate forces in Charleston, South Carolina, opened fire on the harbor citadel of Fort Sumter before dawn on April 12, 1861. The garrison surrendered two days later. Lincoln mobilized 75,000 three-month militiamen for national service, and a great tide of patriotism rolled over the North. Southerners taunted northerners as "doughfaces," effete, moneyed aristocrats and grubbing mechanics who would not fight. Even

---

*Many in Maine were indifferent to slavery—or worse. The federal government hanged convicted slave trader Nathaniel Gordon of Portland in February 1862, a full ten months after the outbreak of war.

some prominent Yankees were skeptical. Oliver Wendell Holmes had raised the issue in the late 1850s in *The Autocrat of the Breakfast Table,* his collection of essays recording eccentric imaginary conversations at breakfast in a Boston boardinghouse. Holmes believed New Englanders, especially upper-class ones, wanted testing and toughening by military service. "I don't believe in any aristocracy without pluck to its backbone," the Autocrat said. "Ours may show it when the time comes."[18]

Chamberlain admired Holmes (he had invited him to lecture at Bowdoin in 1858) and had certainly read the *Autocrat.* After Sumter, it became evident that Holmes's fears of Yankee softness were groundless. Holmes's own son, Oliver Wendell Holmes, Jr., joined the newly raised 20th Massachusetts in the summer of 1861.* All across the North, thousands of young men, Boston Brahmins, office clerks—mechanics too— rallied to the colors. Some Bowdoin students enlisted at the first news of the Sumter attack. Those who stayed home formed two military companies, the Bowdoin Guards and the Bowdoin Zouaves, and drilled in Maine Street. In July the student organ, the *Bugle,* called on the government to arrest Davis and transport him to Brunswick, where a student court would rescind his honorary doctorate. "Bowdoin has a little account to settle with him," the paper said. Chamberlain looked in regularly on the student drills, listening intently to the commands and observing the responses.[19]

The Third Maine, under the command of Bowdoin graduate Oliver Otis Howard, passed through Brunswick in early June, en route to Washington. The regiment contained two companies recruited in nearby Bath, so there was a large turnout at the depot. "Professors and students, forgetting their wonted respectful distance and distinction, mingled together in the same eager crowd," Howard recalled. The excitements were too much for some Bowdoin men. George E. Kenniston, orator of the class of 1861, impulsively enlisted, was wounded at the first battle of Bull Run in July, and spent commencement day in a Confederate prison.[20]

For the time being, Chamberlain confined his patriotic activities to speaking at recruiting rallies and writing recommendations for Bowdoin graduates seeking officer's commissions. Calm gradually returned to the campus. In August, Bowdoin appointed Chamberlain professor of modern languages and granted him a leave of absence to study in Europe

*Holmes was seriously wounded at the battle of Ball's Bluff on October 21, 1861.

during 1862. George Adams presided over a soldiers' aid society at the First Parish Church, and the churchwomen met in the vestry there to fashion comforts for the volunteers. Professor Upham attributed increased student interest in international law to the war.[21]

Down on the Potomac, Lincoln turned to Maj. Gen. George B. McClellan to repair the Bull Run disaster. In the beginning, even the energetic, confident McClellan saw little cause for optimism. "I found no army to command," he wrote, only "a mere collection of regiments cowering on the banks of the Potomac." Chamberlain received firsthand reports of army conditions from Walter Poor, a former student now posted to Fortress Monroe, Virginia, that echoed McClellan's misgivings.[22]

"If you could see the soldiers drill, hear the confused murmur of voices in the ranks drowning the commands of the officers and distracting the attention of the men, could see the beardless boys, and see the lifeless and characterless men who command them, you would not be surprised at the panic at Bull Run or our reverses elsewhere," Poor wrote Chamberlain in October 1861. Superior Confederate leadership and discipline offset the Union advantage in numbers and equipment. The southern social system produced officers accustomed to command, Poor went on, and a rank and file accustomed to obey. "We want cool, self reliant, *self controlling* officers and disciplined, silent, obedient men," Poor said.[23]

The correspondence focused Chamberlain's attention on Virginia. In his methodical way, he resumed the military education Major Whiting had begun long ago. (He asked Poor to explain the difference between a fort and a fortress; Poor replied that a fortress was larger.) Poor's emphasis on the need for leadership struck him forcibly. So did the young man's conviction that it would be a long, hard war. Chamberlain had a wife and two children to support. He had turned thirty-three at the end of September. Nathaniel Hawthorne's dictum might have cheered him, had he known of it: "No man should go to war under fifty years of age," Hawthorne wrote, "such men having already had their natural share of worldly pleasures." He worried about being too old (his hair had begun to turn gray), and about his heavy burden of family responsibility.[24]

Emerson had argued in "The American Scholar," his famous and much-reprinted 1837 oration, that men of ideas should not stand aloof from the controversies of their time. "Action is with the scholar subordinate," Emerson said, "but it is essential. Without it, he is not yet a man." As the political crisis deepened, action drew even with reflection in Emerson's view. " 'Heroes' of the world have certainly needed work and had it and done it well, and it is Heroes that we must try to be," he wrote a friend in 1856. Three years later, Emerson saw John Brown of Harper's Ferry as a hero and a saint.*[25]

At Bowdoin, the scholarly Chamberlain agonized about converting the idea of military service into action. He was at low ebb anyway during the winter of 1861–62. Tuberculosis claimed Horace Chamberlain on December 7, 1861. Lawrence had been with him at the end. They used to talk of making the Grand Tour together; then Horace had dreamed of emigrating to Oregon. His death left Chamberlain nervous and depressed. "That he should be cut down at the very opening of his career, and when he had so much reason to anticipate a prosperous course, seems almost against the order of nature," he wrote Sae. Chamberlain had no one in mind to succeed Horace in the role of friend and confidant. He felt mired in dim domestic and professional routine; Brunswick struck him as more dismal than ever.[26]

Thousands of men were dying now on the battlefields of Virginia and the West. Ulysses S. Grant carried out his successful river campaign in February. In April he claimed a close-run victory at Shiloh, in southwestern Tennessee. The casualty figures there were astounding, nearly twenty four thousand men killed, wounded, and missing on both sides. In May and June, McClellan's Army of the Potomac advanced up the Virginia Peninsula to within view of the spires of Richmond. Then, in a series of counterstrokes known as the Seven Days' battles, Confederates under Robert E. Lee turned what looked like a decisive Union victory into a sharp strategic reverse. McClellan suspended the campaign, leaving some sixteen thousand killed, wounded, and missing on the Peninsula. On July 2, 1862, Lincoln issued an appeal for 300,000 new volunteers.

Chamberlain, beset, dreamed of honor, glory, and a heroic destiny in the murky realm of war. In a series of "fellow citizens" speeches, he urged Brunswick's young men to respond to the president's call. "This war can only be quelled by a swift and strong hand. [The rebels] will have no respect for us until we whip them." Good men were wanted in the crisis. "Come out for your country—answer the call. Be ready to

*Not Hawthorne: "Nobody was ever more justly hanged," he wrote. "He won his martyrdom fairly, and took it fairly."

stand at your post. Come out from your shady retreats." Responding to his own rhetoric, he determined to seek an officer's commission for himself.[27]

McClellan's army shuffled onto the transports and sailed back up the Potomac. Lee reorganized his forces, now known as the Army of Northern Virginia, and prepared for offensive operations in the vicinity of Washington. Northerners were confused, skeptical, sometimes defeatist. Hawthorne captured one element of northern ambivalence, what he called "the anomaly of two allegiances," in an essay in *The Atlantic* magazine. A man's state—Maine or Georgia, Massachusetts or Virginia— "comes nearest to [his] feelings, and includes the altar and the hearth," Hawthorne wrote. The nation, the aggregation of states that Hawthorne styled the General Government, "claims his devotion only to an airy mode of law, and has no symbol but a flag." Sounding dangerously tolerant of rebel motives, he noted that in the South the stronger of the two allegiances had "converted crowds of honest people into traitors, who seem to themselves not merely innocent, but patriotic, and who die for a bad cause with as quiet a conscience as if it were the best."[28]

Chamberlain finally resolved his own doubts. Devotion and duty impelled him to act, though these alone might not have been sufficient. Great issues were being decided down on the Potomac while he corrected themes and pottered in his garden. War offered an outlet for the tremendous physical and emotional energies that had been building in him. On July 14, 1862, he wrote the governor of Maine to request a commission in one of the five new regiments being raised in the state in response to Lincoln's appeal.[29]

"I have always been interested in military matters," Chamberlain wrote Governor Israel Washburn, "and what I do not know in that line, *I know how to learn.*" His age put him just beyond range of criticism for staying home; there were Fannie and the children, too, and useful work at Bowdoin. "But I fear this war, so costly of blood and treasure, will not cease until the men of the north are willing to leave good positions, and sacrifice the dearest personal interests," he went on. With the year's study leave, he would not be forced to resign his professorship. He advised Washburn that he would be free of his college commitments by the first week of August.[30]

The governor offered him command of one of the new regiments. Saying he had too much to learn, Chamberlain asked for a subordinate position; he preferred to earn a colonelcy. Howard, who had returned to Maine on convalescent leave (he lost his right arm at Seven Pines/ Fair Oaks on the Peninsula), encouraged Chamberlain when they met at a rally at the Brunswick depot. His Bowdoin colleagues, however, were incensed. Chamberlain had not consulted them, and they read about his prospective appointment in the *Portland Press*. He attributed their hostility to academic politics; they feared the liberals would fill his vacancy with one of their own. Smyth thoughtfully pointed out that Chamberlain could be crippled in battle or even killed, and thus rendered permanently useless to the college. Smyth did more. On behalf of Bowdoin, he delivered a formal protest to Augusta.[31]

Smyth found an ally in Maine attorney general Josiah Drummond. "Have you appointed Chamberlain Col. of the 20th?" he wrote Washburn on July 22. "His old classmates etc. here say you have been deceived: that C. is *nothing* at all: that is the universal expression of those who know him." This was untrue; Chamberlain had many supporters. "[He] is as capable of commanding a Regt. as any man outside of a West Point graduate," Brunswick physician John D. Lincoln told Washburn. The issue seems never to have been in doubt. On August 8, the governor offered Chamberlain a commission as lieutenant colonel of the 20th Maine Volunteer Infantry. The colonelcy went to Adelbert Ames, an 1861 West Point graduate from Rockland.[32]

Chamberlain accepted the same day. Fannie left no record of her reaction. Though she must have been aware of the general line of her husband's thinking, the actual decision surely came as a terrible shock. Why should this distant event overturn her carefully ordered world? The ground shifted under her feet, altering her private landscape entirely. From a later vantage, Chamberlain's quest seems quixotic, selfish. What about Daisy, now approaching her sixth birthday? What about Wyllys, not quite four and still in skirts? What about his students? Chamberlain had grown a fierce and martial mustache; possibly it emboldened him to face down Fannie's objections as he had those of his Bowdoin colleagues. By mid-August he was established at Camp Mason, near Portland, in temporary charge of the 20th Maine.

There he found a casual, undisciplined mob. Uniforms and equipment had not yet been issued. One young man turned out for duty as officer of the day dressed in a brown cutaway coat, striped trousers, and a silk hat. He carried a ramrod in place of a sword. Though Ames was not expected in camp until the end of the month, Chamberlain could turn to an experienced assistant in Maj. Charles Gillmore of Bangor, who had commanded a company of the Seventh Maine in action on the Peninsula. Gillmore brought some order out of the chaos. He formed a guard and began to instruct the men in drill. Within a few days they were able to form a line and march by the flank.[33]

They were bountymen, leftover recruits from the four new regiments that had preceded the 20th. The initial surge of enthusiasm of 1861 had long since subsided. These men were not unpatriotic; neither were they the innocents of Bull Run days. To encourage volunteering, the federal government paid out $100 per enlistee. The state of Maine added forty-five dollars, and some communities—including Brunswick—offered a further bonus. Most of the rank and file were from small towns and country districts where a cash prize approaching $200 would stretch a long way. Companies A, C, E, G, I, and K were recruited from coastal towns. Companies D and F were from south-central and western Maine. Companies B and H were drawn from the isolated communities of the far north. Eighty-five percent of the men were New England–born. One-third were farmers; more than half were mechanics or laborers.[34]

Gillmore soon had the regiment stamping energetically about the parade ground. New officers turned up. A Chamberlain protégé, Portland lawyer John M. Brown, Bowdoin class of 1860, became regimental adjutant. Another protégé was his twenty-one-year-old brother Tom, who happily came out from behind his store counter to enlist. Tom expected army life to agree with him. "I like warm weather," he wrote Chamberlain; in common with many geographically ignorant Yankees, Tom placed Virginia in the tropics, roughly on the latitude, say, of the Gold Coast. "I hardly ever saw weather so warm but I could stand it well," he added. On the strength of his storekeeping experience, Chamberlain recommended Tom for quartermaster sergeant.[35]

Uniforms arrived and were distributed. Chamberlain's, tailor-made, fit him elegantly. A delegation from Brunswick presented him with a handsome white charger. More to the point, each man received a woollen blanket, a rubber blanket, a haversack, a knapsack, a canteen, a tin plate, a tin dipper, and a knife, fork, and spoon. Sufficient weapons were found to arm two companies. "The camp put on a military appearance, and the regiment, if not a lion, was at least clothed in the skin of that formidable beast," wrote Ellis Spear, Bowdoin 1858, a Wiscasset schoolmaster who commanded Company G. Spear admitted that he "scarcely knew a line of battle from a rail fence." Like most of the rank and file, though, he was keen and willing to learn.[36]

The instructor arrived during the last week in August. Col. Ames, a short-tempered, ambitious, and opinionated regular, twenty-six years old, had been a clipper sailor, rising to first mate, before he entered the military academy. Severely wounded while serving with the Fifth U.S. Artillery at the first battle of Bull Run,* he recovered in time to see action at Garnett's Farm and Malvern Hill on the Peninsula. Accustomed to the crisp efficiency of regulars, Ames found the 20th's picturesque slovenliness appalling. He set to work training the officers and smartening up the men. He seems to have warmed immediately to his second-in-command. Ames described him "a gentleman of the highest moral, intellectual and literary worth." He soon came to appreciate Chamberlain's military qualities as well.[37]

Capt. Charles G. Bartlett of the 12th U.S. Infantry mustered 979 officers and men of the 20th Maine into federal service at Camp Mason on August 29, 1862. That same day, Gen. John Pope's Union army offered battle to Lee's Confederates near Manassas. By the evening of the following day, Pope's forces had been routed and were in full flight toward the Washington defenses. Lee's intentions were unknown, but it could be assumed he would try to exploit the victory of second Bull Run. At Camp Mason, the 20th Maine received orders to entrain for Boston, where the steamer *Merrimack* would be waiting to carry the regiment to the Potomac.[38]

Fannie, with her father as escort, came down from Brunswick September 1, Monday, to see Chamberlain off. She and Adams spent the night in his tent and made their way to the depot early Tuesday morning while he marched the regiment down to the cars. The troop train pulled away from the Portland station, and Fannie soon faded from view. Chamberlain carried with him a New Testament that the Whiting Hall Sunday school class had given him in 1853. He carried, too, the perplexed good wishes of his father. Events had not altered Joshua Chamberlain, Jr.'s states'-rights views. Some of the Brewer patriots already detected a copper tinge to him. " 'Tis not *our war*," the old man wrote Lawrence. All the same, he offered a father's benediction.

*Ames's battery commander mentioned him in dispatches after Bull Run, and he was later awarded a Congressional Medal of Honor for his actions there.

"Come home with honor, as I know you will if that lucky star of yours will serve you in *this war*. Take care of Tom until he gets seasoned to the trenches. Good luck to you."[39]

Alexander
West Point to Manassas, 1857–61

A second lieutenant's duties at West Point were light and reasonably varied: teaching, coaching cadets in boxing and fencing, looking after the affairs of Company A, Engineers. Off duty, Alexander read, played chess, and paid teatime calls on the married officers of the garrison. "I am very pleasantly situated and enjoying myself almost as much as I could anywhere," he wrote his sister Cliff. West Point hardly qualified as one of the exotic places on the map of his childhood imagination. Still, taking Jeremy Gilmer's advice, he decided to wait for something better to turn up rather than request a new assignment so soon.[1]

There were occasional alarms. Sapper units were sometimes detached for temporary service elsewhere. In early November 1857, the War Department ordered Company A to prepare to move to New York City to guard the Treasury vault there. Government agents claimed to have evidence that mobs thrown out of work by the panic of 1857 were plotting to plunder it. "As my monthly pay comes out of the subtreasury, I patriotically obeyed the order," Alexander told Cliff. "It required but little preparation—I only curled my moustache up at the corners." There was no uprising; the engineers remained in barracks.[2]

The anecdote conveys some of the flavor of the 1850s army, a small, widely scattered force officered by men with too much time on their hands. Some, like Alexander, were intelligent, energetic, ambitious. In normal times, the army would offer little scope for their abilities. Others were time-servers, dull men further dispirited by long years at low pay in junior grades. In 1857, Congress approved the first base-pay raise for officers in more than half a century. With allowances, Alexander could expect an income of about $1,400 a year as a second lieutenant. By contrast, Cliff's husband, George Hull, trained, like Alexander, as an engineer, already earned $2,000 annually as superintendent of a Georgia branch railroad.[3]

Hull could count on advancing as far as his talents and Steam Age economic expansion would carry him. Young army officers took their

places at the end of a long gray line of seniority. Col. John DeB. Wal-
bach, the Fourth Artillery's commanding officer, died at age ninety-three
in June 1857. Commissioned in 1799, he remained on the active list to
the final hour of his life. Frontier service offered occasional excitement,
if not promotion. The army garrisoned dozens of outposts from the
Great Plains to California and the Northwest. There were rebellious Indian tribes to pacify, migration routes to map, railroad routes to survey.
Beginning in the summer of 1857, there were secession-minded Mormons to subdue.[4]

Declaring immunity to federal authority, Mormon settlers around the
Great Salt Lake refused to permit the passage of California-bound wagon
trains, attacking several parties and killing some migrants. In June 1857
two infantry regiments and the Second Dragoons set out from Fort Leavenworth, Kansas, on a punitive expedition. Dwindling supplies, storms,
and Mormon guerrilla attacks forced the column into early winter quarters at Fort Bridger, Wyoming, on the eastern slope of the Wasatch
Mountains one hundred miles short of Salt Lake. There the troops settled in to await reinforcements from the east.[5]

Word came for Company A, miners and sappers, at West Point to
contribute a detachment to the relief force. Alexander volunteered for
the expedition and was accepted. The prospect thrilled him. Even so,
he took special care to leave his spiritual affairs in good order. With
Presbyterian high seriousness he gave Oliver Howard, West Point's unofficial chaplain, two books on religion and five dollars for prayer tracts.
"I wish to be thought by my men to be a Christian and have their
sympathy and interest during the expedition," he explained. The sappers
left for Leavenworth in early April 1858, with Lt. James Duane in command and Alexander as subaltern. They joined the relief force in Kansas,
six columns of five hundred men each, the whole ready to move as soon
as the plains grass would support the trains.[6]

Here were the vast, unspoiled regions Aleck had dreamed of penetrat-
ing. The engineers, in company with the Sixth Infantry, marched from
Leavenworth May 6. Three weeks later, at Fort Kearney, the column
turned off the migrant trail for what the topographers believed to be a
shorter, more direct route to Bridger. It followed the South Platte River
to Lodge Pole Creek, then ran along the creek to its headwaters in
the Black Hills before skirting the southern flank of the Medicine Bow
Mountains and crossing the Continental Divide at Bridger's Pass. The
rifle companies camped there for two weeks while the sappers cut a

route through to the old trail. Snow lay thick in the shady spots well into July, and skims of ice formed in the water buckets overnight. Gradually descending through rough country, the column reached Fort Bridger on August 1. News arrived shortly that the Mormons had capitulated. The relief columns were broken up and sent elsewhere. The sappers were ordered to return to West Point.[7]

Though the military operation ended in anticlimax,* the West fully met Alexander's romantic expectations. On the Little Blue River in Kansas, a tornado tore through camp in the middle of the night and carried away his tent, exposing him to a sudden drenching. From Pine Bluffs on Lodge Pole Creek he had his first view of the Rockies. "They loomed high over the prairies with Pike's, Long's & one or two other snow peaks in sight," he wrote, "& impressed my youthful imagination very deeply." Game abounded. The native inhabitants, clad only in breechclouts and feathers, were picturesque too, though apt to be unfriendly. Aleck encountered Pawnee, Sioux, Cheyenne, and Kiowa, and made notes on their languages. Duane let him go off on hunting expeditions during the day in exchange for his taking all the picket rounds at night.[8]

He shot antelope, wolves, wild duck, grouse, sage hens. He seems to have viewed his first buffalo hunt as a sort of rite of passage, a test of manhood. West of Kearney, six of the column's Delaware Indian scouts spotted a small herd and gave chase, soon joined by two wagonmasters and Lieutenant Alexander. The buffalo retreated up the bluffs overlooking the trail and headed southward over the tableland, the nine horsemen in furious pursuit.

Alexander overtook the others and rapidly closed the range. When his horse shied, frightened by the strange, rank scent of the buffalo, he dug in his spurs and struck the animal over the head with his rifle. "At last my grey let himself out, & going through the bunch so close that I could have touched them on either side he placed me alongside of the leader, both bull and horse at their best speed." He lay the gun across his left arm and fired. The bull fell with a crash. Dismounting, he charged the wounded animal and, from a distance of about thirty yards, shot him again. As he finished off the bull, one of the Delawares, "a big fellow named Wolf, 6 ft. 2 in. [and] splendid looking," galloped up. "Few moments in my life have been prouder & happier than that and few

---

*There were, however, casualties. Early on the march, Alexander's West Point classmate John T. Magruder fell into a drunken argument with a settler. The man returned after dark, ambushed Magruder, and shot him dead.

compliments sweeter than hearing Wolf tell the other pursuers, who had all given up the chase & gathered around, 'He make good hunter; he not 'fraid.' "[9]

The return march began on August 9, 1858. Moving rapidly over the emigrant trail, the column covered 1,019 miles in forty-seven stages, reaching Leavenworth on October 3. Ten days later the engineers were back in barracks at West Point. Alexander resumed the familiar garrison routines. Along with his company duties, he assisted Professor Mahan in the engineering department. He studied French and Spanish; analyzed a French army engineer corps' report on the siege of Sebastopol; read *The Ingoldsby Legends* and *The Autocrat of the Breakfast Table*, and feuded with his commanding officer, Col. Richard Delafield, over an accounting for ordnance stores. It was one of those peculiarly intense and drawn-out unpleasantnesses so characteristic of the old army.* Even officers not at cross purposes with Delafield found him exacting, peevish, and cold. Both men gave over many bile-filled hours to the dispute.[10]

Alexander taught fencing, gymnastics, and shooting during the summer encampment of 1859. He angled for a California posting, too, though he suspected Delafield would try to block his bid. He considered applying for an opening under Pierre G. T. Beauregard in Louisiana. "New Orleans would just suit me," he wrote his father. The balls and parties of the West Point summer season provided diversion. At one of these he met two Virginian sisters who were summering in the Hudson Valley. Singling out one of the girls, he soon forgot Delafield, Beauregard, even California. A rowing excursion on the Hudson led to other encounters. Almost before he knew what had happened, Aleck found himself deeply involved with his future wife, Bettie Mason of King George County, Virginia.[11]

She was twenty-four years old, a physician's daughter. Alexander had little to say of the courtship, and the couple's earliest correspondence does not survive. Bettie appears to have been his first serious romantic interest. There had been Miss Church; he could claim no more success in a brief pursuit of Mary Lee, one of Robert Lee's daughters. A belle named Lou Galt struck his fancy, but she turned out to be a pinchbeck girl, "rather destitute of the precious metals, even down to nickel." Aleck's approach seems to have left a lot to be desired. According to

---

*Thomas J. Jackson, serving in a Florida garrison in 1851, carried on a famously stupid and prolonged quarrel over quartermaster procedures with his commanding officer. Jackson quit the army before the dispute could be resolved.

Cliff, he offered one girl a piece of the seat of his breeches as a token of his affection. Possibly his technique had improved by the summer of 1859. In any case, Miss Teen, as Alexander soon began to call Bettie Mason, responded. By the end of the summer they were engaged.[12]

He did not consult his father about the affair, and the patriarch reacted with a mixture of anger and pain when he eventually learned of it. Alexander had promised he would not precipitously "take the oath of allegiance to a feminine power." When he did the very thing, Leopold could hardly restrain himself. "My own mind has settled down to a feeling of utter hopelessness, & I now care little when or whom he marries," he wrote dramatically to his daughter Marion. "*Approval* was out of the question. The most that can be done is to submit to the evil."[13]

A short visit to Bettie in Richmond in early December left Alexander more certain than ever of his feelings. He had taken up winter quarters in New York City, where he and Maj. Albert J. Myer, a clever, versatile army surgeon, tested a new flag signal system Myer had developed as a by-product of his medical school researches into sign communication for the deaf. They presented their findings to the War Department in Washington, and lobbied Congress for a bill to establish a signal corps that would use Myer's "wig-wag" system. In March 1860, Aleck received another temporary assignment, as recording secretary to an ordnance bureau board that was testing several models of breechloading rifle. ("As a good shot, I've also had all the firing to do," he wrote home.) For the time being, at least, he had escaped Delafield.[14]

Alexander courted Bettie and fought his running battle with authority against a backdrop of rising political tensions. Through Bettie's family he heard accounts of the John Brown excitement. One of her uncles, a physician, treated Brown after his wounding in the fighting around the Harper's Ferry arsenal. The government hanged Brown in Charles Town, Virginia, on December 2, 1859. Bells tolled in mourning across the North. In Richmond, Alexander found Virginians outraged at Yankee attempts to make a martyr out of a slave insurrectionist. In New York City he found intense interest in the Harper's Ferry affair, and more sympathy for the southern point of view than he had expected. Like most professional soldiers, he had taken little interest in politics.* Now his southern patriotism flared. "If it *does* come to war you will have one son in it from the commencement, bearing a musket in the ranks if

*Dennis Hart Mahan, a West Point professor for more than forty years, was said never to have voted in a civil election.

nothing else, & if [William] Seward is president his first act shall be signing my resignation," he wrote Leopold.[15]

The patriarch relented early in the new year and gave a belated blessing to the couple. Alexander and Bettie Mason were married at Cleveland, the King George County estate of Roy Mason, another of Bettie's uncles, on an unseasonably warm Tuesday, April 3, 1860. Aleck's sister Sarah Lawton, who had married in 1845, sent an arch acknowledgment of the event. "I think brides are to be sparingly congratulated," she told him, "as nobody can guess what sort of husband any given man will make." Later in the month he took Bettie to Fairfield to meet his father, then on to Atlanta, where they stayed with Cliff and George Hull. After a brief stopover in Virginia, the newlyweds arrived at West Point around July 1. So far, he had been unable to break permanently free of Delafield, who seems to have intervened about this time to block Myer's request for Alexander to join him in New Mexico to test the new signals in a campaign against the Navajo. In any case, no orders awaited him at West Point. He began to search for quarters on the crowded post.[16]

When the chemistry professor, Henry L. Kendrick, offered the Alexanders two rooms in his cottage, they accepted gratefully, bought furniture, and sent out invitations for a modest housewarming. An hour or so before the guests were to arrive, Alexander received orders to relieve his old academy rival Henry Robert as second in command of a sapper detachment at Fort Steilacoom, Washington Territory. He and Bettie sold the furniture, packed their trunks, and sailed from New York in the sidewheel steamer *Northern Light* at noon, August 11, 1860.[17]

It was a difficult passage. At their first stop, Aspinwall (now Colón), Panama, "a miserable little Spanish-negro railroad village built in a swamp," the dirty, overcrowded hotel had a bed for Bettie but none for him. He slept in a chair in a warehouse next door. A man died of yellow fever there during the night. They traveled by rail next day to Panama, and boarded the *John L. Stephens* for San Francisco. A kindhearted shipping line official gave them the steamer's bridal stateroom. Bettie came down with a case of Chagres fever, a variety of malaria, and lay ill in the bridal suite for much of the voyage. Alexander went ashore when the ship put into Acapulco for coal, and devoured a breakfast of squabs and fried plantains. A Frenchwoman dressed as a man served him.[18]

Jeremy Gilmer met the Alexanders at wharfside in San Francisco. California life evidently agreed with Captain Gilmer and sister Lou. "They look stouter and much improved in health," Alexander wrote home.

After a pleasant six days ashore, the couple boarded the steamer *Cortes* for the last leg of the journey, arriving at Fort Steilacoom, at the head of Puget Sound, on September 17.[19]

This was Eden, a pristine country, fertile, rich, and a continent away from the discord of the states, where Abraham Lincoln, the Republican candidate for president, awaited the voters' verdict at home in Springfield, Illinois. Aleck and Bettie began to live an idyll. "As I look back at it now, it seems to have been the last of my youth," he wrote long afterward. "I had a position for life, & an assured support in the profession I loved, & I had only to get the most pleasure that I could out of my surroundings." In the region's mild climate, roses and pansies were still blooming in December. The stupendous snow peaks of the Cascades glittered on the southeastern horizon. A dam on a little stream flowing into Puget Sound formed a small pond in woods a mile or so north of the post. "Here Miss Teen would sit on the bank & read while I, out on a log, could always catch a fine string of brook trout in a little while," he recalled.[20]

Fort Steilacoom had been established in 1849 on a sixty-acre former farm that the government rented from the Hudson's Bay Company. The cottages of Officers' Row were grouped along the northern edge of a wide, grassy parade ground, the barracks opposite. By 1860 the little town of Steilacoom, with a population of three hundred, counted seventy houses, six stores, three hotels, three sawmills, a flour mill, a library, a school, and Roman Catholic and Protestant churches.[21]

Alarms were raised occasionally still, but Aleck had missed most of the action. The garrison commander, Lt. Col. Silas Casey,* did send him north to investigate reports that Yakima bands were threatening the settlements, but he found the hinterland quiet. Nor did another flare-up of the boundary dispute with Britain appear likely. Fighting had nearly broken out on San Juan Island in the Strait of San Juan de Fuca in mid-1859 when an American settler, Lyman A. Cutler, shot a pig belonging to Charles J. Griffin, a Briton. Griffin petitioned a British magistrate to arrest and punish Cutler. The island's dozen or so American settlers requested military assistance. Gen. W. S. Harney, the hard-mannered American commander in the Northwest, ordered a company of the Ninth U.S. Infantry under Capt. George C. Pickett to San Juan Island.

---

*Casey, West Point class of 1826, published a *Study of Infantry Tactics* in 1861 that became a standard reference for Civil War officers of both sides.

The British, characteristically, sent a gunboat, HMS *Satellite,* soon joined at anchor opposite Pickett's camp by two others, *Tribune* and *Plumper.*[22]

Pickett, a dandified Virginian, not very bright but as bellicose as his general, struck off a proclamation declaring the disputed island a U.S. possession. The gunboats threatened to land Royal Marines to drive the Americans away. Pickett vowed to fight to the last man. Casey marched from Fort Steilacoom with 450 reinforcements. Stalemate ensued. As in another boundary dispute with England on the other side of the continent twenty-two years before, the government turned to Winfield Scott. He arrived on October 20, 1859, relieved Pickett, turned back Casey's column, and arranged a truce.*[23]

Harney had since redirected his energies, leaving off the profitless business of provoking the British and Indians to enrich himself. He set the sappers to building roads into remote Harney lands, making his many thousands of acres available for sale to settlers. There were few official duties. With time on his hands, Alexander read, tinkered with a project for an improved artillery shell ("a flat projectile designed to sail like an aeroplane," he wrote later), hunted and fished, and marveled at his surroundings. "Altogether, this is as beautiful & fine a country as I ever saw," he wrote Fairfield.[24]

The Alexanders took possession of a parlor–dining room and an upstairs bedchamber in a trim little clapboard house, painted yellow, that they shared with a bachelor officer. They dined on trout, pheasant, goose, and duck, supplemented by potatoes, carrots, cabbages, turnips, and onions available free from the post garden, and by cranberries, hazelnuts, whortleberries, and raspberries from the surrounding bogs, meadows, and groves. There were long rides into the surrounding country, and walks in the woods. Bettie, a crack shot, competed in post marksmanship contests. They became friends with Tom Casey, the son of the garrison commander, and his wife, Emma, daughter of the West Point artist Robert Weir. There were dances and other jollifications. "Once some wretched traveling minstrels gave a show, & I remember 'Joseph Bowers' sang to the grinding of a coffee mill," Alexander recalled. The officers built a makeshift sleigh, but snow fell infrequently and soon melted in the soft winter air.[25]

The mental collapse of Alexander's chess partner John Ector turned

---

*American and British detachments remained on San Juan Island until 1872, when German emperor Wilhelm I, acting as mediator in the dispute, awarded it to the United States.

out to be the most absorbing event of the winter of 1860–61. Ector, brother-in-law of the post paymaster, Maj. A. B. Ragan, had shown signs of oddness for some time. When he began to rage noisily on religious subjects, Casey detailed two soldiers to nurse him. Late one night he became homicidal, assaulting one of the nurses with a poker. Roused from sleep, Alexander hurried over in his dressing gown and slippers and managed to disarm him. At breakfast, Ector began talking wildly of killing all those on the post who were plotting against him. Alexander coaxed him outdoors and, with the help of half a dozen soldiers, subdued him. Casey ordered Ector to be fitted with a straitjacket and locked up in an outbuilding, his ankles fastened to a staple in the floor.[26]

Aleck encouraged his father to visit, promising that the views of Mount Rainier alone would more than compensate him for the trouble and expense of the journey. But the patriarch had large issues on his mind that autumn of 1860. Leopold Alexander had become an ardent secessionist. He shared many Southerners' almost irrational dread of Abraham Lincoln, who in November won a four-way race for the presidency with 40 percent of the vote. South Carolina seceded in mid-December. The other Deep South states prepared to follow.[27]

No one knew yet what secession might mean. Lincoln said little about his intentions; President Buchanan temporized. State by state, secessionists worked to establish a new nation. In December, Leopold joined the Wilkes County committee of defense. On January 19, 1861, the Georgia convention voted for secession, and hauled down the Stars and Stripes from the statehouse flagpole in Milledgeville. That night there were bonfires and toasts in the little square in Washington. Leopold gave a rousing speech, and a new flag, blue with a single five-pointed star, went up over the courthouse. Only Judge Andrews remained true to his old Whig-unionist convictions. He shut up his house that night, and darkened the windows.[28]

Alexander kept up with developments as best he could. "We suppose from the latest news that Lincoln is elected," he had written Cliff November 11, five days after the balloting, "and if so I *hope* and *expect* to be called in to help secede." For him, there were no ambiguities. He had settled his loyalties. "If [Lincoln] is once inaugurated, it will be too late to oppose him, as the purse and the sword will be in his hands and the Army and Navy are sworn to obey his commands," he went on conspiratorially. "If he is elected I believe the interests of humanity, civilization, and self-preservation call on the South to secede, and I'll go my arm, leg, or death on it."[29]

He put it less melodramatically in his memoirs. "As soon as the *right* to secede was denied by the North," he wrote, "I strongly approved of its assertion & maintenance by force if necessary." He had a second motive, the same one that propelled thousands of men, northern and southern, toward the abyss. "Being young and ambitious," he admitted, "I was anxious to take my part in everything going on."[30]

Meanwhile, he thought through his next move carefully. He knew the sappers were to return to West Point soon, so he decided to delay his resignation, thus saving the price of the passage home. Hundreds of officers were experiencing similar alternating currents of excitement and anxiety, and making similar calculations, political and material. Politics were rarely discussed openly in the old army, but it seemed to be taken for granted that southern-born officers would go with their states. Like many others, Alexander doubted that war would actually come. He assumed the southern states would field an army to defend secession, that the North would ultimately recognize the right, and that bloodshed would be avoided. The crisis began to drain away a substantial minority of the officer corps of the U.S. Army. Eventually more than three hundred of the 1,080 active-duty officers resigned and made their way south.[31]

In his inaugural address, on March 4, 1861, Lincoln spoke concilia-torily. "I am loath to close," the president said; but by then nobody was listening. Toward the end of March the engineer detachment received orders to return to West Point. The steamer *Massachusetts* carried the sappers away from Fort Steilacoom on April 9. Alexander's bird dog, another Ponto, howled a mournful good-bye from the foreshore. At Port Townsend the vessel shifted passengers and cargo to the *Cortes.* An hour or so after the ships parted, poor Mrs. Ragan, who had troubles enough with her crackbrain brother, discovered she had left her poodle Annette aboard the *Massachusetts.* A painful scene ensued. "Mrs. R. could never hope to see Annette again, & her grief was sad to see," Alexander re-called. He assumed one of the ship's crew had thrown the poodle overboard.[32]

The *Cortes* called at Portland, where Alexander bought Wilkie Collins's detective novel *The Woman in White* to read at sea. The *Cortes* fell behind schedule. They passed the outbound Panama steamer near the Golden Gate. A messenger intercepted Alexander at the wharf with new orders that relieved him of duty with the engineers and directed him to report to Lt. James B. McPherson on Alcatraz Island. A second copy of the order awaited him at the Gilmers'. Albert Sidney Johnson, the departmental commander, held a third. He reached the obvious conclusion. The authorities did not want him to continue his journey home.[33]

The next Panama ship would not sail for ten days, so he had plenty of time to talk things over with Bettie. He also used a friend from cadet days, William Sanders, now with the Second Dragoons, as a sounding board. Kentucky-born Dock Sanders turned out to be a fire-eater, the most radical secessionist Alexander had fallen in with up to now. Sanders had unfinished regimental business in Utah, but they agreed to meet in Montgomery, the provisional Confederate capital, late in the spring. Over on Alcatraz, McPherson gave him an unexpected explanation for the new orders. Alexander reconstructed their remarkable conversation many years later. "These orders are meant to say to you that if you wish to keep out of the war you can do so," McPherson told him. "You will not be required to go into the field against your own people, but will be kept out on this coast on fortification duty." McPherson believed war to be certain. It would be long and costly, he said, but there could be only one outcome. The South, poor, agrarian, and backward, could not support its armies in a large-scale conflict. Inevitably, the North would prevail.[34]

McPherson went on to hold out both alternative and opportunity. Alexander could wait out the fighting in safety and comfort. Casualties would thin the engineers' ranks. He could expect rapid promotion. Better still, there were business opportunities. He would have charge of the government reservations in the San Francisco district, thousands of acres of grazing lands. "Buy a flock of sheep & hire a Mexican to herd them & in four years you will be a rich man," McPherson advised. Like General Harney, he could use his official position to speculate profitably in real estate. "Going home," he wound up, "you have every personal risk to run & in a cause foredoomed to failure."[35]

This frank appeal to self-interest failed to move Alexander. With Bettie's approval, he wrote out his resignation and handed it to McPherson. Much later, he elaborated a shaky constitutional rationale for his action, one that closely followed the standard secessionist line. The cause, he said, was *liberty*. He would fight "not for slavery but the *sovereignty of the states*." This was threadbare political philosophy, and in any case his motives were plain enough in the spring of 1861. All across the South, local allegiances were proving stronger than national ones. Alexander's people were Georgians first. When a Pony Express rider reached San

Francisco with news of the bombardment of Fort Sumter, he realized that Georgians were going to war. "If I don't come & bear my part they will believe me a coward," he told McPherson. "I must go & stand my chances." McPherson agreed to forward Aleck's resignation to the War Department. The quartermaster department proved helpful, too, persuading the steamship line to carry the Alexanders eastward for half-fare. They boarded the *Golden Age* for Panama on May 1. Dock Sanders came down to the wharf to see them off.[36]

A superstitious man might have descried ill omens in several events of the return voyage. At Aspinwall, poor Ector, still in a straitjacket, lunged at Alexander, bit at his overcoat, and ripped away a large piece of it. A consumptive died two days into the New York passage. A fireman fell into the ship's machinery during a storm and was crushed to death. Someone misunderstood the report about the stoker and ran along the passageway shouting "Fire!" Bettie asked Aleck to go on deck and find out whether they were sinking. But he no longer cared whether the vessel swam. He lay doubled up in his bunk, miserably seasick.[37]

They reached New York on Friday, May 24. There Alexander learned that Lincoln had mobilized 75,000 militia, and that Virginia, Tennessee, Arkansas, and North Carolina had followed the Deep South out of the Union. News of the shooting in Alexandria, Virginia, of the Zouave hero E. E. Ellsworth* spread through the city. Alexander found the mood disturbing. "It was plain," he said, "that any Confederate ran great risk of being mobbed if it was known that he was on his way south." He also suspected the War Department might try to detain him. With secession severing direct rail connections to the South, the way to Georgia now led through Kentucky, still straining to perserve a precarious neutrality. The Alexanders hurried through their shopping and boarded the Erie Railroad cars for Cincinnati that evening.[38]

Tired, grimy, half-starved, they arrived at sunrise Sunday, May 26, and spent the day recuperating in a hotel. At the station that afternoon, an accommodating stranger helped Alexander, whose bags were stamped U.S. ARMY, settle into the St. Louis train. Taking a seat opposite Bettie, he launched into a long monologue about the Fort Sumter action, which he claimed to have witnessed. None too subtly, he put his Confederate convictions on display. Alexander marked him down at once as a police

*On May 23, 1861, James W. Jackson shot and killed Ellsworth after he hauled down a Confederate flag atop Jackson's hotel, the Marshall House.

spy. He and Bettie quietly left the train at Seymour, Indiana, for their Louisville connection. Misunderstanding their destination, the spy remained aboard when the cars rattled off toward St. Louis.[39]

From Louisville they traveled south to Chattanooga, where, on the morning of the twenty-ninth, Alexander had breakfast with the Confederate war secretary, Leroy P. Walker, who was en route to Richmond, the new Confederate capital. Walker told him a commission as a captain of engineers, dated April 2, awaited him there. After a night in Atlanta with the Hulls, the Alexanders reached Washington, Georgia, around noon on May 30. The patriarch, with Hillie, Marion, and Alice, met them at the village station. Next day Alexander set out, alone, for Richmond.[40]

In home country now, he could let down his guard and reflect. He thought over what McPherson had said about the warmaking capacities of the North and South. The roundabout rail journey had taken him through some of the most thickly settled and prosperous regions of the North. "Every station was a town, & everywhere there were camps and soldiers in regiments & brigades," he had noticed. "And they were all fine healthy looking men, with flesh on their bones & color in their cheeks, thoroughly well uniformed, equipped and armed." Looking out the smutty window as the train crawled through the Tennessee and north-Georgia hill country, he had seen the contrast. There were fewer men under arms—companies here, not regiments. Some men wore militia uniforms; many more were barefoot and clothed in homespun. Only a few carried modern rifled muskets. "Then no one could fail to note a marked difference in the general aspect of the men," he went on. "Our men were less healthy looking, they were sallower in complection & longer & lankier in build, & there seemed too to be less discipline & drill among them."[41]

Richmond was crowded with troops and government officials. An acquaintance offered Aleck half a room at the overbooked Ballard House. He had a short audience Monday, June 3, with Jefferson Davis. The president, a former war secretary and chairman of the Senate Committee on Military Affairs, remembered him from the old army. He directed Alexander to set up a shop for the manufacture of Myer's signal equipment while he waited for permanent orders. Aleck soon grew bored with the project. He felt unimportant, supernumerary. "My commanders have their hands full & can't look after me closely enough to keep me employed," he wrote Bettie. Their manner, he thought, suggested they were too busy to bother with him.[42]

Large Confederate forces were assembling at Norfolk, Yorktown, Fredericksburg, Manassas, and Winchester. Downcast, Alexander waited for an assignment to one of these legions. The days were oppressively hot. In mid-month he sent word for Bettie to join him in Richmond. He idled away the days. "No sign of orders for me yet—a delay which has effectively removed any conceit I may ever have had that my services were worth anything," he wrote her dejectedly June 29. That night, the posting finally came. "I will be serving with the largest army in the most important place, & that too under our *best* general," he wrote her the next day, his mood transformed. Bettie arrived from Fairfield a day or so after he had set out for the front. "I'll pay those yankees for separating us if ever I get the chance," he promised her. On July 2, 1861, Captain Alexander reported to General Beauregard's headquarters in the northern Virginia hamlet of Manassas.[43.]

Part II

THE SOLDIER'S ART

And war began: in other words, an event took place counter to all the laws of human reason and human nature.

—*TOLSTOY, War and Peace*

CHAPTER 4

APPRENTICESHIP

———⋗●⋖———

ALEXANDER
MANASSAS TO FREDERICKSBURG, 1861–62

ALEXANDER KNEW NO ONE AT BEAUREgard's headquarters except his West Point classmate Sam Ferguson, a roughmannered South Carolinian who doubtless needed a prod to introduce him to the others. There had been no cause for worry. The staff made a place for Aleck at the general's table, and found him a bed in the headquarters house near Manassas station. Alexander, clever, impatient, prone to faultfinding, admired Beauregard from the start. He appreciated the general's elaborate New Orleans courtesies and impressive military bearing, and was prepared to overlook his small vanities. "His hair was black," Alexander recalled, "but a few months afterward when some sorts of chemicals and such things became scarce it began to come out quite gray."[1]

Elsewhere in July 1861, other members of the Alexander clan were completing their mobilization. Felix Alexander served as an aide to the Confederate secretary of state, the family's Washington neighbor Robert Toombs. Hillie was in camp outside Richmond with the Ninth Georgia. Alexander Lawton, sister Sarah's husband, commanded the Savannah defenses. Jeremy Gilmer had resigned from the U.S. Army and was en route from San Francisco. At Fairfield, Leopold Alexander, full of patriotism, promised the new government two-thirds of his cotton crop. "We already have *men* enough, & our only want is money—cotton *commands* that, for 'Cotton is King!' " the patriarch declared. He foretold the speedy collapse of the Union regime, and the defenestration of Lincoln and General Scott.[2]

Alexander drafted a dozen privates for instruction in the Myer system and bought a horse, a large, dark bay named Dixie, to carry him over the rolling, still-peaceful countryside south of Bull Run. ("A very sorry, doubtful looking beast," an army friend remarked of Dixie, but Aleck remained loyal to her to the end.) Working rapidly, he set up a network of signal stations along the Confederate line, which ran west to east for six miles along the Bull Run valley from Warrenton Turnpike to the railroad at Union Mills ford. A station atop Wilcoxen's Hill relayed messages from the outposts to headquarters in Manassas. He found Dixie more biddable than his privates. "Some of them are so stupid that I have to knock them down & jump on them & stamp & pound them before I can get an idea in their heads," he complained to Bettie, now established in Richmond lodgings. Even so, he had the wig-wag system in operation within a week.[3]

The Confederates drove off a Yankee reconnaissance force at Blackburn's Ford on July 18, an affair that proved to be the preliminary to the first battle of Manassas.* Alexander experienced hostile fire for the first time when federal guns opened on Beauregard's field headquarters at the Wilmer McLean farmhouse, a half-mile south of the ford. McLean's wife was the widow of one of Bettie's numerous uncles; finding themselves kinsmen of sorts, Wilmer and Aleck became friends. With the aid of a spyglass, Alexander observed the gunners' preparations from a chair in McLean's grassy yard. "They loaded three or four guns, taking quite a time & aiming very carefully, & then they fired all three simultaneously—& in about five seconds all three arrived shrieking in chorus," he recalled. One shot passed through the kitchen, showering bits of mud daubing over the staff's midday meal but injuring no one.[4]

The Civil War's first full-scale battle opened shortly after daybreak on Sunday, July 21, with the light shelling of Confederate positions near the stone bridge that carried the Warrenton Turnpike over Bull Run. This turned out to be a diversion; the federal commander, Brig. Gen. Irvin McDowell, aimed his main effort at the Confederate left. Cannonading and some skirmishing continued at the stone bridge for a couple of hours. At eight o'clock, Beauregard ordered Alexander up to the aerie on Wilcoxen's Hill to report what he could see of the enemy's movements. Beauregard meantime fixed his attention on Mitchell's Ford,

*Federals and Confederates gave different names to many battles, Bull Run/Manassas, for example, and Antietam/Sharpsburg.

where he had concentrated the bulk of his forces for an assault of his own on the federal left.[5]

Alexander stared into the green distance. Something flashed out in the west beyond the stone bridge—the sun's reflection, he decided, off a brass cannon. He adjusted the glass, trained it on the road leading up from Sudley Springs Ford, and caught the gleam of bayonets and musket barrels. Certain, now, that he had spotted McDowell's main force swinging out around the Confederate flank, he signaled to Col. Nathan Evans, commanding at the stone bridge: "Look out for your left; you are turned."[6]

Recalling old army tales of junior officers who had seen a little and imagined a lot, Alexander wrote out a plain-style message for Beauregard:

> I see a body of troops crossing Bull Run about two miles above the Stone Bridge. The head of the column is in the woods on this side. The rear of the column is in the woods on the other side. About a half-mile of its length is visible in the open ground in between. I can see both infantry and artillery.

Evans's cavalry vedettes reported the crossing at about the same time. The two messages together convinced him. Evans collected elements of two regiments, about eleven hundred infantry, and set out for Sudley Springs to contest the federal advance.[7]

Like most battles, First Manassas turned on a series of "what ifs." Had his flanking column fallen upon an unwary enemy, McDowell might have rolled up the Confederate line and continued on to Richmond. "Had I succeeded on that day," McDowell told a friend some years after the war, "I should have been the greatest man in America." He failed, not least because of Alexander's warning and Evans's nimble response. Evans's rearguard action delayed the Federals long enough for Beauregard and Brig. Gen. Joseph E. Johnston to shift strong forces to meet the threat.[8]

Before the Confederates could win, however, a lot of fighting and dying had still to occur. At ten o'clock, Alexander spotted a towering column of cloud off to the west. He reported this, as well as the progress of the federal advance toward Henry House Hill, which he could measure by the battle smoke rising and thickening over the lines. He could see now that the fighting over there would be decisive. Yet Beauregard

and Johnston were idling at Mitchell's Ford at the other end of the
line. Figuring his message had not been emphatic enough to impress
Beauregard, he climbed down from the tower and rode over to report
in person. Alexander called the generals' attention to the dust cloud,
too, suggesting it was evidence of enemy reinforcements. Beauregard,
reluctant to give up his own offensive scheme, hesitated. Johnston advised strengthening the left, where the volume of fire seemed to be on
the increase. Then, suddenly, it swelled to an uproar. "The battle is
there," Johnston said finally. "I am going." Beauregard shortly
followed.[9]

Alexander had been right to insist the battle would be won or lost on
the left. He had been wrong about the dust clouds. The baggage trains
of Johnston's Shenandoah army had raised them, not Patterson's
Yankees coming down from Harper's Ferry. Fresh Confederate forces,
part of Johnston's infantry just off the cars from Winchester, pushed up
to the front. Alexander returned to the Wilcoxen tower. At about two
o'clock, intense flashes of red burning through the smoke told him the
battle was building to a crisis. A new battery opened fire, away to the
left. Whose? He saw a shell burst over the enemy line. That settled it.
Making his way through the wrack of stragglers and the walking
wounded, he reached Henry House Hill in time to witness the Confederates, delivering here for the first time the savage ululation known as the
rebel yell, launch the counterattack that decided the battle.[10]

The federal withdrawal dissolved into a rout. The pursuit, such as it
was, ended almost as soon as it began. At the stone bridge, Alexander
met an agitated Ferguson, who carried orders from Beauregard to halt
the Confederate advance. "Some fool has sent some rumor about
Yankees south of Bull Run down about Union Mills and everything is
ordered to come back," Ferguson told him angrily. Several hours of
daylight remained, and a full moon would be up later. Beauregard,
though, judged the army too disorganized to follow up what already
could be classed a smashing victory. Johnston agreed.[11]

North of the bridge, entire federal regiments had scattered. Bodies of
men and horses lay where they had fallen. Dismounted guns and
wrecked wagons blocked the turnpike. Muskets, haversacks, caps, over-
coats, and canteens were strewn by the roadside. Ahead, Alexander saw a
red-haired, purple-faced Confederate roughing up a terrified little civilian
in a frock coat and silk hat, prodding him with a pistol and threatening to
shoot. "You infernal son of a bitch," the officer shouted in surly tri-

umph. "You came to see the fun, did you? Came to see us whipped & killed. God damn your dirty soul." The prisoner turned out to be Congressman Alfred Ely of New York, out from Washington to observe the battle. Invoking Beauregard's authority, Alexander ordered the officer to holster his pistol and hand Ely over to the provost guard.[12]

Later, toward dusk, he inspected the battlefield and cast a professional eye over the wreckage. Casualties from a New York Fire Zouave regiment were sprawled near a dozen abandoned guns of two federal batteries, many of the horses dead in harness. Three Confederates lay in a heap, killed by a solid shot. "One of them had his arms raised & extended exactly if he were aiming his musket," Alexander noted coolly. Beyond, across Warrenton Turnpike, a neat row of ripening corpses marked the battle line of the Second Vermont.[13]

In the aftermath, leading Confederates agreed that with God's help a great victory had been won, a long step taken toward southern independence. For a time Alexander shared that view. Later, when it became evident that Manassas had settled nothing, a reaction set in. "It is customary to say that 'Providence did not intend we should win,' but I do not subscribe in the least to that doctrine," Alexander wrote. "Providence didn't care a row of pins about it." Johnston and Beauregard contented themselves with a partial victory when instead they should have lashed their forces into hot pursuit that moonlit night. Alexander accepted the conventional argument that Washington could not have been captured on July 22, 1861. Still, why not make the attempt? "We had them routed & on the jump," he wrote, "& just to make history interesting & instructive we ought to have improved this rare occasion to the utmost."[14]

It took nearly a week to bury all the dead, some one thousand altogether. "They have only finished with the enemy today," Alexander wrote Bettie July 27, "burying 83 of them together, principally those red breeches New York Zouaves."[15]

Manassas established the pattern, immutable in the Eastern Theater in the first years of the war, of short, sharp campaigns followed by long intermissions. After First Manassas, the main armies did not join battle for eight months. Alexander witnessed much of the fighting on the Virginia Peninsula in the spring of 1862, but staff assignments kept him out of the line at Second Manassas and Sharpsburg. He approached his work with a level of enthusiasm and intelligence that set him quite apart from the common run. He was "one of the most industrious officers I ever knew," a fellow officer said of him, "and was always doing and suggesting something new." Before he accepted a combat command in late 1862, Alexander established a reputation as one of the most versatile and efficient staff officers in Confederate service.[16]

His duties were astonishingly varied. After Manassas, Beauregard appointed him chief of ordnance for his command, now styled the First Corps, Army of the Potomac; Johnston gave him the same assignment for the Second Corps. He helped train the artillery. He worked to improve the quality of the artillery ammunition, much of which he found "worse than worthless"—prone to tumble in flight, explode prematurely, or both. He experimented with rocket batteries and tested a field telegraph system. He supervised Confederate spy operations in northern Virginia. He tried code-breaking. He set up a workshop for the conversion of sporting weapons for military use and oversaw the repair and distribution of captured small arms and cannon. He became the Confederate service's first (and only) successful aeronaut.[17]

He was healthy, wiry, and strong, in high spirits, restlessly energetic, confident. He had grown a beard, perhaps to compensate for his spreading baldness. Scraggly and ill-kempt, it caused him to look a decade older than his twenty-six years. Life in the field turned out to be not at all unpleasant. He reeked of sweat, leather, horse, sour coffee, bad food, tobacco, and burnt powder. Though he sometimes complained of overwork, he assured Miss Teen, now pregnant with their first child, that the risks were small. "Really & truly now the *danger* of battle to any one man is very little indeed, & in my new 'posish' I will be less exposed even than before," he insisted. He boasted to her of his importance. "I have to be able to supply over 3,000,000 rounds of cartridges to different sized guns, besides artillery ammunition for forty cannon," he said, "& in a battle I would have a great deal to do with posting the Arty. & directing its fire."[18]

By October the Confederates had pushed their advance outposts to within sight of Washington. Working with Beauregard's chief of staff, Lt. Col. Thomas Jordan, Alexander set up a collection system for the reports of Confederate agents in the capital. The spy network included Washington socialite Rose O'Neal Greenhow, who, in one of the war's great espionage coups, had tipped Beauregard to McDowell's advance on Manassas, and two shadowy figures, a freebooting adventuress who called herself Augusta Morris and a noisy, excitable widow named Catherine Baxley. The three, working independently, smuggled out military and political intelligence through, among others, Marylander E. Pliny Bryan, one of Alexander's signalmen.[19]

Rose Greenhow, whose extensive social and political connections made her Jordan's star turn, continued to smuggle out information even after Allan Pinkerton's agents placed her under house arrest in late August. The federals pulled in Mrs. Baxley a few months later, found incriminating documents sewn into her bonnet lining, and held her at the Greenhow house, where she and Mrs. Greenhow evidently met for the first time. By January 18, 1862, both had been shut up in the Old Capitol Prison. Augusta Morris joined them there in early February. Mrs. Baxley did not disguise her strong secessionist sympathies, but claimed to have been unaware of the significance of the papers she had carried north from Richmond. "I will go home and meddle no more with edged tools," she pledged in a bid for release. Mrs. Morris, meanwhile, boldly continued her work, bribing turnkeys to carry out her messages. "You could buy up the whole regiment for $1,000," she wrote one of her contacts.[20]

The network may have been improvisational and crude, but it produced reliable estimates of federal strength. (Pinkerton's Secret Service consistently exaggerated Confederate resources, practically paralyzing the federal command at times.*) During the autumn and early winter, using information passed through Bryan and others, Alexander drew up an order of battle that listed every Yankee regiment by brigade and division. His assessments of Union troop strength, organization, and battleworthiness proved remarkably accurate over time.[21]

Pinkerton's operatives hauled in Bryan in late February. For some reason the spies were never brought to trial; all four were freed in early June. When the women eventually turned up in Richmond, the War Department, baffled, called in Alexander to find out what they wanted. The interviews amused him. The queenly Mrs. Greenhow detested Mrs. Baxley and suspected Mrs. Morris of playing a double game. "One thing each one wanted was that it should be understood that she had been perfectly discreet in every respect, but that the other two had flickered more or less," he said. "Evidently their common calamity had not drawn them together." Alexander fell briefly under the spell of Augusta Morris, who seems to have been quite a beauty. He soon recovered. "Mrs. M I

---

*"They never had any spy worth a cent," Alexander said.

think is not a model of *virtue* however patriotic she may be," he wrote Bettie. "I am going to give her a few hundred dollars of the secret service money & send her off." Mrs. Morris and Catherine Baxley faded from the scene. Rose Greenhow published a lively account of her adventures and became something of a celebrity before she was drowned while trying to run the blockade at Wilmington, North Carolina, in October 1864. Aleck lost all touch with Bryan, whom he had liked. He learned, much later, that Bryan died of yellow jack in Charleston not long before the war's end.[22]

Bettie gave birth to a daughter on November 10, 1861. She sent word that the baby had a full head of black hair, black eyes, a red face, and no teeth—"the exact image of her papa," Alexander joked. He longed to make her acquaintance, but Jordan's spies were reporting McClellan ready to march, and he could not get away. Alexander believed the Confederates were prepared for the test. He greatly respected McClellan's artillery, but was otherwise unawed. "His cavalry is numerous but can't ride & his infantry except the Irish can't fight," he assured his father.[23]

Mrs. Greenhow's sources failed her this time; the Federals did not leave their winter camps. Alexander established Bettie and the child, as yet unnamed, in a house near Gainesville ten miles from the Centreville headquarters. He had begun to refer to her as Secessia, to Leopold Alexander's mortification; the patriarch evidently believed the baby had been so named until he heard that Dixie, Rebelle, and Manassa were other possible choices. The couple eventually called her Bessie Mason Alexander. The landlady turned out to be "a very mean old specimen," Alexander wrote Fairfield, but room and board were reasonable at forty dollars a month, and he could ride over for weekend visits. On a snowy January night there, he saw his daughter for the first time.[24]

The troops endured a harsh winter, wet and raw, with occasional heavy falls of snow. Sick lists mounted. Alexander glumly noted the growing disparity between the opposing forces. "Our army here is much smaller in effective force than *anyone* who has not seen the figures wd. imagine," he wrote one of his sisters. "We have not gained any strength for several months past, while the Yankees are increasing their numbers as well as improving their armament every day." Hardship undermined morale. "I was struck with the universal slouch and depression in the ranks," wrote one visitor to the camps. "Through the whole army was that enervating moldiness."[25]

Confederate leadership failed to improve conditions in the winter cantonments, but President Davis did act to clarify the command structure in northern Virginia. Davis transferred Beauregard to the West, leaving Johnston in sole charge. Though sorry to see Beauregard go, Alexander respected Johnston; he turned down Beauregard's invitation to accompany him west. Ordnance problems, especially those resulting from the bewildering variety of Confederate weaponry, demanded much of his attention. He and his assistant, George Duffey, a middle-aged Richmond jeweler turned gunsmith, fed a steady supply of new and captured rifle muskets to the infantry commands, gradually replacing the old smoothbores with longer-range, more accurate firearms. Alexander found time to visit Bettie and the baby and, in idle moments, worked out complex chess problems with the aid of back numbers of *Chess Monthly Magazine*.[26]

In early March, anticipating McClellan's long-expected offensive, Johnston ordered a withdrawal south to the Rapidan River. The movement shook Alexander out of his comfortable winter routine. "We had been quiet for so long, I had almost forgotten it is *war*," he wrote his father. He supervised the shipment of ammunition and other materiel from the Manassas warehouses and, in a parting shot, blew up the now-famous stone bridge over Bull Run. He managed to salvage a pair of suspenders, two sets of woolen shorts, and some cigarette tobacco before the rear guards fired the depot. He saw his wife and daughter safely into temporary lodgings in Richmond. As relief for Dixie, he acquired a second horse, Meg Merrilies, a bay mare named for the Walter Scott gypsy. He hired a slave manservant, Charley, no last name recorded, fifteen years old, "medium tall & slender, ginger-cake colored, well behaved & good dispositioned," who would remain with him until Appomattox.[27]

McClellan's shift of most of the federal army to the Virginia Peninsula in mid-March forced Johnston to hasten the Confederate withdrawal. Johnston conducted a skillful though at times ragged retreat south and east toward Yorktown. Alexander traveled light, "roughing it a good deal," he said; for several days he could not find a comb to run through his scanty hair, and used a fork instead. He complained about looting and straggling and thought Johnston should shoot a few defaulters as an example to the others. In the confusion, fourteen of Uncle Roy Mason's slaves ran off to the Yankees.[28]

The Confederates, bluffing and playing on McClellan's unnatural caution, held the Federals in front of Yorktown for a month, then began a long, slow retreat toward Richmond. For another thirty days the armies skirmished. The Peninsula was poor country for such work, low and flat, waterlogged, malarial. Marches were epics of difficulty and discomfort. "The roads were but long strings of guns, wagons and ambulances, mixed in with infantry, artillery and cavalry, splashing and bogging through the darkness in a river of mud," Alexander wrote. Artillery and sniper fire were incessant, keeping the troops in a crouch in their flooded trenches from sunrise to sunset. Yankee ironclads steamed up the James and York rivers and heaved enormous shells into the Confederate lines. Alexander, moving about on ordnance business, found himself frequently exposed. "They missed me by twenty yards," he wrote Bettie exultantly after one encounter with sharpshooters.[29]

By late May, leading elements of McClellan's army were close enough to Richmond to hear the city's church bells ring the hours. In his maddeningly deliberate way, McClellan had brought off a strategic coup. "Practically without firing a shot, in two months he just maneuvered us out of Norfolk, & of Yorktown; opened both the James & the York rivers; compelled us ourselves to blow up the *Merrimack*; & established his own pickets within six miles of Richmond," Alexander wrote admiringly. He fretted that a sudden Yankee thrust would trap Bettie in the capital. "If a battle goes against us *as soon as you hear it* start off by the first train," he instructed her. *"By no means think of waiting to hear from me."*[30]

In any event, the Federals had reached the limit of their advance. Johnston made ready to go over to the offensive. Word that the battle was about to open reached Alexander in a Richmond sickbed. Still weak from a mild case of measles, he returned to headquarters the evening of May 30. At midday on the thirty-first, Saturday, Confederate forces struck the Union left wing, caught awkwardly astride the flooded Chickahominy River. Fair Oaks/Seven Pines was a confused and awkward fight. D. H. Hill's troops mauled a federal division under Silas Casey, but a series of misadventures denied Johnston a clear-cut victory. Toward sundown, Alexander and other staff officers were riding near the front with Johnston when the Yankees opened up with small arms and cannon fire. Hit in the shoulder and ribs, Johnston became one of the more than eleven thousand casualties of the battle. Robert E. Lee arrived from Richmond at noon the next day to succeed him in command of what Lee soon designated the Army of Northern Virginia.[31]

Johnston's stroke seemed to freeze McClellan. His powerful army re-

mained in its lines. "All his good strategy went for naught because he
was afraid to wade in & fight," Alexander said of him. Lee had no such
fears, though his reputation did not stand high in mid-1862. Many in
the army regarded him as a mere engineer, a fortifications specialist, a
"King of Spades." He had failed in his only independent command, in
western Virginia in 1861. Alexander, believing the outnumbered and
outgunned Confederates required a bold, risk-taking leader, doubted
Lee would be up to the job. At West Point, Lee had impressed him as
conventional, regulation-bound, cautious. An old army acquaintance,
met by chance a day or so after Lee took over, corrected Alexander's
misconceptions.

"Lee is audacity personified," Capt. Joseph Ives, who had observed
Lee closely as a member of Davis's military staff, told him. "His name
is audacity, and you need not be afraid of not seeing all of it that you
will want to see."[32]

Lee's plans were bold enough, but as with Johnston there were critical
failures of execution. The Seven Days' battles opened on June 25, 1862,
with a federal probe at Oak Grove. Lee seized the initiative at Mechanicsville the following day. Stonewall Jackson fell behind schedule, showed
up late, and failed to carry out his part of the scheme. (His "incredible
slackness" cost Lee a decisive victory, Alexander charged later.) McClellan managed to extricate his army, conduct a fighting withdrawal, and
deal a costly tactical defeat to Lee at Malvern Hill. Still, McClellan's
Peninsular Campaign ended in failure. It is an irony that Lee won a
strategic victory even though little enough went right for him tactically.
(And casualties mounted steeply: seven days, seven battles, more than
twenty thousand killed, wounded, and missing.) At least the Confederate
formations never lacked for ammunition. The Alexander ordnance system worked so well that he could turn over the operation to Duffey and
observe some of the Seven Days' action from the air.[33]

"The battle was just opening at [Gaines's] Mill," he wrote his father,
"& I had a fine view of it & the retreat of the enemy, burning stores
and blowing up ammunition wagons until . . . the balloon leaked so
much that I had to come down."[34]

The contraption had been fabricated from bolts of colorful dress silk,
sealed with a rubbery varnish, and, with pure hydrogen unavailable, filled
with illuminating gas from the Richmond Gas Works. Alexander disliked
heights. He accepted the balloon assignment from Lee with profound skep-

ticism. To his surprise, he found the sensation agreeable; he dosed his occasional giddiness with pulls from a flask of his father's Old Hurricane brandy. There were immediate military benefits too. Signaling with big black cambric balls suspended under the basket, Alexander reported the approach of federal reinforcements at Gaines's Mill and, in several night ascensions, traced the route of McClellan's retreat by the glow of the Yankee campfires. In ascensions from Drewry's Bluff the evening of June 30, he discovered McClellan's camps at Malvern Hill.[35]

His career as an aeronaut ended July 4 when the steamer *Teazer*, from which he had several times launched the balloon, ran aground in the James. A Yankee gunboat shortly appeared and opened fire, scattering the *Teazer*'s crew and forcing Alexander to jump overboard and swim for it. The little vessel floated off the mudbank at high tide. The Federals claimed the *Teazer* as their prize, and with it Lee's air force.[36]

"Drive on, Abram."

The phrase became an Alexander trademark. In the quiet month after the Seven Days, he hired the slave teamster Abram (he again failed to record the last name) from his Virginia owner, rebuilt depleted ammunition stocks, distributed weapons newly produced in Richmond or captured from the Federals, and overhauled the ordnance train. The army rewarded him with promotion to lieutenant colonel. Miss Teen, the baby, and his brother Felix, who had followed Robert Toombs into the army several months before,* joined him in lodgings, "a nice cool house in a shady grove" on the edge of Richmond. This pleasant interlude could not last. Lee planned to test McClellan's successor, Maj. Gen. John Pope, whose elevation had provided occasion for much joking among Confederate veterans of the old army, Aleck among them. "Pope is a blatherskite," he wrote his father.[37]

In mid-August the ordnance train set out in Lee's wake. On August 30, Alexander caught sight of distant smoke, evidence of what turned out to be Pope's humbling at the second battle of Manassas. Pope withdrew the beaten army into the Washington lines; Lincoln shortly banished him to the Minnesota Territory and recalled McClellan. Alexander followed Lee across the Potomac. At Frederick, Maryland, in early September he browsed in a bookstore and left with a five-month-old number of *Harper's Magazine* and an 1860s best-seller titled *Father Tom and the Pope; or, A*

*Toombs had resigned as Confederate secretary of state in July 1861.

Night at the Vatican. He bought three small dishes for his mess chest at a country pottery on the Boonsboro road, paying with a Confederate one-dollar bill. The potter cut a Maryland banknote in half to make fifty cents change. He had a brief reunion on the line of march with Alexander Lawton, now commanding a division in Stonewall Jackson's corps. Felix was somewhere about, too, with Toombs's Georgia brigade.[38]

Alexander went briefly into the line as a freelance rifleman at South Mountain on September 14. He shot a Yankee at a range of six hundred yards, a top-class piece of marksmanship, and retired shortly thereafter with a souvenir, an elongated ball that chipped a rock a few inches from his head. Two days later, he formed a train of empty wagons and rattled off to Harper's Ferry to collect the trophies Jackson had captured there, more than seventy cannon and large stores of ammunition. At Lee's direction, he forwarded guns and ammunition to Sharpsburg, where they were turned against their former owners. On the afternoon of September 17, from the heights near Harper's Ferry, Alexander watched shells bursting and battle smoke rising over the valley of Antietam Creek.[39]

There, according to Alexander, Lee crossed the boundary between audacity and foolhardiness, venturing battle with little to gain and an army to lose. The Confederates claimed a drawn battle. They expected a renewal on September 18, but McClellan did not offer. That night the army withdrew across the Potomac and went into camp north of Winchester, remaining there for five weeks to rest and recruit. Among the wounded were Lawton and Toombs. Cross-grained, insubordinate, and contemptuous of professionally trained officers, Toombs had known an afternoon's glory at the Antietam lower bridge, where his Georgians held off repeated federal assaults for several critical hours. He returned to Richmond with a painful though not serious hand wound. Denied promotion, Toombs reclaimed his old seat in the Confederate Congress, where he made a career of abusing Jefferson Davis. Poor Lawton had been badly lamed by a bullet through the knee, a wound that would keep him out of the field for the rest of the war.[40]

Alexander set up a comfortable camp in a meadow near Lee's headquarters tent and, armed with an enormous, old-fashioned horse pistol, kept his mess well supplied with quail. He shot more than a hundred in a field of broom corn one sunny October afternoon. At month's end, Lee, in response to McClellan's belated return to Virginia, marched the army over the Blue Ridge south to Culpeper. Alexander shortly followed with the ordnance train, rejoining Lee November 4.[41]

A heavy, wet snow fell the night of November 7–8. In the morning, Lee summoned Alexander to offer him command of Stephen D. Lee's artillery battalion. Steve Lee, promoted to brigadier and ordered to Vicksburg, had lobbied hard for Alexander to succeed him. Alexander knew about his efforts, but made no pitch of his own. He attributed this passivity to the same species of fatalism he often ascribed to the Confederate high command. "I was perhaps a little too good a Presbyterian," he said, "& disposed to let happen what would, as if all events were ordered by a Divine intelligence." In this case, Robert Lee disposed. Alexander took charge of the battalion, six batteries, twenty-six guns, manned by Virginians, South Carolinians, and a roughneck company of Mississippi River stevedores. Along with the Washington Artillery of New Orleans, Alexander's command formed the artillery reserve of the First Corps of Lt. Gen. James Longstreet.[42]

Sharpsburg, Steve Lee told him, had been "Artillery Hell." The Yankees had more heavy rifled pieces, and shells that burst most of the time. Confederate gunners were still searching for combinations that could neutralize these federal advantages. Alexander had been critical of Confederate artillery organization from the start. Since June 1861, when he had taken temporary charge of five batteries assembling in Richmond, he had been an advocate of cohesive artillery battalions operating independently. This was then a novel idea. As a matter of common practice, individual batteries were parceled out to the infantry brigades, leaving only a modest general reserve. "This scattering of the commands made it impossible to mass our guns in effective numbers," Alexander argued. In consequence, artillery performance had been disappointing, especially during the Seven Days. By the late summer of 1862, Lee, impressed by the results of concentrated fire at Second Manassas, had become a convert to Alexander's view. The system of independent battalions gradually spread through the Army of Northern Virginia.*[43]

In mid-November a new federal commanding geneal, Ambrose E. Burnside, put the Army of the Potomac in motion for the Rappahannock. Two federal corps pulled up opposite the old colonial town of Fredericksburg on November 17. Lee followed. Swimming over bottomless roads in heavy rain, Alexander's battalion arrived on the twenty-second. While Burnside waited for his pontoon trains, the Confederates

*And, eventually, in the Union army and in European armies as well.

settled into good defensive positions on the south bank. At Longstreet's request, Alexander supervised the siting of the First Corps's guns, some of them along a ridge known as Marye's Heights.[44]

CHAMBERLAIN

ANTIETAM TO FREDERICKSBURG, AUTUMN 1862

A fair-sized crowd of Bostonians turned out to cheer the 20th Maine on the march from the railroad station to the *Merrimac*'s berth. The newspapers were full of the second Union reverse at Bull Run these anxious days; the crowd's huzzahs and the doom-saying headlines combined to make the men jumpy. They clattered up the gangway and into the steamer, and tried to make themselves comfortable. Then the 36th Massachusetts went aboard. The *Merrimac* cleared Boston Harbor with baggage piled high in the passageways, troop decks crowded, hot, sooty, and loud with the ceaseless racket of the ship's machinery. The men seemed to expect disaster. Rumors circulated of a Confederate raider stalking the *Merrimac*. When a tier of overloaded bunks crashed down onto the deck above, there was panic: "She's struck a rock!" The alarm passed, and the ship steamed on southward. The new soldiers gradually became accustomed to their strange surroundings. At least the late-summer seas were calm.[1]

Chamberlain struck up acquaintances with several of the 36th's officers. Their handsome uniforms and accoutrements made him "feel very green and humble," he admitted. He pored over the drill books, memorizing procedures and commands in preparation for long instructional sessions during which Colonel Ames catechized his inexperienced subordinates. He had hardly mastered the first few lessons before the *Merrimac* touched at Alexandria, Virginia, on the Potomac seven miles below Washington. Alexandria was dirty and dilapidated. The inhabitants were sullen. But the Stars and Stripes flew over the town hall, and the scent of southern mint sweetened the balmy air.[2]

The 20th Maine marched into Washington early on Sunday, September 7. War had transformed the dusty, backward capital. Officers, office-seekers, contractors, ambassadors, spies, prostitutes, and parasites of every description jostled for influence, information, pleasure, and custom. In the aftermath of another defeat, Theodore Gerrish, a private in the 20th, saw confusion and demoralization all around. "Regiments of soldiers filled the squares, squadrons of cavalry were dashing along the streets, batteries of artillery, long lines of baggage wagons and ambulances were seen in every direction,'' he wrote. The 20th marched self-consciously and ineptly, each member of the drum corps beating a different time, each man taking a different step. Enduring onlookers' sneers, the regiment shuffled along toward the Washington Arsenal. There Chamberlain oversaw the distribution of Enfield rifle muskets, together with gun slings, cartridge boxes, bayonets, and scabbards.[3]

The newspapers were reporting Lee north of the Potomac. In fact, the van of the Army of Northern Virginia had crossed the Potomac at White's Ford during the night of September 4–5. Lee's objectives were unclear; marching north and west of Washington, he threatened Baltimore, the Susquehanna valley, and Philadelphia as well as the capital. Lincoln and his general-in-chief, Henry W. Halleck, summoned George McClellan, superseded after the collapse of the Peninsula Campaign in July. By the seventh, McClellan had the Army of the Potomac in motion toward Frederick, Maryland, in sluggish pursuit of Lee.[4]

The 20th Maine, one of thirty-five new regiments assigned to the army and barely a month in existence, joined the chase on the morning of Friday, September 12, moving from Arlington Heights northwest along the National Road with the Third Brigade, First Division, Fifth Corps. The brigade, composed of the 16th Michigan, the 12th, 17th, and 44th New York, and the 83rd Pennsylvania, had seen action on the Peninsula and at the second battle of Bull Run. It had been bled down by fighting and further reduced by disease. The 20th, close to a thousand strong, set out with nearly as many men as the other five regiments combined.[5]

It was a killing march. The men staggered under their fifty-pound burdens of arms, ammunition, knapsack, haversack, and canteen. Chamberlain, moving up and down the line on horseback,* found it impossible to keep the ranks closed. The sun burned with an intensity few of these Maine Yankees had ever experienced. Sweat soaked their loose woolen uniforms. Blistered and footsore, thirsty and grimed with dust, they fell out by the dozen. The more valiant among them struggled to keep up, reeling and staggering, but only a fraction of the regiment completed that sixteen-mile march.[6]

In the night, by ones and twos, the stragglers rejoined their companies. The column covered twenty-four miles the next day, and passed through

---

*Field officers were mounted. Company officers marched alongside the men.

Frederick on September 14, Sunday. Ahead, Union forces engaged Confederate rear guards holding two gaps in the dark mass of South Mountain, the Maryland spur of the Blue Ridge. The boom of artillery sounded intermittently. The 20th Maine entered the battle zone on Monday. The men saw hundreds of wounded awaiting attention in temporary sawbones hospitals in houses and yards. The first "johnnies" came into view, prisoners being escorted to the rear—"tall, lank, slouchy looking fellows clad in dirty gray uniforms," Gerrish described them.[7]

The burial details were still at work in Turner's Gap. Fresh mounds marked the graves of the Union dead. There had not been time yet to bury the rebels, who lay where they had fallen among the old oaks, singly and in heaps of three or four. The men stared as they filed past. Chamberlain dismounted for a closer look at one frozen figure, an infantryman of sixteen or seventeen, at rest with his back against a tree. His eyes were open. "This was my enemy—this boy," he thought. He had been shot in the chest. Blood had soaked his shirt, then dried. "He was dead," Chamberlain wrote, "the boy, my enemy; but I shall see him forever."[8]

Chamberlain looked westward from Turner's Gap over the drowsy, sunlit valley of Antietam Creek. Blue-clad Union forces were pushing up the Sharpsburg road. Beyond, the Confederates had drawn up on high ground between the Antietam and Sharpsburg village. From here it seemed like a chessboard war, all the pieces in plain view as they moved into place. It had come about by accident. On the thirteenth, two Indiana soldiers had discovered a copy of Lee's invasion plans, the famous Lost Order, lying in the grass along the roadside. Lee, learning that McClellan had—literally—read his intentions, concentrated his scattered forces at Sharpsburg. The Potomac described a long S a mile or so behind the town, and could be forded only at one place. A powerful, oversized enemy approached. Lee decided to stand and offer battle.

Troops filed into the lines all day September 16, Tuesday. McClellan appeared to be in no hurry to attack. Meanwhile, Stonewall Jackson accepted the surrender of the twelve-thousand-man Union garrison at Harper's Ferry and quick-marched all but one division of his command seventeen miles north to Sharpsburg. The Union Fifth Corps reached the mile-wide valley of the Antietam at about noon on the sixteenth. Later in the day the 20th Maine went into bivouac just beyond the village of Keedysville, behind the center of the federal line.[9]

After dark, musketry sounded every so often away to the north, where

Maj. Gen. Joseph Hooker's First Corps divisions were across the north-ernmost of the three Antietam bridges and moving into position for a dawn advance. Light rain drifted downward during the night. The men of the 20th squatted in the wet grass and awaited events. Shortly after daybreak, Hooker's lines moved through the fog and murk down the Hagerstown Pike toward a field of standing corn. The sun heaved up and burned off the mist. Climbing to the top of a hill, Chamberlain, with several officers and men of the 20th, watched Hooker's battle surge back and forth over the cornfield. Just as it appeared that Hooker might achieve a breakthrough, a large force of rebels burst from the cover of a woods and flashed out a volley that, in one survivor's phrase, "was like a scythe running through our line." Chamberlain and the others watched in awed silence. "We had never seen a battle before," Gerrish wrote. "Whole lines melted away in that terrible carnage." In two hours the First Corps lost twenty-five hundred killed, wounded, and missing.[10]

Toward late morning the Third Brigade, with the 20th Maine, moved a few hundred yards to the south to cover the army trains, the reserve artillery, and the batteries overlooking the center bridge. Shells burst overhead; an occasional solid shot churned through the damp earth. Nobody was hit. A mile to the south, Burnside, commanding the Ninth Corps, delayed his diversionary attack on the lower bridge, leaving Lee free to parry follow-up assaults by the 12th Corps and the Second Corps. At midday the Irish Brigade carried enemy positions in the sunken farm road known afterwards as Bloody Lane, giving McClellan a clear opportunity to break the Confederate center. He allowed it to pass, turning instead to the left, toward Burnside's bridge. By now Burnside had tried several rushes at the graceful little triple-arched bridge, but each had been broken up by a few hundred Georgians of Robert Toombs's brigade firing from thickly wooded bluffs on the opposite bank.[11]

Burnside's troops finally carried the bridge at about 3:00 P.M. The Ninth Corps regiments poured across and pressed the Georgians back. Burnside seemed on the verge of a breakthrough when the sixth of Jackson's divisions, A. P. Hill's—the men having outmarched their own shadows, as the army phrase had it—reached the battlefield from Harper's Ferry. Though he had ample reserves, McClellan turned down Burnside's request for fresh troops; Hill's counterstroke stopped the Yankee advance and stabilized the Confederate right. The fighting gradu-ally died out. At sunset the relative positions of the two armies were essentially unchanged.

The battle of September 17, 1862, America's bloodiest single-day encounter, claimed a total of twenty-six thousand men killed, wounded, or missing. McClellan used the eighteenth to rest and refit, and to bury the dead. At nightfall the Confederates lit cookfires all along the ridge and, under cover of the ruse, recrossed the Potomac. McClellan had missed several chances to break up Lee's army. Even the military innocents of the 20th Maine wondered why he had not thrown the powerful Fifth Corps into the battle. Some twenty thousand of McClellan's seventy-five thousand effectives never saw action.[12]

For the 20th Maine, that was just as well. By 1862 the experts understood that it took at least three to four months to prepare a new regiment for combat. The 20th had been able to keep mostly intact after that first day on the march, but there had been no time for battlefield drill, let alone musketry practice. Many of the men had hardly fired their weapons. Certainly Ames and probably Chamberlain knew the 20th would have stood little chance against A. P. Hill's veterans. Still, the troops had shown themselves steady under their first fire. Halfway through the battle, when the 20th neatly executed a change of position to the right, toward the uproar of the guns, Ames judged it to have passed an important initial test.[13]

Chamberlain's first action came three days after Antietam, when Fifth Corps detachments forded the Potomac for a closer view of the retreating Confederates. A cavalry brigade and the van of the First Division began crossing at Shepherdstown Ford at seven in the morning of Saturday, September 20. Lee's rear guards turned and offered battle. When the 20th Maine reached the ford a little later, the cavalry and some infantry were already returning. Ames took the regiment across anyway, and formed a line of battle on a bluff above the river. Heavy firing sounded away to the right. Ahead, pale forms could be seen flitting among the trees. Soon clouds of white smoke came billowing out of the woods. For the first time the Maine men heard, close up, the weird singing and cracking of minié balls. They returned fire, delivering their first blow to the rebellion. A few minutes later the buglers sounded the recall. The 20th scuttled back down the bluff and formed up on the riverbank.[14]

The Confederates kept up a sharp fire. Chamberlain sat on horseback near a deep place in the fast-flowing river, where several men of a New York regiment had been swept off their feet and drowned, directing the men past the treacherous spot. His mask of imperturbability slipped for a moment when he saw a soldier sit down at the water's edge, remove his shoes and socks, and carefully roll up the legs of his trousers. He prepared himself for the crossing with infuriating deliberateness, as though he had the river and the morning entirely to himself. "Come on, my man," Chamberlain shouted finally, "hurry up, hurry up, or we will both be shot." A few minutes later, Chamberlain's horse was hit near the bridle. In a bravura performance, he remained in midriver, under fire, until the entire brigade had reached the Maryland side.[15]

The 20th went into line in the dry bed of the Chesapeake & Ohio canal,* parallel to the Potomac. This first exposure to battle cost the regiment a total of three men slightly wounded. For the next few days, sharpshooters concealed in a ruined mill on the Virginia bank worked tirelessly to increase the casualty count. Finally a twelve-pounder battery opened up and shelled the snipers out of the rubble. The 20th sent up a cheer as the survivors scrambled up the bluff and fled into the woods.[16]

Chamberlain had led troops in battle; he had shown courage and self-command; he had mastered the main elements of Silas Casey's *Infantry Tactics*. Now, he realized, he had to teach himself to look after the men. The upper Potomac camps were uncomfortable and unhealthy. Maine Yankees were unused to the climate and the unvarying diet of hard bread, salt pork, and coffee. The stench of corrupted flesh poisoned the air for weeks after the Antietam battle. Animal carcasses and human waste fouled water sources. Many officers neglected to enforce sanitary measures. The nights turned cold. The regiment had not been issued greatcoats or tents. Exposure and disease began to take a heavy toll: typhoid, malarial fever, measles. Hospital facilities were inadequate, medicines in short supply. Burial details were at work nearly every day. By the end of October the 20th's sick list contained more than three hundred names.[17]

All this misery pained Chamberlain. Still, short of leading an armed assault on the commissariat, he could do little to speed the arrival of tents, blankets, and clothing. As for himself, he flourished. Cooler weather invigorated him. He seemed not to mind the food. Writing from Brunswick, Fannie asked him to have a photograph made and sent to her. Instead, he posted a lurid word picture of the trials of field service, in a mock-heroic tone that made it clear he found his circumstances inspiriting rather than the reverse. He told his brother Tom he had never felt better in his life.[18]

He slept on the ground, on a rubber blanket; his clothes were begin-

---

*Confederate raiders had blown up the aqueduct that fed the canal.

ning to ravel; disease and privation were endemic; he had gotten nowhere with the army's supply officers; he had been shot at. Taking the
good with the bad, life in the field was a great improvement on Bowdoin.
"Let me say no danger & no hardship ever make me wish to get back
to that college life again," he wrote Fannie. "I can't breathe when I
think of those last two years. Why I would spend my whole life campaigning rather than endure that again. One thing though, I *won't* endure it again."[19]

Chamberlain could draw some tentative conclusions from his initial
experiences. He would have disagreed with Oliver Wendell Holmes, Jr.,
who defined war as "an organized bore." For Holmes, a year's hard
service (he was badly wounded at Antietam) rubbed away all traces of
war's gild of glory. He might have disagreed with another New England
volunteer officer, John De Forest,* for whom combat held roughly the
same appeal as "being in a rich cholera district in the height of the
season." Chamberlain respected military ways and habits. He liked being
in authority. "I wish you could hear Lawrence give off a command &
see him ride along the battalion on his white horse," his brother wrote
home. De Forest admitted experiencing flashes of elation "when the air
is all a yell and the earth is all a flame." Chamberlain knew that wild joy,
too. He had shown no fear at Shepherdstown. A conscientious officer, he
discovered there, is too busy to be afraid. Besides, the antique code of
the de Tankervilles would sustain him. "The instinct to seek safety is
overcome by the instinct of honor," Chamberlain wrote.[20]

He caught his first glimpse of Lincoln's awkward, unlovely form in
early October, when the president visited McClellan's headquarters, conferred with senior commanders, and reviewed the army. Lincoln looked
sad, Chamberlain thought, weighted down with responsibility. A private
in another First Division brigade perceived something more: a shadow
of death. "He looks the same as in his pictures, though more careworn,"
the soldier wrote home; "one of his feet is in the grave." Lincoln issued
the preliminary Emancipation Proclamation a few days after the Antietam battle, decreeing that slaves in rebel-held territory would be free
as of January 1, 1863. Chamberlain reported that many senior officers
disapproved of the measure; Fitz-John Porter, the Fifth Corps commander, denounced it openly.[21]

---

*De Forest (1826–1906) served with the 12th Connecticut in Louisiana and Virginia from 1862 to
1864. His *Miss Ravenel's Conversion* (1867) is one of the few distinguished novels to come out of the
Civil War.

Lincoln probably hoped to gauge the army's temper during the visit. His main purpose, however, was to prod his balky general into action. On October 6, two days after the president returned to Washington, Halleck formally ordered McClellan to cross the Potomac and bring the Army of Northern Virginia to battle. McClellan did not move for another three weeks. Inactivity had mixed results for the 20th Maine. As Private Gerrish noted, "Lead was a much less cruel butcher than disease"; it was usually quicker, too. On the other hand, Ames and Chamberlain used the idle weeks to intensify the regiment's training. The men learned to detest the demanding, rebarbative Ames. "I swear they will shoot him the first battle we are in," Tom Chamberlain wrote his sister Sae. Ames drilled the 20th by the hour, snapping the men from column to line of battle and back into column. He stood aside, glowering, while they fumbled through the nine-step process of loading their rifles. When the regiment had become reasonably proficient in the elementary evolutions, Ames turned the drill over to his second-in-command. The men did not transfer their dislike of Ames to Chamberlain. "Lieutenant Colonel Chamberlain is almost idolized by the whole regiment," one private wrote from the Antietam camp. The men could see how diligently he worked to master the soldier's art. "I *study*, I tell you, every military work I can find," he wrote Fannie. "I am bound to understand *every thing*." He asked her to send him his copy of Jomini's *The Art of War*. He and Ames planned to read it together.[22]

Duty as brigade field officer took him out of camp every third day on long rides of inspection to the Potomac outposts. From the high ground he could see villages, cultivated fields, and, beyond, the lines of the rebel campfires. Jogging along, he would lose himself in daydreams of home. He thought of sending birthday presents to the children, then awoke to the realization that he could offer only a few bits of stale candy and shards of exploded shells. One day he supervised the building of a rough bridge over Antietam Creek; that night he dreamed of leading Fannie over the stream, "& then taking Daisy on my back & swimming while Wyllys looked out for himself & climbed some huge rocks." He hoped to settle them all in Washington for the winter.[23]

Chamberlain led a mid-October reconnaissance in search of Stuart's cavalry, which was running roughshod again in the rear of the Army of the Potomac. At one of the South Mountain passes he experienced the second of the countless near misses that would mark his war career. Some of Stuart's outriders fired on him; a ball tore a hole in his cap.

Safely back in camp, Chamberlain considered the incident. "The 'glory' Prof. Smyth so *honestly* pictured for me I do not dread," he wrote Fannie, referring to the morbid forecasts of his liverish Bowdoin colleague. "If I do return 'shattered,' I think there *are* those who will hold me in some degree of favor. Most likely I shall be hit somewhere at some time, but all 'my times are in His hand,' & I cannot die without his appointing." A serene fatalism helped him repress fear. He convinced himself he had no choice but to accept whatever Providence had on offer.[24]

Lincoln continued to harry McClellan, and on October 27 the reluctant commander finally set the army in motion. The 20th Maine crossed at Shepherdstown Ford the night of Thursday the thirtieth and reached Harper's Ferry the next day. To Chamberlain's eye, the 20th now appeared ready to take its place in the line of battle. He thought the hard work of the last few weeks had transformed the regiment. "In the *army*, & by regular officers, we are already said to be a marked *Regt.*," he boasted to Fannie. "I believe that no other new Regt. will *ever* have the discipline we have now." Harper's Ferry looked poor and rundown; lowering skies and squalls of rain did nothing to improve the town's forbidding aspect. The 20th marched past the ruins of the U.S. Arsenal, where a pile of gun barrels, twisted out of shape by fire and red with rust, stood as an ironic memorial to John Brown's raid. The line of march followed the Loudoun Valley on the east flank of the Blue Ridge, parallel to the Confederates' route through the Shenandoah, on the other side of the mountain spine. The valley had not yet been picked clean; the 20th's foragers supplemented the army's weevily hardtack and corroded bacon with Virginia cattle, sheep, pigs, and vegetables.[25]

The Third Brigade reached Snicker's Gap on November 2 and went into bivouac there, guarding the pass, for three days. Rumor spread that Stonewall Jackson's corps lay nearby, coiled and ready to strike. Chamberlain, exhilarated by life in the open, joked about the outlandish name of the place. "Yet here we are," he wrote Fannie, "expecting a battle with the rebels who are just over the mountain." He went on to assure her of his well-being. "Picture to yourself a stout looking fellow—face covered with beard—with a pair of cavalry pants on—sky blue—big enough for Goliath, & coarse as a sheep's back—enveloped in a huge cavalry overcoat of the same texture & color as the pants—& wearing the identical flannel blouse worn at Portland." To complete this description of a light-opera brigand, he added that he carried two holstered pistols and a cavalry sword three feet long.[26]

Still, home thoughts could be sobering, especially given the likelihood that pale-eyed, bloody-minded Stonewall Jackson would try to make whistles of his bones. He tried not to think of Daisy and Wyllys. "It makes me rather sad," he wrote Fannie, "& then I do not forget I am here in the face of death every day." He asked her to take no special care to remind the children of him—she should let the memory of their father fade. "If I return, they will soon relearn to love me, & if not, so much is spared them." Fannie, too, should put him out of her mind. "Invite the juniors over to spend the evening with some of the young ladies, as we used to do, & keep up your character for hospitality & your spirits at the same time," he advised.[27]

The Fifth Corps proceeded southward, first to White Plains, then on to New Baltimore. Only now beginning to comprehend the scale of the missed opportunity at Antietam, Chamberlain hinted at dissatisfaction with McClellan's generalship. "I see no signs of peace," he wrote Fannie on November 4. "While we will not be beaten, something seems to strike all the vigor out of our arms just at the point of victory." (His ultimate conclusion about McClellan, reached near the end of his life: "The realities of war seemed to daze him.") On the snowy night of November 7, a special courier reached army headquarters at Rectortown with Lincoln's order replacing McClellan with Burnside. The impolitic Fitz-John Porter got the sack too.[28]

The 20th Maine reached Warrenton on November 9. When Burnside put on a farewell parade the next day, the troops cheered McClellan wildly. Chamberlain did not set down his initial reaction to Burnside. Most observers found the thirty-eight-year-old Rhode Islander striking, at least in appearance, with his flamboyant whiskers and his athlete's build. (In what seems to have been a minority view, the younger Holmes described him to a friend as "flabby as a dead jellyfish.") Burnside had not sought the army command, and he never claimed more than modest abilities for himself. Most senior officers judged him incapable of managing large formations in battle.* He had, however, made a powerful impression on at least one personage connected with West Point, from which he had graduated in 1847, eighteenth in a class of thirty-eight. Tavernkeeper Benny Havens admired him greatly. "Old Benny was always talking, even in my day, of Ambrose Burnside," recalled 1857 West Pointer Edward Porter Alexander.[29]

*"He was not fitted to command an army," Grant wrote of Burnside. "No one knew this better than himself."

In any event, another of Lee's officers noted, "Burnside could and would fight, even if he did not know how." In comformance with Burnside's new plan of campaign, the 20th Maine marched for the Rappahannock on November 17. Three days later the regiment pitched camp at Stoneman's Switch on the Aquia Creek Railroad, six miles from Fredericksburg. Expecting to winter there, the men put up log shelters with canvas roofs and began combing the country for firewood, so scarce hereabouts that they soon were digging up stumps for fuel.[30]

Chamberlain instructed Fannie at home to bank the cellar walls, prune the grapevines, and cover the asparagus beds against the cold. She sent him a brief description of their Thanksgiving at the Adams parsonage, a "beautiful dinner, the children all well and perfectly happy, tonight a charming little table of fancy cakes, bright red apples, nuts, candies." Fannie wondered where he had spent the holiday. "You cannot imagine how lonely [I am] this Thanksgiving night, when you ought to be at your own home, with all those who long to see you so," she wrote him.[31]

While Burnside worked out his scheme for the confounding of Lee, the 20th Maine shivered in the comfortless camp at Stoneman's Switch. Chamberlain had done all he could to prepare for the looming battle. "Give my regards to all my friends," he wrote Fannie, "& tell them I am beginning to understand my business."[32]

CHAPTER 5

BLOOD ON THE PLAIN

FREDERICKSBURG,
DECEMBER 1862

BURNSIDE SURELY INTENDED A DOUBLE
bluff. The Confederates expected him to cross the Rappahannock above or
below Fredericksburg, threaten a flank, and force them off the high ground.
Lee learned on the afternoon of November 17 that the Federals were moving toward Fredericksburg. By November 21, two of Longstreet's divisions
were in position to contest a crossing there. Alexander began placing
First Corps guns on the wooded hills west of town the following day. He
paused in his work from time to time to study the federal positions on
Stafford Heights opposite, using a telescope he carried in a special holster on his saddle—"not an opera or a field glass," he explained, "but
a fine large & long spyglass." Alexander looked for the Yankees to come
over near Falmouth, above Fredericksburg, where the Rappahannock
made a sharp southward bend. "I never conceived for a moment that
Burnside would make his attack right where we were strongest," he
wrote.[1]

Alexander knew the country around Fredericksburg well; he and Bettie
had spent part of their wedding trip with Mason kin in the neighborhood. The battalion went into bivouac on the Orange Plank Road, opposite John Guest's house, where the newlywed couple had dined one
evening in April 1860. Casting a soldier's eye over the terrain, Alexander
planted the nine guns of the Washington Artillery in pits on the brow
of Marye's Heights, to cover the open plain between the town and the
hills. He grouped his own batteries in clusters for maximum concentra-

tion in support of key First Corps positions. The light batteries he held in reserve; they could be rushed at short notice to wherever the danger seemed greatest. He calculated distances and firing angles to likely river crossings, to streets leading out of town, and to ravines and dips of ground where infantry could form. Inspecting the lines, Lee suggested deploying the Washington batteries on the reverse slope, so they could be elevated to engage the federal heavy guns on Stafford Heights. Arguing hard, Alexander convinced Lee that the Confederate guns, a mix of obsolescent smooth-bores and modern rifles firing poor-quality ammunition, would be ineffective in a long-range duel with the superior enemy artillery.[2]

Lee and Longstreet had come to rely increasingly on Alexander's eager intelligence, regularly assigning him duties more properly those of Col. James B. Walton, Longstreet's nominal chief of artillery, or even of Brig. Gen. William N. Pendleton, the artillery chief of the Army of Northern Virginia. Longstreet thought so highly of Alexander's engineering skills, noted First Corps chief of staff G. Moxley Sorrel, that he kept him within easy reach of headquarters, more or less on call. Alexander had nearly a free hand in organizing the Fredericksburg defenses. Pendleton did not object to his junior's expanded role. Walton, however, could be touchy about precedence. Only a timely illness—Walton was away on sick leave until December 9, by which date most of the dispositions had been made—postponed a clash of authority.[3]

Still, the seeds of future conflict had been sown. Walton, an auctioneer in civil life, had commanded the Washington Artillery of New Orleans, one of the South's best-known volunteer organizations, since 1857. A Mexican War veteran, now getting on in years, he wore a fine graying *barbe d'Afrique* and reminded his admirers of Napoleon III. Others judged him ponderous, dull, and self-important. Walton had already been passed over for promotion. This rankled; nor did he appreciate being asked to stand aside while Alexander called the shots—literally. Pendleton had no such sensibilities. An 1830 West Point graduate, he taught mathematics at the academy, then abruptly quit the army to take holy orders. He bade farewell to the Episcopal parish of Lexington, Virginia, in 1861 to go to war with the Rockbridge Artillery. He rose to become first Johnston's, then Lee's, chief of artillery. Courtly, benign, remote, gray-bearded, Pendleton closely resembled Lee and was often mistaken for him. He seems to have been more effective as a sort of chaplain-in-chief—in camp, he officiated at prayer meetings and Sunday services—

than as a frontline commander. Younger officers, Alexander among them, were derisive. "A well-meaning man," Sorrel said of Pendleton, "without qualities for the high post he claimed." Years later, Alexander called him unfit and incompetent, "a complete zero" on the battlefield. For now, though, he tried to curb his impatience with his slow-thinking superior.[4]

Alexander had taken over an efficient weapon in Stephen Lee's battalion, and he formed favorable first impressions of the battery commanders: George Moody,* Tyler Jordan, Andrew Rhett, Pichegru Woolfolk, Jr., John Eubank, and William Parker. He struck up friendships with three of his captains—Moody, a pale-haired, large, powerfully built officer; Woolfolk, dark, lively, and good-natured; and Parker, a physician in civilian life (he doubled as battalion surgeon) and a professing Christian. His battlefield ambitions were modest. He only wanted, as he often told Aleck, to "do some good" with his guns. Parker's Virginians were known as the Boy Company for their extreme youth; some were in their early teens. A strict disciplinarian, Parker saw to it that the boys were well behaved and soldierlike, in contrast to Moody's unruly "Tips," so named for the Irish contingent, many of whom were from County Tipperary.[5]

While Burnside waited for his much-delayed pontoon train, the Confederates worked fitfully at their defenses. Alexander placed Rhett's four-gun heavy battery behind earthworks on Marye's Heights. Parker's two rifles went into pits on Stansbury Hill, north of the Orange Plank Road, his two howitzers concealed behind a house nearby. The light batteries of Jordan, Moody, and Woolfolk were hidden in woods, to be run forward at the first appearance of the enemy infantry. Alexander's men dug their gun pits in relative security; for the first time in the war, the opposing pickets negotiated an informal truce and refrained from promiscuous sniping. The Confederates were, however, frequently subject to the disconcerting gaze, distant and godlike, of the Yankee aeronauts. Immense, black, and sinister, the federal captive balloons hoverd over Burnside's camps, as Alexander put it, "like two great spirits of the air."[6]

The pontoons arrived during the last week in November. Burnside, listless, allowed Stonewall Jackson to march the Second Corps down from the Shenandoah and extend Lee's defenses southeast of Fredericksburg. Jackson's arrival gave Lee 78,000 effectives and 275 guns. Burnside idled

---

*A native New Englander, his brother was Dwight L. Moody, a Chicago preacher in the 1860s who later became a leading evangelist.

for a full two weeks, unable to decide how to employ his 120,000 men and three hundred guns. Every morning, new mounds of freshly turned earth were visible on the terraces behind Fredericksburg. The Confederates' two or three tiers of shallow trenches were modest by later standards, but Longstreet assured Lee that his infantry and artillery would dominate the Fredericksburg plain. Longstreet posted three regiments of Georgians in a strong advance line at the base of Marye's Heights, along the Telegraph Road, here sunken three or four feet below ground and revetted with stone: a natural trench, "just breast-high for a man," he said, "and at just the height convenient for infantry defence and fire." All the same, Longstreet showed some anxiety about the First Corps defenses. He called Alexander over during one inspection and suggested siting a spare cannon to cover the open ground in front of Marye's Heights.[7]

"General," Alexander told him, "we cover that ground now so well that we will comb it as with a fine-tooth comb. A chicken could not live on that field when we open on it."[8]

Those, at any rate, were the words Longstreet quoted; Alexander had no recollection of them, though he conceded he might have said something of the kind. Georgians talked that way. Alexander had grown up admiring the Dickensian virtuosity of speech of his slightly older neighbor Dempsey Colley, now serving in the infantry lines at Fredericksburg. ("Now you'll see me kill that hawk so dead he will smell bad in a minute," Colley once boasted.) The blend of assurance, exaggeration, and upcountry pungency in the reply to Longstreet sounds like authentic Alexander. Longstreet had nothing more to say about idle guns.[9]

Burnside wound up his deliberations and decided to force a crossing in the face of the Confederate defenses at Fredericksburg. So obvious a move, he reasoned, had a good chance of catching Lee by surprise. Lee would refuse to believe an opposing commander capable of such a hare-brained scheme. The weather held fair through the first days of December. Rain and snow fell on the fifth; then a cold front passed through and nighttime temperatures dropped into the low twenties. On the afternoon of Wednesday, December 10, word reached the battalion that Burnside intended to move the next day. Longstreet directed Alexander to have the battery animals in harness an hour before daybreak.[10]

Two signal guns boomed at five o'clock on a cold, still Thursday morning, alerting the Confederates to Burnside's first attempt to bridge the Rappahannock. The warning brought hundreds of refugees, mostly women and children, streaming out of Fredericksburg. Alexander's bugler blew

Boots and Saddles, the tents vanished, and the guns were trundled up
to the firing line. Thick, damp fog—"a heavy, smoky mist," according
to Alexander—veiled the narrow valley. The shouted orders of Union
officers were clearly audible, though nothing at all could be seen beyond
a distance of a hundred yards or so. The sounds of Burnside's pontoniers
floated up from the river. Sharpshooters of William Barksdale's Mississippi brigade, concealed in buildings along the waterfront, began firing into the murk. From the heights, only the steeples of the churches
and the courthouse spire were visible, poking up through the layer of
fog.[11]

The bridges had reached more than halfway across the four-hundred-
foot-wide river before rifts in the fog revealed the Yankee combat engineers to Barkdsdale's marksmen. No longer firing blind, they sent the
pontoniers racing back for cover. The sun climbed higher and melted
what remained of the mist. At midmorning, Alexander looked out upon a
spectacular view of Burnside's army. There was an antique splendor to
the scene, 100,000 infantry "standing in great solid squares upon the
hilltops." The Federals were waiting for their bridges, three at
Fredericksburg, two others a mile downstream opposite Jackson's lines.
They made the downstream link in good time, but the Mississippi sharpshooters stopped all work at Fredericksburg. Burnside ordered up a cannonade to root them out. At midday, some 150 guns opened on the city
in an awe-inspiring exercise of Union power. Recalled Alexander:

> Over and in the town the white winkings of the bursting shells
> reminded one of a countless swarm of fireflies. Several buildings
> were set on fire, & their black smoke rose in remarkably slen-
> der, straight & tall columns for two hundred feet, perhaps, be-
> fore they began to spread horizontally & unite in a great
> black canopy.[12]

Alexander held his fire. The Confederates were chronically short of
ammunition, and in any case the rifled cannon, the only weapons able
to reach the Federals on Stafford Heights, fired shells fitted with fuses
that could not be trusted at long range. Anyway, the Yankee barrage
failed of its purpose. Alexander could hear the occasional defiant pop
of musketry even at the height of the bombardment. When the firing
ceased, the pontoniers returned to the partially finished bridges.
Barksdale's snipers opened up and drove them off again. Burnside finally
sent across several boatloads of infantry to clear Fredericksburg. Barks-

dale conducted a fighting retreat, and the short winter day was over before the Federals could complete the bridges and occupy the town.[13]

The Confederates passed the night in line of battle. Burnside's intentions were not at all clear, but Lee expected a powerful attack on Jackson's front, with a light tap on Longstreet's lines as a diversion. Burnside intended to open the battle early Friday the twelfth. As it turned out, he used up the entire day getting into position. Alexander's guns fired intermittently on the pontoons and into streets crowded with federal infantry. Jackson, meanwhile, concentrated the Second Corps, elements of which had been strung out for twenty miles along the Rappahannock, opposite the lower bridges. That night, federal troops ransacked Fredericksburg. Refugees shivered around smoky fires in the woods behind Marye's Heights. The defenders spent a second night on their arms.[14]

The low rumble of artillery passing over frozen ground sounded through the darkness; as the eastern sky began to lighten toward six o'clock on Saturday the thirteenth, Alexander heard Burnside's assault columns forming behind the gray screen of fog. By nine o'clock the mist had evaporated, the pickets and sharpshooters were engaged, and some federal heavy guns had opened an exploratory fire. An hour later, off to the south, three federal divisions, part of Maj. Gen. William B. Franklin's Left Grand Division, began a stately advance across the plain, still lightly dusted with snow, toward Jackson's lines on Prospect Heights.[15]

Alexander rode over to Lee's field headquarters on Telegraph Hill, where the panorama of the developing battle opened up before him: infantry moving on Jackson's front, and long blue columns crossing the pontoons into Fredericksburg. Franklin's attack forced a breach in the Second Corps line, but he failed to develop it. Jackson shortly launched a furious counterattack that whirled the Federals off his end of the ridge. Alexander watched masses of infantry form in the streets of Fredericksburg. There could be no doubt now that the Federals were preparing a major assault. He felt a rush of elation—the near certainty, he said afterward, of an easy victory.[16]

He returned to the gun lines. After a while, Longstreet sent word for him to throw a hundred shells into the town. Alexander directed Moody's twelve-pounders to open an arching fire over the near houses and into the unseen federal columns standing in William Street. Moody's Tips kept up a sustained cannonade despite a sharp counterbattery fire. Rhett's and Parker's rifled guns shelled the river crossings. Toward noon the first Yankees came pouring out of Fredericksburg. The leading assault column (the First Brigade, Alexander learned later, of the Third Division, Second Corps) emerged from Hanover Street, crossed a twenty-foot-wide canal, and wheeled into line of battle in the shelter of a low bluff four hundred yards from the sunken road.[17]

After a brief halt, the advance resumed at the double-quick, the Yankees chanting a nerve-steadying "Hi, Hi, Hi" as they approached the loom of Marye's Heights. Walton's gunners, with two of Alexander's mobile batteries firing over their heads, found the range and began tearing gaps in the assault formation. From Stansbury Hill, Parker's battery sent enfilade fire into the attackers' right flank. The Yankees closed ranks, pushing up to within a hundred yards of the stone wall. Then a bright burst of flame lit up the low wall from end to end, and a blast of musketry scorched the federal line. Every third or fourth man fell. The survivors broke and dashed for cover, collecting behind the scattered houses, seeking the scant protection of board fences or the shelter of little folds of ground, keeping up their courage by delivering a surprisingly brisk return fire.[18]

Wave followed monotonous wave, with identical results. The First Corps guns played on the successive lines as they emerged from the town, crossed the canal, and advanced over the wreckage of their predecessors. The sun thawed the plain, and the passage of thousands of men churned up a sea of black, glutinous mud. Longstreet fed fresh infantry into the sunken road, where the defenders now stood four and five deep, rear ranks loading and passing weapons to the front. The commander of the Second Corps, Maj. Gen. Darius N. Couch, witnessed the disaster from the spire of Fredericksburg courthouse:

> As they charged the artillery fire would break their formation and they would get mixed; then they would close up, go forward, receive the withering infantry fire, and those who were able would run to the houses and fight as best they could; and then the next brigade coming up in succession would do its duty and melt like snow coming down on warm ground.

Eight charges cost Couch's corps four thousand men killed and wounded. "The piles and cross-piles of dead marked a field such as I never saw before or since," wrote Longstreet.[19]

The fighting lapsed on Jackson's front, and the Marye's Heights battle, meant for a diversion, became Burnside's sole effort. To Alexander's amazement, the federal commander persisted in his elephantine tactics. Fresh brigades (belonging, Alexander later learned, to the Ninth Corps) came up on the left of the Second Corps, working their way along an unfinished railroad on the southern edge of town. Clusters of Union troops advanced to within two hundred yards of the stone wall; none got closer. Isolated parties sought shelter in back gardens and outhouses or behind improvised breastworks of the dead and wounded. It was remarkable how steadily the shattered regiments sustained their fire. They "kept the air so full of minié balls that [the] sound was as constant as the flow of water," Alexander noted. The Yankees clearly were not yet ready to give up. They continued to gnaw at the file, though they were only breaking their own teeth. Alexander watched elements of a fresh federal corps (the Fifth Corps, as it happened) tramp across the pontoons and form up in the streets of the lower town, near the railroad station.[20]

A temporary calm settled over the battlefield, though the sniping and cannonading continued at varying levels of intensity. Then, at about three-thirty, with the sun hanging redly a few degrees above the horizon beyond the Confederate left, still another federal formation moved out, following the path, strewn with dead and wounded, of the Ninth Corps brigades. (It turned out to be the First Brigade of the First Division, Fifth Corps, with the Second and Third brigades, including the 20th Maine, preparing to follow.) "The men advanced as far as they could find some partial protection," Alexander observed, "and there they lay down."[21]

Walton's nine guns, meanwhile, were running low on ammunition. Alexander briefly considered running in shot and shell in answer to Walton's plea for relief; it seemed senseless to expose men, animals, and guns unnecessarily. But he interpreted Walton's note as a request to come out of the line. After a moment's hesitation, Alexander collected nine guns from Moody's, Woolfolk's, and Jordan's batteries for a gallop into the Washington Artillery redoubts. He led out aboard Dixie—his "horse de combat," as he now called her—along the Plank Road under heavy artillery fire. Up ahead, a large shell struck the ground, bounced, and came tumbling end over end toward him. "I merely realized that I had no time to dodge, & wondered where it would hit," Alexander recalled. "It passed under the horse's belly somehow." Then one of the guns capsized, further delaying the advance. Walton's gunners limbered up and withdrew. A few moments later, Alexander's battalion made a final dash for the vacated earthworks, racing along under fire in what Confederate veterans would remember as one of the grandest old-style charges of the war. The operation cost the battalion several men wounded, and a dozen horses were hit.[22]

Two advancing brigades of a fresh Union division (the Third Division, Fifth Corps, commanded by Maj. Gen. A. A. Humphreys, whom Alexander had known in the old army) interpreted Walton's departure as the beginning of a Confederate retreat. With a great hurrah, these columns surged toward the stone wall. Alexander could hardly credit this latest evidence of Yankee foolhardiness. His gunners coolly sighted their weapons in the fading light. Off to the north, Parker opened a destructive fire into Humphreys's flank. Wrote Alexander:

> We gave them our choicest varieties, canister and shrapnel, just as fast as we could put it in. It was plainly a disagreeable surprise to them, but they faced it very well & came along fairly until our infantry at the foot of the hill opened.

Burnside ordered one final sprint for the wall, the fourteenth charge of the day. It came after dark, along the railroad cut toward the southern edge of the sunken road. Alexander's guns aimed case shot and canister into the Yankee muzzle flashes. "They certainly gave it up very soon and their flashes died out," Alexander noted. After a few farewell shots, the battalion stood down for the night.[23]

Ammunition chests were refilled overnight, minor damage to the gun pits repaired. Confederate pickets captured a federal courier carrying orders for fresh attacks to be launched at daybreak. Fog again settled in the valley overnight. The sharpshooters went to work at first light, and the federal great guns opened up too. The Yankees did not come. That night, Alexander shifted two of Moody's Napoleons into a ravine on the extreme Confederate left, where they could deliver enfilade fire into the federal skirmishers operating from the banks of the canal.[24]

When it was over, Alexander could not remember what or even whether he had eaten during the battle, or when, where, or whether he had slept. The business at hand consumed him. Early on Monday the fifteenth, he ordered the newly placed Napoleons to open a harassing fire, then turned his attention to a nest of Yankee snipers. They had been shooting, with deadly effect, from loopholes cut in the brick wall of a tannery in a hollow on the edge of town. Only the peak of the tannery roof could be seen. Alexander carefully sighted one of Moody's twenty-four-pounder howitzers, supervised the loading, gave the order to fire, and followed the flight of the shell as it sailed over the curve of the hill, brushing the grass. He heard a detonation, then a cheer from the Confederate pickets. The shell had penetrated the building and burst. Alexander found a headless body in the rubble the next day, along with evidence that several wounded men had been carried away.[25]

Rain fell during the night, lashed by a stiff south wind that carried the sounds of retreat away from the Confederates. They heard nothing, suspected nothing. Dawn revealed an abandoned battlefield. Alexander accompanied a party of skirmishers into Fredericksburg and down to the Rappahannock, where he exchanged stares with an enemy picket on the north bank. He walked out over the plain, taking in the scene with characteristic detachment. Groups of Federals had sought protection behind the weatherbeaten wide planks of broken fences, wood so soft, he observed, that it could not slow, let alone stop, a bullet. Near these flimsy fieldworks the dead lay in high heaps. Corpses formed a level carpet over the sodden open ground. There were only a few surviving wounded. Alexander stooped for a closer look at one miserable Yankee, shot in the head—"a wound which one would have supposed must be instantly fatal, as it was directly through the brain." When spoken to, the dying man replied hoarsely, "Captain, Captain."[26]

Rather ungenerously, Alexander argued that Burnside's assault troops at least ought to have reached the stone wall. "If his men fought as well as *any* of ours, he would have carried the position at Marye's house at the *first* assault," he wrote home a few days after the battle. Confederate casualties on Marye's Heights were light in view of the size of the attacking force: fewer than two thousand killed, wounded, and missing. Alexander's battalion lost one man killed and ten wounded out of more than five hundred engaged. Two casualties elsewhere hit close to home. His friend Ed Lawton (brother of his sister Sarah's husband) was seriously wounded and taken prisoner. He died in a Yankee field hospital. Dempsey Colley was killed, his colorful tongue silenced forever. Word of his death called up memories of tramps in north-Georgia woods, torpid summer afternoons on the banks of the Little River. "He never cared for politics even remotely," Alexander wrote of Colley, "and war ought to have left him alone."[27]

Even the heavens seemed to salute the Army of Northern Virginia, offering a lurid display of the aurora borealis the night of December 14. Alexander admitted later that the celestial omens had misled him, or that anyway he had failed to read the truest lesson in the Yankee pattern of failure. "However badly beaten he never relaxed," Alexander wrote, "& he always came back again."[28]

Alexander had an olympian view of the battle from the terrace of Marye's Heights. Down below, in Fredericksburg, the four hundred officers and men of the 20th Maine compassed Lieutenant Colonel Chamberlain's world. The column picked its way among overturned paving stones, the broken bricks of shattered chimneys, piles of vandalized contents of Fredericksburg parlors. Smoke rose from burning buildings. Shells roared overhead. Walking wounded limped past. Crushed bodies and body parts lay in the streets and dooryards. From above, it looked tidy: General Couch's image of snow falling on warm ground. Down here, Chamberlain saw battle in all its terror and fascination, confusion, ugliness, and pain.

The men had seemed relieved to break camp. Stoneman's Switch was cold and muddy and foul with the acrid smoke of green-wood fires. The Third Brigade sick lists had lengthened. Standard-issue shelter tents, open at both ends, were inadequate to keep out the severe cold. Two men of the 20th Maine froze to death during the night of December 6–7. Four inches of snow fell that night, adding to the misery. Possibly the weather paralyzed Burnside. Forceful and decisive at the start, he had reorganized the Army of the Potomac into three grand divisions of two corps each, then shifted the line of operation to the Rappahannock. There, however, the energy seemed to seep out of him. Senior subordinates were openly contemptuous. Burnside himself freely acknowledged his unfitness for command. "There was a tendency to take him at his word—especially among the high-ranking generals—and the men could not help knowing it," Chamberlain said. You did not have to be a Napoleon to see that Burnside's equivocations had given Lee time to fortify the chain of hills behind Fredericksburg. Finally, trusting to the double bluff, Burnside ordered the issue of three days' cooked rations and twenty extra rounds of ammunition per man, the essential preliminary to battle.[29]

Reveille sounded at three o'clock Thursday morning, December 11. The First Division, Brig. Gen. Charles Griffin* commanding, marched at

*Griffin moved up to command the First Division, Fifth Corps, in late October, succeeding George Morell, left behind when the army recrossed the Potomac.

daybreak and covered five miles before halting in a muddy field in view of Burnside's headquarters at the Phillips House on Stafford Heights. The sound of firing, occasional at first, intensified as the sun drank up the fog. Toward midday the federal artillery opened an earth-jarring bombardment. Chamberlain decided to further his military education by observing the work of one of the regular batteries firing into Fredericksburg. The shelling touched off fires in several buildings near the river. Chamberlain watched the battery send round after round across the Rappahannock and into the thick black smoke hanging over the town. Presently a mounted officer, a member of Burnside's staff by the look of him, approached the battery commander.

"Captain," Chamberlain heard him say, "do you see that white shaft over yonder in the green field above those houses? That's the tomb of Washington's mother. Let your guns spare that!"[30]

Some of the men wondered why the rebels did not reply to the cannonade. The more sophisticated among them suspected a trap. Lee might let them into Fredericksburg; would he let them out? The sounds of skirmishing—small-arms fire, the crack of light artillery—increased in volume, then faded. At dusk, Griffin's division fell back a mile or so and bivouacked in a woods. Word filtered down that the enemy had been driven from the town, and that Union troops were in occupation. Soon their campfires were visible. The enemy's fires lit a crescent along the ridgeline opposite. A collective insomnia came over the 20th Maine. The men sang patriotic songs, Theodore Gerrish remembered, and talked of the victory they expected. After breakfast on Friday the twelfth, the division moved down to the Rappahannock opposite the lower pontoon bridge. There Chamberlain learned that the Fifth Corps, part of Hooker's Center Grand Division, would be held in reserve, as at Antietam. Watching the troops of the Second and Ninth corps cross, he thought he would rather take his chances with the first assault wave than endure the grating anxiety of the wait. There were further delays. The regiment spent a second night in the open.[31]

Chamberlain witnessed Saturday's first efforts to storm Marye's Heights from the north bank. The enemy gunners had the range of the bridges and the streets leading out to the plain, and he could see shells bursting in the town. French's first-wave brigades quick-stepped into the open and began taking casualties right away. Still, they had expected a cannonade. Their ranks closed instinctively and they continued on toward the high ground. Then, all at once, a thin, continuous sheet of flame flashed along the stone wall. "In an instant the whole line [sank] as if swallowed up in earth," Chamberlain recalled.[32]

He watched charge after failed charge. Hancock's division followed French's, Howard's followed Hancock's. That finished the Second Corps. The three brigades of Sturgis's Second Division, Ninth Corps, brought up on the left to support the Second Corps' effort, approached the wall one after the other and were lacerated. Chamberlain could see hundreds of blue-clad bodies lying motionless on the plain. Some of the men in the ranks of the 20th Maine began to cry. Others cursed Franklin, opposite Jackson's lines downstream, for failing to do his part. At one-thirty, word came for Griffin to bring up the First Division to support Sturgis. Hooker tried, without success, to persuade Burnside to suspend the attacks. Griffin sent the First and Second brigades across within the hour. The 20th Maine followed a little later with the Third Brigade, rushing over the swaying pontoons under fire, battle flags flying. Chamberlain heard the hiss of solid shot overhead, and felt the pressure of displaced air as a missile flew past.[33]

The brigade formed up in the lower town, with its left on the Richmond railroad. The men unslung their knapsacks, dropped them on the sidewalk, and moved up Frederick Street. "I held my breath and set my teeth together, determined not to show fear if I could, by will, keep it down," the 20th Maine's adjutant, John Brown, wrote the *Portland Press*, his hometown paper, a day or two later. The cannonade intensified. "Men [were] dying before our eyes," Brown went on, "and fragments of bodies mutilated by shells were lying about." The brigade halted in a muddy street on the outskirts of town, deployed into line of battle, and lay down to await orders. Ames, Chamberlain, and Brown sent their horses to the rear. The First Brigade went forward. On the right, Humphreys's brigades let out a cheer and charged for the stone wall. Then the Second Brigade moved out into the open. Drifting battle smoke obscured his view of the field, so Chamberlain could not tell whether these latest assaults had gained their objectives. Presently the Third Brigade commander, Col. Thomas B. W. Stockton, passed the word for the advance. Ames shouted "Forward," and the 20th Maine set out on its journey over the plain.[34]

"I remember that the sun was setting, nothing else except that I was running up and down the line urging the men on," wrote Brown. The regiment charged at the double quick through gardens, over wire fences, and across ditches. Away to the right, Chamberlain saw a Confederate battery (Moody's, of Alexander's battalion) swing into position to rake the 20th's front. "God help us now," Ames said softly. Men began to drop: a sharp intake of breath, a low groan or burble, then an empty place in the line. The regiment closed ranks and passed over the remnants of Sturgis's brigades, some living, many dead. A few Ninth Corps survivors called out cautions. "Nothing living can stand there," Chamberlain heard someone say. The 20th, veering left toward an angle at the southern end of the stone wall, traversed some thousand yards under fire before reaching the partial cover of a low bluff. There the men fell to the ground and loosed a series of volleys at the stone wall, still a quarter-mile distant.[35]

There had been a dreamlike quality to the advance, as though the power of trance had propelled the regiment toward Marye's Heights. "I saw the 20th Maine coming across the field in line of battle as upon parade, easily recognized by their new state colors, the great gaps plainly visible as the shot and shell tore through the now tremulous line," wrote a rifleman of the 22nd Massachusetts, which had taken heavy losses in the First Brigade charge. Gratitude doubtless fired this soldier's admiration, for the 20th rose, advanced another couple of hundred yards, and took his regiment's place in the line.[36]

One last effort, launched after dark by Getty's Third Division, Ninth Corps: it faltered, too, breaking up some eighty yards short of the wall. The 20th, disoriented, discharged several wild volleys into the night. Getty's right-hand brigade took casualties from the friendly fire of the 20th Maine and its neighbor, the 83rd Pennsylvania. "The greatest confusion existed," Getty's brigadier reported charitably. "Everybody, from the smallest drummer boy up, seemed to be shouting to the fullest extent of his capacity." Over on the right, one of Humphreys's brigades lost several killed and wounded to fire from the rear.[37]

As the shooting died down, the survivors began to confront a new kind of horror. A bitter wind cut across the plain. The temperature dropped. Sweat-soaked from the exertion of the charge, men began to suffer from the cold. Chamberlain had sent his overcoat and blanket to the rear with his horse; he shivered along with the others. The mud froze around the wounded. Presently the wounded began to stiffen and freeze. The wind carried unnerving sounds out of the darkness—the howls of stricken men, the braying of stricken animals. Men still in their senses fired their weapons into the air to attract the stretcher bearers' attention. Most eerie, though, was the murmur of the wounded, a low, steady moan that continued throughout the night. The nasal whisperings of the Confederates were sometimes audible too. The gray wall along the Telegraph Road stood out clearly in the light of a gibbous moon.[38]

Seeking warmth, Chamberlain fitted his chilled form between two corpses and drew a third crosswise for a pillow. Nearby rose a midden of bodies, discarded muskets, knapsacks, canteens. He closed his eyes. "My ears were filled with the cries and groans of the wounded," he wrote a few days later, "and the ghastly faces of the dead almost made a wall around me." He pulled the flap of a dead man's coat over his face. It kept the wind off, but could not shut out that unearthly moaning.[39]

At midnight he got up and roused Brown. They set out across the battlefield; wounded men reached up to touch them and wheeze out a plea for help as they passed. Chamberlain paused every so often to speak a few words of comfort or to offer water. He could do little more. At least the ambulances were at work now along the edge of the plain. Orderlies moved from body to body, seeking out the living by the blue gleam of matchlight.[40]

He returned to his gruesome shelter. Spectral forms roved the battlefield, friend and enemy alike, some in search of blankets or shoes, others to rob the dead. Once, while he slept, a rough hand lifted the coat from his face. When he protested, the intruder moved off apologetically. Somewhere a window blind flapped rhythmically in the wind. It cast a hypnotic spell, calling monotonously: "Never—forever; forever—never." At least that was what Chamberlain thought he heard. The night seemed at once endless and all too short. "We were wishing the hours away," Gerrish remembered, "and yet we dreaded to have the darkness disappear."[41]

The shooting resumed at daybreak. Enemy artillery fired intermittently from Marye's Heights. Snipers were constantly at work. "No man could stand up and not be laid down again hard," Chamberlain said. The accuracy of the Confederate fire made relief or reinforcement impossible. The 20th Maine waited out the day, hungry, thirsty, sore, queasy from breathing in fecal odors and the stench of decomposing flesh. Men learned to recognize the distinctive aural effects of ball, shot, and shell. A minié ball, two-thirds of an inch in diameter and weighing about two ounces, made a heavy *thud* as it struck flesh. Veterans likened the sound of a flight of miniés to a kitten's mewing or to a swarm of irritated bees. Others heard something like *whit-whit*. Solid shot *swished*. Napoleon brass cannon sounded a distinctive *spang!* In the afternoon a large party of enemy skirmishers moved out from the stone wall and into a gully on the brigade's left. The 20th, firing from behind stacks of corpses, helped drive the rebels off. The cannonading continued at intervals. A minié ball grazed Chamberlain's right ear.[42]

Relief came toward midnight on Sunday the fourteenth, after the 20th Maine had been thirty-six hours in the line. The regiment buried its dead on the spot, while overhead the aurora borealis shimmered and flashed—"fiery lances and banners of blood, and flame, columns of pearly light, garlands and wreaths of gold, all pointing and beckoning upward," Chamberlain described it later. The burial parties hollowed out shallow graves with bayonets and shards of shell, and rough-carved the names of the dead on headboards made of broken fence palings.[43]

Making its way carefully through the wrack, the Third Brigade regained the shelter of town. Rumor spread through the ranks that the assault would be renewed at dawn, Burnside himself at the head of it. Troops of all commands were crammed into Fredericksburg. Here was a nightmare scene of another sort, ghastly and comic all at once, like a Bosch canvas. The streets were brightly lit, as though for a carnival. "Groups of men were mixing bread or flapjacks, frying pork or making coffee," one soldier wrote. "Kitchen stoves were in full blast; lighted candles were extravagantly placed on tables. All kinds of music sounded upon the air. Some were dancing, while others were playing cards." There had been a lot of looting. Soldiers flounced about in petticoats and feathers. Many were drunk. The Maine troops spread their blankets on the stone flagging along Caroline Street. Ames moved from company to company, praising the men for their steadiness in the charge.[44]

Shelling and light skirmishing continued all day Monday the fifteenth. Near midnight, Griffin detailed the 20th Maine and two other Third Brigade regiments to return to the front. Chamberlain guessed, correctly as it turned out, that they were to screen some general movement. Ames commanded a section of the thin line; Chamberlain took charge of the regiment. He set the men to work digging shallow rifle pits and throwing up earthworks. The conversation of the rebel pickets drifted over; Chamberlain thought they sounded as anxious as his own people. Rain came down through the inky darkness.[45]

Prowling the front, Chamberlain lost his bearings and made a brief acquaintance with an enemy picket industriously improving his rifle pit. "Throw [the spoil] to the other side, my man; that's where the danger is," Chamberlain hissed. "Don't ye s'pose I know which side them Yanks be?'' the picket answered equably. Chamberlain put on his most authentic Southern drawl and tried to pass himself off as a Confederate officer on rounds. "Dig away then, but keep a right sharp lookout," he ordered, crawling back toward safety.[46]

There were occasional outbreaks of musketry. Presently a junior staff officer rode up and, flustered and gasping, passed the word that the army had recrossed the Rappahannock. "Get yourselves out of this as quick as God will let you," he blurted out. Chamberlain moved off to consult with Ames. They planned a discreet withdrawal. Even-numbered men were to dig while the odd numbers fell back a hundred yards; then the even numbers were to leapfrog over the odd. The process could be repeated until the entire rear guard had collected at the bridgehead. So it happened. The Confederate pickets crept out of their rifle pits and followed at a discreet distance. At one moment a shaft of moonlight shone through a break in the clouds, and a few shots rang out. Nobody was hit. Chamberlain led the regiment across one of the upper bridges at daybreak on Tuesday, December 16.[47]

"They went as they came—in the night," Robert Lee wrote his wife. The battle had been an unrelieved disaster for the Army of the Potomac. The 20th Maine shuffled up from the Rappahannock in a cold rain. Chamberlain cast a backward glance at the Fredericksburg plain and, beyond, toward those leprous hills from which the Confederates had inflicted such terrible punishment. Presently he called a halt. Tired, aching, depressed, he sat propped against a tree, shoulders hunched against the rain. Joe Hooker, passing by, caught sight of Chamberlain and called out a greeting.[48]

"You've had a hard chance, Colonel," he said.

"It was chance, General," Chamberlain answered; "not much intelligent design there."

Hooker, unused to such plain speaking from the mouths of volunteer lieutenant colonels, replied coolly, "God knows I did not put you in."

"That was the trouble," Chamberlain persisted. "You should have put us in. We were handed in piecemeal, on toasting forks."[49]

The final tally showed the 20th Maine to have led a charmed life at Fredericksburg. Ames reported four men killed,* thirty-two wounded. The Third Brigade returns listed 201 killed, wounded, and missing; First Division casualties added up to nearly one thousand. Cumulative losses

---

*The dead were Corp. George Staples and Pvts. Seth Woodward, Henry Chamberlain, and Edward Egget. Pvt. Joseph McNeiley, shot through the lungs, died later in hospital.

were grievous, 12,700 killed, wounded, and missing in the battle—more than two-thirds of that number in frontal assaults on the stone wall at the base of Marye's Heights. There were lots of soldiers in the ranks who, like Chamberlain, thought they could identify the cause of the disaster. "The fault is in our *generals* and *head officials*," a Massachusetts infantryman wrote home. "We fought well, except in a few instances." The men at least had that consolation as they trudged back to their muddy camps at Stoneman's Switch.[50]

Christmas came and went, a cheerless holiday on both sides of the Rappahannock. Alexander gave Charley, his manservant, permission to approach General Lee for a Christmas gift. Lee gave him a dollar. On one of his own visits to headquarters, Alexander took the opportunity to tease Lee about their Marye's Heights disagreement. "It was a mighty good thing those guns were on the brows of the hills when the Yankees charged them," he remarked to one of Lee's engineers in a voice loud enough for the general to hear. Lee let his impudence pass. The guns had performed well despite defective ammunition—the worst supply of any battle in the war, Alexander said. The northern press confirmed the long arm's effectiveness at the time, Alexander claimed, attributing twenty percent of the federal casualties at Fredericksburg to artillery fire, more than double the rule-of-thumb toll of one man in every twelve.[51]

Griffin's First Division set out December 30 on a reconnaissance to the Rappahannock fords, west of Fredericksburg. The First Brigade crossed to the south bank on the thirty-first, skirmished with Confederate pickets, and recrossed on New Year's Day, 1863. The 20th Maine, with the Third Brigade, camped in a pine woods near Richards' Ford for two cold, blustery, but otherwise uneventful days, then returned to the comparative comforts of camp. Alexander obtained a three-day furlough and spent the New Year's holiday in Richmond with Bettie and the child, now living with the Gilmers (Jeremy Gilmer had been chief of the army's Engineer Bureau since October 1862) and others in a crowded house on South Broad Street.[52]

Alexander took the battalion down to the North Anna River in early January, in search of winter pasture for the battery horses. Choosing a campsite in an oak woods near Mount Carmel Church, he set the men to building quarters for themselves and brush stables for the nags. The log huts turned out to be reasonably snug, and the officers' tents even had stoves with chimneys. Food was scarce, though. The troops lived

exclusively on bread and meat, and the army's overtaxed supply system
rarely delivered sufficient of either. Alexander settled in comfortably. He
found room and board for himself, Bettie, the baby, and a nursemaid*
with an old couple, the Worthams, less than a mile from camp. Squire
Wortham, he wrote Fairfield, had "plenty of poultry, potatoes, hot meat,
cabbages, turnips, tomatoes, negroes, little & big, & as good dry oak
wood and light wood as ever warmed a room with three immense feather
beds in it." He looked back on the winter of 1863 as one of the most
agreeable interludes of his life. He could not, of course, foresee that the
war would go on for another two years, producing a quarter-million
more battle casualties. "Ignorance is bliss," he said, "& I shared the
general feeling that after one or two more defeats the enemy would
surely give it up."[53]

Burnside by no means felt ready to quit. He intended to develop the
First Division's year-end sally, but had to stand down when Lincoln, in
dread of another Fredericksburg, forbade a general movement. Dry, cold
weather set in, firming up Virginia's notorious winter roads. Burnside
persuaded the president to approve a new scheme to pry Lee out of his
works. The commanding general came down January 8 to review the Fifth
Corps. Veterans took this, rightly, as evidence that a campaign soon
would commence. Fair weather held, and on the seventeenth the formations were alerted to march at noon the next day. There were delays. Finally,
on Tuesday, January 20, the movement began. The 20th Maine stepped off
in mid-afternoon, again heading for the Rappahannock crossings. Troops
and trains encumbered the roads. As evening came on, a northeast wind
piled up banks of dark clouds. Rain began falling before sunset, continued through the night, and kept up a steady drumming all day on the
twenty-first, turning the countryside into a vast, impassable swamp.[54]

The army foundered in these drowned lands. The troops struggled in
mud up to their knees, the trains were stuck fast, exhausted animals fell
by the wayside and disappeared, as though into quicksand. Rain soaked
the men's subsistence of hard bread, coffee, and sugar. Burnside's staff
recommended calling off the operation. Surprise had been lost. The
federal campfires were visible for miles; at night, Confederate pickets
looked out over a sea of fire. The Rappahannock rose rapidly. Engineer
regiments brought up pontoons. "We could build two [bridges] this

*Alexander paid $1,000 for the slave girl, Amy, in Richmond in the autumn. She remained with
the family until after the war.

afternoon," one of Burnside's engineers advised, "but if we could build a dozen I think it would be better to abandon the enterprise."[55]

Aware that Burnside intended a general movement this time, Lee sent early for Alexander's artillery. The courier arrived at battalion headquarters at one o'clock in the afternoon of January 16; four hours later the batteries were en route to the Rappahannock. The battalion marched late into the night and reached Massaponax Church, nine miles below Fredericksburg, the following day. Alexander remained in bivouac there while the comedy of Burnside's Mud March played itself out. By the twenty-first it was obvious the Yankees were going nowhere. Confederate pickets hurled taunts across the swollen river, and tacked hand-lettered signs to the trunks of bare, dripping trees: "This Way to Richmond," they jeered.[56]

Burnside held out through the twenty-second, though the army did not move at all that day. As a fillip, the regiments were issued a gill of whiskey per man. It was too much for some; one party of drunks touched off a near-riot in the First Brigade of Griffin's division. Finally, on the twenty-third, Burnside admitted failure. The sun reappeared Saturday the twenty-fourth, the day the 20th Maine, wet, hungry, exhausted, staggered back into camp. Alexander's battalion turned around and bogged back to the North Anna. Five weeks before, Chamberlain had boldly challenged Hooker, apportioning him a share of the blame for the Fredericksburg debacle. Now "Fighting Joe," who had conspired to isolate and undermine Burnside, would have an opportunity to apply some intelligent design of his own to the Army of the Potomac's operations. Chamberlain surely winced when the news reached him sometime Sunday that Lincoln had removed Burnside and replaced him with Hooker.[57]

CHAPTER 6

EXCURSION INTO THE WILDERNESS

CHANCELLORSVILLE, SPRING 1863

P

ROUD, BOASTFUL, ENERGETIC, IMPRES-
sive on his white charger, Hooker was a tonic for the worn-down Army
of the Potomac. "In equipment, intelligence, and valor the enemy is our
inferior; let us never hesitate to give him battle wherever we can find
him," he announced in a bracing first general order, issued January 26,
1863. If his self-assurance shaded sometimes into arrogance—Lee, in
disdainful allusion to his nickname, referred to him as "Mr. F.J.
Hooker"—he anyway managed to restore a measure of poise to the
army. Hooker renewed the old McClellan emphasis on drill and discipline, cashiered incompetent officers, improved rations and living conditions. His reforms had an immediate impact in the camps around
Falmouth. "The whole army," wrote Private Gerrish of the 20th Maine,
"seemed to be invigorated with a new life."[1]

The enemy lay in his camps over on the south bank of the
Rappahannock, but the commanding general saw much that required
attention before he could bring him to battle. Hooker dropped Burnside's awkward grand division organization. He caused fresh-baked
soft bread and vegetables to be issued routinely. He sent paymasters
into the camps (one First Division soldier complained he had not
been paid for seven months), and introduced a regular system of
furloughs. As part of a general tidying-up, he ordered the men to
bathe once a week.[2]

The troops responded to Hooker's easy confidence, his nonchalance. He seemed, the journalist Noah Brooks thought, "to regard the whole business of command as if it were a larger sort of picnic." Still, there was a hard edge to Hooker. He meant, for one thing, to stop the high-level intriguing of the kind that had thwarted Burnside. "We knew that Joe Hooker was not that kind of fellow, that no corps commanders would trifle with him, that he would deliberately shoot any man who would dare to disobey him, whether he wore the coarse uniform of a private soldier, or the golden shoulder straps of a major general," Gerrish wrote. After Fredericksburg, the much-maligned Burnside rode among the troops with his hat pulled low over his forehead, either in shame, as most people believed, or to disguise himself. When Hooker appeared in the camps, the ranks responded with genuine cheers.[3]

Winter routines having been established, Chamberlain turned again to the study of war, in an evening vocational school under the direction of veteran Fifth Corps officers. Col. Thomas Stockton, the Third Brigade commander, probably acted as a senior sponsor. Though he was tiring now, Stockton, an 1827 graduate of West Point, drew on long and varied experience: nearly a decade's peacetime service as a regular, command of a volunteer regiment in the Mexican War, and brigade command in the Antietam and Fredericksburg campaigns. Strong Vincent, the colonel of the 83rd Pennsylvania, served as schoolmaster. A native of Erie, Pennsylvania, the son of a prosperous businessman, he worked in the family iron foundry before going on to Harvard, from which he gradua-ted in 1859. Joining a three-months regiment in April 1861, he showed himself to be a strict disciplinarian and a master of drill. One of Vin-cent's men thought him "a dude and an upstart" then; he had reason to revise his opinion later. Vincent had helped run a school for volunteer officers during the winter of 1861–62. This term, he added the lessons of the Peninsular, Second Bull Run, Antietam, and Fredericksburg cam-paigns to the curriculum. Vincent brought his wife down from Erie in January. They used to hack about the countryside around Falmouth, a striking pair on horseback. Chamberlain, alone nights on his hard pallet under drafty canvas, envied the Vincents their companionship.[4]

Col. Patrick O'Rorke spoke authoritatively on the latest in tactics and weaponry. The Irish-born son of a marble cutter, O'Rorke graduated first in the West Point class of 1861.* Though the cadets called him

*His classmate George Armstrong Custer ranked thirty-fourth—out of thirty-four.

Paddy, "he had nothing of the wild Irishman about him," one officer-colleague insisted; he had fought as a regular at First Bull Run, then obtained a volunteer commission as colonel of the 140th New York. One pictures Chamberlain furiously scribbling notes when O'Rorke, equally at ease with theory and practice, rose to address the class. Jeffords of the Fourth Michigan, Welch of the 16th Michigan, Prescott of the 32nd Massachusetts, Gwyn of the 118th Pennsylvania, and Hayes of the 18th Massachusetts were regular auditors. Chamberlain had most in common with James Rice, colonel of the 44th New York. A Yale graduate, Rice taught school in Mississippi and practiced law in New York City before volunteering in May 1861. Rice and Chamberlain were about the same age; both had interrupted promising professional careers; both had young families at home. They became close friends that winter at Stoneman's Switch.[5]

The night sessions covered administrative subjects, too, army ways of doing things, material that Chamberlain found useful on court-martial duty. Most of his cases were petty winter-camp incidents of drunkenness and thievery. Running a drumhead court proved simpler, however, than righting the casual injustices inseparable from military life. One such incident involved the 20th Maine's quartermaster, a ramping bully named Moses Brown, and a sergeant in Company H, George Washington Buck. Buck had stayed behind sick when the regiment left camp for a few days of field drill. Feeling mean, Brown sought him out and ordered him on a woodcutting detail. Brown knew perfectly well that noncommissioned officers were exempt from fatigues. Besides, Buck was on the sick list. He refused the order. Brown cursed him, knocked him down, kicked him, and, after the 20th returned to camp, reported him for insubordination. There were no witnesses; the authorities felt bound to back Brown. They reduced Buck to the ranks. Chamberlain learned the facts a few weeks later, and did what he could to put matters right. By then, though, it was too late.[6]

Chamberlain made use of the liberalized furlough policy in February, taking ten days in Brunswick with Fannie and the children, their first wartime reunion. When he returned, there were officer vacancies to fill, candidacies to evaluate. He had discussed prospective appointments with Governor Abner Coburn during his leave, and they continued to correspond on the subject. One result: Tom Chamberlain's name went in for a lieutenant's commission. There were myriad other details as the fighting season approached. Chamberlain oversaw distribution of the new cap badges and flags, a Hooker innovation intended to simplify identification and build unit pride. Each corps had its own symbol—a Maltese cross for the Fifth Corps, color-coded by division. The Third Brigade flew a triangular white flag with a blue border and a red cross (for the First Division) in the center.[7]

April blew in cold, with a fall of snow the night of the first. On the seventh, President Lincoln reviewed the Fifth Corps from the back of a pony-sized horse. Dressed, as always, in black, he wore his signature tall silk hat; his toes nearly touched the ground. When the pony broke into a trot, the presidential trouser legs rose with the motion, first one, then the other, revealing the white of his underdrawers around the ankles. Some of the men could not help laughing at the figure he cut. Lincoln reviewed the entire Army of the Potomac on the following day. Stoneman led the Cavalry Corps out April 13 on a long raid on Lee's lines of communication. That day, too, Hooker ordered the distribution of eight days' rations and sixty rounds per man. Then the rains came. They continued without letup for more than a week, stranding the army in its camps.[8]

Chamberlain complained to Fannie about having to forage for a dry board to use as a writing desk, and for a candle, pen, and ink. As it turned out, these were the least of his vexations. Though the medical director reported the army as a whole healthier than ever that spring, the 20th Maine now found itself banished to Quarantine Hill. Some medical blunderer had inoculated the regiment with smallpox, probably an instance of vaccine gone bad. By mid-April, eighty-four men were down with the disease; three had died. The regimental surgeon, Nahum P. Monroe, told Ames and Chamberlain the 20th would have to remain in isolation for at least two weeks.[9]

"If in the meantime there is a battle, & I am kept here in a pest house, I shall be desperate with mortification," Chamberlain wrote Fannie. The First Division marched for Chancellorsville in the forenoon of April 27, traveling light with only one battery, two ambulances, and the pack train carrying small-arms ammunition. "We saw our division & brigade move off, & we felt lonesome, I assure you," he lamented in a postscript to her.[10]

Ames, who had been politicking for a brigade command, escaped Quarantine Hill by volunteering as an aide to the Fifth Corps commander, Maj. Gen. George Gordon Meade. His departure left Chamberlain the doubtful consolation of regimental command. He worried about missed opportunities, both martial and financial. He had been named executor of the will of one Captain Badger, a commission, likely to be lucrative, that required his presence in Maine the first Tuesday in May. "You see my perplexity," he wrote Fannie. "I suppose Capt. B intended by appointing me to do me a favor in the pecuniary advantage it would be to execute this trust. If I should give it up now, & then find that I must stay here in this hospital camp ... it would be a great vexation. I feel quite puzzled—*cornered* expresses it."[11]

He refused the Badger job. The First Division crossed the Rappahannock Wednesday, April 29, reached the Rapidan at Ely's Ford late in the afternoon, waded the stream at dusk, camped on the south bank for the night, and pushed on into the densely wooded district known as the Wilderness Thursday morning. On Quarantine Hill, Chamberlain understood that Hooker had thrown a powerful striking force across the river barriers and onto Lee's flank. The battle opened near the crossroads hamlet of Chancellorsville the morning of Friday, May 1. "We could hear the firing plain but there we lay in glorious idleness without being able to lift a finger or fire a gun," one of the 20th's privates wrote home. Chamberlain seethed in his pest house, inactivity trying him almost beyond endurance. While the Third Brigade lay in line of battle near Chancellorsville, he rode over to main army headquarters at Falmouth to appeal to Hooker's chief of staff, Maj. Gen. Daniel Butterfield. He proposed a novel assignment for the 20th Maine: If nothing else, he told Butterfield, the regiment could infect the rebels with smallpox.[12]

Butterfield laughed this off, but did agree to find employment for Chamberlain. That night he detailed the 20th Maine to guard the telegraph wire from general headquarters to Hooker's field headquarters. Strung out along the line, the 20th began to pick up fresh news of the battle. By late Saturday there were intimations of disaster: "Stonewall Jackson has charged upon Howard and the Germans have broken, and run back to the river." It was true; after a long flank march, Jackson had routed Hooker's right flank, the heavily Teutonic 11th Corps under Oliver Howard. The next morning, Sunday the third, Hooker, groggy from a slight wound, his confidence shaken, contracted his lines and ordered Maj. Gen. John Sedgwick to rush the Sixth Corps up from Fredericksburg to reinforce him. "Where is General Hooker?" a worried Lincoln wired Butterfield from Washington Sunday afternoon. "Where is Sedgwick? Where is Stoneman?"[13]

Picket duty at least kept Chamberlain on the move. Confederate raiders cut the wire; friendly troops, ignorant of its purpose, tampered with it too. "I was in my saddle *all* the nights inspecting every inch of the line," Chamberlain wrote Governor Coburn. Following Ames's example, he attached himself to Charles Griffin on Monday the fourth, and managed to get himself into a battle. Griffin advanced one of his brigades a half-mile toward the enemy front, driving in the rebel pickets and skirmishers and probing for the main line of battle. A Confederate battery opened up, and Chamberlain had another horse wounded under him; another near miss. Griffin located the main line, then sounded the recall, his purpose accomplished. Lee, meanwhile, had turned away from Hooker to attack Sedgwick's corps near Salem Church, four miles east of Chancellorsville. After a short, sharp fight, the Sixth Corps retreated across the Rappahannock overnight. Chamberlain went back to patrolling the telegraph line.[14]

Hooker seemed to have fallen into a fit of bewilderment—possibly a drunken fit, too. His only concern now was to convey the army safely back to the camps. Rain began falling Tuesday afternoon. The swiftly rising Rappahannock threatened to carry off the pontoons at United States Ford. Chamberlain came up with the 20th Maine and put the men to work strengthening the bridges. The army recrossed, regiment after bedraggled regiment. The Third Brigade, part of the rear guard, came over at eight o'clock Wednesday morning, May 6. The Fifth Corps had seen little fighting, had taken few casualties, and, unlike Hooker, did not consider itself beaten. "We marched in column at shouldered arms, colors flying and drums beating," one defiant regimental commander wrote. The 20th helped the engineer detachments break up the pontoons, then shuffled a dozen miles through ankle-deep mud, reaching the Quarantine Hill camp late that night.[15]

The ranks viewed the brief, unhappy Chancellorsville campaign as yet another failure of senior leadership. Some said Hooker had been drunk—several men in the 22nd Massachusetts and the 118th Pennsylvania swore they had seen empty whiskey bottles in heaps outside his tent. Chamberlain reserved judgment. "There has been a big battle, and we have had a great many men killed or wounded," he wrote in neat block letters to his daughter. "We shall try it again soon, and see if we cannot make those Rebels behave better, and stop their wicked works in trying to spoil our Country and making us all so unhappy." Released from isolation, the 20th Maine rejoined the Third Brigade on May 17. Changes were afoot. On the eighteenth, Strong Vincent succeeded the elderly, broken-winded Stockton in command of the brigade. Ames's long-sought brigadier's star came through two days later. When he moved over to Howard's corps, Chamberlain moved up to command the regiment.* Promotion and the strong spring sunshine cheered him. "How I should enjoy a May-walk with you and Wyllys," he wrote Daisy, "and what beautiful flowers we would bring home to surprise Mamma. I often think of all our paths and sunny banks where we are always sure to find the wildflowers."[16]

So far as Chamberlain could determine, Hooker had no immediate plans to resume the offensive. He invited his brother John down from Bangor for a visit. "The season is glorious," he wrote him. "Our camp is fine & you would thoroughly enjoy it." He went on to boast of his new command, free of smallpox and soon to be brought up to strength. "We receive the three years men of the 2d Maine tomorrow, & that will make us by all odds the best Regt. from Maine," he told John. As it happened, the 120 replacements arrived as prisoners, under the escort of a Pennsylvania regiment with bayonets fixed.[17]

Part of the Second Maine, mustered in for two years in May 1861, had gone home a few days after Chancellorsville. Those left behind had failed to read the fine print on their enlistment papers. Through some recruiter's trick, they had signed up for three years. When the regiment left for Maine, they rebelled. Their brigade commander treated them as mutineers, holding them under guard without rations for three days. They reached the 20th's camp May 23, half-starved as well as insurgent. From Fifth Corps headquarters, Meade sent word for Chamberlain to shoot any man who continued to refuse duty.[18]

He persuaded Meade to grant him a few days to handle the crisis in his own way. Dismissing the Pennsylvania guard, he ordered the mutineers fed. He heard their version of events and offered to pass it on to Governor Coburn. "You are aware that promises were made to induce these men to enlist, which are not now kept, & I must say that I sympathize with them in their view of the case," he wrote Coburn. He wrote again two days later, reminding the governor that the mutineers awaited word from him. If Coburn rejected their appeal, military justice would grind to its inevitable end. "I have taken a liberal course with them, because they are all good and true men, but I shall be obliged to carry a firm hand," he went on. "They are now ordered on duty, & the orders must be carried out."[19]

Though Coburn declined to intervene, the firing squads were not

*He got a step up in rank, too, to full colonel, and an increase in monthly pay of about thirty-three dollars, to $212.

summoned after all. The mutineers rewarded Chamberlain's patience and tact, most returning to duty within a few days. In the end, only one or two cases went to court-martial. The thin ranks of the 20th Maine were filled out, and only just in time. The First Division broke camp May 28 and marched again for the Rappahannock fords. John Chamberlain would have to catch up with his brothers in the field. On June 3, leading elements of the Army of Northern Virginia set out for the Potomac and beyond.[20]

Religious revival swept through the camps of Lee's army that winter. Parson Pendleton did what he could to encourage this outburst of Christian zeal. Attentive, too, to common religious observance, he came down to Mount Carmel Church, slipped a surplice over his uniform, and baptized little Bessie Alexander. Pendleton and Alexander discussed artillery business as well; Pendleton had delegated reorganization of the long arm to Alexander and Col. Stapleton Crutchfield, Jackson's artillery chief. They recommended completing the process, begun last summer, of grouping all the field artillery in independent battalions answering to the corps commanders. In mid-February, Pendleton endorsed the Alexander-Crutchfield plan, and Lee shortly approved it.[21]

Winter idleness bred military crime, and much of Alexander's business involved courts-martial. As president of a court, he recommended half a dozen death sentences, all for desertion and bounty-jumping, but found martial law inadequate to prevent his hungry soldiers from plundering the North Anna farms. Fowls, pigs, sheep, and even oxen were disappearing at an alarming rate. "The men receive as ration but ¼ lb of fat bacon daily & there is no wonder at their stealing; but it is now such an enormous evil that I am only trying to find a culprit & a color of law to have him shot as an example," he wrote Leopold at Fairfield. Existing punishments were insufficiently severe, he went on, citing as an example the penalty prescribed for a convicted hog thief: forfeiture of all pay and allowances for two years, thirty-nine lashes, and two years in a Virginia penitentiary.[22]

With Longstreet and two-thirds of the First Corps infantry away in southeastern Virginia on detached duty, Alexander was much on his own. Routine battalion duties, such as finding and hauling in forage, repairing harnesses and equipment, and replacing worn-out guns, could be entrusted to his new second-in-command, Maj. Frank Huger (pronounced u'-gee), who reported in mid-February. Aleck and Huger resumed a friendship first formed at West Point. As always, Alexander made time for hunting and fishing. He took his daughter on angling excursions to a creek near the Wortham place, where they caught suckers and other small fry. Bessie helped him fix up a little seine he planned to take along with him when the spring campaign opened.[23]

His promotion to colonel came through in early March. At around the same time, Stonewall Jackson applied for Alexander to take command of one of his infantry brigades—Georgia regiments, his brother-in-law Lawton's former unit. He thought it over and decided against a change. "Except for the increased pay & pride in the compliment," he wrote his father, "I very much prefer the command of my Battn. wh. is as independent & conspicuous as a division of infantry." The infantry vacancy went to another Georgian, Col. John B. Gordon. Despite short rations for men and horses, he pronounced the battalion in "splendid condition" at winter's end. Among his twenty-five guns were four replacements—deadly accurate three-inch rifles captured from the Yankees, and as good as new.[24]

The camps stirred with the coming of spring. "Bettie and I are still together in our nice quarters & enjoying each other's company as if each day were the last," he wrote Fairfield on April 25. He knew by then that she was pregnant for the second time. On the twenty-seventh he set out for Milford Station, where Crutchfield's gunners were test-firing shells filled with new paper time fuses of his design. Even at Fredericksburg, where nearly all the shooting had been at close range, frontline infantry reported casualties from shells that burst prematurely. As a result, the gunners were ordered to fire solid shot exclusively when friendly infantry lay near. Alexander fitted every round in his battalion chests with his own more reliable fuses. He went on into Fredericksburg after the tests for a reunion with friends on Lee's staff, spending the night of the twenty-eighth there. He was still at headquarters the morning of April 29 when word reached Lee that the Federals had thrown pontoons over the Rappahannock at Franklin's old crossing point below the town.[25]

He wired Huger at Mount Carmel to prepare the battalion for the march, a complicated operation: after the guns and caissons of the six batteries came a train of fourteen four-horse wagons carrying provisions, tents, and other baggage for some six hundred officers and men. Huger sent Charley over to the Worthams to inform Bettie of the move and collect Alexander's two horses. Expecting something more elaborate in the way of a farewell, she refused to release the animals to anyone but her husband. Huger had to send an officer along to explain that events would keep Aleck in Fredericksburg whether or not she let his horses go.[26]

Meanwhile, he "played engineer and staff officer for General Lee," supervising the preparation of a line of battle across the Orange Plank Road, west of Fredericksburg. By now Lee knew Hooker's main effort would come from the west. Moving rapidly, three Yankee corps had marched more than eighty miles in three days, crossed two major rivers, and arrived on the Confederate flank. The advance uncovered the Rappahannock fords, freeing two more corps to reinforce the turning column from the north bank. By the evening of April 30, Hooker had seventy thousand infantry in place around Chancellorsville on the eastern edge of the Wilderness, that "wild tangled forest of stunted trees" (Moxley Sorrel's phrase) between Fredericksburg and Orange Court House.[27]

Hooker intended to clear the 120-square-mile Wilderness and bring Lee to battle in the open country beyond. His flank threatened, Lee had another handicap: he would have to accept a battle without Longstreet and most of the First Corps infantry. Nevertheless, Lee decided to divide the army, advancing with Jackson's corps and several stray brigades, about forty thousand men, to meet the Federals in front of Chancellorsville while leaving a detachment of ten thousand in the Fredericksburg lines to hold an estimated forty thousand Yankees under Sedgwick.

Charley sought out Alexander the morning of the thirtieth to report the battalion's arrival. Aleck rode happily among the men and guns. As always, their potential excited him. He afterward emphasized the role that chance played in Lee's greatest victory. Then, though, he felt invincible, as though no opponent, however powerful, could defeat the Army of Northern Virginia. "My spirits rose with a delicious sense of the wicked power of which I was in control, & which I was soon going to turn loose upon our enemy," he recalled. The battalion rested in line that night. Hooker resumed the advance next morning, a bright, mild Friday, May Day. Late in the morning, Lee appeared on the Plank Road, at the head of a dense column. Alexander realized at once that the fieldworks he had laid out were not to be used, at least not today. "We were not going to wait for the enemy to come & attack us in those lines," he wrote, "we were going on the warpath after him."[28]

Lee launched two columns down parallel roads toward Chancellorsville. Alexander's battalion moved down the Plank Road with Jackson's column. After a mile or so the van bumped into the Yankee skirmish line. Alexander called up Woolfolk's twelve-pounders and directed their fire on the skirmishers, who gave ground steadily. Up ahead, on the far side of an extensive clearing, Alexander saw dark masses of Federals forming a line. To the north, in the direction of the Orange Turnpike, heavy firing could be heard. Alexander ordered up more guns. Jackson deployed the infantry on a broad front. Before long the Yankees began to fall back into the woods. Late in the afternoon, Alexander advanced one of his guns to within sight of the Chancellor mansion.[29]

Hooker had halted his leading corps, the Fifth and the 12th, almost at first contact and drawn them into a defensive arc around Chancellorsville, suspending the offensive in hopes that Lee would attack *him*. Alexander bivouacked for the night in a woods just south of the Plank Road. After supper, Parker brought Aleck a cup of coffee, and showed him a small leather bag with ground beans and sugar mixed together. Parker had taken it off a Yankee corpse. "I never before knew how good a cup of coffee could be," Alexander wrote long afterward, "& to this day I never drink a cup of real good coffee, but the picture comes up of the good captain approaching in the fire light, & I hear his gentle voice . . . & he explains in his short quick sentences where the coffee came from." Nearby, Lee and Jackson sat around another fire, plotting. Stuart's cavalry had reported Hooker's right flank in the air—that is to say, unprotected by any natural barrier. To exploit it, Lee opted to split the army into a third part, sending Jackson with three divisions and Alexander's guns through the Wilderness on a twelve-mile flank march out beyond the federal right.[30]

Lee ordered the thirty-thousand-strong column to march at sunrise Saturday, May 2. The lead elements finally moved off at seven o'clock, some two hours behind schedule. Alexander rode up front with Jackson and his staff. He reported Stonewall as "grave & silent" through the morning. Around noon, the Federals sighted the tail of the column through a gap in the forest and sent out a strong infantry force to investigate. The rear guard drove the Yankees off after a sharp exchange. Fitzhugh Lee, scouting ahead with the cavalry, turned up an hour or two later, spoke briefly with Jackson, and led him away into a thicket from which the very end of the enemy line could be glimpsed. "When he came back there was a perceptible increase of eagerness in his air," Alexander recalled.[31]

The column crept on for another mile before Jackson called a halt and ordered the two leading divisions, those of Rodes and Colston, to deploy into parallel lines of battle. There would be no room here for the artillery, so Alexander's battalion went into the third line with A. P. Hill's division. The deployment consumed two full hours. Alexander later estimated the value of daylight this May 2 at a million dollars a minute, but the order to advance did not come until after five o'clock. Finally a bugle sounded; brigade after brigade took up the call. The infantry made slow progress through the tangle of scrub oak and pine, and did not clear the worst of it until close on six o'clock. Then, driving troops of frightened fox, rabbit, deer, and wild turkey before them, the Confederates came bounding out of the forest in full treble cry. The woods evidently had muffled the sound of their approach, for Howard's troops were surprised at their cookfires. His front quickly collapsed. Much of the 11th Corps turned and ran, propelled by the wildest panic, not excepting Manassas, that Alexander had yet seen.[32]

The attackers pushed on through Howard's camps at the double-quick. Alexander, following close behind the first wave, passed a wounded Yankee calling out "Water! Water! Water!" in a strong voice. He had been shot through the forehead; some of his brains were spilling out. Alexander bent down and asked him where he came from. "He changed his cry and began to shout 'New York! New York! New York!' just as he had been shouting for 'Water,' & kept it up as long as I could hear." After a brief check near Dowdall's Tavern, the advance bowled along toward Chancellorsville. Jackson pressed up to the front as darkness came on, determined to finish off Hooker's right wing and force a junction with Lee, now only two miles distant. In the confusion of the rout, friendly troops mistook Jackson and his entourage for prowling federal cavalry. Shots rang out. Jackson, hit three times, dropped off his horse and out of the battle. A. P. Hill succeeded him in command, but only briefly. Hill launched a confused attack that provoked a furious federal cannonade. He and Crutchfield both fell with disabling wounds. Orderlies bore Jackson rearward to the surgeon's tent, where Dr. Hunter McGuire shortly removed his shattered left arm. Stonewall turned over the Second Corps command to Stuart, who sent for Alexander and ordered him to take charge of all the artillery in the field.[33]

At Stuart's request, he spent the night touring the front, feeling for the crooked Confederate line of battle, marking down access roads for the artillery, and scouting for breaks in the woods where guns could be brought to bear on the enemy. Firing broke out from time to time. He came upon a small opening in a dense stand of pine. Only twenty-five yards across, it overlooked the Yankee lines on a cleared plateau called

Hazel Grove. Alexander thought he could fit a battery into the clearing, and a second battery on the knoll just behind it. By now it was close to three o'clock. He rode toward the rear in the pale light of a full moon, past sleeping infantrymen with their rifles at their sides. He awoke Col. Lindsey Walker, commanding one of the Second Corps artillery battalions, and ordered him to alert his batteries for a predawn move. Alexander rolled himself into Walker's still-warm blankets and sank instantly into sleep. "Could death ever come as that sleep did," he wrote as an old man, still savoring the experience, "it would be delicious to die." Walker returned a quarter-hour later and shook him into consciousness. He felt "wonderfully refreshed, as if by a strong cordial." By daybreak he had seventeen guns in line, loaded and ready for action.[34]

For a change, an attack opened on schedule. The Confederate infantry advanced at first light Sunday, May 3, Alexander's artillery booming in support. Bettie told him later she could hear the firing in her room at the Worthams', thirty miles distant. The racket inspired Bessie, eighteen months old, to deliver her longest speech yet: "Hear my Papa shoot Yankee. Boo!" Later that morning Aleck experienced his closest near miss of the war. He could literally follow the flight of the shell with his eye. "I saw this plainly come out of the bushes within ten feet," he reported, "& it seemed to pass my ear within two inches."[35]

The attackers reached Hazel Grove just as the Federals were abandoning it, a "gratuitous gift of a battlefield," remarked Alexander, who at Stuart's command ran all the guns he could collect onto the plateau, some forty eventually, from where they dominated the Chancellorsville clearing. He had a perfect view of the infantry assault. As the Federals became unstrung, Alexander raced back to Hazel Grove to hump the guns up to the new front. They soon were firing into large, confused groups milling around the Chancellor house. "That is the part of artillery service that may be denominated 'pie'—to fire into swarming fugitives who can't answer back," Alexander wrote. He was unapologetic: "One has usually had to pay for this pie before he gets it, so he has no compunctions of conscience or chivalry." As the poet Robert Southey put it, in verse Alexander had committed to memory during boyhood forays into the library at Fairfield:

> They all agreed that revenge was sweet,
> And young Prince Crocodiles delicate meat.[36]

Suddenly the Federals were gone, in full retreat into a strong defensive perimeter around U.S. Ford. Alexander galloped up to the Chancellor mansion, which was now burning fiercely. There were lots of wounded Yankees about. A beautiful Newfoundland dog lay dead in the yard. Lee arrived at noon, completing the union of two of the three wings of his army. The men cheered themselves hoarse at the sight of him. Stuart, who had handled the infantry capably as Jackson's stand-in, was jubilant. "Old Joe Hooker, would you come out of the Wilderness," he kept singing.[37]

Alexander handed over the artillery command to a senior colonel of Jackson's corps and rejoined his battalion. Soon word came to haul his guns off to yet another part of the battlefield. Sedgwick's Sixth Corps had finally carried Marye's Heights at Fredericksburg and was advancing in Lee's rear. Lee sent McLaws's division with Alexander's battalion back down the Plank Road to meet him. Anderson's division shortly followed. Sedgwick's caution here cost him a chance to restore Hooker's fortunes. He allowed light forces to detain him, and only reached Salem Church in the late afternoon. There the Sixth Corps bedded down for the night. The Confederates formed a line of battle across his path and slept on their weapons.[38]

Lee resolved to attack Sedgwick early on Monday the fourth. There were delays. McLaws and Anderson were unsure of where the main Yankee line lay. The sun passed the zenith, and still the infantry had not moved. Lee gave in to a rare fit of temper, his anger mounting as the day wore on. Alexander steered clear of him. "I remember thinking that the quickest & best way to find out about the enemy would be to move on them at once," Alexander wrote, "but the old man seemed to be feeling so real wicked, I concluded to retain my ideas exclusively in my own possession." Sedgwick, meanwhile, resolved on retreat. He had floated the notion of returning to the safe side of the Rappahannock as early as ten o'clock that morning, when he reported some forty thousand Confederates on his front. In fact, Lee had about twenty-one thousand infantry there. The Confederate attack finally got under way an hour before sunset, a clumsy, uncoordinated lunge that the Sixth Corps parried easily.[39]

Anticipating Sedgwick's withdrawal, Alexander marked down points of direction for night firing and sought permission to dip into the ammunition stocks. In what the historian of Lee's long arm called the first instance of Confederate use of indirect fire, Alexander's guns opened on Banks' Ford at ten o'clock Monday night. Despite this harassing fire, Sedgwick had his entire command across before dawn Tuesday. Lee summoned Alexander after sunrise and ordered him to scout gun positions for an attack on Hooker's bridgehead at U.S. Ford. He found good sites for a half-dozen guns, but came away deeply doubtful of the prospects for a breakthrough. He thought Lee, still angry about Monday's failures, had assigned the infantry an impossible task. Hooker's defenses looked impregnable to him. Still, he saw everything made ready and waited out a stormy night. To his surprise, federal artillery opened on his gun pits at daybreak from the *north* bank of the Rappahannock. Hooker had withdrawn the army overnight under cover of the downpour. "Clearly, this decision was the mistake of his life," Alexander observed. He had denied himself a probable Marye's Heights in reverse.[40]

Chancellorsville would be judged a masterpiece, Lee's greatest victory. Alexander had been in the thick of each of the four main components of the battle: the initial dash to meet the Federals on the outer edge of the Wilderness, the flank march with Jackson, the push to Hazel Grove and on to Chancellorsville, and the check to Sedgwick at Salem Church. To him, the result had been as much a matter of fortune as design—especially at the end, when Hooker's unlooked-for exit kept Lee from breaking his army on the breastworks at U.S. Ford. It was "a marvelous story," he would write later, "of how luck favored pluck & skill, & how we extricated ourselves by the boldest & most daring strategy of the whole war." The casualty totals were some thirty thousand killed, wounded, and missing on both sides. The Confederates lost fewer men, but in greater proportion—something like one man in every five, including the irreplaceable Jackson, who died of complications from his wounds on May 10.[41]

Alexander's battalion, less sixty-two killed, wounded, and missing, trudged back down the now-familiar Plank Road and pitched camp in a driving rain. He surrendered to the same "high power" sleep that had overtaken him briefly in Walker's camp. "And about Thursday," he recorded, "Miss Teen was made happy by a telegram from me." He brought Bettie and the child down to Milford Station Saturday, May 9, where they found room and board with Captain Woolfolk's widowed mother at Bowling Green. Aleck spent the month *en famille* at Mrs. Woolfolk's pleasant house, shaded by oak trees, on a hill overlooking the green valley of the Mattapony.[42]

"Drive on, Abram."

Orders for the battalion to join the First Corps at Culpeper Court House reached Alexander in the forenoon of Wednesday, June 3. Bettie chose to stay on with Mrs. Woolfolk. The widow and Colonel Alexander struck a private deal: she agreed to take care of the pregnant Bettie, while Alexander promised to look out for her three sons, Captain Piche-gru, Lieutenant James, and Sergeant Ned, all serving in his battalion. Alexander found the price right, too—$100 a month for room and board, less than half his monthly pay. He whistled for his latest camp follower, a pointer puppy he called Buster, and saw the battalion on the road for Culpeper, sixty miles northwest, by two o'clock that afternoon.[43]

Longstreet had recalled Alexander as part of a larger design, the preliminary movements of Lee's second invasion of the North. Lee left the newly created Third Corps under A. P. Hill (recovered from his Chancellorsville wound and promoted to lieutenant general) in the Fredericksburg lines opposite Hooker. Hill and Longstreet together kept the federals fixed in position along the north bank of the Rappahannock while Jackson's corps, now under Lt. Gen. Richard Ewell, marched for the Blue Ridge.

Hooker launched large-scale reconnaissances in search of Lee's mobile elements. His Cavalry Corps surprised Stuart's command at Brandy Station June 9, touching off what turned out to be the biggest cavalry fight of the war. It was "a great humbug," according to the exacting Alexander. "Twelve or fifteen thousand engaged all day & loss on our side not four hundred," he wrote Leopold. "I rode over the field next day & saw only about twenty dead Yankees—only two killed with the sabre." By June 14, Ewell was across the Blue Ridge at Chester Gap and moving toward Winchester, en route to Maryland and Pennsylvania.[44]

Lee believed that a victory in Pennsylvania would strengthen the northern peace movement and, perhaps, encourage European intervention on behalf of the Confederacy. Alexander knew next to nothing then about Lee's high strategy, but he felt apprehensive about going north. "I only hope for us that we won't cross the Potomac, for I don't believe we can ever successfully invade," he wrote his father. Still, like nearly everyone else in the Army of Northern Virginia, he had absolute faith in Lee. In hindsight, Alexander argued that the Confederates should have remained on the defensive in Virginia and sent reinforcements to besieged Vicksburg, as Longstreet had proposed at the time. But there was an aura of infallibility about Lee in the summer of 1863, an immense prestige. "We looked forward to victory under him as confidently as to successive sunrises," Alexander remembered.[45]

While the armies were carrying out these initial maneuvers, John Chamberlain touched Virginia soil at Aquia Creek and set out in search of his brothers, distributing Christian Commission tracts, Bibles, and

comforts to troops he met along the way. With all the confusion in the
rear areas, not even clergymen were safe; John heard that the Fourth
Michigan's chaplain's throat had been cut the other night, allegedly by
Mosby's guerrillas. But John went on with his missionary work all the
same, conspicuous in a black frock coat and black felt hat. He caught
up to Fifth Corps headquarters near Kelly's Ford on June 11 and, hand-
ing out lemons and Bibles in a field hospital, fell into conversation with
several convalescents from the 20th Maine. They complained of hard usage
and harder officers, John recorded in his diary, then went on to boast
of now having "as good a Col. as is in the Army of the Potomac."
Chamberlain "treats the men like men not as dogs like Ames did," they
told John.[46]

He brought news of home for Lawrence and Tom. The elder
Chamberlains and sister Sae were well. Daisy and Wyllys were in Brunswick under Deborah Folsom's care, for Fannie had resumed her peregrinating ways, moving back and forth between the Boston kin and the St.
Germain Hotel in New York City. "Wyllys asks *where Mama's house is
now*, & Daisy would like to see her, but they are very happy,"
Chamberlain heard at second hand. This hint of instability troubled him,
but he could do nothing about it now. Hooker set the army on Lee's
track, moving roughly parallel with him though a step or two behind.
The First Division broke camp June 14 and reached Manassas Junction
the next day. Chamberlain expected a battle there, a third Bull Run.
But orders came to push on, two more days of hard marching under a
high, hot midsummer sky. Water sources were drying up, and the columns
churned up clouds of asphyxiating dust. There were casualties from sunstroke and dehydration.[47]

Meade detached the First Division June 19 and sent it ahead with
the cavalry to Aldie, on the road to Ashby's Gap. James Barnes, the
senior brigadier, commanded in place of Griffin, who had gone away
on sick leave in early May. Some of the men were skeptical of Barnes,
an 1829 West Point graduate who had left the army in the mid-1830s
to build railroads. It was Barnes who had put the Second Maine mutineers under arrest. There was a strong whiff of the brandy flask about
him, too. Soldiers in one First Brigade regiment reported that Barnes
had been drunk, "reeling in the saddle," on the retreat from Chancellorsville. In the Aldie operation, Barnes's subordinates served him
well. Vincent handled the Third Brigade with special competence. In
concert with Gregg's cavalry division, the brigade, in a long running

fight June 21, drove Stuart's Confederates beyond Upperville and into Ashby's Gap.[48]

Laid low by sunstroke and, probably, by a touch of malarial fever, too, Chamberlain missed the Upperville action. John Chamberlain found him "looking poorly" when he finally overtook the 20th Maine. Chamberlain refused to ride in an ambulance when the march resumed. John trotted along near the head of the column with the colonel and Rice of the 44th New York. They doubtless discussed what the Washington newspapers were now reporting: Confederate columns were north of the Potomac and driving for Pennsylvania.[49]

By June 22, Alexander's battalion had reached Millwood, in the Shenandoah Valley. Infantry detachments operating with Stuart's cavalry held Ashby's and Snicker's gaps while Hill's corps caught up, cleared the passes, and pushed on in Ewell's wake. It had been a hard, straggling three-day march from Culpeper. As usual, Walton let the Washington batteries lead. Alexander's battalion choked on the dust they raised. A man selling applejack along the route did a brisk business until Alexander came along and put him under arrest. One of his best sergeants fell out on the road, along with several privates. When they rejoined the column, he sentenced the rankers to an hour's marching in place, carrying fence rails on their shoulders. He ordered the sergeant to climb a tree and sit in it until further notice. His battery mates gathered around the trunk to rag him about his long, bony, dangling legs. Alexander regretted the punishment almost as soon as he imposed it, "as tending to mortify" a reliable petty officer.[50]

Longstreet had formed the habit, by now hard to break, of turning to Alexander when he wanted important work done quickly and well. On the nineteenth, with the federal cavalry threatening, he sent Alexander back up to Ashby's Gap to lay out a line of battle for McLaws's division. Longstreet changed his mind the next day and withdrew McLaws. When the Yankees (cavalry, with Vincent's Third Brigade) chased Stuart's detachments out of Upperville on the twenty-first, Longstreet ordered McLaws to return to the gap, in company with Alexander's guns. But the federals recoiled, allowing the First Corps to regain the road for the Potomac. Alexander's battalion crossed at Williamsport with Pickett's division on Thursday, June 25. The rest of the corps followed on the twenty-sixth.[51]

Stuart had set out June 24 with most of the cavalry on another flashy ride around the Army of the Potomac. This time, with Hooker forcing the pace, Stuart's antic military behavior proved costly. Federal infantry pushed up between the cavalry and Lee's columns. Stuart lost all contact with Lee. Alexander judged this raid useless. Stuart failed in his primary mission: to screen the Confederates and to keep the army commander informed of the enemy's movements. Lee's three corps plodded northward, denied accurate intelligence for several critical days.[52]

The First Corps passed through Chambersburg, Pennsylvania, on June 27, the townspeople watching in silence from their front porches. A big yellow dog started up a yapping protest as the guns rumbled by. "He charged up to the front fence & reared up on it, & he cavorted up and down, barking furiously, as dogs do when the gate is shut & there are no holes," Alexander noted. Then the dog's little mistress called out in a terrified voice, " 'Ma! Ma! Don't let Beave bite the army!' " The battalion bivouacked a mile or so north of the town and rested for two days. Charley broke into the hospital stores and stole enough brandy to fuel a mild drunk. Alexander punished him with a whipping.[53]

The 20th Maine crossed the Potomac at Edwards Ferry on June 26 and reached Frederick, Maryland, the day after. John Chamberlain described the inhabitants as enthusiastic. "Flags were flying from every window and everybody honored our troops with a smile or at least a look," he wrote in his diary. Veterans saw it differently. Gerrish thought the Marylanders rapacious, profiteering infamously on food and water. "We usually purchased their entire stock," he said, "and as we had no money, told them to charge it to Uncle Sam." Word filtered down on the twenty-eighth that the army had yet another commander, its seventh. In a dispute with Halleck, Hooker had asked to be relieved of command. Lincoln granted the request at once, choosing Meade* to replace him. Maj. Gen. George Sykes moved up to command the Fifth Corps.[54]

Belated news of these developments reached Lee through one of Longstreet's scouts, who turned up to report the enemy across the Potomac and Hooker out of a job. If the information surprised Lee, he did not let it show, though he lost little time in dispatching orders for the army to concentrate near Cashtown, Pennsylvania. When Alexander visited Lee's headquarters near Greenwood on June 30, everyone struck

---

*George Gordon Meade of Pennsylvania, an 1835 West Point graduate, followed McDowell, McClellan, Pope, McClellan again, Burnside, and Hooker.

him as "unusually careless and jolly," despite the wet weather and the now certain fact that the Yankees were close by. Perhaps it was the prosperous look of the countryside that cheered the Confederates: "Big barns, & fat cattle, & fruits & vegetables were everywhere," Alexander remembered. The battalion remained in camp near Greenwood all day July 1. He wrote Miss Teen to let her know a battle likely would be fought soon.[55]

The 20th Maine pushed north from Frederick, twenty-two miles on June 29 (torrents of rain fell that night), twenty-five miles the next day. The punishing pace took a toll on officers and men. Gillmore, now Chamberlain's second in command, fell out sick in Frederick. Chamberlain chose Ellis Spear, the Wiscasset schoolteacher, to fill Gillmore's place. The troops were showing a lot of wear and tear. Their blue trousers had faded to gray. Their blouses were torn and stained. Some men marched in stocking feet, others barefoot; many had fixed brightly colored handkerchiefs around their heads or necks, giving the column something of the look of a refugee swarm. They sent up ragged cheers when the column crossed the Pennsylvania line the afternoon of July 1, Wednesday. Near Hanover there were signs of a recent cavalry fight: broken fences, trampled grain. "Here were scattered along the road cart wheels and half-buried teams and soon dead horses," John Chamberlain wrote. The colonel seemed eager, preoccupied. Gunfire sounded to the west, the deep, measured boom of artillery. The column halted at four o'clock in a meadow west of Hanover. Soon the news spread, "whispers of disaster," according to Chamberlain, of a battle just ended near Gettysburg.[56]

The bugles sounded again as the men were preparing dinner, the familiar slurry of hardtack and bacon. At seven o'clock the Fifth Corps resumed the march, following a local guide on horseback. Presently the moon came up, full and brilliant in a cloudless sky. The country people came out of their kitchens and stood at the roadside to watch the column pass. At a bend in the road, a mounted staff officer approached Chamberlain. Those up front overheard him tell the colonel that McClellan would return tomorrow to command the army. As the rumor raced down the ranks, the men broke into wild cheers. "Everybody said, 'It's as good as 50,000 men,' " John Chamberlain recorded. A little later, speaking in hushed tones, men passed word that George Washington had been sighted, riding over the hills of Gettysburg with the sun setting behind him. "I half believed it myself," recalled Chamberlain.[57]

The dusty blue column trudged on, halting an hour after midnight some three or four miles east of Gettysburg. Twenty miles distant, the bugles were waking up Longstreet's troops. After a breakfast of corn and watery coffee, Alexander's battalion moved out, a lovely march, Aleck remembered, over a good turnpike road that glimmered bone-white in the moonlight.[58]

CHAPTER 7

APOTHEOSIS

GETTYSBURG, JULY 2–3, 1863

THE 20TH MAINE RANKERS, STIFF, SORE, stupid from lack of sleep, formed up in the road between dawn and sunrise. There seemed every prospect that yesterday's battle would be renewed today. Still, the excited awe Chamberlain sensed during the night march had dissolved. The men shuffled along, dragging swollen feet through the ankle-deep dust, as though they were sleepwalking. The sky grew lighter behind them, then, along the horizon, red. Already, at a few minutes past 4:30 this Thursday, July 2, the air felt warm, heavy with the suggestion of oppressive heat later in the day.[1]

The Fifth Corps moved slowly westward, the First Division in the van, reaching the heights southeast of Gettysburg at around seven o'clock. The 20th Maine halted in an open field off the Baltimore Pike. Ahead, Chamberlain could see the northern extension of the federal line and, beyond, the spires and chimneys of the town. The Army of the Potomac had come here because a cavalry detachment decided, yesterday, to stop and fight for the place. Armed with the deadly new Spencer repeating carbines, two brigades of dismounted cavalry held off the enemy infantry until the First and 11th Corps could join the battle. In hard fighting, the Confederates pushed the First Corps off the ridges west of Gettysburg and drove Howard's un- lucky 11th Corps completely out of the town. Union forces rallied late in the day under Winfield Scott Hancock on high ground just to the south. The two damaged corps (Howard's lost four thousand men captured) were soon reinforced. The 12th and Third Corps came up before nightfall. The Second Corps arrived a couple of hours after sunrise, at about the same time as the Fifth Corps.[2]

Hancock's line, conventionally likened to a fishhook, curled around Culp's Hill on the northern end (the barb), followed the curve of Cemetery Hill (the hook), then ran south along Cemetery Ridge for almost two miles (the shank) to a rocky outcrop called Little Round Top (the eye). A taller hill, Round Top, rose up a further three hundred yards to the south. Hancock had seen at once that Little Round Top controlled the battlefield. Enemy artillery placed there could enfilade the Cemetery Ridge position; enemy infantry attacking from Little Round Top could roll up the federal line. The hill commanded the Taneytown Road, the direct route to Washington and the army's escape route in the event of disaster. Hancock sent a 12th Corps division to fortify it Wednesday afternoon. That division withdrew at sunrise Thursday, on the understanding that the Third Corps, now anchoring the Union left, would cover the position. For some reason the Third Corps neglected the task. For most of the day, only a few signalmen held Little Round Top.[3]

Meade had come up during the night. Word spread that he intended to go over to the attack at Culp's Hill, but that front remained quiet through the morning. Some of the Fifth Corps troops used the respite to circulate the rumor of McClellan's return. Henry Hunt, the army's chief of artillery, heard it during an inspection of the Culp's Hill lines. "The boys are all jubilant over it," one man told him. The Fifth Corps veterans hardly had time to plant the McClellan story before they were shifted to the left and rear, behind Cemetery Ridge. Later, the corps moved still farther to the left, near Power's Hill, east of the Taneytown Road.[4]

There, in the shade of an orchard, the men gnawed hardtack, boiled coffee, dozed. Scattered musketry could be heard, nervous pickets sounding off. Chamberlain held the 20th Maine loosely in line of battle. An attack from Culp's Hill seemed unlikely now that the Fifth Corps had changed position. Still, he could expect to be thrown into the fight at any time, and with only the haziest notion of the circumstances. A lot depended on Lee. Chamberlain had no reason to believe Meade would be able to control events. "We knew a battle was to be fought, and a sharp one," he wrote, "but what most impressed our minds was the uncertainty of its plan. Indeed, there seemed as yet to be none. It began the day before as by accident; and it developed itself as it seemed by accident." A regimental commander saw little, influenced less. "Obedience, self-sacrifice and patient endurance are the qualities most in demand for him," wrote one veteran in what could stand as a formal definition of a line colonel's duty. Ignorance made the wait all the harder on the nerves. He felt anxious about his brothers, too, especially John. Tom had been through this before. He had an idea of what to expect. But nothing in his work for the Christian Commission could have prepared John Chamberlain for the shock of a battle exploding around him.[5]

The sun burned down out of a cloudless sky. While the 20th Maine rested in the sultry heat, Meade had begun to investigate an apparent irregularity over on the left, where the Third Corps had gone freelancing. The corps commander, Maj. Gen. Daniel Sickles, a New York lawyer and former Democratic congressman, had been doubtful about the ground assigned him, the low, spongy southern end of Cemetery Ridge. Without permission, he had moved his two divisions across a little stream called Plum Run and onto higher ground a half-mile west of the main line. Sickles's right-hand division formed a line of battle in a peach orchard; part of his left-hand division moved into a rocky ravine called the Devil's Den.[6]

Sickles, a vivid character, headstrong and bold,* nevertheless had second thoughts. He asked Meade to come down and inspect the new position. Meade sent Henry Hunt, who reported that Sickles's initiative had created a large bulge in the line, and that he had too few troops to defend all three sides of it—none at all for Little Round Top. Meade decided to ride down into the salient to scout the ground himself. At around four o'clock, as he neared Sickles's headquarters, Confederate artillery opened from Seminary Ridge. There was no time to pull back the Third Corps now. Shells bursting around him, Meade promised Sickles he would send help. An aide galloped off to alert Sykes to bring up the Fifth Corps to reinforce the salient.[7]

Meade's chief engineer, meanwhile, had ridden up Little Round Top to survey the federal defenses there. Brig. Gen. Gouverneur Kemble Warren, thirty-three years old, an intense, excitable West Pointer,** expected to find a powerful infantry force in occupation. Instead, he met only

*In 1859, in a celebrated scandal, Sickles shot and killed his wife's lover, a grandson of Francis Scott Key. Pleading temporary insanity, he was acquitted—the first successful insanity defense in American legal history.
**His namesake, industrialist Gouverneur Kemble, sent him off to West Point at age sixteen with these words: "We expect you to rank, at graduation, not lower than second." Warren dutifully ranked second of forty-four in the class of 1850.

those few signalmen. One of them reported seeing movement in the woods beyond Plum Run. Warren directed a battery in the Devil's Den to throw over a shot. It revealed the glistening gun barrels and bayonets of a long line of battle. "The discovery," wrote Warren, "was intensely thrilling to my feelings and most appalling." Mastering his emotion, he dispatched a courier to Meade with a request for at least a division to defend the hill.[8]

By now the cannonade was falling heavily upon Sickles's lines. A brigade-sized Confederate force could be seen spilling out of a woods to the left. The shelling stampeded a herd of cattle in Plum Run valley; panicked animals were charging wildly in all directions, bellowing in pain and fear. As Little Round Top came under fire, the signalmen prudently began packing away their flags. Warren asked them to stay a little longer and wig-wag, on the chance the deception might suggest the Federals held the summit in force.[9]

On Power's Hill, the First Division interpreted the opening of the bombardment as the signal to move. Chamberlain led the 20th Maine west toward the sound of the firing. Reaching the Taneytown Road, the column turned south for three-quarters of a mile, then veered west again, onto a farm track. Quick-timing over tilled land and meadows enclosed by stone walls, the division halted at the edge of a wheatfield behind the leftward bend of the Third Corps line. There was a lot of shooting ahead. The cannonade was louder, more menacing here. Chamberlain could see orange flashes of musketry, hundreds of them, through the smoke. The discharges formed a thick mist over Sickles's line of battle. Wounded men limped away toward the aid stations. He watched the First and Second brigades disappear into the murk, and waited for word to follow.[10]

Seven o'clock Thursday morning: Longstreet's gunners were at rest in a grassy wood west of Seminary Ridge. The fieldpieces were parked along the roadside, a country turning off the Chambersburg pike; the battery horses had been watered and let loose to graze. Walton, as senior officer, went off to report to Longstreet. He returned a half hour later with a summons for Alexander from the First Corps commander.[11]

Alexander found Longstreet with Lee on Seminary Ridge, the four-mile-long swell that ran parallel to Cemetery Ridge and about a mile distant. Lee wanted the First Corps to deliver the main assault today, against the federal left, Longstreet explained. Abandoning the fiction that Walton commanded the corps artillery, he told Alexander to scout the ground and take charge of all the guns in the field. To avoid an argument over seniority, he advised Alexander to leave the Washington Artillery in bivouac, out of the battle. He also cautioned him to be sure, when he brought the guns up to the line, to keep out of view of the signal station on Little Round Top. Alexander could see the signalmen from where he stood, sending messages via the wig-wag system he had helped Myer develop for the old army.[12]

Walton had been "overslaughed," to use Alexander's word, and he resented it. Still, his hurt feelings were the least of Longstreet's troubles. He seemed to have fallen into a deep gloom. A forty-two-year-old Georgian, full-whiskered and bearish, steady, cautious, and tough, Longstreet has been described as sulky, petulant, and depressed at Gettysburg. "There was apparent apathy in his movements," his chief of staff, G. Moxley Sorrel, recalled. "They lacked the fire and point of his usual bearing on the battlefield." Longstreet had argued against going up to Pennsylvania in the first place. He had tried twice already to talk Lee out of attacking here, proposing as an alternative a wide flanking movement around the enemy left to force a fight on ground of the Confederates' own choosing. Lee was insistent. He urged Longstreet to open the assault as early as practicable Thursday morning. Alexander claimed, later, that the First Corps could have been ready by eleven o'clock. But Longstreet wanted to wait for all his infantry to arrive. Pickett's division, posted at Chambersburg as rear guard, could not get up before sundown; Evander Law's brigade of Hood's division, marching overnight from New Guilford, twenty-four miles away, had yet to reach the battlefield. Lee gave Longstreet permission to delay the attack until Law was ready.[13]

Alexander's guns, fifty-four pieces from his own, Cabell's, and Henry's battalions, were in position by late morning. Law reported at about noon. Longstreet sent word for Hood's and McLaws's divisions to march for Warfield Ridge, the southern extension of Seminary Ridge, taking care, as Alexander had done, to stay out of sight of Little Round Top. There were mixups and wrong turns. With his instinctive feel for terrain, Alexander had found an easy detour for his artillery. The infantry's tardiness mystified him. Doubling back to investigate, he met the head of one of the columns and sketched out the route he had taken. Nobody wanted to accept responsibility for a change of course. Orders were expected from Longstreet at any moment. When they failed to arrive, the infantry continued its aimless march and countermarch. At least two hours were lost.

Hood's division did not reach Warfield Ridge opposite Little Round Top until after three o'clock. Massing the troops, Law's brigade on the right, Robertson's on the left, the other two brigades in a second line, consumed another full hour.[14]

Lee's orders specified an attack in echelon, from right to left northward along the Emmitsburg Road. Alexander thought the tactical plan "peculiar" even then; in retrospect, he argued that Hood and McLaws should have advanced together, with concentrated force. At four o'clock, while the infantry brigades were still forming for the assault, Alexander's artillery opened fire into the Sickles salient. He had pushed the guns up close, figuring his unreliable ammunition would work better at shorter ranges. Frank Huger ran four batteries to within five hundred yards of the peach orchard for what Alexander hoped would be quick, decisive work. The federal guns on Cemetery Ridge responded with a weight and accuracy that surprised him. The cannoneers began taking casualties right away. In one battery, a man abruptly turned on his heel and strode toward the rear, as though on some vital errand. After a few yards he dropped to the ground, dead. He had been shot while bending low to sight his weapon. Cabell's batteries also suffered. Lots of horses were down over there; men too.[15]

Hood, meanwhile, discovered Sickles's corps in his path, blocking the Emmitsburg Road, which ran northeasterly along the shallow valley between the parallel ridgelines. No one had told Hood about Sickles's move. He cast about for an alternative to what would now be a head-on assault. His Texas, Alabama, and Georgia regiments were among the hardest hitters in Lee's army, even if they were "a queer lot to look at, ragged and dirty," according to James Arthur Lyon Fremantle, a British guards officer traveling with Longstreet's corps. But Hood doubted whether even these matchless attacking troops could evict the Third Corps from the Devil's Den and go on to storm Little Round Top. One of Hood's scouts shortly turned up to report that, unlikely as it seemed, both Round Tops were undefended. Even the cavalry screen had withdrawn. Hood and Law thought they could skirt Sickles, curl around to the right, and overwhelm the enemy's unguarded flank.[16]

Hood sent to Longstreet for permission to try the indirect approach. By now the First Corps commander, twice snubbed, had resolved to follow Lee's instructions to the letter. When Hood persisted, Longstreet repeated his brusque first message: "General Lee's orders are to attack up the Emmitsburg Road." Law followed up with a formal protest for

Hood to forward, with his endorsement, to Longstreet. Again refusing to reconsider, he dispatched an aide to Hood with a peremptory order to get on with the battle.[17]

"I at once moved my brigade to the assault," Law wrote. "Just here the battle of Gettysburg was lost to Confederate arms."[18]

That was hindsight; hardly anyone thought so at the time. In fact, the operation got off to a promising start. Law's and Robertson's lines swept down from Warfield Ridge and over the rough ground in front of Little Round Top. Alexander's guns delivered a heavy fire into the left flank of the Third Corps. The federal batteries kept up an accurate return, though. Two of the guns were blown off their carriages. Moody reported he had too few men to handle his unwieldy twenty-four-pounder howitzers. Alexander sent to Barksdale, commanding the infantry brigade on his left, for assistance. Of the eight volunteers who came over to help work Moody's guns, five were dead or wounded by sunset.[19]

Robertson's brigade cleared the Devil's Den after thirty minutes' hard fighting and prepared to push on across Plum Run to Little Round Top. Lafayette McLaws's division, next in echelon, moved up to the attack. Quite suddenly, the Yankee line began to give way in the peach orchard and along the western edge of the wheatfield. Seeing it waver, Alexander shouted for the dead and wounded animals to be cut away from the teams, freeing the batteries to accompany the infantry. Without a doubt, Sickles's front was crumbling. From here the battle looked to be in its final phase. "I rode along my guns, urging the men to limber to the front as rapidly as possible, telling them we would 'finish the whole war this afternoon,'" Alexander remembered. Heart beating high, he led the guns off the firing line and into a sprint for the peach orchard. The drivers whipped the gaunt, undernourished artillery nags into a lather. Alexander would never again experience anything, anywhere, to match the wild exhilaration of that pounding charge. Guns bouncing, sparks flying, dust boiling up in brown clouds, the batteries gained the orchard, pulled up, loaded, and began loosing shotgun blasts of canister into the Yankee swarm.[20]

The Federals, however, had not been idle during Longstreet's drawn-out preparations, especially on Little Round Top. "It had been heavily reinforced while we were pottering around in sullen inactivity," Sorrel noted. Alexander caught his breath, wiped the sweat from his eyes, and trained his glass on the middle distance. What he saw brought him to earth with a thud. "It was not the enemy's main line we had broken," he discovered, but only Sickles's outposts. "That loomed up beyond us, a ridge giving good cover behind it & endless fine positions for batteries. And batteries in abundance were showing up & troops too seemed to be marching & fighting every where."[21]

Over toward Little Round Top, Law's attack had run into serious trouble. Alexander gave Law such support as he could. Directing the cannonade, he limped around on a sore right knee. A ball had passed between his legs, ripping trousers and drawers and skinning the knee. But he was otherwise unharmed. His guns continued to fire until it became too dark to see.[22]

As the First and Second brigades moved out of view toward the peach orchard, Chamberlain caught sight of a courier spurring to the front of the Third Brigade column. This turned out to be Warren's aide, Lt. Ranald Mackenzie. When Sickles denied his plea for troops to defend Little Round Top, Mackenzie went off in search of Sykes, who told him to apply to Barnes for a First Division brigade. The division commander could not be found. Chamberlain watched Strong Vincent gallop ahead to intercept Mackenzie.[23]

"What are your orders?" Vincent asked the courier.

"Where is General Barnes?"

"What are your orders?" Vincent insisted.

"General Sykes told me to direct General Barnes to send one of his brigades to occupy that hill yonder," Mackenzie said, motioning toward Little Round Top.

"I will take my brigade there."[24]

Out of sight over the hill, Evander Law's right-hand regiments, the 15th and 47th Alabama, were working their way around the federal left. Vincent's initiative now entered the eleven-hundred-man Third Brigade into the race for the key to the battlefield. Vincent rode ahead, up Little Round Top's northern slope, to reconnoiter the ground. Chamberlain passed the order for the 20th Maine to advance. Shouts ran down the column, pitched high to carry above the boom of the enemy cannon. "Fall in! Fall in! By the right flank! Double quick! March!" The regiment jogged along a rutted track, across a rough log bridge over Plum Run, and into a woods at the base of the hill.[25]

Chamberlain studied the landmark. Cleared of timber the previous autumn, Little Round Top had a ragged, scalped look. "It had a rough forbidding face, wrinkled with jagged ledges, bearded with mighty boul-

ders," he wrote; "even the smooth spots were strewn with fragments of
rock like the play-ground or battle-ground of giants." As the regiment
ascended, the enemy artillery (Henry's batteries, with help from Cabell's)
found the range. Several shells exploded overhead. Off to the right,
flame enveloped Sickles's lines in the peach orchard. Below, some five
hundred yards away, the battle for the Devil's Den built furiously toward
a resolution.[26]

Chamberlain rode at the head of the column with his brothers. Bits
of trees and dirt and fragments of granite were jetting about. He needed
a safe place for John, perhaps with Chaplain French and the ambulance
men. A solid shot hummed past. Chamberlain looked around for French.
The chaplain had already moved off, and at speed. A shell had detonated
near him, killing a horse. His own mount, catching its rider's alarm,
carried him swiftly down the line. Reining in abreast of Capt. Atherton
Clark, he began to babble about the near hit. Clark, preoccupied with
closing up the column, listened absently for a moment, then lost patience. "For Christ's sake, Chaplain, if you have any business, attend to
it," he snapped. French went on his way, not to be seen again that day.
Chamberlain dismissed John with instructions to make himself useful
among the wounded. "Shook hands with the Col & Tom & said good
bye—and fell back to the rear amid the whizzing and bursting of shells,"
John recorded in his diary. Inventing an errand, Chamberlain ordered
Tom to drop back to the tail of the column.

"Another shot might make it hard for mother," he told him.[27]

Vincent arrayed the Third Brigade in a quarter-circle just below the
crest, the 16th Michigan on the right, then the 44th New York and the
83rd Pennsylvania. Chamberlain led the 20th Maine beyond the rocky
summit and halfway down the southern slope, which fell away steeply
toward the thinly wooded valley that separated the Round Tops. Vincent
came up. He spoke, Chamberlain remembered, in an awed, faraway
voice. "I place you here," Vincent told him. "This is the left of the
Union line. You understand. You are to hold this ground at all costs."[28]

Chamberlain allowed himself a moment to think, then ordered the
first of the two improvisations that would prove decisive. He deployed
the 20th "on the right by file into line," an unusual evolution, slow to
execute, but with the advantage of bringing the ranks into position facing the enemy and ready to fire. To screen his left, he sent Company B
under Capt. Walter Morrill over toward the eastern base of Round Top.
With Morrill detached, the 20th Maine settled into line with 308 men

and two dozen officers—"all but the drummer boys and hospital attendants," Chamberlain noted. He released the prisoners and the provost
guard, too, including the two remaining Second Maine mutineers and
Lt. Addison Lewis of Company A, in arrest for overstaying a leave.[29]

Around to the right, Hood's lines approached the base of Little Round
Top opposite the front of the 44th New York. Rice joined Chamberlain
for a moment. They could see clearly that the enemy had turned the
Third Corps left. "The Devil's Den was a smoking crater," Chamberlain
recalled, "the Plum Run gorge a whirling maelstrom; one force was
charging our advanced batteries near the wheatfield; the flanking force
was pressing past the base of the Round Tops; all rolling toward us in
tumultuous waves." From a cottage-sized boulder on the summit, Warren
too saw the gray wave rolling toward Little Round Top. He ordered up
two rifled cannon of the Fifth U.S. Artillery, regulars under Lt. Charles
Hazlett, and diverted the 140th New York, the trailing regiment of a
brigade double-timing to Sickles's support. Hazlett's gunners found the
incline too steep for the horses, so they manhandled their ten-pounder
Parrotts up to the summit. Warren, thin, wiry, stronger than he looked,
put his own shoulder into one of the pieces. Hazlett soon had the Parrotts
blazing away.[30]

The Confederate barrage lifted. On cue, the gray lines, the Fourth,
44th, and 48th Alabama of Law's brigade and the Fourth and Fifth Texas
of Robertson's, rushed the Third Brigade center. Volley after volley
flashed out from the crest of Little Round Top. The fighting spread to
the 20th Maine's right, then along Chamberlain's entire front. After
several minutes of rapid firing, Lt. James Nichols, commanding Company
K, alerted Chamberlain to what looked like a strong enemy column
working around the 20th's left and rear. Chamberlain climbed atop a
boulder for a better view.[31]

Did he realize, balanced there on that man-high rock, that this would
be the transcendent moment of his life? Did he think, now, of all those
volunteer officers, not very different from himself, marking time in back-
waters, penned up in garrison at Fortress Monroe, shaking with fever in
some outpost on the Carolina coast, rotting under the subtropical sun
in the Louisiana bayous? Did he wonder at his own strange fortune?
Here he stood, hardworking, determined, restless, overachieving J. L.
Chamberlain, responsible for the neglected left flank of the imperiled
first army of the Republic, his shrunken regiment guarding the high
road to Washington. Brewer boy, Bowdoin student, Bangor seminarian,

professor of rhetoric, husband, father, amateur soldier, hero—this was heady stuff, a consummation no seer could have foretold. Here was glory enough even for doubting, doomsaying old Professor Smyth.

The gray-clad figures looming on the flank of the 20th Maine belonged to the 15th Alabama, reinforced by seven companies of the 47th Alabama under twenty-seven-year-old Col. William Oates. They fanned out over the low ground between the hills, tired and thirsty after a hot pursuit up Big Round Top of a detachment of the Second U.S. Sharpshooters. Pausing on the summit, looking north over the Yankee line, Oates had imagined the damage Alexander's artillery could do from there. As he considered the possibilities, a courier cantered up with a message from Law, commanding the division in place of Hood, who had been wounded in the first minutes of the advance. Law's instructions were to press on to Little Round Top without delay. So Oates had taken a long last look at the Yankee signalmen, energetically working their flags as Warren had told them to do, and moved obediently down the mountain.[32]

On the way, he caught a glimpse of the white tops of a train of supply wagons parked in the Yankee rear and detached a company to drive them into the Confederate lines. Meanwhile, the 20th Maine arrived on Little Round Top's southern slope and began putting up rough breastworks. Vincent's brigade might have beaten Oates to the spot by ten minutes, certainly by no more than a quarter of an hour.* Chamberlain, from his boulder, confirmed the enemy's appearance behind his left, then ordered his second improvisation. He told Spear to bend back the left-hand companies—that is, to refuse the endangered flank. Chamberlain placed the colors with their guard at a boulder on the far left, then ordered a sidestep all along the front. This thinned the line to a single rank, but stretched it to cover double the distance. When Oates's regiments swung into line of battle and charged, the 20th Maine's volley caught them full in the face.[33]

"They poured into us the most destructive fire I ever saw," said Oates.[34]

The attackers dove for cover. But even as the firing died away for the moment on Chamberlain's front, it built to a pitch of intensity on the right. There, Robertson's Texans had broken through the Devil's Den,

*After the war, Longstreet cut the margin even closer. "I was three minutes late in occupying Little Round Top," he told a group of Union Gettysburg veterans. "If I had got there first you would have had as much trouble in getting rid of me as I did in trying to get rid of you."

charged up the west slope of Little Round Top, and driven in Vincent's right-hand regiment, the 16th Michigan. The 140th New York arrived just as the attackers began to flow into the breach. With Paddy O'Rorke out front, the 140th charged the Texans, stopped their momentum, and chased them back down into the valley. The luckless O'Rorke dropped to the ground, shot dead in the first exchange. Vincent slumped, too, hit in the chest while trying to rally the 16th Michigan. A sharpshooter firing from the Devil's Den claimed O'Rorke's brigadier, Stephen Weed. Then Hazlett went down, killed as he bent low to catch Weed's last words.[35]

Opposite Chamberlain, Oates massed his Alabama demibrigade for a second try. Nearly seven hundred strong, the 15th and 47th Alabama sprang howling out of the rocks and scrub. The 20th Maine responded with a well-aimed fire and stopped the assault a dozen yards short of the line. A few minutes later the Alabamans launched a third assault, this time advancing as far as the 20th's fieldworks. The struggle became intensely personal, small groups swaying back and forth over a few yards of broken ground. "The lines [were] at times so near each other that the hostile gun barrels almost touched," Gerrish, fighting with Company H, recalled. The Confederates gradually forced back the 20th's front, so that some of the Maine dead lay within Oates's line.[36]

For the moment, Chamberlain had little to do. Orders were superfluous now, even if they could have been heard above the din. He considered it an essential part of his duty to project a mannequin-like image of coolness and courage that would inspirit the hard-pressed riflemen. No night class in a winter cantonment could teach this aspect of an officer's business. It seems to have come to Chamberlain by instinct. He stood near the regimental colors, sword in one hand, pistol in the other, a solitary figure: such a scene as might have caught the eye of a painter working in the heroic mode. As time passed, even some of those who had been there with him came to see it that way. Memory cleansed the battle of scorched flesh, bloody gristle, filth, nitric stench, terror, animal rage. "Every now and then I meet some small-sized, modest fellow in citizens clothes, that I knew only on horseback in the field, where he appeared to me almost like a centaur, and grand in physical strength," Warren, familiar with the phenomenon, wrote a dozen years after the war. Little Round Top veterans remembered Chamberlain, only just above the average in height, as a giant. Perhaps he was larger than life for an hour or so that afternoon, standing there next to the colors and flourishing his sword.[37]

At times there were more of the enemy than of Chamberlain's own men around him. Oates himself led a party of barking rebels into the 20th's line. The sound of the battle swelled to a roar, like the blast of a fire burning out of control. Rammers clanged against overheated barrels. Men shouted nonsense, sang snatches of hymns, called out the names of wives or mothers, prayed or cursed in hissing whispers. The Maine troops' sun-bleached blouses were dark with sweat, their lips and tongues coated with white residue from bitten-off cartridge ends, their faces gray with burned powder. During the lulls they moved among the wounded of both sides, stripping off their cartridges and—reversing the usual practice in this war—scavenging enemy muskets to replace the Enfields, which, as Chamberlain reported blandly after the battle, "did not stand service" well.[38]

The 20th Maine's casualty count passed one hundred. Chamberlain worried about his thinning line and diminishing supply of ammunition. He had been grazed on the right instep, and a ball had struck the scabbard of his sword, raising a painful bruise on his hip. (He escaped something worse. "I rested my gun on the rock and took steady aim," a veteran of the 15th Alabama wrote him long after the war. "I started to pull the trigger, but some queer notion stopped me. I am glad of it now, and hope you are.") The 20th Maine's center had been so shot away that only a few men remained to defend the colors. Chamberlain sent Tom and one of the sergeants separately down the line to recruit reinforcements in the right-hand companies and the neighboring 83rd Pennsylvania. The Pennsylvanians were vulnerable, too, though their commander promised to extend his left to maintain contact with the 20th. The center held—mostly, Chamberlain decided later, because the enemy failed to recognize its weakness.[39]

Oates had troubles of his own. An hour ago, on Round Top, he had envisioned the end of the Army of the Potomac. Now his regiments were being shot to rags. In the face of a fire so destructive that Oates's line "wavered like a man trying to walk against a strong wind," the Alabamans gave up their third effort and fell back again to regroup. Like Chamberlain, Oates had a brother with him here. Lt. John Oates had been shot in at least eight places; Billy Oates knew, when he passed the word to mass for a fourth charge, that his brother would not survive the battle.[40]

During the last lull, Chamberlain and George Washington Buck, the disrated sergeant, enacted one of those death-scene melodramas that meant so much to Civil War soldiers. Buck had a chest wound, and knew he was dying. He called out hoarsely to the colonel: "Tell my mother I did not die a coward." Chamberlain could hardly fail to respond to such a plea. He paused and bent down for a word with the true-hearted Buck.* "You die a sergeant," Chamberlain told him. "I promote you for faithful service and noble courage on the field of Gettysburg!" He had Buck carried away and laid with the other wounded in a grassy area on the reverse slope of the hill.[41]

Oates allowed Chamberlain no time to savor the bittersweet moment. "Forward, men, to the ledge," he shouted, and again the Alabamans rushed the south slope of Little Round Top. The 20th Maine responded as before. The charge lost impetus just as the 20th's fire began to fall off. All along the line, men were using up the last of their issue of sixty rounds. The 20th Maine had launched thousands of minié balls at the enemy. The Confederates returned thousands of their own, an intensity of fire that shredded trees to a height of five or six feet and sawed one specimen in half near its four-inch-thick base. Now, though, only a handful of Chamberlain's men were able to maintain a steady fire.[42]

And it looked as though the Confederates, stirring again down there in the scrub, were forming for a fifth try. Some of the Maine men prepared to use their muskets as clubs. As it turned out, the Alabama regiments were spent. They had shown almost superhuman endurance: the overnight march, the confused approach to Warfield Ridge, the trip up and down Round Top, four uphill charges. Still, so far as Chamberlain knew, they were as dangerous as ever. Even a halfhearted charge might overwhelm the worn-down 20th Maine. He decided that surprise, psychological shock, and the bayonet were his best weapons. As he prepared to use them, the lieutenant commanding the color company sought permission to range ahead and collect one or two of the wounded.[43]

"In a moment," Chamberlain told him. "I am about to order a charge."

He stepped up to the colors. "The men turned toward me," he wrote. "One word was enough—'Bayonet!' It caught like fire, and swept along the ranks."[44]

Gerrish remembered it differently. Chamberlain called out the full series of commands, according to Gerrish: first "Fix bayonets" and, a moment later, when the low rattle of metal striking metal had run all

---

*Justice eventually caught up with Buck's nemesis, Quartermaster Brown. After the war, he served hard time in the Maine State Prison for robbery.

along the line, "Charge, bayonets, charge." The men hesitated, Gerrish thought. Then a subaltern went forward, shouting for the others to follow. With a wild yell the 20th Maine lurched down the slope, the left wing, in Chamberlain's phrase, swinging out "like a great gate on its hinges." Some of the Confederates stood gaping at the blue line careering toward them, bayonets flashing in the evening sun. A few resumed firing. Others turned and jogged off toward the rear. An officer aimed his big Navy revolver at Chamberlain's face. He missed, or the weapon misfired. With his free hand he offered Chamberlain his sword.[45]

Morrill and his flank guards now made a timely appearance, opening a close-range fire into the Confederate left and rear. Oates, assailed unexpectedly from this quarter, began to see enemies everywhere, volleying and thundering to the right and to the left of him, in his front and behind him too. In his memoirs, he compared the predicament of his 15th Alabama to that of the gallant six hundred at Balaklava.* "Some were struck simultaneously with two or three balls from different directions," he recalled. He had no choice but to retreat. "When the signal was given," he admitted, "we ran like a herd of wild cattle."[46]

The 20th Maine came on, sweeping the valley and, improbably, clearing the entire Third Brigade front of the enemy. The regiment collected scores of prisoners before Chamberlain, chary of a counterattack that might cut him off, called a halt in front of the 44th New York, still in position just below the crest of Little Round Top. Panting, thirsty, sweat-soaked, weak-kneed, the men staggered back up the hill. Many slumped to the ground and fell into a narcotic sleep. It was about six-thirty, and the battle was over here.[47]

The losses could be roughly tallied: for the 20th Maine, ninety or more wounded, between thirty and forty killed or mortally wounded. Behind the lines, at a Fifth Corps field hospital, John Chamberlain had overcome an initial attack of nausea and gone to work among the victims. They arrived in an endless stream. "There were wounded men pouring in from every quarter all needing some help a cup of water or pocket handkerchief," he wrote. "Men without an eye or nose or leg or arm or with mangled head or body would constantly attract your sympathy each looking a little worse than the one that went before." He eventually counted fifty men from his brother's regiment.[48]

There were some fifty Confederate dead in the 20th Maine's immedi-

*"All of us, on both sides, who were in such hot places as that were made to see double and are disposed to exaggerate in favor of our respective sides," Oates conceded.

ate front. The 15th and 47th Alabama reported a total of 123 men killed
and wounded, doubtless a low figure. Chamberlain claimed his regiment
alone took more than three hundred prisoners from five different units.
Altogether, Hood's division lost more than two thousand killed,
wounded, and missing in the July 2 attacks. McLaws lost roughly the same
number. Sickles's two divisions suffered forty-two hundred casualties before
the Confederates finally drove them from the salient. The First and Second
brigades of the First Division, sent into the wheatfield to support the Third
Corps, together reported some 550 casualties; the number of killed,
wounded, and missing in Vincent's brigade exceeded 350.[49]

At nightfall, Hood's division held the Devil's Den and the peach orchard. Law's brigade clung to the northwestern slope of Big Round Top.
But Longstreet's attacks had achieved nothing decisive. On Little Round
Top, James Rice approached Chamberlain through the shadows. The
taller mountain oppressed him. He had asked a supporting brigade, five
regiments of Pennsylvania Reserves under Col. Joseph Fisher, to occupy
it. For some reason Fisher had refused. Rice ordered Chamberlain to
take the depleted 20th Maine up Big Round Top and hold the summit.[50]

The 20th ascended before moonrise, advancing in darkness over rough
ground with bayonets fixed. When enemy pickets opened an uncertain
fire, the regiment rushed the crest and took another two dozen prisoners. Chamberlain deployed his 198 survivors among the rocks and trees
and sent to Rice for ammunition and infantry support. He could hear
the Confederates, some three hundred yards away to the right, improving
their works, piling rock upon rock. One of Fisher's regiments approached, then turned back when the enemy on the lower slope discharged a volley or two. Eventually the 83rd Pennsylvania and the 44th
New York came up to fill out the line. The men slept on their arms.
Chamberlain dozed between half-hourly reports from his pickets.[51]

The opposing lines exchanged a noisy fire at sunrise on Friday the
third, but the musketry soon gave way to a fragile calm. Relief arrived
late in the morning. Rice met Chamberlain at the base of the mountain
and took him by the hand. "Your gallantry was magnificent," the brigade
commander told him, "and your courage and skill saved us." Possibly.
Anyway, Billy Oates thought so. He wrote after the war that the 20th
Maine had spared the Army of the Potomac a decisive defeat. Sykes also
commended him. Adelbert Ames sent a congratulatory note. "I did want
to be with you and see your splendid conduct in the field. God bless
you and the dear old regiment," Ames wrote. "I am receiving all sorts

of praise," Chamberlain wrote Fannie the next day, "but am bearing it meekly." To her, though, he could not contain his pride. "I shall tell of some little incidents, such as my taking officers prisoners & receiving swords & pistols & c.," he promised Fannie. "We captured one whole rebel Regt."[52]

He heard discouraging medical reports about Vincent. Tom survived unhurt. The Second Maine mutineers outlived the battle; so did Lieutenant Lewis, a brave if slovenly officer. ("He may perhaps be allowed to retain his present rank," Chamberlain wrote Governor Coburn, "but cannot expect to be promoted.") John, more or less recovered from Gettysburg's assault on his senses, continued to nurse the wounded, carrying water, rigging canvas screens against the scorching sun, praying over the extreme cases. Their fortitude surprised and touched him. "They will never believe their case utterly hopeless," he wrote. "I [saw] them walking around with broken skulls, with eyes & parts of their face gone with balls in their bodies & through them. They would say, 'Well, I recon, a scratch or so, how do you come off old chap?' They are all very patient and uncomplaining." From the 20th Maine, Billings and Kendall, Estes and Steele, Noyes and Linscott and George Washington Buck needed no succor. They were dead, along with thirty or so others.[53]

"The 20th has immortalized itself," Chamberlain boasted to Fannie. Sometime after one o'clock Friday afternoon, the 20th Maine filed into a woods behind the left center of the Cemetery Ridge line. By then a terrific cannonade had opened, and eleven brigades of Confederate infantry were massing for a famous charge.[54]

With the coming of night, Alexander turned his attention to the details of recovery. He oversaw the care of the wounded (among them Pichegru Woolfolk, hit in the shoulder), the burial of the dead, the shooting of wounded horses, the salvaging of harness from dead animals, the refilling of the ammunition chests, and, finally, the distribution of hard bread and bacon. Servants in search of their masters were a feature of the landscape that night. Alexander's own, inquiring along the line for "Marse Ned," eventually found him in the peach orchard. Charley delivered a haversack of rations and his other mount, Meg Merrilies, to replace Dixie, out of action with a deep gash in the hip. Thinking Dixie would heal, Alexander spared her a bullet.[55]

Later, at Longstreet's bivouac, he learned that Lee intended to renew the battle in the morning, using Pickett's fresh division as a spearhead.

There were no details, but his impression was that the assault would take up where today's had left off, just north of the peach orchard. Longstreet evidently had taken time for a word with Walton, for he instructed Alexander to find a place in the firing line for the Washington Artillery. This and other business occupied him until an hour after midnight, when he built a bed of fence rails and, with Dixie's saddle for a pillow, managed a couple of hours' sleep. First light revealed that he had run some twenty of the guns into exposed positions on the ridge, vulnerable to enfilade from Cemetery Hill. In a near panic, he moved them before the enemy could see well enough to penalize him for the error. A little later, Pendleton came along to inspect the line. He approved Alexander's arrangements without alteration.[56]

Further adjustments were required later in the morning. Lee had decided overnight to shift the point of attack northward, toward the federal right-center on Cemetery Hill. Motioning toward an umbrella-shaped clump of trees that marked the spot, Lee told Alexander to lay down a converging fire there. Alexander repositioned the guns without mishap, though the enemy batteries threw over an occasional shell. By ten o'clock he had the five First Corps battalions in line on gently rolling ground along a mile-long arc: from south to north, Henry's opposite Little Round Top, his own (under Huger) in the peach orchard, the Washington Artillery (under a subdued Walton, who made no attempt to supervise guns other than his own), Cabell's, and, finally, Dearing's battalion, which had come up with Pickett. He chose to stay with Dearing's guns astride the Emmitsburg Road, figuring he could best observe the effect of the fire from there. Pendleton offered him nine short-range howitzers from Hill's corps. He posted these guns in reserve, to be brought up, when the time came, to advance with the infantry.[57]

Lee had high expectations for the bombardment. "It was not meant simply to make a noise," as Alexander understood it, "but to try & cripple [the enemy]—to tear him limbless." As usual, ammunition stocks were limited. He could count only on what he had in the limbers and caissons. Subtracting canister, useless for long-range work, he estimated a hundred rounds per gun—enough for ninety minutes' rapid firing. Longstreet told him to keep one of Pickett's couriers at hand, to carry the word to Pickett when the moment came to launch the assault.[58]

In later years, Alexander scathingly criticized the planning for the July 3 battle. Lee could hardly have chosen a worse point of attack, he argued; the infantry had to cross fourteen hundred yards of pasture and grainlands swept by cannon fire from the full two-mile length of Cemetery Ridge. Lee's artillery arrangements were faulty, too. Hill's guns were underemployed. Ewell's artillery, which could have taken the federal line in enfilade, contributed little to the result. It had been Pendleton's responsibility to arrange for all the artillery to work in concert. In any event, fifty-six guns of the Second and Third corps never fired a shot. Alexander learned afterward that only one of Ewell's five artillery battalions joined in the bombardment that preceded Pickett's Charge.[59]

Still, he expected success that afternoon, though he knew the enemy had as many guns as the Confederates, with more and better ammunition and a superior position on high ground, behind fieldworks, in a compact line along which infantry could be rushed to threatened points. "The fact is that like all the rest of the army I believed that it would come out all right, because General Lee had planned it," he explained. Fremantle, the British observer, sensed something even more damaging than this unqualified trust in Lee: an "utter contempt," he put it, "felt for the enemy by all ranks."[60]

Longstreet was the exception. He had profound respect for the Yankees up there on Cemetery Ridge. Alexander saw little of the First Corps commander during the early part of the day. Longstreet was still sunk in gloom, even less inclined to attack today than he had been yesterday. He had failed again to persuade Lee to abandon the offensive. "The enemy is there," Lee told him, gesturing toward Cemetery Ridge, "and I am going to attack him there." Alexander, meanwhile, took encouragement from a camp rumor that Lee meant to throw every available rifleman into the assault. In fact, Longstreet had fewer than fifteen thousand infantry. He claimed, later, to have told Lee that no fifteen thousand men anywhere could carry Cemetery Hill. Whether he said that or not, Longstreet now conveyed to Alexander his absolute lack of confidence in the project. Longstreet's first note, sent at around noon, rocked Alexander back on his heels.[61]

> Colonel. If the artillery fire does not have the effect to drive off the enemy or greatly demoralize him, so as to make our effort pretty certain, I would prefer that you should not advise Gen. Pickett to make the charge. I shall rely a great deal upon your good judgement to determine the matter, & shall expect you to let Pickett know when the moment offers.[62]

Reading this, Alexander experienced a sort of epiphany, a flash of insight that revealed all the manifold hazards of the enterprise. "It was no longer Gen. Lee's inspiration," he realized, "but my cold judgement based on what I was going to see." Longstreet, of course, often turned to Alexander for advice on technical and engineering questions. Aleck liked being taken into his general's counsel. But this carried matters several stages further. The responsibility for touching off a battle belonged to Lee. Alexander wanted no part of it, though all at once he could think of a dozen reasons for canceling the attack.[63]

He showed the note to Ambrose R. Wright, a Georgia brigadier who was with him when Longstreet's courier rode up. After talking it over with Wright, he sent this reply:

> General. I will only be able to judge of the effect of our fire on the enemy by his return fire as his infantry is but little exposed to view, & the smoke will obscure the field. If, as I infer from your note, there is any alternative to this attack, it should be carefully considered before opening our fire, for it will take all the arty ammunition we have left to test this one thoroughly & if the result is unfavorable we will have none left for another effort—& even if this one is entirely successful it can only be so at a bloody cost.[64]

The courier returned shortly, carrying a second note from Longstreet. Alexander raced through it, then handed the scrap over to Wright. It read:

> Colonel. The intention is to advance the infantry if the Arty. has the desired effect of driving the enemy's off, or having other effect such as to warrant us in making the attack. When that moment arrives advise Gen. P. and of course advance such Artillery as you can use in aiding the attack.[65]

"He has put the responsibility back on you," Wright said. Longstreet surely knew Alexander would be unable to offer unqualified assurance that the Yankee guns had been silenced. With luck, he thought he might manage a temporary suppression of the enemy fire. Achieving that, and with help from Hill and Ewell, the attack might possibly succeed. Wright's brigade had pierced the Cemetery Ridge line yesterday, though it had quickly been driven back. Alexander asked Wright to assess the odds of another try.

"Well, it's mostly a question of supports," Wright told him. "It's not as hard to get there as it looks. The real difficulty is to stay there after you get there—for the whole infernal Yankee army is up there in a bunch."[66]

The exchange with Wright seemed to restore Alexander's balance. He decided to settle the question of Pickett before the cannonade opened. Once the firing commenced, there could be no turning back. Then, in an act of faith, he convinced himself that Lee had attended to all the details, including the critical supporting assignments for Hill and Ewell. Lee could see the entire battlefield. He held all the threads in his hands. Colonels commanding corps artillery, however able, had no business interfering with the plans of great generals. Meddling colonels stood little chance of ever becoming generals themselves. "Half the day had been spent in preparation," Alexander said. "I determined to cause no loss of time by any indecision on my own part." Still, he made his customary thorough job of it. Before answering Longstreet, he rode rearward for a word with Maj. Gen. George C. Pickett, quondam hero of the San Juan Island Pig War.[67]

Pickett's war career had fallen some way short of distinguished. Some of his colleagues found him dull-witted and trivial, though Longstreet seems to have been fond of him. Notwithstanding his long, girlish, perfumed ringlets, Fremantle thought him "altogether a rather desperate-looking character." Alexander meant just to "feel his pulse," as he put it, about the assault. He did not mention Longstreet's forebodings. Pickett, he saw at once, could barely suppress his excitement. His spirits were soaring and he seemed certain of success. At 12:40 P.M. by his watch, Alexander dispatched this note to Longstreet:

> General. When our arty. fire is at its best I will advise Gen.
> Pickett to advance.[68]

Pickett formed his three Virginia brigades in two lines. Pettigrew massed on his left, with Trimble's two brigades behind the left center. Wilcox held his brigade in reserve, to be employed where it would do the most good. Probably as a salve, Longstreet assigned Walton and the Washington Artillery the honor of opening the bombardment. The booms of two signal guns duly sounded, one after the other.[69]

Alexander marked the time as one o'clock. "As suddenly as an organ strikes up in church," he recalled, "the grand roar followed from all the guns." The Confederate line seemed all at once to erupt. "All their batteries were soon covered with smoke, through which the flashes were incessant," wrote Henry Hunt, Meade's artillery chief, who witnessed the display from Little Round Top. The guns, leaping and bucking with each discharge, fired at a steady rate of fifty rounds an hour. Hunt's batteries responded tentatively at first, then with increasing weight. There were, again today, more enemy guns in action than Alexander had expected. He had planned to sustain the cannonade for fifteen minutes or so, then unleash Pickett. He could see now that a far greater effort would be required to silence even some of the federal guns. Alexander seriously underestimated the duration of the bombardment. Possibly his watch stopped. Possibly, in the excitement, he simply misread it. For whatever reason, he lost track of a full sixty minutes. The cannonade continued for nearly two hours. "I could not make up my mind to order the infantry out into a fire I did not believe they could face, in such a hot sun," he wrote. He held back, hoping for some outward sign of success, for as long as he dared. Alexander put the time of the first of his two notes to Pickett at 1:25 P.M. It was probably 2:25. The message read:

> If you are to advance at all you must come at once, or we will not be able to support you as we ought. But the enemy's fire has not slackened materially, & there are still 18 guns firing from the cemetery.[70]

He had reserved the nine howitzers for this moment, but the aide he sent to guide them to the front returned to report that they were nowhere to be found. Alexander learned later that "some general" (it turned out to be Pendleton) had sent the guns to a more sheltered place without telling him. He now considered how he could replace the absent flying column, which he had expected to be limbered up, chests full, and ready to charge.[71]

As Alexander puzzled out the problem, the federal fire seemed to slacken. Taking up his spyglass, he thought he could detect movement in Hunt's batteries near the clump of trees. At least some of those eighteen guns appeared to be pulling out. "If he does not run fresh batteries in there in five minutes, this is our fight," he told himself. The minutes passed. A gap of some four hundred yards opened in the Yankee line. On this evidence, Alexander decided the cannonade had inflicted more hurt than he had supposed possible. By now many, perhaps most, of the federal guns had stopped firing. He sent a second note to Pickett:

> The 18 guns have been driven off. For God's sake come on quick, or we cannot support you. Ammunition nearly out.[72]

Alexander's bombardment *had* done substantial damage to the batteries near the clump of trees. There were a dozen spectacular caisson explosions. Many horses were hit. The commander of the federal Second Corps artillery reported one-third of his men killed or wounded. But much of the shooting went long, into the rear echelons. The frontline infantry suffered little. The falling off of the federal fire had come by order of Henry Hunt, partly, perhaps, as a ruse—it fooled Alexander—and partly to conserve ammunition for use against the Confederate infantry.[73]

Three o'clock approached. Alexander waited for Pickett's brigades to turn up, praying the Virginians would be more punctual than Hood had been yesterday. Presently Longstreet joined him at his post among James Dearing's batteries. Alexander told him some of the Yankee guns had traveled; Pickett could expect a fair start. Longstreet made no reply. Alexander added that most of his batteries had burned down their ammunition stocks to between five and fifteen rounds per gun. This caught Longstreet's attention. He seized on it as a last chance to stop what he regarded, rightly it turned out, as folly.[74]

"Go and halt Pickett right where he is, & replenish your ammunition," Longstreet told him.

"General, we can't do that. We nearly emptied the trains last night."

Longstreet did not answer for a moment. Then he said, "I don't want to make this attack. I believe it will fail. I do not see how it can succeed. I would not make it even now, but that General Lee has ordered & expects it."

Again, Alexander had the impression that, at a word from him, Longstreet would suspend the operation. He said nothing. Longstreet would have to fight his battle alone. Pickett's arrival broke the awkward spell. His division emerged from the shelter of the woods, advancing in common time, about a hundred yards a minute, with lines dressed and flags unfurled.[75]

Alexander mounted and spurred over for a final word with one of Pickett's brigadiers, Richard Garnett, an old army acquaintance. Garnett had taken a terrific kick from a horse a day or two before, and he had left an ambulance to lead his brigade in this charge. Alexander wished him luck, then turned back to collect guns for the advance. He detailed those with at least fifteen remaining long-range projectiles, eighteen guns altogether, to accompany the infantry. The others were to worry the federal artillery until Pickett closed. With this last order, he cantered

over to join the guns pushing forward on Pickett's right, across the valley
beyond the Emmitsburg Road.[76]

The enemy guns poured an accurate fire into the oncoming waves of
infantry, though the shelling did not break up the formations. Rifles
posted on Little Round Top did the most damage, tearing into the flank
of Kemper's brigade on Pickett's right. Kemper's command left a trail
of dead and wounded as it advanced. Alexander never forgot his encounter with one of Kemper's infantrymen. His mouth and chin had been
shot away and he sat, stunned and mute, with his back to a rail fence.
"As I halted my horse this poor fellow looked up at me, & I even noted
powder smut showing on the white skin of the cheek," Alexander remembered. He studied the victim for a moment, then continued on
across the valley. The guns were taking heavy casualties, in men and
horses too.[77]

The Confederates swept upslope through the high grass. A blue haze
of musketry smoke rose and spread over the federal line. Alexander saw
an enemy column come out from behind breastworks and swing into
line of battle on Pickett's right flank. He directed a sharp fire into these
Yankees—Stannard's Vermont brigade, he learned later. By now he
could see almost nothing through the billows of smoke, though the
sound of the firing told him the battle had reached a crisis. Building
steadily, it rose to the loudest roar he had ever heard.

It was a short, unequal struggle. "Fredericksburg!" some vengeful Federals shouted. Stannard's brigade formed one-half of the vise that
pressed the life out of Pickett's Charge. The other half, two resourceful
infantry regiments and a detachment of skirmishers, aimed volley after volley into the Confederate left. Garnett was shot and killed near the stone
wall that here formed the main federal line. Another of Alexander's old
army comrades, Lewis Armistead, leaped the wall and dropped to the
ground, mortally wounded, within arm's reach of the muzzle of a Yankee
cannon. Lost Cause diehards afterwards memorialized the spot as the
high water mark of the Confederacy. Alexander kept up the cannonade
a little longer, until the falling off of musketry and the appearance of
the first of Pickett's fugitives convinced him the charge had failed. In
an "absurd and tragic" postscript (Alexander's words), Wilcox advanced
his brigade, far too late to do any good. Another two hundred men
killed and wounded were added to the Confederate casualty lists. As
Wilcox's troops recoiled, Alexander ordered all his guns to cease firing,
to save their few remaining rounds to cover the retreat.[78]

The charge cost more than six thousand casualties altogether, close to half of the total engaged. Pickett survived. He had hovered about in the rear of his division during the final agonizing phase of the battle. Now, dazed, seemingly in shock though physically untouched, he proceeded slowly back to Seminary Ridge. Lee rode up, alone, to Alexander's post near the Emmitsburg Road. Expecting a counterstroke, he had shaken off his retinue and come to rally the beaten infantry. Alexander thought Lee actually *wanted* the Yankees to attack. "He had the combative instinct in him as strongly developed as any man living," he said of Lee. A stranger, neatly dressed, equipped with field glasses and a pocket pistol, presently joined Lee and Alexander. The three spoke at length, but Lee did not introduce the younger men (the stranger was the British Coldstream Guards officer Fremantle), perhaps, Alexander thought, "on account of my disreputable pants with my naked knee showing." He did look more like a powder boy than a senior officer, begrimed, coatless, sweat-drenched, his symbols of rank barely visible on the collar of his gray shirt.[79]

Lee guided his horse Traveller into the backwash, calling out words of encouragement to the survivors. "It was all my fault," Alexander heard him say. He considered that a fair assessment, then and later. "Had [Pickett] been properly supported the result would have been very different," Alexander wrote his father two weeks after the battle, echoing Ambrose Wright. Fremantle thought Lee's bearing sublime at this critical moment, when it seemed certain the Yankees would come booming down from Cemetery Ridge. "If the enemy or their general had shown any enterprise, there is no saying what might have happened," Fremantle wrote. The enemy did not come.[80]

Alexander ordered the horses watered and ammunition brought up. Disorganized infantry continued to flow past. The Yankee guns ceased firing. Alexander could not fathom why. True, he expended ammunition as though he were paying for it, shell by shell, out of his own pocket. "But that was because our supply was always scant," he explained. "It is generally the poorest economy in the world to save ammunition in battles." At dusk he ordered the batteries towed to concealed positions behind Seminary Ridge. Finishing long after dark, he went off in search of his battalion. Huger had gone into bivouac near a big barn being used as a field hospital. In two days the battalion had lost more than a quarter of its complement in killed and wounded, about 140 men. (The dead included the sergeant whom Alexander had punished for straggling.)

Losses of horses were great, too—more than a hundred. Alexander, overcome with fatigue, discovered a heap of wheat straw inside the barn, lay down in it, and slept.[81]

The 20th Maine survived Alexander's cannonade without injury, and had no part in the July 3 battle. On Saturday the fourth, Independence Day, Chamberlain led the regiment on a reconnaissance beyond the peach orchard toward Seminary Ridge. He encountered none of the enemy, but only dead and wounded men and horses. In one small field he counted five hundred dead of both sides, and a thousand dead animals. All around, corpses were beginning to bloat and blacken in the heat. Blood and carrion drew clouds of flies. The remains of a burnt-out barn held several charred bodies—wounded men, evidently, who had been unable to escape the flames.[82]

Returning to Little Round Top, the regiment buried its own dead, each grave marked, as at Fredericksburg, with a headboard made of ammunition boxes, the victim's name carved into the soft wood. Chamberlain sent out details to dig shallow graves for the enemy dead. He visited some of the casualties, billeted on farms in the neighborhood. After noon, rain began to fall in swaths, further evidence of what veterans of Fredericksburg and Chancellorsville already knew: that sustained heavy cannonading disturbed the atmosphere and created the conditions for a deluge. At the Fifth Corps hospital, John Chamberlain helped move some of the wounded into a grove where they could be sheltered from the downpour. "Never mind," one man told him. "We are not long for this world."[83]

John, who had heard no news of his brothers, made his way to the 20th Maine's camp later in the day. "If I ever shook hands heartily I did so then as I looked on Lawrence & Thomas alive," he wrote in his diary. He spent the night there, wet and trembling with chills. Overwrought and physically ill, he could be counted a Gettysburg casualty too. John felt strong enough to accompany the regiment on the march next day, Sunday. "The further I rode the thicker the ground was strewn with dead & dying with muskets whole & broken & bent & shattered with knapsacks & blankets & rubbers, with shells & shot, & now & then bullets of iron that came from the bursted shells & some of those deadly explosive rifle shots the Rebels use with such deadly effect," he recorded. Minié balls and shrapnel recognized no distinctions, John discovered: "Rebels & Yankees [were] side by side, the rough features of the hardy working man & the pale delicate lineaments of the student or the family pet.''[84]

All too quickly, the frightfulness became commonplace. Recovering his nerve, John began collecting letters, gilt buttons, and other souvenirs from corpses. "One man got 60$ in greenbacks & some Confederate money and a very chaste gold ring (ladies)," he reported. In the ruins of a burned farm building, experienced scavengers scraped charred bodies with sticks, rubbing away the blackened flesh where the pockets were supposed to be, hoping for "some prize wh. had withstood the flames." John appropriated a tent and two rubber ground sheets. The stench was tremendous, indescribably vile. He grew accustomed to that, too, and noted with surprise that his appetite had returned.[85]

The column trudged on into the night, halting finally near Marsh Creek, ten miles from Cemetery Ridge. Wet weather and indecision stalled the pursuit on the sixth. Chamberlain used the time to write his battle report, while the details of the Little Round Top fight were still vivid. He said farewell to John, who turned back for Washington. Rain fell intermittently. Strong Vincent died in a field hospital July 7. "I grieve much for him," Chamberlain wrote Fannie; he asked her to post a note of condolence to Vincent's widow in Erie. The Fifth Corps passed near the old Antietam battlefield on the tenth. In the van, the 20th Maine skirmished with enemy rear guards on the Sharpsburg pike, losing two men killed and six wounded. "We are now making rapid marches & expecting another big fight somewhere in this vicinity," Chamberlain wrote the Maine adjutant general from near Williamsport on the Potomac.[86]

Meade had given the Confederates a long headstart on the retreat, and still more time to entrench along the flooded Potomac. By daybreak on the fourth, wagonloads of Lee's wounded were en route to Virginia, while the Confederate main body stood in line, expecting Independence Day fireworks from Meade. In the event, he only sent out light reconnaissances. Longstreet's corps withdrew from Seminary Ridge after dark, in what Alexander recalled as one of the heaviest rainfalls he had ever experienced.[87]

The battalion parked in a soggy meadow overlooking the Fairfield Turnpike to await its place in the line of march. Alexander, Huger, and a couple of others got hold of an old door and sat on it through the night, the rain, as warm as milk, streaming off their rubber coats. Every half hour or so, someone splashed down to the road to see what infantry command chanced to be passing. The battalion finally entered the traffic stream at six o'clock Sunday morning, the fifth. Alexander managed to get off a telegram to Bettie, knowing she would be frantic for word from him. Stopping at a sparsely stocked country store along the route, he bought bits of thread and yarn for her, items that had become almost impossible to obtain in Virginia.[88]

The column pushed on until one o'clock in the morning of Tuesday, July 6, halting near Monterey Springs after nineteen hours on the road. Through the mist, Alexander could see the lights of a large spa hotel up in the hills. It struck him as incredible that a normal business should be going on there. To compound the insult, he mislaid his hat and had to resume the march with a handkerchief tied around his head. The battalion continued southward through rain and mud for another twelve hours, clearing Hagerstown, Maryland, before stopping for the night. There were scattered fights as Meade's cavalry brushed against the rear guards.[89]

The leading elements of the Army of Northern Virginia reached the Potomac July 7, and took up positions covering the crossings between Williamsport and Falling Waters. After several days of rain, the river ran far too deep for fording. The Yankees had broken up the pontoon bridge at Falling Waters, and it would be several days before a new one could be improvised. Lee summoned Alexander to help lay out a line of battle. Meade granted him three days of undisturbed work. "The enemy pursued us as a mule goes on the chase of a grizzly bear—as if catching up to us was the last thing he wanted to do," Alexander said. The first federal infantry did not appear until the tenth. Alexander encountered Lee in an oak wood that morning, a Friday. The commanding general greeted him with unusual warmth, then questioned him closely about the strength of the lines. Alexander assured him they would hold.[90]

The sun shone finally. Cherries and raspberries were ripe and abundant. Alexander foraged corn, potatoes, and fat chickens from a farmer one bright afternoon, stewed it all together in a great pot, and served it up to all comers that evening. Some of the guests remembered that ragout as the best meal they had ever eaten. Meade threatened, but did not attack. Meanwhile, fatigue parties were at work stripping the siding from every old house and barn in the district. When the engineers nailed the last rough plank over the pontoons on the night of July 13, the army tramped dryshod to the Virginia side.[91]

Alexander argued, later, that Meade should have attacked along the Potomac for all he was worth. He could have ended the war at Falling Waters. Coupled with the fall of Vicksburg on July 4, the destruction of Lee's army might have finished the Confederacy. At the time, many veterans of the Army of the Potomac assumed the last great battle had been fought. "This war, I suppose you can see, is rapidly coming to a close issue, & the *heavy fighting* is nearly over," Chamberlain wrote Fannie. The forecast turned out to be hopelessly wrong. Chamberlain and the others had failed to account for the Confederates' extraordinary recuperative powers. "Our next move I can't conjecture, tho' I think Gen. Lee means to fight, and we are all anxious for it, thinking that we had not a fair showing at Gettysburg," Alexander wrote his father in a letter dated July 17, just two weeks to the day after Pickett's disastrous charge.[92]

Part III

———✦———

CATACLYSM

For thirty days it has been one funeral procession past me, and it has been too much.
—Gen. Gouverneur K. Warren

CHAPTER 8

BARREN WINTER

———◆———

ALEXANDER
EAST TENNESSEE, 1863–64

"**I** DO NOT THINK WE CAN EVER SUCCESS-
fully invade," Alexander wrote home after Gettysburg. The final stages
of the retreat, from Bunker Hill to Culpeper, eighty-nine miles, were as
difficult and dangerous as the early ones: pelting rain, swollen streams,
frequent skirmishing. Breakdowns of horses forced Alexander to draft
some officers' mounts into the battery teams. Straggling and illness were
widespread. Lee, Alexander thought, wore an anxious look, as though
he had begun, for the first time, to doubt the army's ability to endure
and fight on.[1]

The battalion rested for a few days, then moved on to Orange Court
House and five restorative weeks in camp. Alexander supervised the overhaul of the guns, carriages, and caissons, resumed his experiments with
fuses, and devised a method of raising the light howitzers on skids so
they could be worked as mortars. He engineered the transfer of his
friend Joe Haskell to be battalion adjutant. The mess assimilated another
new member, an English officer named Stephen Winthrop, on extended
leave from H.M. 22nd Regiment of Foot. Looking for a war and liking
long odds, Winthrop ran the blockade at Charleston, made his way north
to Lee's army, and attached himself to Longstreet during the Gettysburg
battle. Longstreet passed him along to Alexander. Stout, muscular, energetic, with an oval face and a prominent nose, Winthrop craved the
stimulus of controlled violence, on the battlefield and elsewhere. He was,
for instance, a skilled butcher of livestock. "If anything had to be killed

he loved to do it," not out of cruelty, Alexander noted, drawing a fine distinction, "but destructiveness!"[2]

The stragglers caught up, the sick got better, the lightly wounded returned to duty, rations improved. Lee lost that worried look. Alexander remained as confident as ever. "There were still a few men left in the country who could be brought into the ranks," he observed, "and boys were growing up every day to be fit for soldiers." Longstreet granted him a five-day furlough to run down to Bowling Green to see Bettie, now entering her eighth month of pregnancy. He served on an artillery board; as always, technical work of this sort engrossed him. Alexander formed a friendship with one of the members, Col. Snowden Andrews, a rare and lucky officer with a tale to tell. When a shell fragment tore open his side at Cedar Mountain in August 1862, Andrews became one of the few men ever to see his own liver and survive to describe it.[3]

Longstreet revived his proposal to shift large forces west, this time to the relief of Braxton Bragg, who had fallen back to the vicinity of Chattanooga under pressure from the federal Army of the Cumberland under William S. Rosecrans. Lee endorsed the idea, though Richmond withheld final approval for three weeks. Orders to march for the railroad at Petersburg only reached Alexander the night of September 8. The battalion struck tents early on the ninth. Huger commanded on the march while Alexander, with Longstreet's permission, returned to Mrs. Woolfolk's for a few extra days with Bettie, due to give birth any moment. McLaws's and Hood's divisions went on ahead, some elements entraining on the eighth and ninth; the first troops reached Atlanta the evening of the twelfth. Alexander's battalion loaded September 17, the guns lashed to flatcars, the horses in stock cars, the men in boxcars. Longstreet left the Washington Artillery in Petersburg with the survivors of Pickett's division, finally disencumbering himself of Walton, who continued to carry the title of corps artillery chief.[4]

The Federals, meanwhile, had seriously complicated matters for Longstreet, who had assured Lee he would reach Bragg in two days. Ambrose Burnside, transferred west to command the little Army of the Ohio after the Fredericksburg debacle, occupied Knoxville on September 2, severing direct rail connections from Richmond to Chattanooga. Burnside's presence in Knoxville discounted the Confederacy's sole strategic advantage, that of interior lines by which forces could be moved rapidly from point to point. Denied the direct 550-mile route, Aleck Lawton, now army quartermaster general, sent the First Corps on a long roundabout through the Carolinas and Atlanta. The route followed light lines of varying gauges, and required several time-consuming changes of train. There were occasional mishaps. During one night stage, a stock-car door flew open and several horses tumbled out; they were recovered along the roadside next morning. Alexander learned from the telegraph operators at Kingsville, South Carolina, that Bragg had fought and won the battle of Chickamauga September 19–20. Roughly seventy-five hundred of Longstreet's infantry arrived in time to decide the outcome. Alexander heard, later, that his West Point mentor Jim Deshler had been killed on the second day of the battle.[5]

The rickety cars clanked on westward over warping tracks and crumbling roadbeds at an average speed of less than four miles an hour, reaching Atlanta the afternoon of September 23. The battalion staff joined Aleck that evening for dinner at the Hulls'. The journey resumed before dawn the next morning, another twenty-two hours to cover 110 miles to the railhead at Ringgold, Georgia, completing the trip of 843 miles in seven and a half days. During the day, word reached the Hulls that Bettie had safely delivered twins on the twenty-first. George Hull wired the news on to Ringgold. The telegram never reached Alexander. He caught up to Longstreet on Chattanooga Creek on the twenty-fifth, leaving Huger to equip the battalion and march it up to the line.[6]

Bragg won a clear tactical victory at Chickamauga, then let Rosecrans's still-powerful army withdraw into the Chattanooga defenses. Longstreet and others called Chickamauga a hollow triumph, costly and without meaning. "Everybody seems to be disgusted at his incapacity," Alexander wrote his father. "Bragg has no plan & won't do anything." Longstreet prepared for an early resumption of the offensive, sending word to Alexander on September 27 to bombard the Chattanooga lines next day, as a preliminary to an infantry assault. Bragg canceled the operation and ordered a general cannonade for October 5, hoping to shell the Federals out of their crowded camps. It had small impact, partly because of ammunition failures. Alexander's battalion, posted on the north slope of Lookout Mountain, engaged in a regular exchange with a "vicious little battery" posted in Moccasin Bend of the Tennessee River. "It nearly buried itself in the ground under high parapets, and fired up at us like a man shooting at a squirrel up in a tree," he recalled. Aleck's gunners shifted lots of earth about, but otherwise caused no harm. The duel began to seem like a metaphor for Bragg's effort: the Confederates static and ineffective, the Yankees defiant.[7]

Woolfolk, still recuperating at home from his Gettysburg wound, sent word to Alexander that he had become a father twice again. Mother and twins, a boy and a girl, were well. Mary Clifford offered condolences. "We all sympathize with you," Cliff wrote, "for while twins are a great affliction any time it is doubly so for you & [Bettie] now." In a gloomy postscript, she added that she had fitted out a convalescent's room for him, just in case.[8]

Longstreet continued to lobby for a campaign of maneuver, though without success; he and Bragg could agree on nothing. A strict disciplinarian, bad-tempered and dyspeptic, of debatable competence, Bragg inspired all but universal dislike. His senior generals were in open revolt. Rumor had it that Bragg shot a man every day, though Alexander admitted he witnessed only one execution during his brief season with the Army of Tennessee. He graded Bragg's abilities as modest at best. "And to be entirely frank," he went on, "there were some who did not hesitate openly to say he was simply muddle headed & especially that he could never understand a map." Longstreet considered Bragg unfit to manage an army, and said so openly.[9]

Longstreet proposed a wide swing to the west, toward the federal railhead at Bridgeport, Alabama. He directed Alexander to scout the approaches and prepare a scheme for assaulting the town. Alexander set out for Bridgeport on October 10 via the village of Trenton, Georgia. The name struck sparks of recognition. As a child, mere mention of it had filled him with terror. An especially strict and severe boarding school operated in Trenton, a Wackford Squeers sort of place, remote and inaccessible behind the long loom of Lookout Mountain. His father used to threaten to send him there for his misdeeds. Aleck spent a night in the village hotel before moving on through rough, picturesque country to Bridgeport. He returned to Longstreet on the twelfth with what he considered a first-rate plan of attack. Nothing came of it, in spite of a strong endorsement from President Davis during his mid-October visit to Bragg's demoralized army. The siege dragged on. Ulysses S. Grant arrived and in late October forced open the Cracker Line to carry food, forage, and ammunition into Chattanooga, effectively smashing the Confederate lock. A few days later, Bragg ordered Longstreet to march against Burnside at Knoxville.[10]

Longstreet complained, later, that first word of the Knoxville venture reached him as a camp rumor November 1. That at least gave him an opportunity to think the problem through, with the sound of Alexander's guns firing ineffectually into Chattanooga as accompaniment. When Bragg summoned him to a council two days later, Longstreet told him such a project might succeed if sufficient forces, say twenty thousand men, were made available, and if the balance of the army withdrew to safer positions behind Chickamauga Creek. Bragg ignored both caveats and sent Longstreet northeast with twelve thousand men—the force he had brought from Virginia, supplemented by a pontoon train, eight guns of Leyden's artillery battalion, and four small cavalry brigades under Joseph Wheeler.[11]

Longstreet called Alexander's batteries down from Lookout Mountain the night of Tuesday, November 3. The battalion marched east to Rossville, then to Tyner's Station, where rail transportation was supposed to be available as far as Sweetwater, forty miles below Knoxville. Longstreet's demands overwhelmed the lightly built Tennessee & Georgia line. Alexander's battalion waited in camp at Tyner's Station for five or six days. Victuals and winter clothing were scarce. Game, however, abounded in the Tennessee woods. "Col. Alexander has partridge every day," an envious cavalryman wrote home. He shot rabbits, quail, and, a first for him, a woodcock. The bird's fine, lustrous eyes and sleek plumage made, he thought, as exquisite a picture as he had ever beheld. The battalion started for Sweetwater on November 10, the long train of flatcars wheezing out of the station at three o'clock in the afternoon. The underpowered engine kept running out of fuel; the men had to jump down at regular intervals to gather wood to fire the boiler. After a chilly sixty-mile run, the battalion reached the end of the line early in the morning of the eleventh.[12]

Bragg had refused to supply Longstreet with staff officers who knew the region, or even with detailed maps, so Alexander spent the next two days in the saddle, reconnoitering. He had for company Maj. John Clarke, Longstreet's newly joined staff engineer. They found the country people cool, suspicious, and divided in their loyalties. He and Clarke approached a brick farmhouse, a substantial dwelling for the district, to inquire about roads and Tennessee River crossing points. A girl of eight or nine came to the door.

"Sissy, are any of the grown people home?" Alexander asked.

She looked him over, then replied, "What I wants to know is are you a Reb, or a Yank, or a bushwhack?"[13]

Alexander supervised construction of a pontoon bridge over the Tennessee at Hough's Ferry and watched the first troops cross during the evening of Saturday, November 14. Burnside, with about 22,000 men, sent out a mobile force to delay the Confederate advance. The federals skirmished with Longstreet's van at Lenoir's Station at dusk Sunday, then fell back overnight to Campbell's Station, thirteen miles southwest of Knoxville. The Confederates followed over roads axle-deep in mud. During the afternoon of the sixteenth, Alexander's battalion deployed in broad, open meadows and shelled Burnside's front while Hood's division, temporarily under Micah Jenkins, the senior brigadier,* reached out for a flank. The firing made "a pretty show," Alexander recalled, but defective ammunition again discounted the result. Army of Tennessee stocks were even worse, he now saw, than those of the Virginia army. Shells tumbled, failed to explode, blew up in the tubes. In any case, the enemy discovered the flank march and safely withdrew.[14]

By the afternoon of November 17, the Confederates were approaching the outworks of Knoxville. The next day, Wednesday, Longstreet ordered the Yankee pickets driven in, the main line developed, and the town invested from north of the Holston River. The skirmishers encountered serious resistance only along the main road, where a brigade of dismounted cavalry, armed with fast-firing carbines and protected by a breastwork of fence rails, barred the way. The enterprising Yankee brigadier turned out to be Dock Sanders, last seen escorting Aleck aboard the Panama steamer in San Francisco in May 1861. ("He had changed his politics" since then, Alexander noted dryly.) Sanders's troopers repulsed the Confederates with ease. Longstreet, impatient, called for Alexander to run up his guns and blast the Yankees out.[15]

He found a covered approach to a house some three hundred yards from Sanders's front, and sited Taylor's battery of four twelve-pounder Napoleons in the yard. With Longstreet's authorization, he concealed two South Carolina infantry regiments in a swale, with orders to charge at his command. Moody's twenty-four-pounders limbered into the open and delivered a steady fire from a range of eight hundred yards. Then Taylor's Napoleons whistled round after round of solid shot into the breastworks. The impact sent fence rails flying; presently, Yankee troopers could be seen deserting the line. On Alexander's signal, the South Carolinians surged to within forty yards of the enemy line. There they halted, dropped to the ground, and began to return fire.[16]

Alexander stamped his feet in rage. "They had it if they'd gone on!"

*Barely recovered from his Gettysburg wound, Hood had his right leg shot off at Chickamauga.

he shouted, jumping about and waving his arms. His distress evidently moved Winthrop. He drew his saber, squared his elbows, and put spurs to his horse, reaching the South Carolinians just as they were rising to resume the advance. As Winthrop bore down on the stacked rails, a dozen defenders fired up at him. Alexander saw him slump in the saddle. The attacking infantry, meanwhile, vaulted over the breastworks. Sanders was shot in the abdomen in the charge and carried, mortally wounded, to the rear.[17]

Afterward, Alexander, Huger, and Haskell rode back to see about Winthrop. Alexander ordinarily steered clear of operating rooms, "with their instruments & loose pieces piled up, which are ugly things for soldiers to see," but made an exception today. They found the hospital quartered in a big brick country house. Buster trotted along at their heels, his first occasion under a roof. When the party mounted the staircase, the dog, large-pawed and awkward, refused to follow. Buster tried the stairs after much cajoling, moving "gingerly as an elephant," Alexander recalled, and safely reached the long second-floor hallway. There the joy of his achievement overcame him. "He raced around, & up & down, a time or two, & then, a window at one end being open, he took a flying leap through it," Alexander went on. Buster alit in a clump of thick grass, staggered for a moment, then bounded away unhurt. Aleck and the others laughed themselves sore, all except poor Winthrop, part of whose collarbone had been cut away and resected, and who lay trussed up in bandages, still dazed from surgery.[18]

Longstreet closed on Knoxville and probed for a point of attack. Fort Loudon, a Confederate-built earthwork bastion on the northwest edge of town, appeared to offer the most promising approach. Alexander sited his guns to enfilade the position, now renamed Fort Sanders after the defunct brigadier, and rigged a battery of twelve-pounder howitzers for high-angle fire. By Sunday, November 22, he had everything ready. Then one of Longstreet's staff officers discovered a hill on the south bank of the Holston from which rifled cannon could enfilade a long section of the enemy line. Longstreet directed Alexander to ferry Parker's four ten-pounder Parrotts across. Alexander objected, largely because he mistrusted the long-range ammunition.* Longstreet insisted. Two days were lost in shifting and siting the guns. Alexander reported Tuesday evening that Parker could open fire at sunrise Wednesday, the twenty-fifth. Long-

---

*Parker's battery fired 120 long-range shells during the Knoxville siege, Alexander reported. All but two tumbled or burst prematurely.

street again postponed the assault, this time to await the arrival of two infantry brigades Bragg had decided belatedly to send him.[19]

These troops arrived later on Wednesday, together with Bragg's chief engineer, Gen. Danville Leadbetter, who had supervised the construction of Fort Loudon in 1862. Alexander conceived an instant dislike for Leadbetter, a self-important 1836 West Pointer who at once began to bombard Longstreet with advice, most of it faulty. When word reached him Wednesday night that Longstreet had postponed Thursday's assault, he blamed the delay on Leadbetter. Longstreet and Leadbetter rode off together on a scout Thursday. That evening, Alexander received orders to return Parker's guns to the north bank and prepare to operate against the other end of Burnside's line, at Mabry's Hill, northeast of town.[20]

Used to being Longstreet's chief adviser on engineering questions, Aleck resented being ignored, especially when he knew Leadbetter had it all wrong. He could hardly object, though, because Longstreet himself had gone over the ground. On Friday, after Wheeler's cavalry drove in the Yankee pickets, Longstreet examined the Mabry's Hill sector more closely, this time in company with Alexander and the division commanders. He at least showed himself capable of admitting a mistake. "Everywhere we saw open level ground obstructed by a creek & artificial ponds, without cover anywhere," Alexander recalled. "Even Leadbetter had not a word to say." Longstreet reverted to the original plan.[21]

By now several days had been lost, though the odds for success still seemed better than average. A storming column could approach under cover to within two hundred yards of Fort Sanders. Through a flaw in Leadbetter's original design, the defenders were unable to deliver head-on fire from some parts of the fort. Alexander believed his guns, operating at close range, could suppress the enemy fire long enough for the infantry to cover the distance, cross the dry ditch in front of the works, and scale the parapet. Longstreet fixed the attack for Sunday, November 29. At the last minute he decided to drop the opening bombardment in favor of a surprise rush at first light. Alexander, his role now reduced to firing off the signal guns, again suspected Leadbetter's influence.[22]

Before midnight, as a preliminary, the skirmishers were to turn the Yankee pickets out of their rifle pits. This they accomplished easily, though Alexander thought the only result had been to alert the enemy. A fine, half-frozen mist fell through the night. The storming column formed in the dark, three brigades abreast in line of battle, no guides, no special instructions—as though, Alexander said, they were about to charge into a wheatfield. He fired three signal guns, then directed a slow shelling of the fort. The infantry advanced in the twilight of dawn. Alexander stopped firing at the first chorus of rebel yells. He could see muzzle flashes in the dim light. The sound of musketry never rose to any great volume, and it gradually died away. Alexander assumed McLaws's division had carried the position. In fact, McLaws had been thoroughly mauled. The infantry found the ditch to be several feet deeper than advertised, the sides of the parapet slippery with ice. McLaws, doubtless recalling Longstreet's (and Alexander's) assurances that the trench would be no obstacle, had neglected to provide scaling ladders. The attackers milled about for twenty minutes, taking casualties, then streamed back to the start line.[23]

Losses approached eight hundred killed, wounded, and missing. Longstreet prepared to try again, but canceled the attack when a courier arrived with a telegram from Richmond reporting Bragg's defeat at Missionary Ridge. A second message followed, this one from Bragg: Sherman had set out from Chattanooga to relieve Burnside. Longstreet decided to allow Sherman to come on to within a day's march, then withdraw to the northeast, toward Virginia.[24]

The trains started for Blain's Cross Roads on December 3, the infantry following in a cold rain the next night. The half-frozen troops set fire to fences along the roadside, kindling flame at the angles where the rails crossed, lighting up the route for miles. This knack for starting fires in a downpour amazed Alexander. Many men were shoeless. In Alexander's battalion, the drivers gave their footgear to the cannoneers, who had to walk. Breaking precedent, Longstreet allowed the troops to swap shoes with Yankee prisoners.* Horseshoes also were in short supply. During the siege, the Confederates had fished dead animals out of the Holston River to recover shoes and nails. Now the drivers destroyed wounded or broken-down horses for their shoes. The ragged column rested briefly at Blain's, eighteen miles from Knoxville. Alexander chased away two hungry infantrymen trying to rustle a pig. One, retreating into a woods, turned and fired at him. He missed by ten yards or so. The First Corps labored on, fifteen miles Sunday, December 6, a further seventeen miles on the eighth, then nine miles on the ninth, to the neighborhood of Rogersville, where Longstreet called a long halt.[25]

---

*"When a man is captured his shoes are captured too," one philosophical Yankee was heard to say.

After a sharp rearguard action December 15 at Bean's Station, the Confederates withdrew across the Holston at Cobb's Ford. Alexander selected a good winter campsite on south-facing slopes thickly grown with hardwood, and with a good mountain stream nearby. The country yielded adequate food supplies for a change; corn still stood in the fields. With conditions so favorable, Alexander asked Longstreet for a furlough. Longstreet granted him a generous sixty days, and he set out December 28 for Washington, Wilkes County. Bettie, with three infants and a nurse in train, had reached Fairfield a few weeks earlier, after an epic journey over the Confederacy's ramshackle railway system. Aleck had only himself to look after; even so, he nearly succumbed to exposure. The mercury dropped to near zero. The cars were cold, crowded, slow; he found little to eat at the stations, though at one he did manage to acquire a sweet potato, which he sliced and heated on the stove in the car. In spite of everything, he reached Fairfield ahead of the letter carrying word of his leave. Everyone was at supper. Cynthia, waiting at table, recognized his footfall and announced "Mars Porter" before she caught sight of him.[26]

Bettie introduced him to the twins, christened Edward Porter II and Lucy Roy. He inspected the outbuildings and visited the lot and rode the fields. Fairfield seemed unchanged at first glance. Far from the fighting and the army camps, the plantation bore few outward marks of war, though a closer look told Alexander the fat days were gone, probably for good. There was less meat, largely on account of a shortage of salt for curing. Fairfield produced more vegetables and sweet potatoes, less cotton. Machine-made items such as caps, buttons, and shoes were unavailable. Leopold Alexander had no footwear to distribute to the Fairfield slaves in the winter of 1864. Coarse Osnaburg cloth replaced wool for the slaves' winter clothing.[27]

Leopold's health remained robust, and his mood lightened with Bettie and his grandchildren about the place. Commotion in the nursery broke what had become an oppressive stillness at Fairfield. At the patriarch's urging, Aleck dropped down to Savannah for several days to visit his aunt Louisa and her banker husband Anthony Porter, who looked after his financial affairs. Sure of eventual Confederate victory, he instructed Porter to invest his disposable income in government bonds.[28]

Alexander regretted the Savannah trip ever afterward. On his return, Leopold handed over a telegram from Longstreet. He would not have resented a summons for field service, but the general sent for him to testify in a court-martial of Lafayette McLaws. Longstreet, McLaws, Jenkins, Evander Law, and others had feuded throughout the Knoxville campaign. Possibly they picked up the habit from Bragg and his disputatious band. At any rate, Longstreet accused McLaws of inadequate preparation for the Fort Sanders assault, and especially for failing to equip the storming column with scaling ladders. Alexander thought the charges exaggerated and unlikely to stick. Nevertheless, he dutifully caught the next train for Richmond. When he reached the capital he learned that the McLaws court was in recess. By then it was too late to return to Fairfield, so he billeted himself on his sisters and determined to sample such pleasures as Richmond had to offer.[29]

These were plain enough by the winter of 1864, even in the patrician circles Alexander frequented. "I don't know how people live here now who depend on daily buying for daily bread," Sally Lawton wrote their father. "Prices have run up almost to the fabulous. Beef $5 per lb—sugar $20—meal $50 per bushel—butter $10—bacon $8—flour *not to be had*." There were so-called starvation parties; the guests provided musical entertainment, the hostess bread and butter. Aleck passed the time with his West Point friend Tom Berry, now lieutenant colonel of a Georgia regiment. Berry liked his liquor hard, a taste that had slowed his rise in the service. Sally took a reforming interest in Berry, and tried to cure him of dipsomania and fix his promotion at the same time.*[30]

He also saw a great deal of Jeb Stuart—on one occasion, in mortifying circumstances. They met in a photographer's gallery, Stuart with a veiled woman on his arm. He presented her as an old friend of Aleck's. When she parted the veil, Alexander looked perplexed. "Don't you know her?" Stuart asked, beginning to laugh a lot. It was Mary Lee, whom Aleck had courted with a deflating lack of success at West Point. He had not seen her since 1858. "The floor would not swallow me up so I had to shake hands & stammer out a little conversation which I commenced by telling her that I never would have known her which wasn't very complimentary," he confessed to Bettie. He backed out of the gallery with nods and an awkward bow, and a promise never meant to be kept, to call sometime.[31]

Alexander did, however, drop in on Adj. Gen. William Mackall at the War Department, who told him that Joseph Johnston, Bragg's successor in command of the Army of Tennessee, had applied for him as chief of artillery. The position offered wider scope for Alexander's abilities and

*Berry never achieved high rank in Confederate service. He died shortly after the war, probably of drink.

an overdue promotion to brigadier. Pendleton had recommended Aleck for advancement the previous November, but nothing had come of it, largely because of caste considerations involving Walton, the senior artillery colonel. Now, with promotion in view, he declined (in keeping with his long-standing private policy) even to acknowledge interest in the job. He *was* interested, he wrote Bettie, "as being the more prominent & complimentary & as being nearer to you." Officially, though, he told Mackall to do whatever he judged best for the army.[32]

As it happened, Lee refused to let Alexander go. He proposed Pendleton instead, sending him to Georgia on an inspection tour in hopes, Longstreet let slip a few weeks later, that Johnston would "take a fancy to him and keep him."* Jefferson Davis told Sally Lawton that Aleck was one of the few officers Lee absolutely would not part with. Now that the issue had been decided, he allowed himself some private grumbling. "It is a little unfair on me as neither Lee nor Longstreet ever secured my promotion when I was not wanted elsewhere & now they retain me in an inferior position," he wrote Bettie. But he went on to declare himself content with whatever might come his way. "I always feel better satisfied when my wishes are not consulted or gratified, for then I feel sure the whole matter is *providential* & that my path is chosen for me by a wiser judgement than my own," he wrote her.[33]

News of the proceedings infuriated the patriarch, who charged the delay and confusion to Jefferson Davis. Leopold accused him of blocking Aleck's promotion as retribution for the family's friendship with the ranting Toombs, Davis's bitterest political antagonist. "He has treated Ed with great injustice," Leopold wrote his daughter Marion. "No thanks to *him* when Ed is promoted—all to Ed himself for the character he has achieved without the help of anybody." His conspiracy theory quickly fell apart, however. Alexander's long-sought step came through March 1, 1864. Walton's transfer to the innocuous post of inspector general of field artillery created the opening. Alexander carried a brigadier's commission in his pocket when he boarded the train March 2 for the return to Tennessee.[34]

The mountain winter had been severe, with heavy falls of snow. Food and forage were scarce. The battery horses were thin and weak, hardly fit for field service. At least the men were better shod, no longer leaving trails of blood in the snow; Lawton had shipped three thousand pairs

---

*Johnston did not fancy Pendleton. The job went first to Francis Shoup, then to Robert Beckham. Beckham was killed in action near Columbia, Tennessee, in November 1864.

of shoes to Longstreet's corps. The days were overcast and numbingly cold. Alexander faced the brittle east-Tennessee winds in a stout jacket and a pair of thick blue "soldier pants" Huger had scavenged for him. With Walton out of the way, Longstreet formally appointed him chief of corps artillery, and he turned energetically to the task of preparing the command for the spring campaign. He assembled a regular staff: Winthrop, Joe Haskell, and three newcomers, Bettie's seventeen-year-old brother Willie Mason as aide, John Middleton as quartermaster, and Dr. William Post as surgeon. Huger stepped up to command Alexander's battalion.[35]

The first days of reentry into the harsh world of the army camps were always the hardest. Then, too, he had begun to feel the first stirrings of war-weariness, a state of mind that had the effect of inducing flights of domestic fantasy, dreams of Bettie and the children. "Little Bess shall be a great musician," he decided. "Eddy shall be a high spirited little fellow governed principally by his own self respect which he shall be taught to value above any pleasure or temptation & Lucy shall be our own sweet little pet to be our comfort in our old age when Bessie is married & Eddy at the Southern West Point." Then reality would intrude. The mountains were full of bushwhackers, deserters from both armies who preyed on both sides indiscriminately. Hunger had become endemic. The fighting would begin again soon. "Tell Bess that Papa loves her & Buster says 'Bow Wow I love Bessie when she is a good girl,'" he wrote, as much to cheer himself as to draw a laugh out of the little girl.[36]

The battalion moved up to Greeneville, Union politician Andrew Johnson's hometown and now Longstreet's headquarters, March 8. Alexander and his staff boarded with the Union-loyal Crawford family. The country people thereabouts were hardbitten and dour, consumed by political and personal feuds. "Scarcely a week passes but there are murders & hangings & shootings between the bushwhackers & Union & secesh citizens and our soldiers," he wrote Bettie. Alexander, who had a gift for getting along with all sorts, found the Crawfords civilized by comparison. Mrs. Crawford discouraged her children from singing Yankee songs, and she sometimes sent up food to supplement the Confederate officers' meager fare.[37]

The officers sometimes suffered more from famine than did the rank and file. New commissary regulations gave them responsibility for feeding their servants and ostlers as well as themselves. This left Alexander, who had the hired slaves Charley and Abram to provide for, doubly short. Officers could, of course, buy provisions from such stocks as were available. But every mess was in this market. Without the boxes of bacon and dried peas his father shipped regularly from Fairfield, he might have gone seriously hungry. Nor did his eye fail him. Hunting in the snow one afternoon, he brought down twelve partridges with twelve shots, gallantly offering six of the birds as a gift to the wife of Gen. Simon Bolivar Buckner. He tried peacock ("phenomenally tough") and, during one lean stretch, hawk. Resourceful as ever, Alexander had Charley cruise the slaughter lots for butchers' leavings. "We rarely had difficulty in cheating a butcher out of a whole beef's head," he recalled. "And when a beef's head is skinned & chopped up & boiled all day it makes a big camp kettle full of one of the most delightful & richest stews in the world." The stuff kept well, too, congealing into a hard mass from which thick slabs could be sliced for a cold breakfast or lunch on the march.[38]

Where would the First Corps fight? Against whom? In March, Lincoln turned the prosecution of the war over to his relentless western generals. Grant, now in supreme command, shifted his headquarters to the Army of the Potomac in the field. Given Grant's fighting record, the Confederates could expect Meade, still nominally the army commander, to be considerably more aggressive in Virginia this spring. In the west, Sherman threatened a move on Atlanta. Alexander awaited word on whether Longstreet's corps would march for Johnston or return to Lee.

Longstreet offered a third alternative, but his proposal to invade Kentucky did not find favor. Orders came in late March for the First Corps to rejoin the Army of Northern Virginia. Mrs. Crawford organized a farewell party, setting out cakes and other treats and inviting several young ladies in for the occasion. Alexander supplied brandy and sugar for the egg nog. The First Corps broke camp March 28, following the line of the Holston River toward Bristol, in southwestern Virginia. Snow fell, then rain, then snow again. Alexander reached Bristol on March 31 after a wretched four-day march, palliated only by an enjoyable evening at the country house of an elderly Confederate brigadier named A. E. Jackson, called "Mudwall" to distinguish him from the better-known Confederate hero of the same name.[39]

Hunger turned the soldiery thievish and insubordinate. Alexander reprimanded one of his officers for failing to punish two men accused of robbing an old woman of bacon and flour. An officer-led soldier mob stormed the Bristol commissary storehouse the night of April 1, plundering bacon, bread, and other provisions. The guard opened fire; two men were killed, one a lieutenant; four were wounded and several others captured, among them another lieutenant. Alexander thought Longstreet should hang the officer without trial. His own gnawing hunger shriveled any sympathy he might have felt. He wrote Bettie that foraging for two meager meals a day used up most of his time and all of his energy.[40]

The First Corps entrained for Charlottesville on April 11. All at once, life became supportable again. Alexander found a good billet in an empty university dormitory. The sun appeared for the first time in three weeks, and he rode over to Monticello one bright afternoon for a tour of the Jefferson place. He made a flying trip to Orange Court House for a visit with Lee's staff. He found his friends there in good spirits, confident about the coming campaign, though they too had suffered a hard winter and there were shortages of every sort of equipment and provision. But they still had Lee. Grant had beaten every Confederate he had met in the West; he had not yet met Lee. Alexander returned to camp with the feeling that things were going to turn out all right after all. Longstreet's corps started for Gordonsville on April 22 and went into bivouac in that vicinity to await Grant's opening move.[41]

Lee came down from Orange on Friday the twenty-ninth to review the First Corps. Battle flags flying, the two infantry divisions and all the artillery massed in the broad pastures of a cleared valley. Even after fifty years, Alexander could recall every detail of the pageant. It marked, he saw in hindsight, the beginning of the end of the Army of Northern Virginia. To his last hour, the memory of men and guns drawn up in the brilliant spring sunshine retained a surpassing power to stir him emotionally.

"In imagination I can see today the large square gate-posts marking where a country road led out of a tall oak wood upon an open knoll in front of the center of our long double lines," he wrote in 1907. "And as the well-remembered figure of Lee upon Traveller rides between the posts and comes out upon the ground, the bugle sounds a signal, the guns thunder out a salute, Lee reins up Traveller and bares his good gray head and look at us, and we give the 'rebel yell' and shout and cry and look at him once more.

"A wave of sentiment seemed to sweep over the field," he went on.
"There was no speaking, but the effect was as of a military
sacrament."[42]

CHAMBERLAIN
VIRGINIA, HOME, AND WASHINGTON, 1863–64

With Lee's escape, the euphoric mood drained slowly out of the Army
of the Potomac. Chamberlain knew months of tedium after those intox-
icating hours on Little Round Top. The army marched, halted, marched,
halted, scrimmaged, halted. Hardship, illness, occasional danger: these
were the normal conditions of army life, but with no compensating advantage that Chamberlain could discern. In bleak moments one could
not help dwelling on the inescapable fact that, despite the fifty thousand
Gettysburg casualties, not a lot had changed. Meade let the Confederates
slip away at Williamsport. The campaign ground on. "The procrastina-
tion and delay soon removed whatever elan the troops possessed," the
historian of the Fifth Corps wrote. On July 15, the First Division, with
Charles Griffin again in command, doubled back to Sharpsburg and over
South Mountain to Burkettsville, a hard, hot march of twenty-five miles.
Two days later the column crossed the Potomac on the pontoons at
Berlin, a less than triumphal return to the barren landscape of northern Virginia.[1]

At Berlin, Chamberlain heard the first reports of the draft riots in New
York City, three days of incendiarism, rampage, and murder touched off
when the newspapers published the names of the first group of army
conscripts. The mobs, largely Irish, ransacked draft offices and the Second Avenue Armory, hunted down and assaulted blacks, set fire to the
first floor of abolition journalist Horace M. Greeley's *New York Tribune*
building. They burned the Colored Orphan Asylum down to the ground.
On orders from Washington, two brigades of regular troops were detached from the Fifth Corps and rushed north to help restore order.
The regulars left with the sincere good wishes of many of the volunteers.
"If they but carry out our sentiments, every traitor in New York City will
be shot," a Massachusetts soldier wrote home. The troops put down the
mobs with a heavy hand. Estimates of the number of killed and wounded
ran as high as one thousand.[2]

Fannie, Chamberlain learned to his dismay, had been in the city during the uprising. He had supposed her in Brunswick. "But New York!" he wrote her in exasperation. "It is not safe to get away is it? I wish you were at home. You should have been there before." A few weeks earlier, he had floated the notion of selling the Potter Street house, arguing that with Fannie so often away, he might as well put the family into lodgings and save the expense of housekeeping. He soon dropped the idea, concluding, perhaps, that she would be even more likely to ramble if deprived of a permanent home base.[3]

The Fifth Corps advanced down the Loudoun Valley, then turned eastward for Manassas Gap. Elements of the Third Corps skirmished inconsequentially with Confederate rear guards at Wapping Heights the afternoon of July 23. Early next morning the First Division set out on what veterans remembered as one of the hardest marches of the war, up the steep, overgrown slopes of a craggy hill, the summit of which offered spectacular views of the Shenandoah Valley, as well as blackberries in profusion. There was no sign of the Confederates, however; they had disengaged safely during the night. The division scuffed back downhill and took the road for Warrenton, halting just beyond the town on the twenty-seventh for a few days' rest.[4]

By now, troops and animals were in a state of near collapse, jaded, ill-clad, and undernourished. Jumping fresh meat and soft bread were dimly remembered luxuries of a fabled past. The men crawled with lice. ("Nothing but boiling will kill them," one man explained, "and for three weeks no one has had a chance to boil a shirt.") The commissary issued clothing and shoes, new shoddy* to replace raveled uniforms and broken-down government brogues. In one First Brigade regiment, three men marched in dirty white shirts and underdrawers; their blouses and pants had literally rotted off them. Meade, following Lee, pushed the army up to the Rappahannock. The First Division camped for several days near Bealton Station, a country halt, one building and a water tank on the Orange & Alexandria Railroad, then moved up to the river at Beverly Ford.[5]

Two full months of unrelieved marching and fighting had reduced Chamberlain to a state of near-exhaustion. Gillmore, his nominal second-in-command, remained away on what amounted to a permanent sick leave. Surgeon Monroe had resigned after Chancellorsville, and the 20th fought the entire Gettysburg campaign without a medical officer. Along

*A composite woolen material for making army uniforms. The word soon came to define anything cheap and inferior, or any person considered mean, contemptible, or counterfeit.

with his own and Gillmore's duties, Chamberlain assumed some of the responsibilities of the blue-pill men. His highly developed sense of stewardship compelled him to accept the added burdens without complaint. "I consider it an officer's first duty to look after the welfare of his men," he wrote Governor Coburn. Even so, he was relieved when the newly appointed assistant surgeon reported during the third week of July. The regimental commander himself became one of Dr. Abner Shaw's first patients. "I had to be surgeon & father as well as colonel to such an extent that I fell sick myself," he explained to Coburn. At the end of July, Chamberlain requested a twenty-day furlough, enough time to take the cars north and recruit his strength at home. The brigade surgeon diagnosed him as suffering from "nervous prostration."[6]

He arrived in Brunswick on the afternoon train August 6, and felt well enough to speak that evening at a First Parish Church Thanksgiving service for the Gettysburg and Vicksburg victories. ("Capital," George Adams rated his son-in-law's oration.) He soon lapsed into a recovering-hero routine at home. There were romps with Daisy and Wyllys, breakfasts at the Tontine, acquaintances in to tea, dinners at the parsonage, reunions with Bowdoin colleagues. Still, the interlude seemed unaccountably strange. He felt constrained, oddly out of place in these once-familiar surroundings. Even so, he had posted a request to extend his leave when James Rice wrote asking him to return to camp so he could get away for a short visit home. Chamberlain, now senior colonel of the brigade, could not refuse him.[7]

Reporting at Beverly Ford on August 23, he learned that Rice's promotion to brigadier had come through. Rice moved over to a First Corps command, and on the twenty-fourth Griffin gave Chamberlain temporary charge of the Third Brigade. Pvt. Oliver W. Norton, the brigade bugler, an admirer of both Vincent and Rice, expressed reservations about the new commanding officer. "[He is] a former professor in a college and a very fine man," Norton wrote home, "though but little posted in military matters." Griffin had hardly a flicker of doubt, though he knew Chamberlain's commission dated back only a year or so. He had read the Little Round Top reports, and discussed the action with senior First Division officers. Griffin resolved to try to confirm Chamberlain in permanent command.[8]

The riot-delayed draft resumed in New York City on August 19, and bountymen shortly began arriving to fill out the depleted regiments. Most proved, in time, to be steady soldiers. Still, the system encouraged abuse. Crowds of bravos, confidence men, gamblers, and other sinful characters offered themselves as substitutes for draftees, accepted the enlistment bounty, and bolted at first opportunity, usually to repeat the process again and again, pocketing the government's cash each time. In August, five bounty-jumpers posted to one Fifth Corps regiment, the 118th Pennsylvania, were hunted down, captured, and court-martialed. Meade ordered them to be shot.[9]

The full corps paraded to witness the executions on the brisk afternoon of Saturday, August 29, massing by columns of regiment along the lip of an immense, bowl-shaped meadow. The funeral procession, five black coffins each borne by four soldiers, slow-timed into the meadow while a band played the Dead March from Handel's *Saul*. Dressed in blue trousers and white shirts, the condemned men crossed a bridge over a narrow stream, halted at the foot of their freshly dug graves, and took seats on the edge of their coffins, facing the firing party thirty paces distant. The chaplains, a Roman Catholic priest, a rabbi, and two Protestant parsons murmured words of consolation. The prisoners were blindfolded with strips of white bandage. A bugle sounded Attention. The provost marshal called out an order and the firing party, sixty muskets, one in every twelve loaded with a blank charge, closed in long strides to within a few feet of the graveside. The marshal's next command instantly converted the prisoners into corpses. "There was a gleaming flash, a line of curling smoke, a sharp crash like the report of a single rifle," recalled Theodore Gerrish. The impact tumbled four of the men into their coffins. The fifth remained erect. Someone gave him a shove, and he fell gently into place. The band struck up "The Girl I Left Behind Me," and the columns filed slowly back to camp.[10]

There is no surviving record of Chamberlain's reaction, though he evidently described the executions in detail in a letter to his sister. "What a dreadful thing to witness!" Sae Chamberlain wrote back. His own handling of a capital military offense had been quite different, and the Second Maine mutineers had proved, almost to a man, to be reliable soldiers. Draftees were reporting now to the 20th Maine and other regiments of his brigade. He expected trouble, but thought he could meet it. "I trust we can manage them with enough skill & prudence to save them from desertion & its inevitable consequence—shooting," he wrote Coburn. "I don't want any of that business with Maine men." In the ranks, the shock of the judicial killings soon wore off. Meade's intentions were only partly realized. Many men felt some sympathy for the victims,

and resented having been forced to watch the spectacle. "Poor privates
must suffer for *their* crimes, but officers for the same offense are dismissed, or imprisoned for a few months," one soldier wrote home.[11]

The pattern of cool weather held through early September, reminding
Chamberlain of Maine at that season. He began to get the "feel" of
brigade command, though he knew loneliness there in the headquarters
compound upon the hill overlooking the Rappahannock. Camp life, with
its regular rounds and predictable routines, deepened the ache of homesickness. The visit to Brunswick had not been all he had hoped for. He
regretted the missed opportunities. "How I wish I could sit with you &
Daisy at some communion table; if we could only get rid of the association of formality & factitious if not forced feeling—how happy such a
season would make me," he wrote Fannie. He acknowledged, regretfully,
that to his children, Fannie, too, he had become a changed man, ab-
stracted, solemn, awkward in their presence.[12]

His friends, meanwhile, were doing all in their power to ratify his
assignment to brigade command. Griffin, a thirty-seven-year-old West
Point veteran of the Mexican war and frontier campaigns, a tough, austere, acerbic regular,* recommended a brigadier's star for Chamberlain—the first such endorsement he had ever made. He also petitioned
Meade's headquarters to break with common practice and permit Chamberlain to continue to serve with the First Division. Rice, Barnes, Sykes,
Howard, and Meade also sent in recommendations. Vice President Hannibal Hamlin, a Maine man himself, wrote Lincoln on Chamberlain's
behalf. "He is a superior man and has proved himself an efficient, brave
and gallant officer," Hamlin wrote the president.[13]

Lincoln did not approve the appointment. Chamberlain suspected that
Senator William Pitt Fessenden, Hamlin, Coburn, and other Maine
Republicans had, for some reason, failed to bring sufficient political
pressure to bear. Hamlin and Fessenden were strong antislavery men.
They may have wished to reserve their patronage for a more ardent
emancipationist. In any case, the Fifth Corps had long since fallen out
of Republican favor. It was McClellan's favorite corps; a former commanding officer, Fitz-John Porter, had been bluntly critical of the administration. Griffin made no secret of his high regard for McClellan. His
reputation as a loose cannon (he had openly and vehemently denounced

---

*One of Griffin's brigadiers, New Yorker J. J. Bartlett, affected gaudy dress, even in the field. Once,
when he approached Griffin at a rest halt, Griffin glanced up and said, "Well, Bartlett, when will
the rest of the circus arrive?"

Pope during the Second Bull Run campaign, and Meade had almost sacked him for his outspokenness after Gettysburg) probably damaged Chamberlain's chances. Griffin held out loyally for him, actually declining to receive officers sent from Meade's headquarters to take charge of the Third Brigade. Chamberlain remained in command through most of the autumn.[14]

Still officially colonel of the 20th Maine, he continued to involve himself in regimental affairs. Gillmore, venturing out of hospital at last, took over the 20th in late August. (He would be gone again in October.) Chamberlain pressed for Tom's promotion to captain and command of Company G. Ellis Spear, a newly made major, was Gillmore's understudy. He found a solution to the problem of Lt. James Nichols of Brunswick, who had helped raise the regiment in the summer of 1862 and had been a brave and reliable officer on Little Round Top and elsewhere— when sober, anyway, a condition he could rarely maintain for long, at least in camp. Chamberlain fobbed Nichols off on the cavalry, "in the belief," he wrote the governor artlessly, "that a new sphere of duty might give him a better opportunity to reform." He campaigned for better medical services, too, negotiating with Charlotte Elizabeth McKay, a free-lance nurse from Maine, to set up an improved model of brigade hospital.[15]

As summer shaded into autumn, Washington increased the pressure on Meade to bring off a battle. With Longstreet's corps away in Tennessee, the Army of the Potomac could mass overwhelming superiority. Meade moved up to Culpeper on September 16, obliging Lee to withdraw behind the Rapidan. The Fifth Corps pushed on in late summer heat to an advanced position three miles beyond the flyblown town ("as nasty a hole as I ever beheld," one ranker complained), camped on a ridge, and idled away two weeks. Meade's caution here cost him some of his advantage in numbers. On orders from Washington, the 11th and 12th corps were peeled away from him September 25 and sent to Chattanooga to reinforce the besieged Federals there.[16]

Lee responded by going over to the offensive, marching west in a series of sidesteps aimed at outflanking Meade. For a month the armies maneuvered, the Federals falling back along the line of the Orange & Alexandria Railroad, always a step or two ahead of Lee. There were hard, chafing marches and occasional fights, including a sharp one, ending in a decided Confederate reverse, at Bristoe Station October 14. Jeb Stuart retaliated five days later, routing a federal cavalry division at Buckland

Mills. These affairs determined no larger issue. "If either side gained any advantage there was little disposition shown to follow it up," said Gerrish, articulating a fairly common view in the ranks. Lee failed to cut Meade off, though he did force him to retreat more than forty miles and give up a long stretch of the O&A. The Confederates ripped up the track as they retreated to safer positions behind the Rappahannock.[17]

There was little glory here for the Third Brigade. The marching and countermarching, northwest to southeast and back again, further undermined Chamberlain's health. It forced him, too, to abandon the promising medical alliance with Charlotte McKay. Over the last days of October she followed him from Fairfax Station to Gainesville to Warrenton, just missing him at each place. She finally caught up to brigade headquarters at Auburn. There Chamberlain told her the army probably would remain in motion; no time now for hospital reforms. Mrs. McKay returned, disappointed, to Washington.[18]

The Federals trailed after Lee, rebuilding the railroad as they went. Early on November 7, a cold, clear, breezy Saturday, Chamberlain led the Third Brigade through clouds of wind-stirred dust toward Rappahannock Bridge, where a north-bank stronghold, comprising two earthwork redoubts and a long curve of rifle pits, covered the Confederate withdrawal. Around noon, the column ascended a wooded ridge overlooking the Rappahannock plain and halted. Word came a couple of hours later to deploy into line of battle and advance across the plain to the river.[19]

The van of the Fifth Corps emerged from the sheltering woods at three o'clock and moved out along the left of the railroad. The Sixth Corps came on over rougher ground on the other side of the O&A. Enemy artillery opened a brisk fire from the redoubts. Bugler Norton, riding with Chamberlain, noted that much of the shooting went long. After about a mile, a courier rode up with orders for Chamberlain to throw two of his regiments forward in support of a strong skirmish line working its way through dry grass toward the Rappahannock. The skirmishers gradually cleared the Fifth Corps' front, reached the river, and took possession of the Confederate rifle pits.[20]

The federal artillery played on the redoubts for more than an hour, though with little visible effect. The Confederates kept up a steady return fire. Scouting ahead, Chamberlain had another horse shot under him— Charlemagne, a recent acquisition; the animal survived his wound.*

*And returned to Maine with his master.

Chamberlain concealed his main line, exposed to the cannonade and to long-range musketry, as well as he could and awaited developments. Toward five o'clock, John Sedgwick, commanding Meade's two-corps right wing, ordered the Sixth Corps to attack the main redoubt.[21]

The storming column, composed of the Fifth Wisconsin and the Sixth Maine, advanced in the evening twilight, bayonets fixed. Unexpected reinforcements arrived in the form of the First Division skirmish line, assembled out of detachments from all four of Chamberlain's regiments, including fifty men from the 20th Maine, now under the command of Ellis Spear. These troops drifted across the railroad embankment and joined the charge. The attackers covered the ground in a rush, burst into the main redoubt, and held fast until supporting Sixth Corps troops could arrive to confirm the result. The spoils were seventeen hundred prisoners, four guns, eight battle flags, and a pontoon train—as complete a minor victory as any in the war.[22]

As a sort of tribute, the Third Brigade skirmishers sent some seventy prisoners, including five officers, to Chamberlain. His command remained in position overnight. Bugler Norton sounded "The General" before dawn on the eighth, and the brigade marched to Kelly's Ford. The full Fifth Corps crossed later in the day, advanced a couple of miles, then returned to the north bank after discovering that Lee had stepped back out of reach behind the Rapidan. The Third Brigade camped in the open, without tents or fires. Around midnight sleet began to fall, changing to snow a little later. When Chamberlain awoke, an inch of snow covered his thin blanket, and a bitter wind was blowing out of the north.[23]

Exposure brought on a sharp attack of the "ague-fit" that had enfeebled Chamberlain at intervals since June. Malarial fevers accounted for fully one-quarter of all reported Civil War illnesses, and the autumn of 1863 turned out to be an especially severe malaria season. The editors of the official medical history of the war described the initial symptoms: "feelings of languor, weariness and indisposition for physical exercise or mental work, depression of spirits, yawning, aching in the bones and soreness in the muscles, with creeping or chilly sensations along the spine, loss of appetite and perhaps nausea." These were followed by "chills, perhaps developing into rigors, and accompanied with goose-skin, shrunken features and lividity of the lips and nails, and with internal congestions manifested by nausea, irritability of the stomach, epigastric pain, splenic or hepatic uneasiness, hurried respiration, rapid, irregular or slow pulse, irritability of temper, headache, confusion of mind, drowsiness or even stupor or coma." In the last stage, the cheeks were flushed, the mouth dry, and the tongue furred; breath came short and fast and the pulse pounded full and strong.[24]

During the second week of November, as the brigade moved camp from point to point, Chamberlain experienced increasingly violent alternations of fever and chills. Malaria victims were rarely bled as late as 1863, but other treatments were almost as crude. Army doctors reached first for quinine, the universal malaria specific. Systematic doses failed to improve Chamberlain's condition. If dissolved in whiskey, as it often was, the potion doubtless made him feel worse; he had never acquired much of a taste for liquor. The brigade surgeon may also have prescribed mercury, salts (for the bowels), and opium. For the most severe cases, enterprising medical men might also try blue pill (for cases of furred tongue), Hoffmann's anodyne, ice if available, hot drinks, aromatic powders with camphor, and Fowler's solution.[25]

When the attacks persisted, the medical staff advised sending Chamberlain north. He resisted leaving, evidently expecting this bout to pass as had the others. He collapsed completely during the weekend of November 14–15. The 20th Maine's adjutant wrote Fannie to report him seriously ill, causing consternation in Potter Street and at the parsonage. A surgeon-escort helped him aboard a train for Washington. Chamberlain made the journey semiconscious, eyes glittering with fever, in a drafty cattle car fitted out with rough plank benches. He checked into the Seminary Hospital in Georgetown, D.C., November 19. In the first years of the war, army hospitals were reserved for private soldiers; the government expected ailing officers to look out for themselves. By late 1863, though, a few officers' hospitals had been established. The old system suited Chamberlain, who had little use for the convalescent's table. By early December he had recovered sufficiently to discharge himself and head north to Brunswick for an extended sick leave.[26]

Illness left him sallow, dangerously thin, weak, easily tired. The aftereffects of quinine made him giddy and hard of hearing and caused a ringing in his ears. Hunkered down in Potter Street, he kept largely to himself and his family. He avidly consumed news from the fighting fronts, where the reports were mixed. In Virginia, Meade aborted the short Mine Run campaign without bringing Lee to battle and ordered the army into winter quarters around Culpeper. At least there remained the afterglow of Grant's and Burnside's successes in Tennessee. Christmas with Daisy and Wyllys helped restore his spirits, and he gradually recovered his strength. By the new year the worst had passed.

Chamberlain continued to oversee 20th Maine business. Tom had been caught up in a flurry of politicking in camp at Rappahannock Station, using such influence as he possessed on behalf of a sergeant in Company H who wanted to become an officer. The company commander reported Tom to the colonel, writing indignantly that two other men were more qualified, that he expected to be consulted in the selection of his subalterns, and that in any case the sergeant had done nothing to earn promotion. Word reached Chamberlain, too, that Nichols had finally left the regiment, and that Chaplain French intended to post his resignation any day.[27]

In mid-January, declaring himself fit to return to duty, he began to press Griffin and others about regaining the Third Brigade command. Instead, he received orders to report to a court-martial in Washington. Fannie joined him there in mid-February, leaving Deborah Folsom in charge of the Brunswick household. He and Fannie took in the sights of the dirty, ill-kept, crowded, overpriced capital. The respectable theater provided an occasional diversion. *Hamlet* and *Richard III* played alternately at Grover's in March, and an opera company came to town to perform Charles-François Gounod's *Faust*. They saw one of the Booths play Shylock in *The Merchant of Venice*.[28]

He found the judicial assignment irksome. Taking a break from the dull round of hearings in mid-April, he conducted Fannie over the Gettysburg battlefield—the first of his many returns. He clamored to be in on the opening of the spring campaign. "My health is very good & will be better when I get to the field which I have been trying to do for a month," he wrote Cousin Deborah. He lobbied with such persistence that one of his judicial colleagues accused him, perhaps half-seriously, of entertaining a morbid desire to be shot.[29]

The adjutant general responded with an order directing him to report to a court-martial in Trenton, New Jersey. Chamberlain learned there that Grant had crossed the Rapidan on May 4. In two days of confused fighting, the Battle of the Wilderness, Grant made his first acquaintance with Lee and the Army of Northern Virginia. On the ninth, just as he fell ill with another onrush of fever, Chamberlain renewed his plea for release from the court. Illness and worry cast him down. A singleminded desire to return to Virginia consumed him. Reports from the front were sketchy, but it was beginning to look as though Lee had stalled Grant's offensive in the Wilderness. Then Grant clawed out around the Confederate right toward Spotsylvania. On the tenth, word reached Chamberlain at last that he was free to go.[30]

"I left Lawrence at the Depot waiting to take the Philadelphia train for Washington," Fannie wrote Deborah Folsom. "He was very anxious for me to go back to Washington again with him, but I thought it was not best." If Fannie was being tiresome, Chamberlain had been still more so, driven by his neurotic anxiety to rejoin the Army of the Potomac. His courtship of the widowmaker surely pained and baffled her. At the least, a nominal struggle between love and duty seemed owed to her. It turned out to be no contest. Chamberlain passed through Washington and on into the zone of battle, overtaking the 20th Maine near Spotsylvania Court House toward the end of the second week in May.[31]

CHAPTER 9

THE ENDLESS WAR

ALEXANDER
END GAME, MAY–JUNE 1864

Now AND AGAIN, SOME DELICACY MIGHT still be obtained for the camp table. Alexander, Joe Haskell, Fred Colston, and the rest of his sharp-set staff were making a late breakfast of fat shad roe the morning of May 4, Wednesday, when word arrived that Grant had marched. Enemy cavalry had crossed the Rapidan shortly after midnight. The infantry was following. The four thousand wagons of the federal ammunition and supply trains were churning up clouds of yellow dust on the roads for the Rapidan fords. Alexander pushed his plate away, the roe forgotten. Longstreet alerted him to have the guns ready to move at once on signal from First Corps headquarters.[1]

Grant's intentions were plain. He intended to converge on Richmond with four separate forces: the large and powerful Army of the Potomac, and smaller armies in the Shenandoah, in western Virginia, and at Fortress Monroe. At the same time, his junior partner Sherman would advance on Atlanta. Already, Sherman's cavalry raiders were spreading alarm in north Georgia. At Fairfield, Bettie had begun to keep a loaded pistol on her dressing table. Aleck, meanwhile, went about his work with his usual air of bright-eyed optimism. He believed Grant could be checked. Political circumstances favored the Confederate cause; soon it would be election season in the Union states. "The quarreling & the rise of gold at the North foreshadow trouble for them at home besides what we are preparing for them here," he wrote Bettie. Lee would rise to any challenge from Grant and George Meade. Alexander's faith in Lee remained boundless.[2]

He judged his command, three battalions, with a fourth en route to him from Southside Virginia, to be in fair condition except for horses. He was 130 short, and had nags to draw only fifty-two guns. He worked all day in preparation for the long march, some forty miles, from the Gordonsville camps to the probable first battlefield. "Horses are being fed, beds rolled up & all the bustle of breaking camp is in full blast," he wrote his wife during a short break. He saw the batteries onto the road a few minutes after four o'clock. The column moved north and east at a brisk pace, rested from midnight till dawn, then continued on until four o'clock Thursday afternoon, when Longstreet called a halt at Richard's Shop on the Catharpin Road, a blister-raising thirty-six miles from Gordonsville, but still a dozen miles short of the goal.[3]

Coming from the west, Lee planned to strike Grant at right angles as he pushed south through the Wilderness jungle. Alexander later questioned why Lee had allowed the First Corps to camp so far from the prospective battlefield, leaving Longstreet unavailable for the opening phase of the action when the Federals, strung out on the few good roads leading from the Rapidan, were most vulnerable. Marching with Longstreet, Alexander did not hear the first rolling volleys of the battle of the Wilderness; hindsight revealed their symbolic significance. "Now, from the 5th of May, until the next 9th of April, the two armies were under each other's fire every day," he wrote. Grant had the advantage of numbers, nearly twice as many troops as Lee—more than 100,000 to 62,000. And he had something more, according to Alexander, who had heard much about the Union commander from his old army friend Longstreet, a quality all his predecessors lacked: the moral courage to fight the Army of the Potomac without letup, for all it was worth.[4]

Lee made contact according to his design. The Confederates stopped the initial advance May 4, Thursday, but lacked the strength to turn the check into a reverse. That evening, Lee sent word to Longstreet at Richard's Shop to come up to the relief of A. P. Hill's corps on the Orange Plank Road. Longstreet resumed the march at thirty minutes past midnight, a local guide leading the column north from the Catharpin Road. The First Corps reached Parker's Store at first light Friday and continued up the Plank Road toward Hill's lines, three miles distant. At five o'clock, a quarter-hour after sunrise, firing broke out to the left, on Ewell's Second Corps front. Then, abruptly, with Longstreet's infantry still a mile or more away, the battle exploded on Hill.[5]

The federal Second Corps, Hancock's, struck Hill at both ends and collapsed his flanks onto the center. Longstreet's infantry jogged toward the firing in a double column, eight men across, that filled the broad, straight Plank Road. Soon large groups of Confederates came into view, moving in the wrong direction, streaming back along the verges in what Alexander, riding up front with Longstreet, characterized as "a perfect rout." Joe Haskell called over to an infantry officer to ask whether the men were being turned around. "No, God damn 'em," came the reply. "They are running."[6]

In the melee, Alexander saw Lee himself spur to the front, as at Gettysburg ten months before. A federal battery began throwing shells from a pine woods beyond a clearing. The head of Longstreet's column swung into line of battle. At Lee's approach, the Texas brigade sent up a howling protest: "Lee go back! Lee to the rear!" Somebody grabbed Traveller's bridle and turned him toward Longstreet, whom Lee evidently had not yet seen. A dense mass of blue appeared in the road. A moment later a steady, rolling volley flashed out from the Confederate line. "It told Hancock & Meade & Grant that Longstreet had arrived," Alexander wrote exultantly. Hancock's assault columns were stopped along the entire front.[7]

Alexander escorted most of the guns back to Parker's Store—they were not much use in this blinding country—and rejoined Longstreet at about nine o'clock, just as Hancock renewed the attack. Ninety minutes of persistent effort yielded no gain anywhere on the First Corps line. Longstreet began to consider a counterstroke. Lee's chief engineer, Maj. Gen. Martin Smith, returned from an early-morning scout to report finding what he believed to be the unsupported tip of Hancock's left flank. Smith also told Longstreet about an unfinished railroad cut, overgrown now, that he thought would enable three or four brigades to work up close under cover.[8]

Longstreet chose Moxley Sorrel to lead the attack. He gave Sorrel, who had never before commanded troops in battle, detailed instructions, then dismissed his chief of staff with what might be taken as the definitive statement of his tactical method: "Hit hard when you start," Longstreet told Sorrel, "but don't start until you have everything ready." Sorrel galloped off to collect the assault troops, four infantry brigades, some five thousand men. As Hancock's second effort faltered, Longstreet sent Alexander across country to find Stuart's cavalry and scout sites for guns to support Sorrel's advance.[9]

He met Stuart on a path in the deepest Wilderness, flatlands thickly grown with new-leaf saplings thirty feet high and no thicker than a man's arm. Like a squire showing a neighbor over his estate, Stuart escorted Alexander all around the cavalry lines. Skirting an open field, he carelessly pushed an aide out front to flush the Federals. Bursts of orange instantly lit up the dark edge of the wood, revealing a long line of enemy skirmishers. The aide lay low in the saddle and regained cover unhurt; the horse took a minié ball through the nose. "He kept up a constant snorting and blowing of blood on Stuart & myself," Alexander complained. Finding no place for artillery in this wasteland, he spurred back toward Longstreet's headquarters.[10]

On the way, he fell in with Joe Haskell, who passed along a report of calamity: Longstreet had been shot. Sorrel's attack had been a perfect success. The Confederates spilled out of the woods, knocked over Hancock's end brigades, and, in Alexander's phrase, "rolled them up like a scroll." Over on the Plank Road, Longstreet saw visions of a great left wheel that, picking up Hill's and Ewell's corps, would overwhelm Grant's army and throw the remnants back across the Rapidan. He sent word for Kershaw's division (Joseph Kershaw had succeeded McLaws after Knoxville) to double-time to the front. Longstreet, Kershaw, and several other officers pushed on up the Plank Road. Away to the right, from the cover of a thicket, a party of Confederate riflemen sighted the entourage, mistook it for advancing Yankees, and opened fire. "Friends," Kershaw shouted. "They are friends." The impact of the ball lifted the broad-beamed Longstreet out of the saddle and dropped him down hard. He had been shot through the throat, a possibly mortal wound, Haskell, quoting a surgeon, told Alexander.[11]

Dazed and dripping blood, Longstreet hissed out orders from a stretcher: Let Charles Field, the ranking division commander, take charge and, using everything he had, gain the Brock Road just ahead. He spoke briefly to Lee, urging him to force the pace. Inevitably there were delays. Not unnaturally, Field wanted time to get a feel for the battle. Lee decided to straighten the crooked Confederate lines, a time-consuming project. Hancock's corps, granted a four-hour reprieve, fell back and re-formed behind sturdy defenses.[12]

Strange things happened in "that repulsive district," as Sorrel called the Wilderness. The loss of Longstreet seemed to paralyze the First Corps. Alexander thought his absence more costly than Jackson's in similar circumstances on practically the same ground a year ago. The advance did not resume until four o'clock. The woods were afire by then;

even Hancock's heavy log-and-earth breastworks were burning in places. Field's tardy effort achieved nothing. At the time, Alexander believed Longstreet's wounding alone had saved the Army of the Potomac from destruction. He never wavered in the belief. The Wilderness battle claimed more than 25,000 casualties, two-thirds of them Federals. Some of the wounded, unable to walk or crawl, burned to death or were asphyxiated in the smoking woods.[13]

There were no formal engagements on Saturday the seventh, but only constant sharpshooting, heat and thirst, stinging woodsmoke, swarms of biting insects, and the reek of carrion, human and animal. Toward sundown Alexander received word to start the artillery for Spotsylvania Court House; Grant's trains had been sighted heading in that direction. Burnside and Hooker had given up after their setbacks in this part of the world, especially Hooker, who was easily spooked. Grant kept going, south and east in a renewed effort to move out in front of Lee and block the Richmond road. Lee correctly anticipated Grant's play. For the moment, though, on the chance it might be a feint, he could risk releasing only the First Corps from the Wilderness lines. Even if the Confederates won the race, the First Corps, now under Richard Anderson, would have to fight alone all day Sunday if Grant chose to provoke a battle.[14]

Alexander thought well of Anderson, a South Carolinian whom he had known slightly in the old army. Perhaps recalling Longstreet's sulks and mood swings, he went out of his way to emphasize Anderson's equable temperament. Sorrel left a sharper portrait of this colorless officer. Brave, to be sure, Anderson was also "inert, indolent, and by no means pushing or aggressive," Sorrel wrote. "He seemed to leave the corps much to his staff, while his own meditative disposition was constantly soothed by whiffs from a noble, cherished meerschaum pipe." Anderson acted out of character Saturday night. Figuring nobody could sleep anyway in those haunted, smoldering woods, he advanced Lee's start time by five hours, putting the infantry in motion at ten o'clock. Alexander led the guns on a swift, choking trip over secondary roads fetlock-deep in dust, rejoining the infantry at the Po River crossing at daybreak. The column paused for breakfast and an hour's rest, then regained the road for Spotsylvania.[15]

The halt nearly cost Anderson all the advantage of his early start. Alexander encountered Fitzhugh Lee's cavalry falling back toward the Po bridge under pressure from enemy infantry, elements of the Fifth

Corps, now under Gouverneur Warren. He directed two batteries of John Haskell's* battalion to accompany the leading infantry brigades hastening to Fitzhugh Lee's relief. The riflemen were just settling into the light breastworks the cavalry had assembled when the Federals charged, three brigades strong. Expecting lightly armed cavalry, they shied when confronted with several volleys of heavy musketry. Anderson fed Field's division into the improvised works and instructed Alexander to lay out a credible line of battle. He placed his old battalion on the edge of a pine thicket on the left, giving Huger's guns a commanding sweep over the open ground the Yankees would have to cross if they decided to come again. They came once more, then twice again. But they always came one division at a time, and were easily repulsed.[16]

By midday, Warren's corps had been fought to a standstill and Alexander could turn his attention to the defenses at Spotsylvania Court House, where John Haskell's battalion, firing from exposed positions, had been hit hard. Alexander moved along the line in search of cover for Haskell's guns. He paused to cadge a drink from an infantry captain, taking a moment, in the southern manner, to pass the time of day. A federal battery measured the range and opened fire just as Alexander handed the canteen back. "Three shells exploded together, just short of us and a little high," he remembered. "The whirring and whizzing of the fragments filled the air, & they tore up turf all around." Remarkably, neither officer was hit, though one shard ripped a button off Alexander's coat front, and another tore away half the captain's sleeve. But a two-inch-square piece struck Dixie with a loud *spat*. Alexander had been told, somewhere, that a once-wounded horse, hit again, will always squeal in a certain characteristic pitch. Dixie now let out a shriek unlike anything, human or animal, he had ever heard. Great gouts of blood gushed from her neck. She reared; he threw himself clear; she landed heavily on all fours, shocked and disoriented, and began to race around wildly.[17]

Seeing the commotion, Stephen Winthrop galloped up to volunteer his special services. "General, she's mortally wounded," Winthrop sang out. "Shall I put her out of her misery?" Alexander nodded. The Briton drew his revolver and took aim. "Hold on," Aleck called at the last moment. "I guess she'll live to carry her own saddle to the wagon train & save our packing it." On examination, Dixie turned out to have a flesh wound, ugly but treatable. In a few weeks she had quite recovered.[18]

*Brother of Alexander's aide Joe Haskell.

Warren, meanwhile, called for assistance and prepared to renew the battle. Meade ordered an immediate attack, but Warren and John Sedgwick's Sixth Corps were slow to combine. The operation did not get under way until six o'clock, around the time the van of Ewell's corps arrived to reinforce Anderson. Alexander brought into action nearly every one of his fifty-four guns. They "butchered the Yankees in piles," Alexander wrote home; Confederate casualties were "miraculously small." The rest of Ewell's corps moved up during the night to extend Anderson's line.[19]

Next day, Monday, the opposing sides worked away at their entrenchments, the federal pioneer troops equipped with picks, shovels, and axes, the poverty-stricken Confederate infantry picking at the earth with bayonets and tin cups. Hill's corps arrived during the afternoon. Snipers exchanged a deadly fire throughout the day. A Confederate marksman claimed Sedgwick, fifty-one years old, a bachelor devoted to the game of solitaire, as he inspected the Sixth Corps front. A twelve-pound shot flew into the bore of one of Moody's twenty-four-pound howitzers. Huger recovered the ball and fired it back out of one of Taylor's Napoleons. "It seemed to know the road," he reported. In a chance meeting with Stuart, Alexander learned that Sheridan's cavalry corps had started for Richmond and that the Confederate troopers were about to set off in pursuit. Alexander found him in high spirits. Laughing behind his flowing Old Testament beard, Stuart guyed him again about the encounter in the photographer's gallery with Mary Lee.[20]

The Spotsylvania lines described a semicircle facing north, with a bulging salient in the center. Alexander considered the bulge, known as the Mule Shoe on account of its shape, a poor piece of military engineering. Besides, the Confederates had neither the time to fortify it adequately nor the troops to occupy it. Yet it served an important, perhaps decisive, unintended purpose. The salient so alarmed and attracted Meade that he decided to recall Hancock, who had started two divisions across the Po in a sortie against the Confederate left. The flanking operation, if pursued, "might have ruined us," Alexander argued afterward. Instead, Hancock returned to the north bank to lend his weight to an assault on the Mule Shoe.[21]

Warren's corps opened the attack on Anderson's front at three-thirty Tuesday afternoon. The Confederates, with heavy artillery support, broke up his seven-brigade charge. Warren tried again, but only lengthened the casualty lists. At six o'clock, three brigades of the Sixth Corps, now under Horatio Wright, entered the fray on Warren's left. They made modest gains at the apex of the Mule Shoe, then were driven back by a counterattack. At sunset, on Warren's right, Hancock launched the final assault of the day: like the earlier ones, a failure.[22]

Sharpshooting and cannonading continued through the eleventh, Wednesday, while Grant planned another try at the salient. Yankee marksmen pushed their outposts to within fifty yards of the First Corps positions. The enemy light batteries poured a stream of shot and shell into Anderson's works, a relentless bombardment that tore away at the thin pines that shaded and partially screened Alexander's old battalion. Three of Huger's guns were struck by solid shot and wrecked. But "our lines are generally strong," Alexander wrote home, "and I would like nothing better than to have the enemy attack them with every man he has." He heard Stuart had been wounded, seriously from the sound of it, in a cavalry clash at Yellow Tavern, near Richmond.[23]

Grant's preparations involved a series of casual troop movements that Lee wrongly interpreted as the preliminary to another flank march. Accordingly, he sent orders to withdraw all the frontline guns at nightfall so the army might slip quietly away ahead of the enemy. The artillery chiefs of Ewell's and Hill's corps executed the order literally. Alexander allowed himself a good bit of latitude. Visiting each battery, he saw that the ammunition chests were mounted, the gun carriages lined up, and the exits cleared. When the time came, the guns could be swiftly and silently drawn out, hitched up, and driven away.[24]

Rain fell steadily overnight, slackening to drizzle toward dawn. Hancock signaled for the advance a few minutes past four-thirty. Steering by compass through the murk, twenty thousand infantry ghosted along in a dense column twenty men deep. Alexander heard muffled cheering before anything became visible. Some picket firing broke out. Then the Federals swarmed out of the fog, hurdled the parapet, and overwhelmed the Mule Shoe defenders, capturing four thousand prisoners and twenty-two cannon. Recalled belatedly from their rearward parks, the guns had arrived in two long lines just in time to surrender. Only two of the pieces managed to fire at all.[25]

Meanwhile, Burnside launched a diversion on Hill's front and Warren opened with artillery and pushed his skirmishers up to Anderson's lines. Alexander's gun crews, standing to their weapons, delivered a slow, steady fire. Warren chose not to convert the demonstration into an assault. At the base of the salient, Ewell rushed in fresh troops to seal the gap in his lines. Hancock kept up the pressure, but could not exploit the opening. With five more or less intact brigades, Ewell counterattacked, stopped Hancock's advance, and, improbably, drove the Federals back to the edge of the parapet.[26]

But it was early still. Hancock turned the Confederate breastworks the other way and held most of what he had gained. Grant ordered Warren and Wright to follow up Hancock's success. The fighting continued all day in the rain, the fire rising to a pitch of intensity never before seen or heard in this war. Musketry felled an entire forest in front of the salient, which now became the tight, self-contained killing ground known as the Bloody Angle. Bodies of the dead and wounded from earlier attacks were literally shot to pieces.[27]

At eleven o'clock, after a long delay, Warren advanced Griffin's and Cutler's divisions over the open ground that Alexander's guns had flailed during Sunday's fighting. By common consent, the defenders allowed the enemy to approach to within a hundred yards before opening fire. The Federals stood it for a few minutes, then fell back into a hollow. A little later, a terrific volume of noise boiled up out of the ravine. The firing—it sounded like a battle down there—continued for nearly two hours. Afterwards, Alexander could find no mention of this action in any federal report, or any explanation in the Confederate accounts. He eventually concluded that Griffin's and Cutler's divisions had been fighting *each other* for all that time.[28]

Grant fed reinforcements into the Bloody Angle all afternoon, drawing infantry from Burnside and Warren when it became apparent that their attacks were going nowhere. Night came, but the fighting went on in the downpour. Toward midnight an oak, twenty-two inches thick at its base, toppled into the Confederate lines, cut in two by gunfire. Its fall injured several men in a South Carolina regiment. Finally, at one o'clock in the morning on Friday, May 13, Lee authorized a withdrawal. The survivors dropped back to a new line across the base of the salient. Hancock possessed the Mule Shoe fully at last, a dubious prize on an unlucky day.[29]

Only the sharpshooters were consistently homicidal after daybreak, though the artillery kept up an intermittent fire. Stuart, Alexander learned, had died of his injuries. The federal wounded lay in the mud in front of the First Corps lines; incredibly, a few men downed in the initial assaults five days ago were still alive. "We had noticed one who had occasionally raised himself to a sitting posture," Alexander reported.

"Today he was trying to knock himself in the head with the butt of his musket, making several feeble efforts." Alexander's glass brought him close. He struggled weakly for a while, then was still. The blows had hardly seemed sufficient to kill, yet he did not move again.[30]

The Confederate skirmishers ventured out of the trenches early on Saturday the fourteenth. They found the Yankee works vacant. "We felt like boys out of school," Alexander recalled. "For a little while the strain would be off. We could walk & sit outside the trenches, & shells stopped coming around." He toured the debris-strewn fields. Someone had stripped the man who had been clubbing himself. Alexander noticed he had decorated his skin with beautiful tattoos of eagles, flags, and other patriotic devices. Where had the living enemy gone? Overnight, Warren and Wright had marched cross-country to take up positions for an attempt on Lee's right. Bad roads, mud, drizzling rain, pitch darkness, and exhaustion stalled the initiative. Lee shifted the First Corps rightward to cover the new front. The troops settled in for a period of trench warfare.[31]

The experience adumbrated the troglodyte world of the Western Front of 1914–18. Rain fell day after day. Men fought, fed, and rested in knee-deep wastewater. Chronic night fogs brought on chills and fever. "Until the seventeenth I never even took off my vest or pants," Alexander complained. Sleep became prized above all else, even tobacco. Still, he assured Bettie, he fully expected to live to make old bones. "I am much less exposed than I used to be as Battn. Comdr. & now when we are fighting in pits I always dismount & go in under cover of the parapet," he insisted. Anderson's troops at least had a respite from heavy fighting. From the sixteenth to the twenty-first, the only actions of note occurred on the other end of the line. In the most significant, Grant attacked Ewell in the old First Corps works on May 18. The operation failed utterly.[32]

Grant gave up on Spotsylvania—the Federals lost in excess of fifteen thousand killed, wounded, and missing in the fighting there, for a total of more than thirty-three thousand since May 5—and started Hancock on a wide swing around the Confederate right, hoping Lee would turn, follow, and risk his army in the open. Lee did not react; Alexander concluded later that he had never known of the trap Grant set for him, using Hancock as decoy. Instead, Lee retreated some thirty miles to Hanover Junction, behind the North Anna River.[33]

The First Corps started after dark on Saturday, May 21, marching all night over firm roads. Alexander left the column Sunday morning to call on Squire Wortham and his wife. The Worthams seemed pleased to see him again, though they knew the Confederates were rushing through and that the Yankees were close behind.* "About the least they could expect would be to lose all their poultry & live stock, & to have all their fences burned," Alexander said. The battalion crossed the North Anna and went into camp Sunday afternoon near a farmhouse outside Hanover Junction. When Alexander inquired about chickens, the farmer refused to sell any.[34]

The enemy turned up sooner than expected—the next morning, in fact, May 23, Monday. A battery firing from north of the river announced Grant's appearance. Several shells dropped into the farmyard, making refugees of the farmer and his family. "I say, won't you sell me those chickens now?" Alexander called out to his retreating back. He rode over to the North Anna bluffs to oversee the distribution of the artillery, then joined Anderson and his staff to await events. He found the corps commander pacing the yard behind his headquarters, a fine brick country house, and drawing placidly on his meerschaum. Aleck checked in with a small party of aides and couriers near the house. A moment later a shell whistled into one of the chimneys, loosing a cascade of bricks. Catlike, he jumped onto the sill of a cellar window and pressed himself flat against the sash. He escaped with painful bruises on his ankles and feet. A courier was buried in the rubble and killed, and one or two others were injured.[35]

Warren's Fifth Corps crossed at Jericho Ford and went into line of battle on A. P. Hill's front. Hill attacked at six o'clock. Unable to sustain an initial success, he broke off the battle with a loss of about fifteen hundred men. In consultation with Lee, Alexander helped lay out the First Corps line that night. As they conferred, a teamster and a mule struck up a noisy argument nearby. Lee and Aleck were deep in discussion when the commanding general, notorious for his softheartedness toward animals, broke off to reprimand the muleteer. Lee had a peculiar way of shaking his head when worried or angry—"snapping at his ear," the younger officers at his headquarters called it. Ignoring Lee, the teamster went on abusing the animal. Lee paused again and snapped at his ear.

"What are you beating that mule for?" he said finally.

*Forty-eight hours later, Grant and Meade conferred at a makeshift table set up in the broad aisle of Mount Carmel Church, near Alexander's winter camp of 1862–63.

Alexander expected the anger in Lee's voice to turn the man to stone. It did no such thing. In a cracker whine, he sang out:

"Is this any of you-r-r mule?"[36]

The Confederates braced for another of Grant's trademark dawn visits. He did not appear on May 24, or the next day or the day after that. "They wanted to attack us," Alexander said. "They crossed the river for that purpose. And their engineers & their generals looked at our beautiful lines with longing eyes for several days. But they always shook their heads & said it would not do." On the twenty-sixth, the Federals stepped back from the North Anna, turned southeast, and tried once again to outmarch the nimble Army of Northern Virginia.[37]

They crossed the broad Pamunkey at Hanovertown, twenty miles northeast of Richmond, and advanced to the marshy fringe of Totopotomoy Creek. Lee followed. On Tuesday the thirty-first, Fitzhugh Lee's cavalry reached the road junction of Cold Harbor, north of the Chickahominy, near the old battlefields of the Seven Days of 1862. Lee determined to strike Grant's left flank there. Possibly the strain of retreat had begun to wear on Lee; perhaps the intestinal disorder he had brought down from the North Anna made him even more aggressive than usual. For whatever reason, Alexander thought Lee had never before seemed so impatient to attack.[38]

He selected the First Corps for the job. During the night, Longstreet's veterans, three divisions now that Pickett had rejoined, pulled out of the Totopotomoy lines and passed in the rear of Ewell's command.* The column covered the eight or nine miles to Cold Harbor in deep silence. "A man with his eyes shut would only have known that anyone was on the road by the occasional rattle of a canteen," Alexander wrote Bettie. "It reminded me of Byron's description, 'Some thought about their children, wives and friends / And others of themselves and latter ends.'" Anderson attacked with two brigades at dawn Wednesday, June 1, but made no headway against Sheridan's dismounted cavalry. Anderson tried again, but the federal troopers, armed with Spencer carbines, held on for the late-arriving infantry. When the Sixth Corps reached the battlefield at midmorning, Anderson called off the operation.[39]

The other First Corps brigades waited in the road during the assault, random fire occasionally reaching the front ranks. Without orders, troops here and there began to entrench; the urge to dig had become

---

*Now under Jubal Early. A fall from his horse at Spotsylvania had incapacitated Ewell.

instinctive. With the enemy up close, Anderson accepted these works as a rudimentary line of battle. Alexander sited the guns at suitable points. The lines were slightly concave, the country flat and thinly wooded—favorable conditions for converging fire. Alexander instructed the battery commanders to run the guns out in front of the breastworks whenever possible.[40]

Two enemy corps attacked toward the end of the workday. The worn-out defenders dropped their entrenching tools, shouldered their muskets, and checked the assault after an hour's hard fighting. Forgoing sleep, the Confederates labored all night on their defenses. The Federals did not test them Thursday. A hard rain began falling in the afternoon, laying the dust and breaking a long spell of intense heat. Beyond the gray curtain, Grant's army massed for another dawn assault.[41]

The Yankees—Hancock again, with Wright's corps and W. F. Smith's 18th Corps on loan from the Army of the James—advanced through the pine woods and swamps of Cold Harbor at first light Friday. Alexander met them with sweeping crossfires. The initial assault lasted only eight minutes. Meade persisted, even though Grant sent word he could suspend the attacks if they looked as if they were failing. The heaviest fighting surged up in front of the First Corps. "Since 5½ o'clock we have repulsed fourteen assaults," Kershaw reported in a note to Anderson at eight o'clock. "We are sustaining little loss—damaging the enemy seriously. My line is all right and very strong." The Federals kept up some show of aggressiveness until early afternoon, but they had lost heart. Grant intervened and stopped the battle at one-thirty. By then the ground was "black with the dead," John Haskell remembered. Cold Harbor cost the Federals a further fifty-six hundred killed, wounded, and missing, most of them in the first hour. Lee lost fewer than fifteen hundred.[52]

Still, the Confederates were beginning to see the logic of Grant's operations: If he kept at it, he would sooner or later wear the Army of Northern Virginia out of existence. "Ultimately such a bloody policy must win, and it makes little difference to them, as the vast majority of the killed and wounded are foreigners, many of whom can't speak English," a First Corps staff officer wrote home, expressing a common view. The staffer knew, probably, that reinforcements—more than forty thousand since May 5—had largely made up Grant's losses. Even so, the Union commander was trading at a discount. "Among every one thousand men," Alexander wrote, "there is a certain percentage who have initiative, courage & are leaders; a larger percentage who will make sturdy followers only; & a residue who are shirkers." In only a few weeks, the proportion of shirkers in Grant's army had risen dramatically.[43]

The armies passed another brief season in the Cold Harbor trenches, "the eight days of greatest hardship the army ever endured," according to Alexander. The troops huddled in ditches a yard wide by two feet deep, protected by a parapet less than three feet high. Two ranks were in residence day and night, the men wet, hot, filthy, crawling with vermin, and, worst of all, sleep-deprived. Rations were carried in and the wounded and dead carried out under cover of darkness. Alexander moved up and down the line countless times during the course of the workday, bent double, scrambling apelike over or around the dozing infantry. At nightfall he retired to the rear, made for an uncontaminated creek, and luxuriated in its cool bath.[44]

The sharpshooters practiced from early dawn until last light. When Taylor's gunners elevated a damaged Napoleon, thirty-seven musket balls spilled out of the breech. Shot rolled around in all directions over the Cold Harbor plain. In a dash across one exposed stretch, Alexander dropped the envelope containing his pay for the month of May—$301 in new Confederate bills, worth about twenty-five dollars in gold. He advertised for the packet, affixing a scrawled note to the crook of a stick and sending it down the line, passed from hand to hand. His wages were returned anonymously a day or two later. An expert marksman, Alexander took his turn as a sniper. The work, he found, demanded specialized skills. "It was not shooting at a whole man," he said, "but generally only at an edge, or corner, exposed for a few seconds behind some obstacle. If any larger fraction, it was jumping across some gap and harder to hit than a snipe." The corps staff's morale remained steady enough, even in the face of all this misery. At headquarters, officers boasted of garnishing Ohio-cured bacon with Connecticut onions, blockade-breaking provisions shipped from Nassau via Wilmington and on by rail to the fighting front.[45]

Grant, Alexander knew, was no mere butcher, but a thinking soldier of great ability. His next move, across the James River to Petersburg, ought to have ended the war. Four vital rail lines met at Petersburg. Lee could not victual the army if these communications were cut. He would be forced to abandon Richmond, the industrial, political, and psychological heart of the Confederacy, and fight his weaker army in open country. But Grant had blunted his weapon in the Wilderness and at Spotsylvania and Cold Harbor. He seized the Petersburg opening, but his exhausted army no longer had the strength to close the issue.

The Yankees marched during the second week of June, swiftly, secretly, deceiving Lee entirely, in what Alexander called "the most brilliant stroke in all the Federal campaigns of the whole war." It began at night-fall Sunday, June 12. "Enemy gone," Alexander wrote in his diary the next day. The Fifth Corps crossed the Chickahominy at Long Bridge and went into line of battle to cover the movement of three corps to Wilcox's Landing on the James. A fourth corps came around by ferry to City Point, on the south bank. The transports unloaded, then steamed upriver to carry other troops across. By late morning of the fifteenth, Wednesday, the 18th Corps stood in front of Petersburg; Hancock would shortly arrive with the Second Corps. The Sixth and Ninth corps, soon joined by the Fifth, lay in camp at Wilcox's, waiting for Alexander's old army friend James Duane, Meade's chief engineer, to complete his extraordi-nary pontoon bridge over the James. Duane started the half-mile-long, thirteen-foot-wide bridge ("the greatest the world has seen since the days of Xerxes," Alexander thought) at four o'clock Wednesday, and finished before midnight. Federals crossed in a ceaseless stream over the next forty-eight hours.[46]

"It was all accomplished without mishap, and in such an incredibly short time that Lee refused for three days to believe it," Alexander wrote. The old man's intuition failed him for once. He did not discover that Grant had gone until after daylight on the thirteenth. Even then, he misunderstood the movement. The First Corps waited in camp all day on the fourteenth as Beauregard, commanding at Petersburg, sent out the first calls for assistance. Just beyond earshot, Alexander watched one of Beauregard's couriers, Col. Samuel Paul, put the case for rein-forcements to Lee. Alexander thought Lee disliked the message or the messenger, perhaps both. ("And I imagined a new military precept, to be taught in the schools," he recalled, "that *personae gratas* should always be selected for messengers.") Lee refused to credit Beauregard's claim that Grant had thrown significant forces across the James. Davis, in Rich-mond, dismissed it, too, with a slighting comment on Beauregard's ten-dency to sensationalize.[47]

At dawn June 15, the First Corps took the road for the Drewry's Bluff crossing, but Lee changed his mind and suspended the movement. "That was the time & place, the day & hour, when the last hope of the Confederacy died down & flickered out," Alexander said later. Smith's corps, sixteen thousand strong, assaulted the Petersburg lines at seven o'clock that evening. Over the next three days the Federals attacked again and again: first Smith, then Smith and Hancock, then Hancock, Wright, Burnside, and Warren. Beauregard's scratch force, fewer than thirty-five hundred men, including the home guard, at the start, grudgingly built up to a total of about fourteen thousand, stood for more than sixty hours against the full weight of Grant's army.[48]

This, in Alexander's view, was the crisis of the Civil War. He never lost his enthusiasm for the "if" game; what-might-have-beens fascinated him for as long as he lived. What if Lee had rushed the First Corps to Petersburg on the fifteenth? Beauregard checked the Yankees with militia, light cavalry, and second-line artillery. Longstreet's veteran infantry surely would have delivered such a blow as Grant had never felt before, a defeat of incalculably greater scope than Cold Harbor, a disaster to rock the northern financial markets, undermine the Republican party's political foundations, and dry up enlistments.

Instead, the First Corps idled in the dust near Malvern Hill. "Grant had gotten away from US completely & was fighting *Beauregard*," Alexander said. "The Army of Northern Virginia had lost him, & was sucking its thumbs by the roadside 25 miles away, & wondering where he could be!!!" The First Corps crossed the James the morning of June 16, but only to keep Benjamin Butler's harmless little James army bottled up at Bermuda Hundred. Lee finally ordered Kershaw's division to Petersburg shortly after midnight June 18. An hour or two later, the last in a long line of couriers from Beauregard, liberally quoting prisoners' statements, convinced Lee of the full measure of Grant's achievement. He sent word for the balance of the army to follow Kershaw.*[49]

The Federals attacked throughout the day on Saturday the eighteenth. Alexander reached Petersburg around nine o'clock and helped conduct the First Corps infantry into line. These veterans were hardly tested; the corps diary described the federal efforts as "feeble." Alexander brought his guns up to the front after dark—"of all the moonlight nights I can remember, perhaps the most beautiful, the whole landscape bathed & saturated in silver," he wrote. Grant did not renew the battle. Federal casualties from May 5 totaled sixty-six thousand—more men than the

---

*Only Hill's and Anderson's commands were available. Lee sent Early's corps to the Shenandoah Valley after Cold Harbor to counter the federal threat there.

entire Army of Northern Virginia had mustered at the outset of the campaign. Still, Lee had missed his last, best chance. "This army cannot stand a siege," he had told A. P. Hill a few weeks earlier. Lee saw it then; in hindsight, Alexander recognized, too, that after Petersburg the end would be only a question of time.[50]

CHAMBERLAIN

SLAUGHTER PENS, MAY–OCTOBER 1864

Chamberlain rejoined a bled-down 20th Maine at Spotsylvania around May 15. More than a hundred men had been killed or wounded in the Wilderness, one name in every four on the regimental muster roll. Private Gerrish was among the casualties, shot in the left ankle on the first day of the battle, though not seriously enough to warrant immediate attention. For two days he lay under a tree outside the field hospital awaiting his turn, lacking even a blanket for comfort, drifting in and out of consciousness, listening to the keening of men in pain and the far-off drone of the fighting. On the second day, the walking wounded shuffled in with news of disaster: Lee had seized the Rapidan fords and cut off Grant's retreat. "We had expected so much from General Grant, and now he was to be defeated as other generals before him had been," Gerrish wrote, conveying the disappointment, tinged with an invalid's apathy, he had felt then. As it happened, the tale-bearers were wrong. Grant resumed the offensive, sending the Army of the Potomac out around Lee's right toward the Richmond road.[1]

The Fifth Corps had seen more hard fighting at Spotsylvania. Casualties mounted at an unprecedented rate. "I just live, father," an infantryman in Griffin's division wrote home, "and that is about all." Chamberlain's particular friend James Rice was mortally wounded May 10, shot in the hip leading a hopeless charge. Three young officers of the 20th Maine were casualties too—Morrell killed, Melcher and Prince wounded. Grant allowed Chamberlain little time to mourn. "He was like Thor the Hammerer; striking blow after blow, intent on his purpose to beat his way through, somewhat reckless of the cost," Chamberlain said. He had barely taken over the 20th Maine from Ellis Spear when Griffin, in pursuit of Thor's aim, chose him to lead a group of seven miscellaneous regiments in a head-on charge against Longstreet's veterans. Griffin thought better of the idea and amended the order. Chamberlain carried out the operation under cover of night, advancing Griffin's lines half a mile with slight loss.[2]

The 20th Maine huddled in rifle pits under sniper and artillery fire—lucky, well protected, probably both, for Chamberlain reported only one casualty during his first few days in line. A heavy cannonade fell on the regiment the morning of May 18 as Grant tried a two-corps assault on Ewell's front. Chamberlain watched it break up in failure. "Lee is holding us very stiffly," Chamberlain, writing under fire, reported to Maine governor Samuel Cony. "We are not pushing him in front, but are moving to turn his right & that of course brings us nearer to Richmond." After this latest setback, Grant accepted another drawn battle. "The victory, so far as there was any, rests with Lee," Charles Wainwright, the Fifth Corps artillery commander, wrote in his diary. At midday on Saturday, May 21, Warren's corps pulled out of the line and marched by the left again, toward the North Anna River.[3]

Chamberlain showed no resentment in returning to his regiment, doubtless recognizing that Thor's way meant vacancies were certain to appear in the brigade commands, and sooner rather than later. After all, he noted, the hammering business was hard on the hammer. Griffin found appropriate work for him, military odd jobs, usually of a dangerous kind. "I was often put in charge of peculiarly trying ventures, advance and rearguard fights, involving command of several regiments," Chamberlain recalled. The first such assignment came his way on the march to the North Anna. Chamberlain led the Fifth Corps advance, ranging out front with the skirmishers.[4]

A wisp of blue smoke rose from a wooded hillside ahead, just beyond a narrow, tree-lined stream called Pole Cat Creek. An instant later the report sounded and a cannon shot tore through the column, killing a man in the 118th Pennsylvania. Chamberlain detailed the 118th and the 20th Maine to work around the battery's flank while two other regiments approached from the front. The flanking column halted at the edge of the creek. The men began to mill about noisily. After a while someone had the bright idea of throwing an old section of wooden fence across the stream. The racket would have awakened the dead. It certainly alerted the enemy. Chamberlain looked on helplessly as the Confederates limbered up and galloped away.[5]

Pushing on, Griffin's division reached the North Anna at Jericho Ford about three o'clock Monday afternoon, May 23. Deserters and other helpful persons reported Lee's army drawn up in line of battle near Hanover Junction, south of the river. Warren, appearing nervous and excited, stood on the north bank hurrying the infantry across. By nature "apt to take freaks," according to Charles Wainwright, not always a friendly witness, Warren had cause for anxiety. Grant already had concluded that he had been promoted beyond his competence. His staff work had been excellent, at Little Round Top and elsewhere. He had proved himself to be as brave as a lion. But Warren had trouble managing large bodies of troops. He could not keep to schedule. His attacks were ill-concerted. At Spotsylvania, Grant told Meade to relieve him if he thought another commander would do better. He also faulted Warren for his inability to delegate lesser tasks. Grant might have fired him on the spot had he seen him at Jericho Ford this afternoon, directing traffic when he should have been up front, spying around for weak places in the Confederate line.[6]

The 20th Maine forded the chest-deep river, scaled the bluff south bank, and stood guard while the engineers threw over a pontoon bridge. By five o'clock, Warren had the entire corps across. The First Division moved inland and formed a line of battle along the edge of a country lane. At six, Confederates of A. P. Hill's corps assailed the bridgehead. Lysander Cutler's division gave way on the right, but a well-directed response from Wainwright's artillery disrupted the advance and Warren rushed up troops to check it. The 20th Maine lay under a sharp fire for nearly two hours. Toward dusk, Hill broke off the battle and withdrew. A series of powerful thunderstorms bowled through during the night, lighting up the skies and flooding the newly dug trenches. The front remained quiet, except for skirmishing, for the next two days. Then, on Thursday, May 26, Grant ordered still another move by the left.[7]

Chamberlain led the 20th Maine back across the North Anna in a hissing downpour. The full corps idled in the rain and mud for several hours to allow the Sixth Corps to pass, only resuming the march toward first light Friday. The route, southeast again, ran through plantation country as yet untouched by war. "We plundered without stint, and completed our inroad only when everything had disappeared before the gun and knife," one soldier admitted. Despite these forays, the column covered thirty miles before halting for the night. Officers and others too proud to steal could buy asparagus, peas, and early lettuce along the route. The rain had stopped and the roadside camps were pleasant: fireflies alight, night sounds—frogs, crickets, an occasional lonely owl—homely and pleasant.[8]

Next morning, in glaring sunlight and oppressive heat, the corps reached the Pamunkey and crossed on pontoons to Hanovertown. On the twenty-ninth, Sunday, Griffin's division pushed beyond Totopotomoy Creek. Next day a heavy Confederate force struck the Fifth Corps's right-hand division under Samuel Crawford. The enemy could find no opening there and withdrew early in the evening. Warren ordered the corps to entrench. The 20th Maine settled into line near Bethesda Church, three miles north of the crossroads at Cold Harbor.[9]

Chamberlain lay on the outer edge of the storm of June 3. In a minor action, the First Division overran the enemy rifle pits in front of Bethesda Church, but failed to pierce the main works of Early's corps, 150 yards beyond. The 20th Maine reported another twenty-five men killed, wounded, and missing in this halfhearted operation. Word filtered down during the afternoon of terrible losses at Cold Harbor. The attacking infantry evidently had anticipated disaster. Some of the men had written their names and addresses on slips of paper and sewn them to the backs of their coats, "so they might be recognized upon the field," one of Grant's aides wrote, "and their fate made known to their families at home." After Cold Harbor, regimental commanders were no longer asked for daily returns of casualties. When Chamberlain sought an explanation he was told, confidentially, "Because the country would not stand it, if they knew."[10]

He left the 20th Maine on Monday, June 6, for what would turn out to be the final time. Warren sent for him to take charge of five small Pennsylvania regiments from two Fourth Division brigades, consolidated to form a new First Brigade in Griffin's division. He also asked Griffin to write another recommendation for Chamberlain's promotion. Meade forwarded it, along with a dozen others, to the War Department a few days later. The reorganization caused some hard feelings. Warren had passed over the senior First Division colonel, William S. Tilton, in Chamberlain's favor. Cutler, the Fourth Division commander, resented having one of his brigades taken from him. Explaining the shuffle to Meade's adjutant general, Warren noted that the Pennsylvanians had performed poorly of late, especially at Spotsylvania, and that their apologists blamed Cutler, though he had been in charge for only a few weeks. Warren hoped a fresh start under a capable new commander might bring a change for the better.[11]

The command comprised the 121st, 142nd, 143rd, 149th, and 150th Pennsylvania, late of the defunct First Corps, plus the 187th Pennsylvania, a new regiment that mustered eight hundred men, nearly as many as the other five combined. Chamberlain called the regimental commanders together, introduced himself, and outlined his expectations for them. They seemed to appreciate his collegial way of doing business. "This little talk did us good," Horatio Warren, the commanding officer of the 142nd Pennsylvania, told Chamberlain later. The troops were allowed to bathe and were issued new kit: blankets, haversacks, canteens, shoes. Rations were plentiful and varied. ("Grant feeds well," one infantryman reported.) Chamberlain led the brigade out of the Bethesda works on June 7 for a turn of picket duty amid the huge cypresses, willow oaks, and swamp magnolias of the Chickahominy bottoms. *Mal aria.* This was unwholesome country, the earth saturated, the atmosphere heavy with the odor of rotting vegetation. Outpost work was tiring, unglamorous, and often dangerous, though preferable on the whole to confinement in the Cold Harbor trenches, where the slightest stir would provoke a volley or even bring a battery into action.[12]

Attrition: It was the sum of misadventure and accident, the neat hole in a man's forehead when a sharpshooter found his mark, mangled bodies under a sun shelter collapsed by shellburst. Warren took the wastage hard. For one of the early Spotsylvania battles, he had dressed himself in full ceremonial uniform, trimmed with a general officer's yellow sash. Now, a month later, he looked seedy, haggard, and care-worn. "He is certainly one of the most tender-hearted of our commanders," Theodore Lyman, a member of Meade's staff, said of him. Wainwright found him apathetic and uncommunicative. "He seems to have sunk into a sort of lethargic sulk, sleeps a great part of the time, and says nothing to anyone," Wainwright observed. One soldier's fate, not an especially uncommon one, haunted Warren during these Cold Harbor days: the boy buried a friend in a shallow roadside grave one afternoon, then became a corpse himself a quarter-hour later.[13]

Grant launched his great initiative, the movement across the James, the evening of Sunday, June 12. The Fifth Corps set out at dusk for Long Bridge on the Chickahominy, crossed on pontoons before dawn the next day, and entrenched near Riddell's Shop to screen the passage of the Second, Sixth, and Ninth corps. The column resumed the march after nightfall and reached the James at Wilcox's Landing Tuesday after-noon. Salt breezes blowing over the river, here a mile wide, cleansed away the miasma of the Chickahominy. The high green banks of the broad James reminded Lyman, and no doubt other homesick New

Englanders, too, of the Narragansett Bay approaches to Newport. Steamers ferried the Fifth Corps infantry across to Windmill Point on Thursday the sixteenth. The artillery and trains crossed by Major Duane's remarkable bridge downstream.[14]

Chamberlain had the advance southwest from the James, a sixteen-mile night march through forsaken country, houses abandoned, farms untended, dust thick in the superheated air. Like many field officers, he had developed the knack of napping in the saddle; the company offices and the ranks had no choice but to shuffle along in heavy-lidded misery. Chamberlain called frequent brief rest halts. The ranks were grateful; the habit earned him mild censures for tardiness from higher authority. The First Brigade reached the battle zone an hour after midnight and bivouacked in the rear of Burnside's corps. Smith's corps, the first to arrive, had opened the battle for Petersburg; over the past two days Smith, in concert with Hancock and later with Burnside, had captured several strong points in the ten-mile-long system of redans and trenches covering the southern and eastern approaches to the town. But the defenders held on in the main works, even though up to now they had received practically no help from Lee, who was still north of the James, trying to puzzle out Grant's intentions.[15]

"All goes on like a miracle," Charles Dana, an assistant war secretary assigned to Grant's headquarters, reported early in the operation. In his understated way, Grant sounded equally pleased. The army had withdrawn from the Cold Harbor lines, marched fifty miles, crossed two rivers, and beaten Lee to Petersburg, he wrote chief of staff Halleck in Washington—all this "without the loss of a wagon or piece of artillery." By the seventeenth, though, Dana sensed trouble. Gains were slight in comparison with the effort expended. Losses in commissioned officers and senior petty officers were beginning to tell. "The men fight as well," Dana thought, "but are not directed with the same skill and enthusiasm." The Fifth Corps moved into line on Burnside's left June 17, Friday, and prepared to join a general advance at dawn the next day.[16]

Warren saw the corps into action shortly after four-thirty Saturday morning, then retired to his tent for a nap. Out there in the gloom, the forward lines were strangely quiet. The skirmishers, stepping over the dead from yesterday's battle, approached the enemy rifle pits and found them empty. They crept up to the main works; these were abandoned too. Overnight, Beauregard had quietly withdrawn to a shorter line, a chain of redoubts connected by a heavy infantry parapet that ran along high ground west of the Norfolk Railroad. The Second Corps assaulted twice, failed twice. Slowed by rough ground, the Ninth and Fifth corps could not get up in time to attack in concert.[17]

The morning passed in confusion. Reports reached army headquarters that Confederate First Corps troops were moving up to the Petersburg front. Several hours were consumed in reconnoitering the new line and in carrying out other preliminaries to be regarded as important in the circumstances. Meade, his temper and anxieties rising sharply together, ordered a general assault for noon. Warren replied that he could not possibly start before one o'clock. "Everyone else is ready," Meade shot back. Burnside, too, was balky this morning. The command system seemed to be breaking down. At 2:20 P.M., his patience exhausted, Meade ordered each corps to attack at all hazards, without reference to the others.[18]

Chamberlain's brigade had broken camp at first light and moved out on the left of the First Division. After a while, word came to halt. There was a long delay. The sound of the Second Corps battle could be heard away to the north. The advance resumed at 10:30 A.M., the division massing for an attack north of the Norfolk Railroad. From the left, a Confederate battery posted out in front of the main works fired steadily into Griffin's line of battle. By now Warren had thrown off his lethargy and was moving restlessly from point to point. He spurred over to Chamberlain and directed him to silence the enemy guns.[19]

Forming a column of fours, Chamberlain led the brigade across a bridge over the railroad cut, then deployed under cover of a woods, four veteran regiments in front, the 142nd Pennsylvania and the oversized 187th Pennsylvania, here going into action for the first time, in the second line. Chamberlain rode in a brigadier's usual place, the open ground between the lines. In obedience to a premonition that he would be shot in the stomach today, he had strapped his blankets to the front of the saddle, covering his middle. The thick woolen roll might slow or even stop a missile. The lines passed through the woods and into a clearing, pushing the enemy infantry before them. The shelling intensified. Ahead, the skirmishers opened fire. Chamberlain pushed the 142nd into the first line to extend his left and cover the full front. As these dispositions were being completed, a shell burst near him, wounding his horse and killing the brigade flag bearer.[20]

He disentangled himself, caught the flagstaff, and continued on foot. The enemy guns disappeared behind an infantry screen. Glancing back,

Chamberlain could see that the brigade had ranged far out in front of the rest of the division. He found concealment behind a rail fence, overgrown with brush and briars, that ran along a slight swell overlooking a shallow, well-watered ravine. The Confederate works at Rives' Salient were in plain view beyond. Chamberlain ordered the men to lie down on the reverse slope. A sergeant in the 143rd Pennsylvania recalled watching him pace the line, calling out words of encouragement to the men.[21]

There were occasional shell bursts and a lot of sharpshooting. Chamberlain sent word for artillery support; after a while, a twelve-pounder battery appeared. He helped site the guns just below the crest, muzzles resting on the grass. Studying Rives' Salient through his field glasses, Chamberlain counted at least a dozen cannon. Fresh troops were filing into the works; he estimated three thousand infantry in his immediate front. At army headquarters, Meade seethed over the delays ("The general was in a tearing humor," Lyman reported) and finally snapped out the order for Hancock, Burnside, and Warren to attack off their own hook. Chamberlain's men dozed in the hot sun.[22]

An officer wearing lieutenant colonel's shoulder straps approached with what he claimed were orders from Warren to advance at once. Chamberlain did not recognize the courier. The instruction sounded vague and had not come through the usual channels; his brigade lay exposed and, as far as he could tell, entirely without supports.

"Do they send a verbal order, and say nothing about whether I am to attack alone, or with the entire army?"

"I understand that you are to attack alone," the lieutenant colonel said.[23]

Chamberlain struck off a note: The First Brigade had advanced a mile beyond the division front; its left flank hung in the air; enemy infantry and artillery were strongly entrenched on dominating ground; and the brigade would have to negotiate a bog under a converging fire. "From what I can see of the enemy lines," he concluded, "it is my opinion that if an assault is to be made, it should be by nothing less than the entire army."[24]

The staff officer* promised to deliver the note. He returned shortly with word that supporting troops were on the way and that the First Brigade was to lead a general attack timed for three o'clock. Chamberlain

---

*It may have been Lyman, though he made no mention of carrying orders to an advanced brigade in his detailed account of the events of June 18.

called the six regimental commanders together. Tactics did not signify here. He simply told them to clear the swamp as rapidly as possible, without stopping to fire, and to make a lot of noise as they advanced. The lines could re-form on higher ground for the final charge. Chamberlain dismissed the six with instructions to return to their regiments and repeat the orders to their company commanders, who in turn were to explain them to the men.[25]

Cutler's division passed behind the First Brigade and deployed on the left. When the Second Brigade of Griffin's division appeared on his right, Chamberlain established contact with its left-hand regiment, the 21st Pennsylvania Cavalry (dismounted and converted to infantry after the Wilderness), then went over for a word with Cutler. The Fourth Division commander sounded confused and angry. As it turned out, Cutler had some excuse for ill temper. "What [one of Warren's couriers] handed me as an order was only a blank piece of paper, and I am at a loss," he said. Cutler ranked Chamberlain and seemed disinclined to accept his junior's interpretation: that Warren meant for Cutler to join Griffin's command and charge in step with it.[26]

Horatio Warren wrote later than every man in his regiment realized that the assault stood no chance of success, and that failure would carry a high price—"death and sure annhiliation," in his (redundant) phrase. Warren and the other regimental commanders dutifully passed along Chamberlain's instructions. Chamberlain paused to deliver a short oration: no stage fright today, no stutter, no evident anxiety, in spite of the premonition. A veteran of the 143rd Pennsylvania recalled that a fair number of men in the first line were within earshot, and that Chamberlain's words seemed to have a steadying effect. The full speech sounds windy now, but it had the ring of authentic feeling then, and anyway the content hardly mattered, only the tone. "We know that some must fall, it may be any of you or I," Patrick DeLacy quoted Chamberlain as saying, "but I feel you will all go manfully and make such a record as will make all our loyal American people grateful." A few minutes later, sometime between three-thirty and four o'clock, Chamberlain drew his saber and called out the commands for the advance.[27]

The eighteen hundred officers and men of the First Brigade kicked over the rail fence and jogged down the hill into the ravine, spongy ground there, a fifty-yard-wide patch of swamp grown thick with alder, briars, and brush. A brook ran along the far side. In freshet, it had incised a deep washout at the edge of the slope rising from the opposite bank. Beyond, the ground inclined gradually to the Confederate works. Chamberlain ordered an oblique to the left, and the lines moved down into the swale.[28]

The first line struggled through mud and briars, flailed by a crossfire of musketry and artillery. The formation soon broke apart. Independent parties of riflemen emerged from the thickets, crossed the stream, climbed out of the gully, and charged up the lower slope through rows of drought-stunted corn, "yelling," said Horatio Warren, "like a pack of infuriated devils." On the left, Cutler's troops faltered almost at once. DeLacy could see a great mass of them withdrawing. On the right, the unhorsed 21st Pennsylvania Cavalry charged several times despite mounting losses. Chamberlain's 187th Pennsylvania, coming up with the second line, staggered under its first heavy fire, panicked, turned about, and headed for the rear.[29]

Right, left, and center, the assault was a sorry affair. The First Brigade blamed Cutler, whose division arrived late and departed early. On the right, a Second Brigade veteran alleged the First Brigade's failure to follow through with the initial charge had contributed to the heavy casualties in his unit. Lyman, watching from an open field, thought all the attacking troops went in grudgingly, without spirit. Met with a concentrated fire, "they sullenly fell back a few paces and lay down, as much to say, 'We can't assault but we won't run.' " Here, Lyman thought, were the cumulative effects of the Wilderness, Spotsylvania, Cold Harbor. "You can't strike a blow with a wounded hand," he said.[30]

Chamberlain witnessed neither the collapse of the Rives' Salient attack nor the rout of the 187th Pennsylvania. He was shot in the washout as he turned half around to shout an order. He felt a sharp sting, in the back, he thought at first. In fact, the ball passed through him from hip to hip. He let the point of the cavalry saber drop to the ground and leaned heavily upon the hilt. Balanced there, he tried to call out to rally the others, but his voice faded to a whisper as his systems began to shut down. His blood flowed freely, soaking his drawers and his blue trousers and running down his legs. He sank slowly to the ground.

Two subalterns carried him into a clearing out of the direct line of fire, where a dozen others lay seriously wounded. He sent one of the aides away in search of the senior regimental commander, who would have to take charge of what remained of the brigade. A few voices cried out for water. Some of the men were bent into strange, tortured shapes. Chamberlain lay on his back, staring up into the hazy sky, his own dark blood wetting the ground. Dust and battle smoke tinged the sinking sun with copper. A full moon would be on the rise soon. Presently two soldiers approached with a stretcher. Chamberlain motioned them to take the others first; he expected to die among the bleached stones of the little clearing.[31]

William Tilton came over from the 22nd Massachusetts, Second Brigade, to stand in for Chamberlain. He found chaos. Large groups were milling about in the backwash; these could be re-formed, but other parties were trapped on the slope, unable either to resume the advance or withdraw. Tilton heard that Meade had ordered a renewal of the assault, and the arrival in his rear of three regiments from the Third Brigade seemed to confirm the report. He got the skittish 187th Pennsylvania back into line, sent out details to clear away brush in his front, and anxiously awaited the word to advance.[32]

At army headquarters, Meade had regained his composure. Perhaps, like Hooker at Fredericksburg, he decided he had lost the number of men his orders required him to lose, and could stand down now. "When you conclude that nothing further is practicable straighten your lines and make your connections secure," Meade wrote Warren and Burnside at six-thirty. "I am quite satisfied that we have done all that it is possible for men to do, and must be resigned to the result." Warren reported that he hoped to get all the Fifth Corps dead and wounded—upwards of one thousand men, he said then, undercounting by half—off the field by the end of the evening.[33]

The stretcher bearers ignored Chamberlain's weak protests, carried him out of the clearing, and found a place for him in the grass behind one of the twelve-pounders of Bigelow's Ninth Massachusetts Battery. After a while, two of Bigelow's gunners picked him up and delivered him to the division field hospital. Warren and Griffin visited him there, giving Chamberlain the opportunity to make what he regarded as a last request. "He expresses the wish that he may receive recognition of his service by promotion before he dies for the gratification of family and friends, and I beg that if possible it may be done," Warren wrote Meade at nine-thirty. Someone, probably an aide at Fifth Corps headquarters, released Chamberlain's obituary to the newspapers.[34]

Meanwhile, Tom Chamberlain, having learned of his brother's wounding, collected Abner Shaw, the 20th Maine's surgeon, and Morris Townsend, surgeon of the 44th New York, and led them to the First Division hospital. They found Chamberlain on the ground, under tall pines, his face gray in the moonlight, touching feet with his friend George Prescott, colonel of the 32nd Massachusetts. The division surgeons gave Prescott a slight chance of life, Chamberlain none. The wound had begun to clot, and his trousers were stiff with dried blood. After a while the orderlies lifted him onto a rough table and cut away his clothes. Probing, Shaw, Townsend, and the division field surgeon, Dr. R. A. Everett, discovered that the ball had entered Chamberlain's right hip, struck and splintered the hipbone, and, in its passage, cut the bladder and urethra. They swabbed the wound, cleaning out bits of cloth and bone, extracted the ball, which lay just below the surface on his left side, and made some crude repairs, sewing up the bladder and reconnecting the severed urethra. Shaw and Townsend sat with Chamberlain, who was insensible from loss of blood and a heavy dose of pain-dulling morphine, from midnight to dawn.[35]

Prescott died on Sunday. A stretcher party came for Chamberlain and transported him, in relays, sixteen miles to City Point. Townsend, attending, did what little he could for the patient's comfort. He somehow survived this journey under a relentless sun, and even found the strength to take up a pencil and scrawl a farewell note to Fannie:

> My darling wife I am lying mortally wounded the doctors think, but my mind & heart are at peace Jesus Christ is my all-sufficient savior. I go to him. God bless & keep & comfort you, precious one, you have been a precious wife to me. To know & love you makes death & life beautiful.
>
> Cherish the darlings & give my love to all the dear ones Do not grieve too much for me. We shall soon meet Live for the children Give my dearest love to Father, mother & Sallie & John. Oh how happy to feel yourself forgiven God bless you evermore precious precious one Ever yours Lawrence.[36]

Townsend saw Chamberlain aboard the steamer *Connecticut,* bound for the Naval Academy Hospital at Annapolis. Fannie learned late that night that he had been shot. She set out from Brunswick in the middle of a prostrating heat wave—the mercury reached one hundred degrees Fahrenheit—and with Daisy sickening for the measles. Word reached the Brewer branch of the family on June 21. "Recovery doubtful," the wire informed them. The ill tidings stunned the household. "It is strange that as well as we knew that we have been liable to hear this news for two years it seemed as great a shock to us as though you had never been exposed," Sae wrote her brother a few days later. "We could almost annihilate distance and fly to you."[37]

Much of the credit for Chamberlain's survival went to Shaw and Townsend. Unlike the anonymous sawbones at the division hospital, jaded, blood-soaked, inured to the grossest sights and sounds, they had a personal stake. Still, Chamberlain had suffered shocking wounds to delicate and essential parts. Civil War medical techniques were primitive, even in the surest hands. (When Oliver Wendell Holmes, Jr., took a ball in the heel at Chancellorsville, surgeons shoved a carrot in the wound to keep it open for draining.) Chamberlain's surgeons inserted a catheter to drain the wound and carry away urine discharges. As parts of him began to heal, a half-inch fistula formed around the catheter. It would become inflamed from time to time, causing him pain—sometimes searing, all-but-insupportable pain—at intervals for the next fifty years.[38]

He had the gratification, real for him, of achieving brigadier's rank. Grant formally approved Chamberlain's promotion June 20. Charles Gillmore, still carried on the books as lieutenant colonel of the 20th Maine, delivered the commission, along with a copy of the Senate's confirmation of the appointment, on a visit to Chamberlain on July 3–4. He found the patient in a steep, potentially fatal decline. The surgeons, Gillmore wrote John Hodsdon, the Maine adjutant general, blamed the constant seepage of urine. The condition would persist, they said, causing abdominal ulcers that would eventually kill him. The Chamberlains in Brewer again were told that Lawrence was near death. They sent John Chamberlain down from Bangor to be with him at the end.[39]

When John arrived July 16, the crisis had passed. Not for the last time, Chamberlain had confounded medical authority. "The most excruciating of his pains have ceased, and his wounds have healed greatly," John wrote Hodsdon. "The surgeon who has just come in tells me I can assure Gen. Chamberlain's friends that his danger is considered passed, and his recovery certain." According to John, he had already begun plotting his return to the army.[40]

Chamberlain lay three months in Annapolis, gradually regaining his strength. The uneven pace of recovery frustrated him. He would come on strong for a time, then relapse. When he felt well enough, he would move about the hospital, politicking among the soldiers, canvassing votes

for the critical autumn elections. Lincoln's position seemed irredeem-
able at summer's end. With Grant's Virginia campaign widely regarded
as a failure, a mere siege, Republicans schemed to drop the president
in favor of a candidate with at least a small chance of winning. Then, at
a stroke, Lincoln's prospects improved. Sherman entered Atlanta
September 2, eclipsing the Virginia disappointments and practically en-
suring the president's reelection.[41]

Oath-loyalty, a reflex respect for established authority, and self-interest
led Chamberlain to support the incumbents: Lincoln the Republican,
Samuel Cony the War Democrat. George Adams's abolitionist convictions
had made him an early Lincoln partisan. War simplified and coarsened
Adams's political aims. "I am for peace, for not prolonging this terrible
war. Therefore for fighting," Adams wrote Chamberlain September 6.
"I will not whine, nor grumble. Stand by, stick to it, hold on, trust in
the Lord. That's my politics, & that's my religion. And so I vote for
Cony & Lincoln." His son-in-law could not have expressed his own views
more succinctly.[42]

As Chamberlain mended, his friends began to consider how he would
occupy himself when he became fit again. Lincoln's restored fortunes
offered prospects of preferment for an invalid hero. Bowdoin sent word,
through Adams, that he would be welcome to return at any time. Adams
rightly suspected that Chamberlain's ambitions had outrun the Department
of Modern Languages. "I have imagined all along that, if you *live to leave*
your present position, many openings will offer themselves more inviting
than this," Adams wrote, catching Chamberlain's attitude perfectly. From
Annapolis, Chamberlain settled his immediate future. Fannie's condition
(she was due at year's end) evidently had no bearing on his decision.
"I long to be in the field again doing my part to keep the old flag up,
with all its stars," he wrote the governor.[43]

Chamberlain was furloughed on September 20; he passed his thirty-
sixth birthday, September 28, 1864, in Brunswick. A long, painful climb
had brought him to life's crest—the even divide, he put it many years
afterward, when he was well along on his journey down the far slope.
During these autumn weeks at home, his thoughts returned often to the
opening lines of Dante's *Inferno:*

> *Nel mezzo del camin di nostra vita,*
> *Mi retrovai per una selva oscura*
> *Che la diritta via era smaritta.*

("Midway the path of life, I found myself in a gloomy wood, where the right way out was perplexed," in Chamberlain's own translation.)

Fannie supervised his slow convalescence. As autumn wore on, the Army of the Potomac began to exert its familiar hypnotic pull. He saw his way clearly. "I believe in a destiny," he wrote his mother, gently informing her of his intention to return to Virginia. Pain sometimes clouded his senses, he tired easily, he could not mount a horse or walk a hundred yards without assistance. His wife escorted him to the Brunswick depot on October 29 and helped him aboard the southbound cars.[44]

CHAPTER 10

THE LAST CAMPAIGN

JUNE 19, 1864–APRIL 12, 1865

Heat, dust, racket, the ceaseless singing of deadly objects overhead: "Severe sharpshooting and artillery practice, without intermission, day or night," Alexander noted in his diary June 19. The enemy line butted up close. From it, the Federals could launch raids, the sharpshooters practice undisturbed. Grant built a second line just to the rear, a permanent defensive system of enclosed forts. Small garrisons could safely be left in these strongholds, freeing mobile forces for strikes against the Confederate flanks. With finical attention to detail, Alexander supervised the siting of the batteries, the strengthening of the parapets, and the digging of bombproofs for the troops.[1]

Siege conditions tested all his considerable powers of invention. Alexander's workshops turned out one ingenious contraption after another: wooden mortars, protective sharpshooters' boxes, bullet-proof oak shields for fieldpieces. He ordered twelve light Coehorn mortars from the Tredegar works, and trained a newly joined but weaponless artillery company to use them. He looked after his private interests, too, scavenging the minié balls and unexploded shrapnel that were deposited like dew every night in the lines. The ordnance department offered a pound of scarce English birdshot for four pounds of spent iron and lead, an exchange that fit him out hand-somely for the autumn partridge season.[2]

A sharpshooter's bullet found him during one of these junkyard expe-ditions, his haversack barely half full—or anyway so ran the legend that grew out of the incident. Alexander recalled it differently. He had been studying the enemy works opposite Elliott's Salient for several days. The lines were badly sited here; dead ground out front offered a sheltered avenue of attack. The Yankees aroused his suspicions by maintaining steady fire on the salient, even when observing a tacit truce elsewhere. Alexander surmised an approach under cover of a sap roller.* He went down into the salient each morning convinced he would see one of these outlandish antique machines rumbling toward him. The real explanation took form in his mind as he started back after his morning observation of June 30. "They were coming underground," he decided, as certain of it as though he had actually witnessed the sinking of the shaft. "They were mining us!"[3]

He heard the pop of a rifle; an instant later the ball struck the sun-baked ground, bounced, and buried itself in his left shoulder. The arm went numb. Aleck stood motionless for several seconds, hoping, idiotically, to deny the Yankee marksman the satisfaction of a confirmed hit. Then he regained his senses and started downhill to safety. Shock and a slight loss of blood left him woozy. He found a soldier to help him back to his camp. Winthrop, catching sight of him leaning heavily on the escort, thought he had been gravely wounded. He lay down under a tall pine to await the corps surgeon. Dorsey Cullen arrived presently, examined the wound, and congratulated him. The bullet had missed both artery and joint. Cullen gave him chloroform, enlarged the opening with forceps, and dug out the ball. "It was a calibre .58, with the impression of the cross threads of my coat stamped in the lead as if done with a steel die," Alexander said.[4]

It meant a furlough, of course. Next day he could walk and ride about without discomfort. He called at Lee's headquarters to deliver the warning about the mine. The commanding general was unavailable, so he spoke to his chief of staff, Charles Venable. Venable had a visitor, Francis Lawley, the *London Times* correspondent. Eavesdropping, Lawley volunteered his own observations, scoffing when Alexander estimated the length of the gallery at five hundred feet. He insisted, in the know-it-all manner of newspapermen, that such a long tunnel would be impossible to ventilate. Still, when Venable passed along Alexander's report, Lee ordered the engineers to begin countermining.[5]

Aleck left Petersburg July 4 and reached Fairfield, 475 miles distant,

*A large cylindrical basketwork object, a sort of mobile breastwork, used to cover troops digging a sap trench toward the enemy lines.

six days later, covering the last seventeen miles on foot. Sherman had become the obsession of upper Georgia. The gentry were busy hiding or sending off their silver and other valuables in anticipation of the arrival of the Yankee anathema. Alexander heard that James McPherson, commanding one of Sherman's armies, had been killed, sniped out of the saddle north of Atlanta. Alexander recalled their talk on Alcatraz Island in April 1861, and McPherson's prediction of a long, bitter war and a foredoomed Confederacy. Hood, meanwhile, replaced Joseph Johnston, relieved for lack of aggressiveness in Sherman's front. Word came that the Federals had touched off an enormous explosion under Elliott's Salient, creating the hecatomb known as the Crater. The Yankees, it turned out, had started work on the mine only five days before Alexander discovered it.[6]

He returned in mid-August to find the army in good spirits. Rations were adequate for a change. Looking ahead to winter, he sent to Fairfield for two or three pecks of dried tomatoes and okra. "Our standing dinner is either okra soup or rice, peas & bacon boiled together making what we call 'Hopping John,'" he wrote Bettie. This could be varied by dinner with the Camerons in Petersburg. William Cameron's blockade-rich table offered quantities of all but forgotten peacetime luxuries: lobster and salmon, fresh vegetables, ham, chicken and roast pig, ice cream, pound cake, fruitcake, almonds, raisins, dried figs, grapes, pears, claret, Green Seal champagne, sherry and madeira.[7]

Still, Lee's immobilized army chafed under the enforced idleness of the siege. The Federals shelled Petersburg indiscriminately. Lee could find no effective means of reply. Alexander proposed to retaliate by breaking the unofficial truce that generally prevailed on the front lines. Yankees could be slaughtered as they took the evening air. "We can kill a great number of them with a volley," he observed, "& are perfectly justifiable in doing it when they fire on our women & children." Sherman continued to cast a pall. Everyone's anxieties seemed fixed on Grant's brilliant junior. He marched into Atlanta September 2. "I hope & pray that you don't have to leave Washington, for I don't know where you could go," Aleck wrote Bettie on the fifth. Cameron temporarily lightened his burden of worry with a gift of three bottles of sherry, three of port, one of French brandy, and a jar of English pickles.[8]

Discounting the tonic effect in the North of Sherman's victory, Alexander continued to find reason for optimism in Yankee politics. George McClellan, the Democratic nominee, appeared to be a formidable opponent for Lincoln. Should McClellan win in November, Lincoln would be unlikely to prosecute the war with energy, Alexander thought. Discreet contacts could be established with McClellan, who would inherit a dilapidated war machine. Once he examined its worn-out parts, he might be amenable to a settlement—independence for the Confederacy, with free-trade guarantees and a defensive alliance to enforce the Monroe Doctrine.[9]

Alexander had little understanding of politics, northern or southern. He misread the Union electorate, misjudged Lincoln, and reckoned entirely without Grant, who remained in firm control of the armed forces. Grant shattered the metronomic siege routine September 29 with a lunge at Lee's left flank. The attackers overran Battery Harrison on the outer Richmond lines, inducing Lee to rush the First Corps to the threatened spot. Alexander directed a cannonade in support of a counterattack on the thirtieth. The Federals easily checked the five-brigade assault. Alexander thought the troops had fought behind breastworks for so long they had lost the knack of offensive operations. Lee was forced to concede the enemy's gain here; apprehensive about these southeastern approaches to Richmond, he kept Alexander on twenty-four-hour alert over the next few days. "I have to stick on the line like I was part of it," he complained to Bettie. He managed to satisfy the commanding general despite the weakening effects of an attack of dysentery. He cured himself with a concoction from his own pharmacopeia: chloroform, brandy, peppermint, and laudanum.[10]

Increasing pressure on the Richmond lines induced Lee to shift his headquarters to the north bank of the James. Alexander followed with the rest of the First Corps staff, pitching camp in a farmyard halfway between Chaffin's Bluff and Richmond. Lee sent word to him the afternoon of October 6 to prepare two artillery battalions for a strike at dawn the next day on the federal flank north of the Darbytown Road. Lee asked Alexander to join him as his entourage passed his camp two hours after midnight. Alexander finished breakfast by one-thirty and was smoking a cigarette by the fire when Charles Venable cantered up, flustered and clearly in a hurry.

"Aleck, come on!" Venable called. "The Old Man is out here waiting for you and mad enough to bite nails."

Alexander reminded Venable of the meeting time Lee had set.

"Yes, two o'clock was the hour he told us all last night, but now he swears he said one."

Alexander mounted and spurred over to Lee. The commanding general greeted him stiffly. Alexander pointed out that, according to orders, he was in fact a little early.

"One o'clock was the hour, sir, at which I said I would start," Lee answered in a chilly voice.

They rode on in silence. After a while, Lee turned to Alexander and asked him to summon the guide who would lead the column cross-country to the jump-off point for the attack. Taken aback, Alexander replied that no one had instructed him to arrange for a guide. "Well, sir," Lee said, "when I was a young man and had a march to make in the morning I never went to bed until I had procured some citizen of the neighborhood who could conduct me." Aleck swallowed the reprimand and held his tongue. Presently the party reached a fork in the road. Lee went up to a cottage just beyond the turning and roused the occupant, a slight elderly man dressed in a flowing nightshirt.

"Ought I to have taken that right-hand road back yonder?" Lee demanded, without preamble.

"Ah, may be so yes; may be so no," the startled citizen replied in a thick French accent. "Vere 'bouts do you vant to go?"

Though the effort nearly caused him physical injury, Alexander choked back his laughter. In any case, the results of the morning's operation froze his inward smile. After initial successes, the Confederates were driven off with more than thirteen hundred irreplaceable casualties. Battle losses, attrition in the trenches, illness, and desertion were draining the life out of Lee's army. A few Confederates began to think the unthinkable: the conscription and arming of slaves, with emancipation at war's end for those who served. Alexander heard that the Yankee black troops had fought well enough at the Crater—as well as the whites, anyway. (He noted, too, that "there had been a great deal of unnecessary killing" of blacks trying to surrender.) Charles Field, one of the First Corps division commanders, strongly favored using slaves in combat. Alexander remained doubtful. "I believe they may be made to fight tolerably," he said, "but am much opposed to it as inhuman & unchristian & bad policy. We could never *rely* upon them at all."[11]

Alexander probably expressed the prevailing view in the army, where at least the matter could be freely debated. The mere suggestion of arming blacks outraged most civilian opinion-makers. "If slaves will make good soldiers our whole theory of slavery is wrong," Georgia senator Howell Cobb declared. He doubtless spoke for the great majority of his constituents. Slaveowners, of course, were not inclined to risk their property. "I am often astounded when I recall how cheerfully our old people sent their sons into the war and how universally they flinched at sending their negroes," John Haskell wrote Alexander after the war. Hiring out slaves for menial labor was evidently another matter. Alexander reported that slaves had relieved white teamsters in many commands, and that more than a thousand were continually at work on the Richmond fortifications.[12]

Longstreet returned from convalescent leave in mid-October, cheering Alexander and the First Corps staff, who, with winter coming on, had little else to celebrate. The nights turned cold and rations were short. Troops were deserting in significant numbers. Armed bands stole provisions, clothes, and boots. Alexander chased away a group of thieves lurking near his camp one night. Possibly they knew Cameron had supplied him with a bolt of good flannel for shirts, and that his brother Felix had given him a fine piece of calfskin from which he planned to run up a pair of high-topped cavalry boots. With money and good connections, Alexander could make himself comfortable. Private soldiers got what the army could give them, which meant they were barefoot, in rags, and half-starved.[13]

Static warfare offered unlooked-for advantages. Alexander had a full autumn social calendar. He saw a lot of the Gilmers and the Lawtons and their large circle of acquaintances. Aleck proposed a family reunion: the patriarch could come up from Fairfield, visit his five children now in or near Richmond, and return by hog-killing time. While he was at it, Leopold could have a word with Hillie, who was drinking too much, avoiding his brothers and sisters, and otherwise giving cause for worry. "Hilly has never invited me to a meal or indeed pressed me to call at all," Alexander complained. The reunion failed to come off. Alexander consoled himself by constructing snug winter quarters, a large canvas tent with a real chimney and a board floor. He sewed two thick Hudson's Bay blankets together to make a warm sleeping bag. The pointer Buster wandered off, was reported missing, and reappeared to find two rival dogs, Breeches and Petticoats, in occupation. Cameron offered to run a bale or two of cotton out of Wilmington for him, a lucrative trade that could net him many times his brigadier's pay—and in gold.[14]

His anxieties mounted with the approach of the new year. Where was Sherman? Why had Hood started for Nashville when the Yankees were known to be marching in the opposite direction? "I hope & pray that

Sherman may be brought to great grief yet, or at least will not have time to get to Washington," he wrote Bettie. Alexander learned early in December that the second half of his prayer had been heard; Sherman's left wing passed well to the south of Fairfield. Otherwise, there were only ill tidings. Mary Cliff returned to her Atlanta home to find it ransacked; even the locks and doorknobs had been stolen. "I can't myself bear the idea of ever going back there to live," she wrote Louisa Gilmer. In mid-December, Union general George Thomas destroyed Hood's army in front of Nashville. Sherman entered Savannah December 21, a triumphant end to his 285-mile march to the sea.[15]

In the Richmond lines, Alexander imagined Bessie, three years old, hanging up her Christmas stocking for the first time, and the twins, fifteen months, drooling over holiday confections. "How I would like to be Santa Claus for her," he wrote home. He spent Christmas Eve with the Camerons: plum pudding, figs, nuts, fruitcake, champagne, eggnog. Mrs. Cameron gave him a beautiful pair of gauntlets and a steel shirt collar. Cameron quietly took him aside and told him the fancy goods he had ordered would not be arriving after all. The blockade-runner had gone aground under Yankee guns at the mouth of the Cape Fear River.[16]

Chamberlain found the First Brigade broken up, his six Pennsylvania regiments scattered. Griffin gave him two new regiments, the 185th New York and the 198th Pennsylvania. The reconstituted First Brigade, though the smallest in the division, at least carried a good band on the muster roll—one of the best in the corps, Tom Chamberlain thought. Chamberlain's command lay on the left, the extreme westward extension of the Petersburg lines. Distance and the press of business kept him from satisfying his curiosity about Rives' Salient, scene of his June 18 near-martyrdom. He wanted to go back and study the ground, to reassess what had seemed an impossible assignment there. As it happened, he did not return for a second look until 1882.[17]

Chamberlain believed he could survive life in the line, even if it remained to be seen whether he had stamina enough for mobile operations. For the time being, the Potomac army went on fulfilling its destiny "to kill and be killed without decisive actions," in Theodore Lyman's phrase. The siege guns and mortars kept up a steady, uninspiring fire. The sharpshooters were rarely idle. There were occasional raids on the enemy outposts, but most nights the frontline troops observed a tacit truce, exchanging news, trading tobacco for coffee, and sometimes joining in a hymn sing.[18]

The loyal states reelected Abraham Lincoln the first Tuesday in November. The soldier vote went overwhelmingly to the president. Chamberlain thought the result showed that the men's allegiance to principle exceeded their attachment to McClellan, who remained immensely popular with the Potomac veterans. "They were unwilling that their long fight should be set down as a failure, even though thus far it seemed so," he wrote. The Fifth Corps gave Lincoln 5,176 votes to 2,079 for McClellan. The corps's Maine soldiers voted 290 to 74 for Lincoln.[19]

Chamberlain's first real test came during the second week in December. The Fifth Corps, reinforced by a division from the Second Corps, a cavalry division, and a sixteen-gun artillery train, broke camp early on Wednesday, December 7, for a raid on the Weldon Railroad. The Federals had cut this vital supply line just south of Petersburg, forcing the Confederates to use a roundabout wagon route for the final leg. Warren's orders were to smash up a further twenty miles of track between the Nottaway and Meherrin rivers. Griffin's division marched fifteen miles to the Nottaway, halted for the evening, and crossed on pontoons at two o'clock Thursday morning. After a short rest, the column continued on all day, reached the railroad after dark, and at once began the work of destruction.[20]

Chamberlain described the process in a letter to his sister. "You take a Regt. or Brigade & form them up along the track, select a spot where the rail is easiest to get at, & all hands take hold & raise it up—up— until over it goes, upside down & with the sleepers or 'cross-ties' still attached & on top," he wrote Sae. Then the rails were broken up at the points and laid over a pyre of crossties, "balanced so that the weight of the ends will bend the rail nearby double when heated." The troops were kept at it until midnight. Newman Smyth, Professor Smyth's son, now a lieutenant in the 16th Maine, watched admiringly as the more skilled among the men twisted red-hot rails into the shape of a Maltese cross, the corps symbol.[21]

"The road ran on a straight line through the woods," Smyth remembered. "As far as we could see our corps was stretched along it, ripping up the rails and putting them across piles of blazing sleepers." Snow fell Friday night, then turned to freezing rain. The troops discovered plentiful supplies of applejack to take away the chill. Drunkenness and straggling were endemic. The column passed one man collapsed in an alcoholic stupor along the roadside. Rebel bushwhackers following close behind stopped and slit his throat.[22]

Guerrillas fell on and murdered a half-dozen stragglers. The Fifth Corps troops retaliated by burning dwellings and barns along the return route. Chamberlain had no stomach for this kind of warfare, which until now had been largely confined to the Shenandoah and interior Georgia. His heart went out to the victims, who were mostly women and children. "It was a sad business," he wrote Sae. "I am willing to fight men in arms, but not *babes in arms*." In biting cold, Warren's corps marched for Petersburg. Lee sent out a field force under A. P. Hill to try to cut Warren off, but there were only minor skirmishes, none involving Griffin's division. Chamberlain led the First Brigade back into camp the afternoon of December 12.[23]

"Lawrence stood the march well and is very well now," Tom Chamberlain wrote home to Brewer. Tom thought he had never looked better. This was wishful thinking, or else Tom needed spectacles. Chamberlain had not been fit for field service, and the hard chances of the Weldon raid left him weak and ill. His wounds were painfully inflamed. "I shall have to take the knife again," he wrote his brother John, "& am making up my mind where to have it done."[24]

In a New Year's letter, his mother implored him to give up the army. "Surely you have done & suffered & won laurels enough in this war to satisfy the most ambitious," Sally Chamberlain wrote. "I hope you will soon go to the hospital and avoid the coming battles, which must be terrific." He left for Philadelphia around January 13, submitted to a surgical procedure there, and reached Brunswick to begin another convalescence around the twentieth. He arrived home to find that Fannie had given birth on January 16, to a daughter she named Gertrude Lorraine.[25]

The last flicker of a dismal Christmas died out in the New Year's dinner for the Army of Northern Virginia, "a miserable copy of the Yankee Thanksgiving," in Alexander's resentful view. For the fifteen hundred men of his command north of the Appomattox, the commissary supplied 182 pounds of meat, a quantity of moldy bread, and four or five bushels of turnips and potatoes. By comparison, the Yankee Cavalry Corps hospital at City Point served out generous portions of turkey and chicken, cheese, bread and butter, cranberry sauce, tomatoes, celery, apples, peaches, pies, and cakes.[26]

Alexander had hoped for a winter furlough, but a New Year's circular from headquarters discouraged requests for leave. He proceeded glumly with his work on the Dutch Gap defenses. One of his mortar batteries fired day and night at Butler's pioneers, who were digging away at a canal at an acute bend of the James there in an effort to turn the heavy Confederate batteries at Howlett House, north of Bermuda Hundred. Alexander sited guns to cover the expected approach of the Yankee ironclads and sank obstructions in the channel. He experimented, too, with electrically detonated torpedoes, planning to stock them as thick as catfish in the James.[27]

A fortuitous kick from a skittish horse gained him the furlough he longed for. As he inspected the lines near Howlett House on January 7, Dixie stumbled and threw him off, startling his companion's mare, who lashed out with a vicious blow to his ribs. One appeared to be broken, an injury that Alexander thought would rate a convalescent leave—a few weeks with Bettie, now five months pregnant. "I hope that my partially crippled state will procure me the indulgence," he wrote her next day. "I would have every rib broken rather than fail in it." It was a painful, confining injury, and it bought him thirty days.[28]

By February 13, the day Alexander left Fairfield to return to the army, Sherman's advance had penetrated deep into the Carolinas. Detouring to avoid the Yankees, Alexander encountered his father's longtime friend Alexander Stephens, the Confederate vice-president, at a night halt in the little town of Alston, South Carolina. Stephens and other senior Confederates had met ten days earlier with Lincoln at Hampton Roads to discuss possible terms for peace. The vice-president spoke freely about the conference, mentioning what he had interpreted as an offer of cash compensation for emancipated slaves. (Stephens claimed, later, that Lincoln had proposed a $400 million settlement with slaveowners.) Alexander always believed that Lincoln *had* made a firm offer, redeemable with the return of the rebellious states to the Union. At the time, of course, he argued boldly for full independence. Stephens seemed utterly discouraged, Alexander thought, certain that disaster loomed.[29]

He continued on foot to Winnsboro, where he found a place in a train full of refugees fleeing Sherman. He reached Charlotte, North Carolina, on the seventeenth and spent the night in a hotel parlor with fifty other travelers, including the entire population of a girls' school in flight from the rapacious Yanks. ("The snoring in the room that night was something phenomenal," he said.) Arriving in Richmond February

19, he returned to his vigil along the James. He found the troops burning the abatis in front of the fortifications to keep warm.[30]

Sherman's advance pinched Richmond's remaining lines of supply, forcing Alexander's gunners to subsist on cornmeal intended for the battery animals. On a diet of four pounds of hay a day, the nags barely had strength enough to draw the guns. There was one compensation: the army began issuing generous rations of hard cider. Alexander's mess mixed egg yolks into the applejack to create a cocktail called a Tom & Jerry.[31]

Misery bred fantasies of postwar idylls. Alexander dreamed of himself in Brazil, a shakoed, aiguilletted officer in Dom Pedro's forces. He and Bettie would have a large family of fine children, too many to count. She would look after the orchards, gardens, and chickens. He would scratch away at artillery drawings in a cool office. They both would be grateful for their ignorance of Portuguese, for no callers would come to disturb them. "Dont think it is all castles in the air Dear One," he wrote her, "for U know it won't take *much* after the war to make us happy." Alexander began accumulating gold to finance their southward flight, should it become necessary. He closed out Charley's wage account at a Richmond bank, converting seven hundred dollars in Confederate currency into a ten-dollar gold piece. He sold a pistol at auction and hoped for substantial profit from a bale of cotton that Cameron had smuggled out for him. He bought several shares in the blockade runner *Coquette*, which sailed for Nassau in mid-March.[32]

Like many Confederate soldiers, Aleck remained confident of the army's ability to endure. Much later, looking back in wonder, Alexander attributed this blind faith in eventual victory to Southerners' religious character. "They believed in a God who overruled all human affairs, & who in the end brought the right to prevail," he wrote. His sisters had sent their children home to Georgia and were themselves packing to leave, but Alexander saw no prospect that Richmond would be abandoned. He allowed himself to credit a rumor that Johnston had beaten Sherman in North Carolina. On March 25, Lee launched what would prove to be his last offensive operation, a push toward Fort Stedman at Petersburg. The breakout failed, with losses approaching thirty-five hundred. Even this setback failed to shake Alexander. "This army appears to be in good spirits & its numbers are sufficiently respectable to make me feel very hopeful of the result," he wrote the day after the Fort Stedman battle.[33]

Grant opened the last campaign Wednesday, March 29, sending

Sheridan's cavalry with strong infantry support out beyond the Confederate right, toward the road junction of Five Forks. Over on the James, Alexander supposed this to be just another raid. The Yankees delivered a powerful cannonade into the Petersburg lines that night. A hard rain fell through the day Thursday, turning the roads into rivers of mud. Alexander passed the time rereading an old favorite, *The Ingoldsby Legends.*

> *The castle was a huge and antique mound,*
> *Proof against all th' artillery of the quiver,*
> *Ere those abominable guns were found,*
> *To send cold lead through gallant warrior's liver.*
> *It stands upon gently rising ground,*
> *Sloping gradually to the river,*
> *Resembling (to compare great things with smaller)*
> *A well-scooped, mouldy Stilton cheese—but taller.*[34]

But Lee recognized the threat. Five Forks covered the Southside Railroad, Lee's lifeline. He stripped the Petersburg front to assemble a strike force to counter this latest and most dangerous of Grant's leftward movements. Sheridan routed Pickett at Five Forks on Saturday, April 1, turning the Confederate right: the fatal blow. Grant ordered a general assault on the Petersburg front for first light Sunday. Lee prepared to evacuate Petersburg and Richmond. The thin Confederate lines held through the day,* giving Lee time to put the artillery and supply trains on the road. In Richmond, Davis ordered the Confederate government to flee.[35]

Alexander spent Sunday down on the James, making preparations to release another school of torpedoes into the river. He returned at sundown to find the camp deserted except for servants. Orders had arrived late in the afternoon for a withdrawal that night. He passed the word to all the commands along his twenty-four miles of line. The stationary guns and mortars were to be spiked, their crews armed with muskets and converted to infantry. The light batteries were to limber up and march on Richmond. Alexander would meet them at Mayo's Bridge with final instructions.[36]

He and Charley entered the capital a little after ten o'clock. Alexander

---

*Lee's engineers named one of the threatened strongpoints for Alexander. The Federals called the same work Fort Whitworth.

called first on Gilmer and Lawton, who reported that his sisters had gotten safely away that afternoon. He moved on to his sister-in-law Lucy Webb's, where a large, noisy crowd of officers had gathered. He met Charles Field there, and Wade Hampton Gibbes, another of his brothers-in-law. A war widow, Lucy Webb found consolation in nursing; by the spring of 1865 she was deeply experienced in the art of taking care of needful soldiers. Her kitchen operated full blast, turning out plateful of biscuits and meat. Officers were eating as much as they could hold, and filling their pockets and haversacks with the surplus. The men were in good spirits; the women, who would have to stay behind, were nervous and depressed. Jennie Gibbes drew Alexander aside and begged him to look after her husband.[37]

He took up station at Mayo's Bridge two hours after midnight. The streets were crowded, every house ablaze with light. There was scattered firing, the provost guard opening on looters. An old woman pushed a wheelbarrow full of blankets up the street, emptied the contents into an open cellar door, and turned back the way she had come, doubtless for another load. Alexander followed her to the Danville railroad depot. He found the station dimly lit, deserted except for the old woman and one or two others, and well stocked with goods. He helped himself to an English bridle, a thick felt horse blanket, and a fat slab of bacon. "The old woman worked well & steadily at her blanket business," he observed, "& she seemed to pack her cellar full of bales." He fitted the cloth and bridle onto Dixie and rode back to the bridge.[38]

Richmond showed black against the wavering glare of the fires. Toward daybreak a series of terrific explosions sounded; it was the Confederate river fleet at Chaffin's Bluff blowing up. A burning barge drifted under the canal bridge and set some of the floor planks alight. The sun climbed above the horizon—a clear, bright morning. The last of the batteries crossed. Alexander followed and turned for a final glance at the abandoned capital. "The black smoke hanging over the city seemed to be full of dreadful portents," he thought. Then he started for Amelia Court House, thirty-five miles distant.[39]

En route, Alexander met an acquaintance from cadet days, the Virginian John Saunders, who had been a groomsman at his wedding. Today, April 3, was his fifth wedding anniversary. "I don't think I have ever been more depressed," he wrote Bettie that night.[40]

Chamberlain's Maine friends arranged for the Bath district port collectorship to be offered him. This was a sinecure; not much work would be required, and his body could heal in the fusty quiet of a small-port custom house. Chamberlain turned it down. "I owe the country three years' service," he wrote his father. "I am not scared or hurt enough yet to be willing to face to the rear, when other men are marching to the front." True, Fannie, Daisy, and Wyllys needed him, the newborn too. "But there is no promise of life in peace, & no decree of death in war," he went on. Besides, his army prospects had never been better. He meant to gather the rewards of his suffering. "I had a great deal rather see another man in that Custom House, than see another next commander of the First Division," he said, clinching the argument. He did make one concession: he promised he would not feel obliged to lead any more charges.[41]

As always, field life invigorated him. "One would not think me fit to walk a half mile if I was at home; but here I ride as fast & far as the best," he wrote Sae shortly after his return to the First Brigade. Even the steady drumming of the late-winter rains did not depress him. Every so often a mild sun would appear in the mottled sky, and the toads were whistling in the bogs. There were periodic military pageants, such as the one on March 8 when Julia Grant and other celebrities visited Fifth Corps headquarters and reviewed Griffin's division.[42]

The grand movement (Grant's words) opened before dawn the last Wednesday in March, Sheridan's cavalry corps swinging out beyond Hatcher's Run, riding southwest for Dinwiddie Court House. The Fifth Corps, led by Warren, followed. The Second Corps, with Humphreys standing in for the invalid Hancock, advanced on Warren's right. Grant had two objects in view. If all went according to plan, Sheridan and the infantry would turn Lee's right, pry the Army of Northern Virginia out of Petersburg, bring it to battle, and end the war. At the least, Sheridan could cut loose from the Potomac army and raid the Southside and Danville railroads, choking off Lee's supplies and breaking his last link with Johnston in North Carolina.[43]

Chamberlain's brigade had the advance, through flat country, rocky, heavily wooded, and scored by sluggish streams that swelled quickly in hard rains. The column reached the Quaker Road after noon and turned north, toward the White Oak Road extension of the Petersburg lines. Up ahead, skirmishers reported the Gravelly Run bridge burned and enemy infantry behind cover on the north bank. Chamberlain led part of the 185th New York across the waist-deep stream and signaled for the rest of the command to follow. The enemy light forces fell back slowly, picking up strength as they withdrew. Regrouping around the buildings of the Lewis farm, the Confederates flashed out a volley or two, then retired behind breastworks along the edge of a belt of thick timber.[44]

There Chamberlain struck something hard—a full division, it turned out. The veteran Confederate infantry abruptly checked his advance. His two regiments stood for a decent interval, then began to backpedal, both flanks crumbling. "The brigade held better than I have seen our men do for some time, and fell back fighting," noted Charles Wainwright, who now ordered up one of his batteries to help extricate Chamberlain. Griffin appeared, saying little but making it plain that he expected the advance to resume. Chamberlain re-formed his line under Griffin's eye and aimed his second effort at a heap of dirty yellow sawdust near a mill just beyond the Lewis farm.[45]

Forgetting his pledge to Sae, he spurred ahead of the charging infantry. Approaching the dust heap, he tugged sharply on the reins to check his mount, Charlemagne; the animal reared in response and at that moment something struck Chamberlain in the chest, just below the heart. He collapsed onto the horse's neck and felt blood there. The ball had passed through Charlemagne, glanced off the brass frame of a hand mirror in Chamberlain's breast pocket, followed the curve of his ribs, exited out the back seam of his coat, and sped on to its next target, the pistol case of the aide riding alongside him, a subaltern named Theodore Vogel. The impact knocked Vogel right out of his saddle.[46]

Griffin came up to find Chamberlain stunned witless and covered with blood, mostly the horse's but some of his own, too. "My dear General, you are gone," Griffin murmured. Chamberlain groggily denied it. Still dazed, his bridle arm bruised and useless, he rode toward the right flank, where a confused fight swirled, chest-to-chest in places, much like another Little Round Top. He saw Horatio Sickel, commanding the 198th Pennsylvania, drop off his horse. Charlemagne went to his knees, weak from loss of blood. Chamberlain continued on foot and entered the melee just as the lines around him began to recede. Hard-looking gray-clad figures closed in. As at Fredericksburg, he brazened it out by posing as a rebel officer. A few obedient Confederates followed him back to his own lines and were handed over to the provost guard.[47]

To the left, the 185th New York bounced off the enemy breastworks and began to break up under pressure of a Confederate countercharge. Chamberlain saw the regimental commander, Gustavus Sniper, colors in hand, struggling to restore order. Mounting a stray horse, he cantered over to help. "My man," he called down to a lost-looking corporal, giving him a sharp slap with the flat of his sword, "if I can only get you to stand here for a minute I can form a line." From this rallying point he delivered another of his inspiriting harangues; soon a solid knot of men had collected around him. "Try the steel," Chamberlain shouted over to Sniper. Wainwright's Napoleons arrived and opened fire. A short time later, fresh infantry, three full regiments, appeared.[48]

Griffin withdrew to a discreet distance and let Chamberlain manage the battle. Soon the cannon were delivering roundshot into the enemy breastworks. Chamberlain signaled the advance. The Confederates fell back in fair order, leaving little groups of stragglers to be taken captive. Griffin, following, pushed up Bartlett's Third Brigade to the intersection of the Quaker and Boydton Plank roads, less than a mile from the Confederate outworks covering the White Oak Road position.[49]

The afternoon's work could be judged a success. Warren congratulated Chamberlain and promised to write the president for an official commendation. He otherwise had fallen into one of his periodic bullying moods—probably, Wainwright thought, because the wagons carrying his supper and sleeping tent were late coming up. "These awful fits of passion are a disease with Warren," he observed in his diary. Perhaps it was the casualty list that deranged Warren. Losses were heavy, four hundred killed, wounded, and missing in Chamberlain's brigade alone, nearly a quarter of its strength.[50]

Toward dusk, a cold rain began to fall. Burial parties scooped out shallow graves; working in relays, the stretcher bearers carried off the wounded one by one. Less critical cases lay under the dripping trees, awaiting help. Chamberlain walked among them. He caught sight of Sickel, half-prone and holding a shattered arm; Sickel insisted on staying until the others were removed to shelter. Then he paused over the broken form of Maj. Charles Maceuen of the 198th Pennsylvania. Chamberlain had befriended Maceuen, whose family were connections of Meade's. He knelt in the mud beside the body. Something in his manner caught Sickel's attention. "You have the soul of the lion and the heart of a woman," Sickel called softly to him.[51]

The downpour turned the roads to quicksand, swamping Grant's grand movement. Lee sent George Pickett west along the White Oak Road with five infantry brigades to reinforce Fitz Lee's cavalry at Five Forks. Grant prodded Sheridan to push north to that crossroads. Pickett arrived and began to entrench before Sheridan's mudbound troopers

could cover the five miles from Dinwiddie Court House. Over toward
the White Oak Road, Chamberlain's command—his brigade and Edgar
Gregory's, now operating with him—held the left of the Fifth Corps
front along a marshy branch of Gravelly Run.[52]

Grant warned Warren to expect an attack here. At the same time, he
suggested Warren push ahead the next morning, Friday, and probe the
White Oak Road defenses. Warren accordingly moved up Ayres's and
Crawford's divisions, with Griffin in reserve this time. The sun broke
through at about ten o'clock. Ayres started thirty minutes later, a sortie
that soon developed into a full-blown battle, touched off when three
Confederate brigades lunged at Warren's left, just as Grant had pre-
dicted. The attackers, part of Anderson's command and under the overall direction of Lee himself, found a fat unexpected target in Ayres. His
left-hand brigade gave way, and soon the better part of the division came
streaming back through Crawford's lines. The panic spread to Crawford's
ranks. They stampeded too. Fugitives from both divisions plunged across
the creek and jogged on through Griffin's lines.[53]

Fighting on good defensive ground, Griffin's troops checked the assault while Warren restored order in Ayres's division. Grant, through Meade,
sent word for the Fifth Corps to resume the offensive. Warren and Griffin
approached Chamberlain, still black and blue from Wednesday's battle. "I
tell Warren you will wipe out this disgrace, and that's what we're here
for," Griffin explained. Then Warren spoke: "Will you save the honor
of the Fifth Corps? That's all there is about it." Chamberlain could hardly
resist such flattery. For once, he failed to find words for a suitably ornate
reply. He simply agreed to try.[54]

The 198th Pennsylvania waded into the stream. The 185th New York
followed, then Gregory's regiments. The attack had spent itself by now,
and the Confederates were on the recoil, falling back without much
resistance. Chamberlain regained all the lost ground. As at Rives' Salient
ten months earlier, the momentum of the advance carried him into an
isolated position, an open field this time, in front of a fieldwork. Warren
could not decide whether to send him forward or recall him. Figuring
his losses would be severe either way, Chamberlain argued for pushing
ahead. Ayres could follow, he suggested, consolidating whatever gains he
might make.[55]

He sent Gregory's brigade around to the right, through a woods, with
orders to creep in close and send up as great a racket of musketry as
he could manage. Gregory's fire would be the signal for the First Brigade

to charge. "We went with a rush," Chamberlain recalled; it carried the brigade over the breastwork and beyond the White Oak Road, driving the defenders into the main works a few hundred yards to the east.[56]

Chamberlain considered it an achievement of critical importance, magnified later when he learned that no less an eminence than Robert Lee had been directing operations in his front. The lodgement severed direct communication with Pickett, six miles to the west at Five Forks, and gave Grant a pivot on which Lee's right could be turned. The decisive moment would have come sooner, Chamberlain claimed, if only Sheridan had been able to push up to Five Forks Friday afternoon. Instead, his troopers were entangled with Pickett down at Dinwiddie Court House and sending up distress calls to the Fifth Corps infantry.[57]

Chamberlain overstated the case. True, Pickett had beaten Sheridan's cavalry to Five Forks, then driven it back on Dinwiddie. True, Sheridan now asked for the infantry Grant had offered him a day or so earlier. Senior Fifth Corps commanders thought Sheridan had ridden into more trouble than he could handle. In a way he had, but he saw opportunity too. "[Pickett's] force is in more danger than I am," Sheridan told Grant's aide Horace Porter on Friday evening. "If I am cut off from the Army of the Potomac [he] is cut off from Lee's army." If Warren's infantry could only get up to him in time, Sheridan thought he could bag Pickett's command entire.[58]

By late afternoon, heavy firing could be heard to the southwest, toward Dinwiddie. Warren wondered aloud whether he ought to send help in that direction. Chamberlain suggested Bartlett's brigade, and Warren started Bartlett before dark. When Pickett discovered Bartlett's infantry in his rear that night, he retired into the Five Forks entrenchments. Grant and Meade could not have foreseen Pickett's withdrawal. Anxious about Sheridan, intent on seizing the chance to clap onto Lee's right and rear, they issued a series of conflicting orders Friday night. "Within the space of two hours, Warren received orders involving important movements of his entire corps, in four different directions," Chamberlain wrote. The most explicit of these reached Warren at eleven o'clock. It instructed him to disengage from the White Oak Road, march for Dinwiddie Court House, and seek out Sheridan.[59]

Sheridan mistrusted Warren, judging him timid, balky, uncooperative. Even Chamberlain, a Warren loyalist, conceded that he could be indecisive. "He thought of too many things," Chamberlain said. Grant complicated matters by alerting Sheridan to expect Warren by midnight, obviously an impossibility in the circumstances. Still, Sheridan had every right to expect Warren's three divisions, fifteen thousand infantry, to be in place by daybreak Saturday. They were, after all, only four or five miles away. In fact, only Ayres had arrived by first light. Crawford's and Griffin's divisions did not even start from the White Oak Road until five o'clock, forty-five minutes or so before sunrise.[60]

Chamberlain learned after midnight that the Fifth Corps had been detached from Meade and assigned to Maj. Gen. Philip Henry Sheridan. Chamberlain and his friends were well aware of Sheridan's unruly temper, his penchant for self-promotion. Alexander Webb, Meade's chief of staff, wrote later of the "repressed contempt" that officers of the Potomac army felt for Sheridan. "We kept our heads and hearts as well as we could," Chamberlain recalled, "for we thought both would be needed." The rain had stopped, though the roads were still slippery and ankle-deep in mud. The joke went the rounds: *Have you been through Virginia? Yes, in several places.* The column approached Sheridan's lines. Cavalry appeared. Chamberlain caught sight of Sheridan's swallow-tailed battle flag, two stars on red and white, and spurred ahead to report.[61]

"Why did you not come before? Where's Warren?"

"He is at the rear of the column."

"That is where I expected to find him."[62]

Sheridan cut short Chamberlain's flurried attempt to explain, turned, and splashed up the road toward Five Forks. Warren did not report to Sheridan until eleven o'clock. Grant, meanwhile, authorized Sheridan to relieve Warren if he thought it necessary. ("I was very much afraid that at the last moment he would fail Sheridan," Grant wrote later.) The approach march resumed at around one o'clock, hard going, two hours to cover two miles, over a narrow road churned to ooze by the passage of cavalry. The corps formed in line of battle near Gravelly Run Church, Ayres on the left, Crawford on the right, Griffin again in reserve.[63]

At around three o'clock, Chamberlain joined a group of senior officers huddled with Sheridan in front of the church. He watched Sheridan etch his battle plan in the sodden ground with the point of his saber. Warren took notes and sketched a rough map. Yet it sounded simple enough. The cavalry would charge the right front of the two-mile-long Confederate line, while the Fifth Corps advanced to the White Oak Road and wheeled onto the enemy left, which ended in a ninety-degree angle, or return, some 150 yards long. Sheridan told Ayres to aim for the hinge of the angle; Crawford was to charge it head-on.[64]

Sheridan, barely five feet tall, compactly and powerfully built, his hair cropped so short it looked, someone said, like a coat of black paint, paced back and forth, pounding fist into palm, while Warren completed his arrangements. Porter, who was with him for most of the day, thought Sheridan as "restless as a racer struggling to make the start." Finally, at around four o'clock, Warren gave the order to advance. Sheridan mounted his black charger, the fabled Rienzi.* "I'll ride with you," he called over to Ayres.[65]

Somehow, Warren's attack veered off course. Probably his handmade map was faulty. Ayres's division came out of a stand of pine and brushed the angle, where Crawford should have been; Crawford marched off to the right, a full thousand yards away from the battle. The right-hand brigades of Griffin's division followed Crawford. Chamberlain could see the gap widening between Ayres and Crawford. Ayres, he now realized, was fighting alone, and evidently caught between two fires. Griffin was nowhere in sight. Warren had gone off in pursuit of Crawford. On his own initiative, Chamberlain drifted to the left, toward Ayres. He told Gregory to trail him, and sent word of his movements to Bartlett, next in line.[66]

The First Brigade emerged from the woods, crossed a muddy stream, and pushed up a rough ravine. Griffin appeared in the distance and, using his hands, motioned for Chamberlain to go over to the attack. The demonstration abruptly stopped the crossfire on Ayres. Riding toward Ayres, Chamberlain encountered Sheridan. "That's what I want to see! General officers at the front!" Sheridan called to him in his piercing voice. Chamberlain began collecting miscellaneous troops, including a lost brigade from Ayres's division, to throw into the battle. The lines exchanged a rapid series of volleys. Sheridan reappeared, looking aggrieved. He leaned toward Chamberlain and shouted, "You are firing into my cavalry!" Chamberlain denied it, though First Brigade riflemen might well have been shooting high, over the angle and the main front and into the Yankee troopers. "Don't you fire into my cavalry, I tell you," Sheridan repeated. Then, a few moments later, he called out, "We flanked them gloriously!"[67]

It was over by sundown. Chamberlain's brigade swarmed over the parapet and, after a short hand-to-hand fight, oversaw the disarming of more

---

*Sheridan named Rienzi for the Mississippi hamlet where he acquired him, not for the Roman patriot or the Wagner opera. The horse died in 1878 and was stuffed and displayed for many years in a museum on Governor's Island, New York.

than one thousand of Pickett's veterans. Crawford's off-course advance led him fortuitously into the Confederate rear, where a four-gun battery and several hundred prisoners fell into his hands. Some forty-five hundred Confederates were rounded up altogether. "We are coming back into the Union, boys," Wainwright heard one captive say. Pickett, as at Gettysburg, had lost most of his command. This time, though, he witnessed hardly any of the debacle. He, Fitz Lee, and others were enjoying a bake of Nottaway River shad some two miles from the battlefield. An acoustical fluke carried the sound of the fighting away from Pickett. He did not even know he had been attacked until a party of federal cavalry rode into his picnic ground.[68]

Chamberlain learned of Warren's fall from one of Griffin's staffers. His peregrinating habits ("looking after details and making ingenious plans," as Lyman put it) finally brought him to grief. Warren had been away in pursuit of Crawford when Sheridan wanted him with Ayres. Toward sundown, Warren sent word via his chief of staff that he had reached the Confederate rear. In a fit of choking rage, Sheridan blurted out that Warren had been nowhere near the fight; he told the aide to carry the message back to Warren, then summoned Griffin to take command of the corps. Warren certainly had been up front, at least during the final stages of the battle. A veteran of the 91st New York remembered him riding up and down the line, waving the corps colors. "Now, boys, follow me," he kept saying. "This is the last fight of the war."[69]

Chamberlain met Sheridan on the White Oak Road, pushing west to Five Forks. He felt uneasy being alone with him. Indeed, Sheridan, still overwrought, seemed to require at least one more victim. Bartlett rode up and unwittingly offered himself, reporting excitedly about Crawford's capture of some enemy cannon. "I don't care a damn for their guns," Sheridan said shrilly, "or for you either, sir! What are you here for? Go back to your business, where you belong. What I want is that Southside Road!"[70]

Calming down, Sheridan suspended the pursuit for the night, permitting the jaded infantry a night's rest at Five Forks. Porter carried the news of the victory back to Grant, who at once wrote out the order for a general assault on Petersburg. Chamberlain, Griffin, and other officers gathered around a fire at the crossroads. Sheridan appeared out of the darkness. For a change, he modulated his voice. "I may have spoken harshly to some of you today," Sheridan said, "but I would not have it hurt you. You know how it is: we had to carry this place, and I was

fretted all day until it was done." The speech revealed something of
Sheridan's extraordinary powers; whatever bitterness the Fifth Corps officers may have felt melted away in the warmth of his words. Gouverneur
Warren, meantime, rode dejectedly toward the rear, out of the battle,
out of the war, his career wrecked. He reached Meade's headquarters
around midnight. Lyman, who liked Warren, rummaged around and
found him something to eat.[71]

Alexander reached Amelia Court House at sunrise Wednesday, April
5, after a two-day journey over impossible roads. Bettie had cousins in
Amelia, the Misses Smith, and they invited him in for breakfast: eggs,
chicken, different kinds of bread, waffles, butter. Here was plenty in the
midst of famine. For some reason the commissariat had failed to deliver
rations to Amelia, where Lee had directed the scattered commands to
concentrate for the march south to Danville. After breakfast, Alexander
halted the best-equipped batteries and sent the others on west to
Lynchburg, out of harm's way.[72]

Stripped to fighting trim, the army moved at one o'clock, heading
south for Jetersville. Alexander rode up front with Lee, alert for an
opportunity to hammer Sheridan's cavalry as it crossed his line of march.
But the cavalry screen reported Sheridan advancing with heavy infantry
support, two army corps, too powerful a force to challenge with any
prospect of success. With the enemy astride the route to Danville, Lee
ordered a change of course north to Amelia Springs, then west for Rice's
Station on the Lynchburg railroad.[73]

The column marched deep into the night, a pleasant one for the season.
A young moon lit the way through peaceful countryside. Alexander came
upon Gilmer and Lawton and rode companionably with them until a
couple of hours after midnight. After a short rest, he rose to survey a
line of battle covering Rice. Lee intended to stand there, collect rations,
and let the trains close up. Alexander waited anxiously for the columns
to appear. Custer's troopers, he heard finally, had broken into the line
of march, taken guns and prisoners, and burned a long line of wagons—
among them the vehicle carrying Alexander's sword and best uniform.
The Yankees had taken Frank Huger at gunpoint. Custer kept Huger,
whom he had known at West Point, up front with him all day, like a
bear on a leash, gave him a good dinner, and relieved him of a pair of
fancy spurs his father had brought back from Mexico in 1847. Worse
still, infinitely worse, word came that Ewell's rear guard and Anderson's

command, with nearly a third of Lee's infantry, had been cut off and smashed at Sayler's Creek.[74]

The disaster forced Lee to restart what remained of the army. Alexander turned the battle line over to a cavalry rear guard after dark and steered Dixie west for Farmville, where rations were reported to be available. A cold, hard rain fell. He floundered through a sea of chilled mud, needing eight hours to cover the six miles. Buster disappeared during the night, his uncanny ability to find the First Corps artillery in all weathers failing him here at the last.[75]

To his surprise, he saw the van of the army crossing the Farmville bridges to the north bank of the Appomattox. By some misadventure the rear guards had failed to burn High Bridge downstream, so the Yankees were across too. There could be no pause here, though the troops were issued two or three days' rations of meat and bread as they shuffled past. Lee summoned Alexander early Friday and ordered him to fire the two bridges. Grant had forced another detour, Lee explained, showing Alexander the first map he had seen since leaving Richmond. They might still reach Lynchburg by alternate roads, Lee went on, but a brief glance at the map convinced Alexander that Grant had driven the Army of Northern Virginia into an escape-proof trap, the jug-shaped peninsula between the Appomattox and the James. "There was but one outlet, the neck of the jug at Appomattox Court House," Alexander saw, "and to that Grant had the shortest road." Lee saw it just as clearly, of course. That night he opened the exchange of notes with Grant that led, within forty-eight hours, to the cease-fire that ended the war.[76]

The ranks understood too. "Don't surrender no ammunition," Alexander's gun crews called out as he overtook them on the march. No officer had been more careful of powder and shot than Alexander; the men reminded him of his war-long frugality now. "Let us shoot up this ammunition first if we got to surrender," somebody offered. The column trudged on all night Friday. Alexander rode until he nearly dropped out of the saddle from exhaustion. By now the army had begun to fall apart; sometimes, and especially at night, friends were to be feared equally with foes. There were reports of intentional shootings of officers. Alexander pushed on until the early hours of Saturday, when, faint with fatigue, he found a hideout in the woods where he could sleep without fear of Dixie being stolen.[77]

The eighth, Saturday, turned out to be a quiet day, fatally quiet, an ominous suspension of the continuous, shifting last battle. The sun shone after several days of lowering skies. Alexander managed to scavenge a teakettle and a skillet. Cheered by these small additions to his kit, he allowed himself a moment's hope. Then reason prevailed. He remembered that map; Sheridan's troopers were racing for the neck of the jug. Aware the game was up, Lee called a halt at sundown. Alexander sank instantly into a deep sleep, his first full night's rest in a week.[78]

Regaining the road at first light April 9, Palm Sunday, four years to the day after he and Bettie had left Fort Steilacoom, he caught up to Lee's retinue on the Richmond-Lynchburg turnpike just as the sun cleared the horizon. Lee had halted on a hill looking south toward the village of Appomattox Court House, where John Gordon, with a few thousand infantry, was launching a last attempt at a breakout. Lee motioned for Alexander and led him off the road to a felled oak log, where the old man took a seat and began picking absently at the bark.

"We have come to the Junction, and they seem to be here ahead of us," Lee said finally. "What have we got to do today?"[79]

Alexander repeated what the gunners had told him: They were willing to burn down to the last round to force a way through to Lynchburg. Lee answered that he had too few infantry for the job. Given the opening, Alexander advanced a scheme of his own, one he had been turning over in his mind for several days. He had told Charley he expected the Yankees to prosecute the rebel generals as traitors, and he had no intention of trying to stare down a firing party. He intended to flee the country and make his way to Brazil, just now starting a war with neighboring Paraguay.* Still, one last chance remained. The troops, he told Lee, could scatter in small groups with orders to rally on Johnston in North Carolina or, failing that, report to their home-state governors.

"What would you hope to accomplish by that?"

Delay, Alexander went on, might lead to better terms than those that "Unconditional Surrender" Grant would be likely to offer here. The old hope of foreign intervention might be reviewed. At worst, the individual states could negotiate more favorable agreements with the federal power. Anything would be preferable to surrender. By now Aleck had worked himself up to an extreme pitch of emotion. "We are proud of the record of this army," he blurted out, his eager, unlovely features aglow. "We want to leave it untarnished to our children." If Lee resented the imputation, he gave no sign of it. When Alexander had finished, he delivered

*Brazil emerged the winner after a long, vicious struggle in 1865–70 that cost Paraguay three-quarters of its population and more than fifty thousand square miles of territory.

a lengthy meditation addressed, perhaps, as much to himself as to the young officer seated next to him:

Yes. The surrender of this army is the end of the Confederacy. As for foreign help, I've never believed we could gain our independence except by our own arms. If I ordered men to go to Gen. Johnston few would go. Their homes have been overrun by the enemy & their families need them badly. We now have simply to look the fact in the face that the Confederacy has failed.

Suppose I should take your suggestion & order the army to disperse & make their way to their homes. The men would have no rations & they would be under no discipline. They would have to plunder & rob. The country would be full of lawless bands, & a state of society would ensue from which it would take the country years to recover.

And as for myself, while you young men might afford to go to bushwhacking, the only proper & dignified course for me would be to surrender myself & take the consequence of my actions.

If the men can be quietly & quickly returned to their homes there is still time to plant crops & begin to repair the ravages of the war. That is what I must now try to bring about. I expect to meet Gen. Grant at ten this morning and surrender the army to him.

So Lee had decided. He ended by saying, gently, that Grant *had* offered terms, generous terms. Alexander could think of no possible reply. The monologue restored to Lee all his former aura. Aleck felt not awestruck, as before, but diminished now in the great man's presence. "I was so ashamed of having proposed to him such a foolish and wild cat scheme that I felt like begging him to forget he had ever heard it," he wrote later. "It seemed now an inestimable privilege to serve under him to the very last moment, & that no scene in the whole life of the Army of Northern Virginia would be more honorable than the one which was now to close its record."[80]

Lee returned to his headquarters tent off the Stage Road to prepare for his interview with Grant. When Alexander saw him a couple of hours later, he had changed into a full suit of new uniform, with sword and sash and an embroidered belt, boots, and gold spurs. Lee knew as he set out that Gordon's assault had failed. Enemy infantry, two brigades under Chamberlain, other Fifth Corps units, and part of E. O. C. Ord's James army, had arrived to plug the neck of the jug. Longstreet asked

Alexander to mark out a rearward position on which the sagging lines could re-form. He chose a fair one, in open country behind the Appomattox, the last line of battle in the history of the Army of Northern Virginia.[81]

Chaos ruled in the front lines: the troops were confused about truce flags and temporary cease-fires. Custer galloped up to Longstreet's front and demanded the immediate surrender of Lee's entire army. Some of the frontline infantry, ignoring the white flag Custer carried, pulled one of his aides off his horse, disarmed him, and went for his boots. "I appeal to you for protection," Custer shouted excitedly to Hampton Gibbes, whom he had known at West Point. John Haskell recognized Huger's spurs and asked Custer how he had come by them. Sounding embarrassed, Custer said he had offered to take care of the spurs for the captive Huger. Longstreet ended the farce by brusquely ordering Custer back to his own lines.[82]

Grant could not be found; Lee returned, his errand unaccomplished. Alexander fixed him a sort of chair of fence rails, arranged under an apple tree just coming into leaf. He stayed with the general for a few minutes, quietly rolling and smoking a cigarette. Then he moved off. Longstreet spoke briefly to Lee; members of his staff approached every so often; but the old man hardly stirred. He sat quietly, alone with his thoughts.[83]

Finally, at around one o'clock, one of Grant's aides cantered up on a plump seal bay and led Lee away to Appomattox Court House. Alexander climbed a grassy knoll and kept watch on the village. A couple of hours later, Lee on Traveller appeared in the distance, moving toward the Confederate lines at a slow trot. Alexander formed his gunner troops in the road, officers and men, and asked them to uncover their heads in a silent salute. One or two men shouted a hurrah; then others. A mob of infantry came crowding in at Lee's approach. After a while the cheering died away and the old man spoke.[84]

"We have fought the war together," Lee said in a thick voice. "I have done the best I could for you. My heart is too full to say more."[85]

Chamberlain had the advance nearly every day. The westward pursuit continued with scant regard for such details as rations, rest halts, and construction of fieldworks. "Sheridan does not entrench," Chamberlain said. "He pushes on, carrying his flank and rear with him—rushing, flashing, smashing." Word reached the column Monday, April 3, that Richmond had fallen. By the fifth, a week after the opening of the campaign, Sheridan had knocked Lee off the direct route to Danville and his hoped-for junction with Johnston.[86]

Grant drove men and animals to the limits of endurance. "We almost lined the road with exhausted mules," Newman Smyth recalled. Enemy stragglers were rounded up by the hundreds. The Confederates left a trail of now-useless equipment: wagons, arms, haversacks, and Dutch ovens, hundreds of them, upended, their stubby little legs kicking the air. The column slogged on all day Saturday the eighth, and then into the night, a maddeningly slow march, delayed interminably while the Army of the James passed across the Fifth Corps's front. Griffin did not call a halt until midnight, twenty-nine miles from the start and six miles short of Appomattox Court House.[87]

A cavalry courier arrived during the night with a note from Sheridan, addressed to any commander willing to pitch in. Striking a match, Chamberlain read: "If you can possibly push your infantry up here to-night, we will have great results in the morning." He roused the bugler and got his own and Gregory's brigades onto the road. At dawn, another of Sheridan's staffers approached, also looking for infantry. He persuaded Chamberlain to break away from the column, turn onto a side road through the woods, and double-time toward the sound of battle at Appomattox Court House. His two brigades overtook the hard-pressed cavalry just after sunrise. Off to the left, he could see infantry from Ord's James army taking position astride the Lynchburg pike. Soon two Fifth Corps divisions arrived to fill the gap between Chamberlain's and Ord's troops. The final Confederate charge broke up on a continuous, impenetrable infantry front.[88]

Sheridan's cavalry wheeled out of line, squadron by squadron, for a dash around the left to complete the envelopment. Chamberlain's troops drove the Confederates from the crest of a rise. From there he looked down into the valley of the Appomattox and on what remained of Lee's army, beaten now, helpless. The lines swept forward into the village. Disorganized groups of enemy infantry put up a token resistance. Presently a single horseman approached Chamberlain's front, riding slowly, showing a length of clean white cloth. The courier said he had come from Gordon, the Confederate commander here, to arrange a cease-fire while Grant and Lee discussed surrender.[89]

The word struck Chamberlain dumb. The Confederates had been on the run since Five Forks, but this was the first he had heard of surrender. No rumor of the exchange of notes had reached him. For a moment a sort of paralysis set in. Then, collecting himself, he sent the courier up the line to Griffin. A little later, around nine o'clock, two officers on horseback approached his front. One he recognized, a Connecticut cavalryman named Edward Whitaker. The other, wearing Confederate gray, carried a white towel. "This is unconditional surrender," Whitaker told him.[90]

Still, nobody had authorized him to stand down. Chamberlain resumed the advance, though at an easier pace. A cannon shot whistled into the line of the 185th New York and killed a subaltern there: the Army of the Potomac's last battle fatality, Chamberlain later claimed. The cease-fire order reached him at around ten o'clock. The troops stacked arms and began to mill about. Chamberlain trailed a group of senior officers into the village, which consisted of a half-dozen houses, a bare-shelved dry-goods store, lawyer's offices, and the red-brick courthouse. Sheridan, hard-mannered and unsentimental, and Gordon, an old-school young Southerner, sententious and prolix, met, with predictable results. For a moment it looked as though the shooting would start up again. Less eminent persons conversed in small groups. Chamberlain overheard two officers renewing a prewar, probably old army, acquaintance.[91]

"Well, Billy, old boy, how goes it?" the Union officer said.

"Bad, bad, Charlie, bad I tell you; but have you got any whiskey?"[92]

The truce expired at one o'clock; the gatherings broke up as the hour approached. Griffin quietly ordered Chamberlain to re-form his lines and prepare to make or receive an attack. He mounted and awaited events. After a while he sensed a commotion behind him. Turning in the saddle, he saw Robert Lee ride past, "superbly mounted, richly accoutred." Grant, plainly dressed, swordless, his sword hand tucked in a pocket, followed a few minutes later.[93]

They met in the McLean parlor, where Lee signed the document surrendering twenty-eight thousand officers and men of the Army of Northern Virginia. Though Grant forbade ostentatious celebration, Roman candles improvised from captured fuses and launched out of muskets streaked through the overcast now and then. The bivouacs were otherwise quiet. "Campfires of our hundred thousand men and no picket firing . . . how queer it seems," Tom Chamberlain wrote home. James Longstreet came into Chamberlain's camp that night. "Gentlemen," he said, "I must speak plainly. We are starving over there. For God's sake, can you send us something?" Toward midnight, Griffin sought out Chamberlain to tell him he had been chosen to command the formal surrender ceremony.[94]

Alexander collected his parole, together with letters of recommendation from Lee, Longstreet, and Parson Pendleton, who addressed his to the Emperor of Brazil. The three-by-eight-inch paper, headed "Paroled Prisoner's Pass," read:

> Brig.-Gen. E. P. Alexander, chief of artillery, 1st Corps, A.N.V. of Ga., has permission to go to his home and there remain undisturbed with four private horses.
>   W. N. Pendelton. Brig.-Gen. & Chief of Artillery

Virginia had anyway become a less hazardous locale. "There was nobody trying to shoot us," Alexander noticed, "and nobody for us to shoot at." He prepared to start for Washington City and an interview with His Excellency the Brazilian ambassador. He sent Dixie and Meg south with the Haskells, who were riding home to Abbeville, South Carolina. Abram, his slave ostler, had disappeared a few days before the surrender, taking advantage of the confusion to slip away to freedom. Charley stayed to the end. Alexander saw him off with the ten-dollar gold piece he had bought in Richmond. Charley headed north for Manassas, in search of whatever might have survived of his prewar life.[95]

By the oddest of coincidences, Alexander encountered Wilmer McLean, Bettie's uncle-in-law, on one of his errands into the village. Alexander had experienced his first hostile fire at McLean's farm near Manassas on July 18, 1861. To escape the war, McLean had moved two hundred miles south, to Appomattox. "What are you doing here?" he demanded angrily of Aleck. Alexander tried to explain. McLean would not be appeased. "These armies tore my place on Bull Run all to pieces," he said. "And now just look around you. Not a fence rail is left, the guns trampled down all my crops, and Lee surrendered to Grant in my house." Souvenir hunters wrecked McLean's parlor, but filled his pockets too: some officers actually paid for their keepsakes, Sheridan, for one, laying out twenty dollars in gold for the table at which Grant wrote out the surrender terms.[96]

Alexander formed the artillery, now the property of the Army of the James, in a single half-mile-long line along the Stage Road. He could do nothing for the starving battery horses; they had not been fed on the retreat, and the Federals had no forage to spare. Returning to camp, he collected his belongings: $200 in gold borrowed from Hampton Gibbes, his parole, the testimonials to his skill as an artillerist. On the morning of Wednesday, April 12, he rode out of Appomattox and into an unknown future. The guns were still standing unattended in the road. Many of the horses were down now in the mud, nickering softly and unable to rise.[97]

In Brunswick, exploding fireworks, ringing bells, and shouting awoke George Adams early Monday morning, April 10. His wife illuminated the parsonage with candles in celebration of Lee's surrender. For a moment the future seemed as bright as the glow in the Adamses' windows. "I would not for a fortune have missed the experiences of the last two weeks," Chamberlain wrote Sae. "Father said in his last letter to me that 'the glory of battles is over.' But if he had seen some of these we have had of late he would think differently."[98]

Another day of glory awaited him. Chamberlain never knew why Grant chose him to command the surrender ceremony. Griffin showed partiality too, giving him the old Third Brigade, with the 20th Maine, and asking Bartlett, now commanding the First Division, to take the day off and leave Chamberlain in sole charge. He formed the division along the Stage Road at first light on the chill, gray morning of April 12, the Third Brigade on the right, down near the river. On the far side of the valley the Confederates were striking and folding their tents and forming ranks for the last parade.[99]

The ragged column, John Gordon in front, came swinging in route step across the valley. Chamberlain had decided beforehand to offer a formal military salute: tribute to an honored enemy, to be sure, and recognition, too, of all that his comrades had suffered at Shepherdstown Ford and Fredericksburg, at Gettysburg, in the Wilderness and at Spotsylvania and Cold Harbor, in front of Petersburg and along the White Oak Road. As Gordon approached, Chamberlain called out the order to carry arms—the marching salute. The First Division snapped to attention, from right to left all along the line, from the riverbank to the courthouse. The ranks were silent, "an awed stillness," in Chamberlain's words, "as if it were the passing of the dead." Gordon looked up in surprise. Then, with a flourish of his sword, he made an elaborate reply. A moment later, Gordon signaled for the infantry to return the courtesy: "honor answering honor," according to Chamberlain.[100]

The brigades paraded past, halted, faced the Union ranks, dressed the lines, and stacked arms. The Yankees stared at Lee's soldiers with unconcealed curiosity. "As a rule they were tall, thin, spare men," Private Gerrish of the 20th Maine remembered, "with long hair and beard of a tawny red color." When the time came to fold the battle flags, many of the rebels wept. "I pitied them," Chamberlain wrote home, "from the bottom of my heart." It was a drawn-out, day-long agony. After dark, fatigue parties set the surrendered small-arms ammunition ablaze. The fires cast a lurid last light over Lee's dissolved army.[101]

The Fifth Corps marched out of Appomattox in the rain on April 15. Word of President Lincoln's assassination reached Chamberlain the next day, Easter Sunday, in camp near Farmville.[102]

Part IV

TOUCHED WITH FIRE

*The reader will please to remember that there is
a great deal of uncertainty in war,
not only before but after.*
—John W. De Forest

*It is so easy to fight battles on paper, so different
from fighting them successfully on the ground.*
—Gen. John Gibbon

CHAPTER 11

ANOTHER COUNTRY

---⇒≫⊰⊱⊱⇐---

GEORGIA AND MAINE, 1865–73

BATTLES, TOLSTOY SAID, SETTLE NOTHing. The ten thousand battles, engagements, actions, affrays, and skirmishes of the American Civil War left the essential question unanswered: How were whites and blacks to live together? The matter of allegiances, at least, could be regarded as decided. Forces "as irresistible as those of a volcano" created a *nation* out of the loose and feuding federation of sections, Alexander would argue. He thought posterity should be grateful to the South for having fought the issue to the bitter end, even at a cost of 620,000 soldier deaths.[1]

In April 1865, though, the restored nation struck him as a foreign and hostile place. "It was as if I had suddenly died and waked up in an entirely new & different world," Alexander wrote of the first days after the surrender. "There are no words to tell how forlorn & blank the future looked to me." He clung to the Brazil scheme as to a lifeline. Then, too, he found some comfort in the kind attentions of yesterday's enemy. The Federals he met could hardly have been more solicitous; one prewar acquaintance offered him the loan of a month's salary in greenbacks. Even in defeat, Aleck retained his old skill in making friends with powerful men; he rode to the railhead at Burkeville in a party that included Grant's onetime patron, the Illinois congressman Elihu Washburne. He assured Alexander there would be a liberal peace, and that he need fear no reprisal. Lincoln's generous policies, Washburne said, could not fail to win over the defeated South.[2]

Reaching Richmond via City Point on Good Friday, April 14, he put

up at Lucy Webb's and called on Robert Lee at his Franklin Street
mansion. Lee strongly disapproved of his plan to hire himself out to the
Brazilians. On Easter night, Alexander heard the first rumors of Lincoln's murder. Confirming the story, Edward Ord, commanding the occupation forces in Richmond, gave him a pass for Washington City but
advised against using it; the killing, Ord's manner suggested, had
changed everything. Alexander went anyway. The streets of the capital
were aswarm. Lines of people waiting to view Lincoln's body, lying in
state at the White House, reached a half-mile down Pennsylvania Avenue.
Alexander felt conspicuous and utterly Confederate in spite of his civilian
coat, trousers, and black-dyed U.S. Army private's greatcoat. "The passion and excitement of the crowds were so great," he thought, "that
anyone merely recognized as a Confederate would be instantly mobbed &
lynched." The ambassador of Brazil, frankly afraid that Alexander's mere
presence would ignite a riot in front of his embassy, said he could do
nothing for him. He recommended an appeal to the Brazilian consul in
New York.[3]

When that official proved no more helpful, Alexander abruptly
dropped the notion and sent word to Fred Colston, who had intended
to follow him, that the Brazil venture was off. He sailed from New York
April 23 for Hilton Head in the steamer *Arago*, his valise packed with
Yankee stuff for Bettie: yards of shirting, a soft gray silk called pongee,
and a bolt of fine dark red-striped dress cloth. At Hilton Head he caught
the coastal steamer for Savannah, where Anthony Porter turned over to
him his only asset to survive the wreck of the Confederacy, some shares
of Southwestern Railroad stock.[4]

For a few weeks, Washington, Wilkes County, became the crossroads
of the failed Confederacy. Richmond political refugees and parolees
from Lee's and Joseph Johnston's armies streamed through the town in
the thousands. Nearly all of Alexander's close kin were gathered there.
He surprised his brother-in-law Lawton in the village square as he made
his way home from the depot toward midday Thursday, May 4. The
Haskells had sent on the letter outlining his plans, so everyone supposed
him Brazil-bound. Bettie, Lawton told him, had experienced a difficult
childbirth and remained weak, ill, and bedfast.* Even so, some instinct
alerted her to his approach that mild spring afternoon. "As I opened

* The child, a girl born April 7, 1865, died in infancy.

the door," Alexander remembered, "she was in the middle of the room advancing to meet me."[5]

The first U.S. troops entered Washington the next day, federal cavalry in pursuit of Jefferson Davis, who had convened his last cabinet meeting in the offices of the Washington bank only two days earlier. Aleck regretted missing Davis. Still under Lee's influence, he had hoped to persuade the fugitive president to follow "the proper and dignified course" and surrender. As a temporary haven for Davis, Washington became a suspect place. Before moving on, the cavalry sloughed off a provost guard, including a detachment of black troops, to police the town.[6]

The provost gave Alexander permission to carry sporting arms and travel about on a horse, and otherwise left him alone. The authorities did, however, summon Leopold Alexander for questioning about an itinerant sharp named Fulton. He had talked himself into a wartime (probably Methodist) pulpit in Washington. When the patriarch and other leading citizens discovered that Fulton had married, fleeced, and abandoned several women, they ran him out of town. Toward war's end, Fulton made his way through the federal lines and swore out a complaint that he had been persecuted in Georgia for his Union convictions. Leopold admitted as much to the Yankee officials investigating the charge.

"Yes," he told them, "Fulton's union sentiments were exactly what we objected to."[7]

The patriarch's wit might flash out still, but the new order, enforced by armed blacks in blue United States uniforms, mortified the Wilkes County gentry. Local government went bankrupt—the county treasury reported a balance of $3.85 in Confederate currency. More Yankee troops arrived. Highly colored accounts of their outrages began to circulate. The federal commander, Brig. Gen. Edward Wild, a Massachusetts soldier/physician who had led black troops in Virginia and North Carolina, evicted Julia Toombs and her pregnant daughter from the family mansion and established an officers' quarters and a freedmen's school there.* "We have not even an errand boy now, for George, the only child left on the place, is going to school!" complained Fanny Andrews, the unrepentant rebel daughter of the whiggish Judge Andrews, who had remained quietly loyal throughout the war. A party of

---

*Robert Toombs barely escaped arrest, leaving by the back door as the Yankees came in through the front. He eventually reached England and lived briefly in exile there.

soldiers bayoneted a dog named Jeff Davis. Former slaves squatted in vacant houses, pitched tent cities, settled in brush arbors in the woods. They stunned whites by refusing to work without wages. In some instances, they sustained themselves on corn and livestock stolen from their former masters.[8]

Petty clashes were common as black people began to assert their freedom. The Yankees fined young Charley Irvin fifteen dollars for beating a freedman who, claimed Irvin, had spoken insolently to his mother. Fanny Andrews reported that blacks sometimes refused to step off the sidewalks to allow white ladies to pass. Dr. French, the missionary in the Freedmen's Bureau office ("a whang-nosed fanatic," Miss Andrews called him), remarried thirty-three black couples in a mass ceremony. Freed men and women took surnames and refused to answer when addressed as "uncle" or "aunty" or "maum." Wild and French were said to dine with blacks two or three times a week. White Yankees mixed with freed slaves at dances and other jollifications.[9]

Aleck, meanwhile, mooched about Fairfield with too little to do, though he did manage to celebrate his thirtieth birthday, May 26, 1865, with a last bright burst of action. Davis had left behind a fortune, as much as $500,000 in minted coin and banknotes, in charge of a treasury official named Crump. The Federals shortly relieved Crump of his burden and, on May 24, sent it north from Washington under a light cavalry guard. A band of ex-Confederates attacked the specie train that night. A few shots scattered the guard, and the renegades moved in to fill their saddlebags with ten- and twenty-dollar gold pieces. Alexander organized a posse from members of the local militia, caught up with and arrested several of the robbers, and returned to Washington with $20,000 in coin—the only part of the loot ever to be recovered.[10]

The chase and capture were temporary fillips; Alexander's children were steadier compensation. Bessie, age four, and her father were old friends by now, but he hardly knew the twins. Eddie, approaching his second birthday, spoke a patois—"a Choctaw jabber," Aleck called it— that no one but his twin sister could understand. Bettie used to call Lucy over after one of these outbursts and ask Ed to repeat it. Lucy obliged with a fluent, perfectly enunciated translation. Still, the blue devils often assailed him. He had no vocation, no income, no country. He began to dream again of going abroad.[11]

Few of the army comrades whose fates were known to him were much better off. His brothers-in-law Willie Mason and Hampton Gibbes kept a grocery in Petersburg. "It makes me very, very sad, as I sit down in my store and see the Yankees go riding by, to compare our situation now to what it was one year ago," Mason wrote him. (Since he had been half-starving in the Petersburg lines the year before, shopkeeping must have been hard service.) Walter Taylor, one of Lee's aides, found a place with a hardware dealer in Norfolk. But Frank Huger could land nothing and was "roaming the whole country in search of employment," Mason reported. One-armed John Haskell was jobless, too, and newly married besides. Richard Anderson, a onetime Army of Northern Virginia corps commander, worked as a day laborer on a South Carolina railroad gang. Charles Field taught school in Kentucky and barely earned enough to support himself. Thinking Aleck might be short of money, Mason offered him a loan of thirty dollars.[12]

As summer advanced, Alexander investigated various possibilities. Lawton sponsored him for an engineering opening on the Augusta-based Georgia Railroad. "I think Ed could save that road thousands every year over & above his salary," Leopold wrote loyally. Pendleton tipped him to a vacant chemistry professorship at the Virginia Military Institute in Lexington. Robert Lee's eldest son, Custis, now professor of engineering at VMI, wrote to say he had heard Aleck would be offered the chair and to urge him to accept. The place remained a shambles, Custis Lee admitted, hardly touched since David Hunter's Federals burned the buildings, books, and apparatus in 1864. Still, the salary of $1,800 sounded reasonable, provided, of course, that the Virginia legislature consented to appropriate the funds to pay it.[13]

He turned down the VMI offer. The railroad position appealed to him, but he had a rival for it, and a meeting in Augusta with the line's senior management left him doubtful of success. He and Jeremy Gilmer talked of emigrating to California and setting up as civil engineers there. He inquired about the Georgia agency of the new National Express Company. He considered trying to borrow $1,500 to open a grist mill. Meanwhile, he accepted a temporary job, at $250 plus expenses, recording mortgage deeds for a Georgia Central Railroad loan with the clerk of every county through which the line passed.[14]

The assignment kept him away from Fairfield for most of October and November, relieving some of the strain on Bettie. Restless, discouraged, in a chronic state of irritation with the Yankees, Aleck had been a difficult man to live with that summer. No discouragement, however, could dam the flow of his ideas. The deed job gave him the chance to see the country and, at the same time, scout for a farm to rent the following spring. He had it in mind to settle Bettie and the children in the country while he continued to search for permanent work. "I can fix U up with provisions to last it out—poultry &c. to speculate on & then plant it *all* in cotton," he suggested. She, too, felt deep anxiety about the future. "We may eke out a living," Bettie wrote him. "I suppose after a while you will get *something* to do." He at least could go abroad and *act.* Duty and convention kept her in Fairfield, waiting for something to turn up.[15]

Not long after he set out, Bettie forwarded the startling news that the patriarch meant to take a wife. "Your new mamma is to be—well, no other than my dear friend Mrs. Glenn!!!" Jane Marion Glen, forty-four years old, robust, lively, and already twice a widow, had moved to Washington in 1862 to be near one of her brothers, the Presbyterian parson. Bettie insisted Aleck return to Fairfield in time for the wedding; otherwise it might look as though he disapproved of Mrs. Glen. Bessie applied her own form of pressure, subtle but effective. "Tell him to come back in three years, I love him so much, " she instructed her mother.[16]

Gilmer, meanwhile, began to show an entrepreneurial inventiveness rivaling Alexander's. His latest scheme involved speculation in mules. Gilmer would borrow the capital, say $1,200, and send Aleck into the country districts for likely-looking animals to buy and ship to Savannah. Gilmer thought mules would sell in town for between $140 and $150 each—double what Alexander would have to pay. The partners would divide expenses and profits. Gilmer also had designs on a Savannah wood yard. John Gordon, he told Aleck, was interested in shipping Georgia kindling—soft dry pine, split and bundled—to the New York City market. Possibly the three of them could go into the forest-products line together.[17]

Gordon, thirty-three years old in 1865, had done well in the war, rising from captain of an upcountry militia company called the Raccoon Roughs to a corps command at Appomattox, where he had received and returned Chamberlain's last salute. Success in the army had fueled his ambitions. Gordon intended to rise quickly out of the postwar ruins. He showed himself willing to undertake almost any moneymaking scheme; at one stage of his postwar climb he wrote testimonials for an all-purpose medicine called Darby's Prophylactic Fluid. Within a year or two, Gordon would launch a political career through a secret terrorist organization of ex-Confederates known as the Ku Klux Klan.[18]

At Christmas, Alexander heard from another army connection, his former battery commander William Parker, now building a medical practice in Richmond. The hand of occupation evidently lay heavier there than in Wilkes County, where planter power had been in ascendancy since the late-summer departure of General Wild. "If the disgusting Yankees would quit us, if I could never again see a detestable blue uniform, I would be comparatively comfortable," Parker wrote him. He took no interest in the fate of the United States, which he regarded as a foreign country. "I would not be *sorry* if tomorrow the whole bauble were blown into a thousand pieces," Parker went on. "Let us stand by calmly and see the ship go to wreck."[19]

Alexander preserved Parker's "rebel letter" as a curiosity, but he had little bitterness in him. He accepted the outcome as unalterable. The Yankees, for all their bluster, had left the old social and racial order intact in upcountry Georgia, and anyway politics could never hold his attention for long. Nor did his political attitudes mature with the years. Alexander eventually came to a curious conclusion about Confederate war aims: the South, he decided, had not fought for independence or states' rights or even to preserve the old plantation aristocracy, but for compensation for slave property! The South would have gotten it, too, had Lincoln lived. With mental sleight, Alexander transformed the hints Stephens and Washburne had dropped into established fact. "Lincoln intended to give us the four hundred million gratuitously, after the surrender, just because he felt we were *entitled* to compensation," he would write. Lincoln did favor compensation, but his cabinet officers were unanimously opposed, and congressional Radicals were hardly likely to have endorsed payoffs for slaveowners. Yet Alexander convinced himself that only the president's murder had blocked the deal.[20]

Leopold Alexander and Jane Glen were married December 5, 1865. The question of Alexander's living began to resolve itself a week before Christmas, the advent of a new mistress of Fairfield doubtless giving urgency to the process. The University of South Carolina offered him the chair of mathematics, with a $1,000 annual salary, a "good dwelling house," and a twenty-five-dollar tuition fee for each student. Alexander debated the advantages and drawbacks of academic life in correspondence with Custis Lee. "There is too much of the same thing about it," Lee admitted.* On the other hand, a professorship offered security. Early

---

*Robert Lee had become president of Washington College, VMI's small, obscure, and nearly bankrupt Lexington neighbor.

in the new year, Alexander sent his formal acceptance to the university trustees in Columbia.[21]

Anticipating unrest, even violence, as news of Lincoln's killing spread, Chamberlain ordered a double guard around the Farmville camp. Toward evening he rode out to meet Griffin and Ayres, and the three generals together called on George Meade. They found him in a state of gloomy excitement, convinced that rebel conspirators were about to destroy the government and seize the capital. Meade thought the army would have to march on Washington and install Grant as dictator until constitutional authority could be restored.[22]

As it happened, the machinery of succession worked smoothly. Andrew Johnson, the vice-president, had sworn the oath of office some thirty hours before word of the assassination reached Chamberlain. The Fifth Corps marched on Easter Monday, April 17, though not for Washington. With Bartlett's transfer to the Ninth Corps, Griffin assigned the First Division to Chamberlain and ordered him to move up to Burkeville to guard the Southside Railroad.[23]

Chamberlain arranged a "funeral in the field" April 19, in observance of Lincoln's burial. The headquarters tents were hung with rosettes of crape, and the senior First Division chaplain, a Roman Catholic priest named Egan, summoned to deliver a memorial address. The division formed in a hollow square at noon. Chamberlain and the priest stood on a platform of ammunition boxes, Griffin and other ranking guests nearby. At Chamberlain's nod, Father Egan began his eulogy. The troops were soon awash in a flood of Victorian oratory. *Agnus dei:* evil hands, animated by the spirit of rebellion, had struck down an innocent, generous, merciful man. "And will you endure this sacrilege? Can heavenly charity tolerate such crime under the flag of this delivered country?" Egan paused, transfixed by his own eloquence. Chamberlain thought he saw some of the men open and close their hands, as though feeling reflexively for their weapons. He took hold of the priest's elbow and whispered something in his ear. Egan seemed startled at first. But the spell had been broken. With this call to duty, the priest finished with a prayer for obedience that restored calm within the agitated ranks.[24]

Chamberlain's brigades stretched out along the railroad. War had burned through this part of Dinwiddie County the first week in April, and there were scenes of desolation all around. Civil authority had collapsed. Gangs of bushwhackers and freedmen harassed the locals. Chamberlain moved quickly to restore order. He distributed confiscated Confederate commissary goods. When these proved insufficient, he took control of private stocks and handed out food and other necessities according to need. He assigned abandoned vehicles and animals to people capable of making a livelihood out of them.[25]

Chamberlain's attitudes toward the freed slaves were ambivalent. The freedmen were unruly, sometimes violent, eager to work off the resentments of slavery. Whites hated and feared them. Chamberlain thought blacks preyed on defenseless whites. "They not unnaturally banded together," he said of the freedmen, "and without much serious organization and probably without much deliberate plotting of evil, they still spread terror over the country." Chamberlain recognized that the former slaves were landless, homeless, hungry. The abolitionist Wendell Phillips had foreseen this: the Emancipation Proclamation, he had said, "frees the slave and ignores the negro." But Chamberlain had little fellow feeling for these unsettled people. His orders, as he interpreted them, were to keep the peace, not to use his powers to help freedmen adjust to radically altered circumstances.[26]

The whites of Dinwiddie County appreciated Chamberlain's efforts. In late April, a citizens' delegation proposed to honor him with a farewell dinner. He declined with a pretty speech. The Fifth Corps marched for Richmond early on May 2. Next day, the column passed through the Petersburg lines and into the city. Gouverneur Warren commanded there, and the troops cheered him enthusiastically as they swung past his headquarters at the Bolingbroke Hotel. The corps pushed on for Richmond at a leisurely pace, reaching the former Confederate capital the morning of May 6. After a brisk march past the drawn-up 24th Corps, with Meade and Henry Halleck looking on, the column continued on through Richmond and across the Chickahominy before stopping for the night near Hanover Court House.[27]

Authority set a killing pace for the final stages of the march. The men, slogging along day after day over rough, ragged roads, were increasingly resentful. "It seemed as if somebody was as anxious now to be rid of us as ever before to get us to the front," thought Chamberlain. A violent thunderstorm burst over the column late one afternoon, lightning forking out of a blue-black sky, pulses of flame leaping along the tips of the bayonets, in Chamberlain's phrase, like rivers of fire. A bolt struck one of the division ambulances, killing the driver and horses and stunning the occupants inside. The Fifth Corps pushed on late into the wet night.

Around midnight, finally, the column halted (in a floating bog, according to Private Gerrish of the 20th Maine) for a few miserable hours' rest. Next morning, Friday, May 12, the corps cleared Fairfax Court House, then ascended Arlington Heights, overlooking Washington City.[28]

A low bank of fog hid the capital. The rising sun gradually burned it off, revealing the outlines of the city, soft and lovely in the vaporous atmosphere. The troops knocked together permanent camps on the heights. In partial compensation for the hard march, they were given eleven days to prepare for the government's Grand Review of the victorious armies. Senior officers took turns standing each other dinners. Chamberlain entertained George Adams, down from Brunswick with news of Fannie and the children. The First Division officers worked up an elaborate testimonial for Jack Griffin. Chamberlain ordered a pin from Tiffany's of New York, a miniature battle flag, the red Maltese Cross on a white field, bordered with diamonds, with a thousand-dollar diamond in the center. He delivered a florid presentation speech. Griffin responded in kind, though with comparative brevity. Then Chamberlain pinned the device onto Griffin's uniform coat. The evening broke up with the singing of "Auld Lang Syne."[29]

The Army of the Potomac started up Pennsylvania Avenue for the Grand Review at nine o'clock on the clear, bright morning of Tuesday, May 23, Meade's headquarters in the van, then cavalry, provost troops, the engineers (they brought their pontoons along), and finally the infantry at cadence step: the Ninth Corps, with the Fifth and Second corps following. Crowds formed several deep on both sides of the avenue. Buildings were draped with banners and flags and, in tribute to Lincoln, swaths of black bunting. Spring blossoms had been fashioned into thousands of garlands. Scores of bands took up the familiar wartime marching tunes.[30]

Chamberlain watched the 36th Massachusetts step past in the Ninth Corps line of march; the 36th and the 20th Maine had sailed from Boston together in the old *Merrimac* in September 1862. The ranks kept perfect order, "the swaying of their bodies and the swinging of their arms as measured as the vibrations of a pendulum," according to one observer. Chamberlain led the Fifth Corps advance along the broad thoroughfare toward the White House. A girl darted into the street and thrust a garland toward him. She startled his horse; the animal reared, and the officer riding behind him caught the prize. The volume of sound swelled to a roar: cheering, the blare of massed bands, artillery salutes like the trumpeting of a bombardment.[31]

The president, Grant, Sherman; Edwin Stanton and the other cabinet officers; Supreme Court justices; congressmen and governors; envoys and other dignitaries from abroad watched from a reviewing stand opposite the White House. As the head of each column approached, President Johnson invited the senior commanders to dismount and join him on the stand. Chamberlain ascended at his signal. The president, someone noted, sat stiffly, holding his hat by the brim and waving it mechanically, left to right, as the troops passed. Chamberlain watched in silence. The 20th Maine went by, a few remaining Little Round Top veterans among the bountymen, then the following Third Brigade regiments and the other two brigades.

"So passed this First Division," he thought, "and with it, part of my soul."[32]

Chamberlain returned on Wednesday for the review of Sherman's army, then descended gently to earth. There were mundane matters to attend to, the thousand and one details of mustering out. He had his immediate future to settle too. Chamberlain had been invited to stay on in the army. As Warren had promised on the Quaker Road, he had been recommended for brevet major general. Griffin and others were working to gain the permanent rank for him, but he did not expect them to succeed. "The political gentlemen of Maine have not particularly inter- ested themselves in me," he complained to Sae. Even so, he still had hopes of a patronage appointment.[33]

His wounds flared again, raising the prospect of further surgery. Dis- turbing reports reached him about his brother John. He had been hem- orrhaging from the lungs—by the sound of it, the same consumptive condition that had claimed Horace in 1860. John was living in New York, trying for a job under government that would provide a livelihood but not drain away his strength. Their mother asked Lawrence to use what- ever influence he had on John's behalf. "It may save his life," Sae wrote.[34]

The Arlington Heights camps were breaking up. The 20th Maine veter- ans were mustered out June 4. A few weeks later, Meade published the order formally disbanding the Army of the Potomac. Chamberlain ar- rived home toward the end of July, prepared—nothing else had turned up—to reclaim the Bowdoin professorship of rhetoric. Hearing that

Grant would be in Portland around the time of commencement, Chamberlain invited him to Brunswick. Rather surprisingly, he accepted. Grant and his wife came up on the afternoon train August 2. Oliver Howard and Chamberlain led him into the First Parish Church for the commencement ceremony, Julia Grant on Chamberlain's arm. Next day, Bowdoin conferred an honorary degree on the conquering general. At dinner afterward, Howard spoke, Chamberlain too. With a smile and a bow, Grant declined his hosts' request to prolong the oratory.[35]

Fannie's baby, Gertrude Lorraine, seven months old, died the evening of August 14. George Adams officiated at her funeral three days later. Grief and the recurrent pain of his wounds left Chamberlain depressed and weak. He had vowed, in the autumn of 1862, never to return to the old claustral Bowdoin life. "I won't endure it again," he had said then. Yet here he was. He had lost his bearings, for now anyway; he had not found in civil life a moral equivalent of war. Chamberlain had hardly settled into the Potter Street house before he began planning a history of the Fifth Corps. It seemed a way of recapturing some of the intensity, drama, and high purpose that had passed so abruptly out of his life.[36]

Lawrence and Fannie Chamberlain celebrated their tenth wedding anniversary on December 7, 1865. He gave her a double-banded gold-and-diamond bracelet from Tiffany's, an extravagant gift that only temporarily relieved the stresses at work just below the bland surface of their married life. Wartime separation had perhaps damaged it more than Chamberlain knew. Now, without much consultation with Fannie or regard for her wishes, he began to consider such political opportunities as might be open to a soldier/hero—in his case, politics as an extension of war.[37]

Though he sounded ambivalent himself, Chamberlain nevertheless encouraged his friends to promote his candidacy for governor. "I am summoned to Augusta to see some of the gentlemen interested in having me nominated," he wrote Fannie wearily. "I hate these things." In June 1866, Maine Republicans, quelling their doubts about whether he stood with Congress or the president on Reconstruction, chose Chamberlain to lead the state ticket. When he won the governorship by a landslide in September, Fannie declined to accompany him to Augusta.[38]

By some quirk of wind or fate, the high-walled campus of the University of South Carolina survived the burning of Columbia on February 17, 1865, though many of the buildings were in an advanced stage of decay: leaking roofs, broken windows, great chunks of plaster falling off walls. The university had shut down during the war. Now, in February 1866, the dormitories housed part of Columbia's large burned-out population. The army used one building as a military prison, and the Freedmen's Bureau had an office in another. The Alexanders shared a house on campus with J. L. Reynolds, professor of mental and moral philosophy.[39]

The South Carolina capital, "long rows of ruined houses and unsightly piles of chimneys," in the words of one historian of the period, stirred slowly back to life. The university had reopened in January with six professors and twenty students. Alexander saw his courses fill as the term wore on—a windfall, given the twenty-five-dollar-per-student tuition fee. He found the students so poorly prepared, however, that he spent most of his first year on remedial algebra. He did not offer his first engineering course until January 1867.[40]

The Alexanders made friends with the university's two distinguished faculty members, the scientific brothers LeConte, planter's sons from Liberty County, Georgia. (Alexander Stephens had once tutored them.) Aleck turned out to be an excellent teacher, affable and popular. He and Bettie acquired new housemates in the spring, friends as well as kin—Hampton and Jennie Gibbes and their two children. Aleck thought theirs a poor apology for a house, three symmetrical rooms on each of three floors. "Not a closet nor one single *convenience* of any sort," he complained. Five rambunctious children careered about the place. With the coming of warm weather he planted gumdrops and other candy in a tree in front of the house. The ruse kept the young ones out of doors, under its branches, for most of their waking hours: in South Carolina, the Alexander children learned to their astonishment, candy grew on trees.[41]

At James Longstreet's suggestion, Alexander decided to take up writing a history of the First Corps. Longstreet had settled in New Orleans, where he headed an insurance company and prospered briefly as a cotton factor. But he quickly made enemies of diehard Confederates and other mythologizers of Lee and Jackson. Longstreet criticized Lee, especially for Gettysburg, and attributed much of Jackson's reputation to the flabbiness of his opponents—second-string federal commanders, most of them, especially in the Shenandoah Valley. Deadliest of sins, he called on Southerners to cooperate with the Republican party. The South had lost, and must now accept the consequences, said Longstreet; Southerners replied by hurling their newly coined slur at him: scalawag. A soldier by training and habit, not much given to deep thinking on political matters, Longstreet probably regretted ever having spoken out. But, with his characteristic tenacity on the defensive, he never retracted a word.[42]

Longstreet accused his political enemies of distorting his military record and turned to Alexander to set it straight, to peel away legend from history with the same precision he brought to twoscore Army of Northern Virginia battlefields. Industrious as always, Alexander sent dozens of ex-Confederates printed forms that asked for firsthand details of when and where a particular command had fought; numbers of men engaged; hours of action and positions on the field; troops on either side; armament; rounds or volleys fired; casualties. The results streamed in, the forms piling high on Aleck's desk.[43]

Alexander the military historian eventually would rival Alexander the soldier and put Alexander the political analyst in the shade. (The South won the main question, "Who is the best man?" even though "we lost the minor point of self-government," he wrote George Pickett.) For now, he contented himself with collecting material and remained on the alert for professional opportunities. "I am looking out for a good RR for you," Longstreet wrote only two weeks after he arrived in Columbia. In September 1866, he turned down the University of Georgia's offer of the chair of civil engineering at an annual salary of $2,000.[44]

Leopold and Jane Alexander went to Columbia for a long visit early in 1867. Aleck took them around to meet his academic friends, Robert Barnwell, the university president; the LeContes; Alexander Haskell, now teaching law and soon to be married to the youngest of the patriarch's offspring, nineteen-year-old Alice. It was an agreeable life, Leopold found; Ed was even making a little money—he had sixty tuition-paying students, a $1,500 supplement to his salary. The blackened heart of Columbia was being rebuilt. The antebellum and Confederate leadership had regained power under Andrew Johnson's malleable provisional governor. The occupation forces were greatly reduced. "Black codes" were established; where necessary, especially in country districts, night riders of the Ku Klux Klan enforced them with the pistol and the gibbet. When Johnson, a Tennessee unionist with a morbid dread of black emancipation, vetoed the Civil Rights Act of 1866, it began to look as though the worst had passed. "The old southern leaders must rule the South," Johnson decreed from the White House. With his connivance, many of the social patterns of slavery times were restored.[45]

Then Radical Republicans struck back. The first congressional Reconstruction Act, March 2, 1867, reopened all the old questions, overturned the conservative order, and granted a share of political power to blacks. The Reconstruction Act divided ten states of the former Confederacy into military districts. (It exempted Tennessee, the only Southern state to ratify the Fourteenth Amendment, which guaranteed all persons equality under the law.) Garrisons were reinforced. The act empowered U.S. troops to enroll voters—black voters—and supervise fair elections that would allow democratic state constitutions to be written and adopted.[46]

Congressional Reconstruction was, the historian Eric Foner has written, "a radical departure, a stunning and unprecedented experiment in interracial democracy." Black voters formed a majority in South Carolina. They helped choose a new state legislature, overwhelmingly Republican and one-half black, in 1868. The Radicals charged the university's racial barrier; the legislature's funding act for 1869 barred distinctions in admissions on the basis of race, color, or creed. Such developments froze white southerners' blood. When Alexander and his friends decried the evils of Reconstruction, they were talking about black political power, educational opportunity, and economic gains.[47]

Stephen Winthrop wrote from England to commiserate with Alexander on "the dreadful state of things in the South"; he thought Radical policy cruel and unjust. "What revengeful, cantankerous beasts the Yanks must be to go bullying the South as they are doing," Winthrop went on. The British ordered things differently: "I am glad to say our House of Lords have just thrown out the 'Irish Bill' which those miserable radicals carried through the Commons." Another ex-soldier, William Oates (Chamberlain's adversary on Little Round Top), wrote to say he had not given up. "I am one of those who do not believe the cause is lost," Oates told Alexander. "I believe that it is only stifled by force & will again be revived & ultimately triumph."[48]

Oates, of course, turned out to be right. In several states the Klan launched a murderous offensive against blacks and their white Republican allies. John Gordon became the Klan's Grand Dragon in Georgia in 1868, and nearly won the governorship. (The Georgia legislature elected him to the U.S. Senate in 1873.) Gordon grudgingly admitted to a congressional investigating committee in 1871 that he had been a Klan member, but said he knew nothing of murder, beatings, arson attacks on black schools and churches, or other crimes. He did, helpfully, offer names—among them Aleck Lawton's—of other supposed Klan leaders.

Alexander's boyhood friend Dudley DuBose, a son-in-law of Robert Toombs, led the Wilkes County Klan, reputed to be one of Georgia's most violent chapters. The Klan helped elect DuBose to Congress in 1870.[49]

There is no evidence that Alexander endorsed the Klan's campaigns of violence, and he could well have been ignorant of the Klan connections of some of his friends and kinsmen. Still, neither he nor his faculty colleagues in Columbia had any wish to participate in experiments in interracial education. Alexander Haskell and John LeConte resigned in the autumn of 1868, after a large black vote helped to elect Ohio-born Robert K. Scott governor. The carpetbagging Scott had commanded a brigade in Sherman's march to the sea, then served as a senior Freedmen's Bureau agent in South Carolina. Joseph LeConte followed his brother to the University of California in March 1869, the same month two blacks were elected to the university's board of trustees. Alexander stepped up his search for a new job, and revived the old notion of emigrating to California. Robert Lee and John LeConte wrote him recommendations for academic appointments.[50]

Unsettling news reached Alexander from all points of the compass. Peace was taking a heavy toll of his friends. George Moody survived four years in the Army of Northern Virginia only to become a murder victim. A courtroom adversary assassinated him as he worked late one night in his Port Gibson, Mississippi, law office. Yellow fever claimed Willie Mason not long after he had found promising work as a clerk in a New Orleans coalyard. Pichegru Woolfolk died in the collapse of a gallery at the Virginia capitol in Richmond. Winthrop returned to England from the Argentine, where he had failed at farming, and could find no permanent work. He wrote Alexander that he wished the war could be fought over again, so he could be in it from the start this time.[51]

Still, there were private joys, and even some material successes. Two new members joined the Alexander nursery, Adam Leopold, born July 24, 1867, and Willie Mason, named for Bettie's brother, born November 23, 1868. Revealing a taste for speculation that would grow on him over the years, Alexander bought a city lot in Columbia for $973 in March 1868 and sold it at year's end for $1,200. He also purchased ten thousand acres on North Island at the mouth of Georgetown harbor, South Carolina, for $766—an astonishingly low price even in the depressed economy of the postwar Low Country. He thought the estate—his "barreny," he called it—could be developed for hunting, fishing, and sea bathing and eventually sold to northern interests for three or four times what he had paid for it. He plodded on with his math and engineering classes. By September 1869, though, he felt confident enough in the future to re-sign the professorship. With financial assistance from his father, he went into business for himself. Alexander and several partners built a factory to process meal and oil from cottonseed, products for which, they be-lieved, all manner of uses might be found.[52]

"Great chance to see, and be seen," an army acquaintance wrote Maine governor-elect Chamberlain. "Don't get dizzy-headed." That seemed unlikely, though Chamberlain did show a tendency to stray from the party line. His views were generally more conservative than main-stream Republicans'. Despite some misgivings (he objected to granting freed slaves the vote), he supported the Fourteenth Amendment and more often than not backed Congress over the president in the struggle for control of Reconstruction policy.* He also favored strict terms for ex-Confederates. "War is not a game where there is everything to win and nothing to lose," he told the Maine legislature in his first annual address in January 1867. "Those who appeal to the law of force should not complain if its decision is held as final." He sounded not unlike his fellow Republican, James Longstreet of New Orleans.[53]

Pensions for widows, aid for war orphans, war debts, jobs for returning soldiers: such were issues that confronted the governor of Maine in the immediate postwar years. Chamberlain proved a popular chief executive, though he made—actually seemed to court—a small but bitter corps of enemies. Chamberlain offended the state's powerful temperance move-ment by refusing to establish a special constabulary to enforce Maine's tough liquor laws. He believed a one-mission state police force would threaten civil liberties. Nor could he please the liquor lobby, probably because he left the restrictive laws undisturbed. He did not seem to care whether such stands cost him at the polls. "The loss of the rum vote is no great grief," he wrote Thomas Upham, the Bowdoin emeritus temper-ance crusader and abolitionist.[54]

Chamberlain signed death warrants of condemned criminals, the first Maine governor in recent memory to do so, arguing that the law either should be carried out or struck off the books. He ordered the execution of a rapist and murderer (a former slave, as it happened, who Chamber-

*In 1866, Maine was one of only six northern states that allowed blacks to vote.

lain believed had shown no remorse for his crime) over the opposition of religious groups and other opponents of judicial life-taking. "Many are bitter on me about capital punishment," he wrote his mother early in 1869, "but it does not disturb me in the least." His investigations of corruption in war-debt claims led to threats on his life. They made no impression on him. "I do not think I have a particle of fear in me of anything that walks or flies," he went on. "I go on in the strength of conscious rectitude & you can't scare me." By and large, the majority of voters saw things Chamberlain's way. He won reelection in 1867, 1868, and 1869.[55]

Transitions: After two years of recurring illness, John Chamberlain's lungs failed him for the last time in August 1867. Tom Chamberlain married John's widow, Delia, in 1870. Sae wed the Brewer merchant Charles Farrington in 1867; their firstborn, a son, died in infancy. There were continuing conflicts in the Chamberlains' marriage. Fannie categorically refused the role of governor's lady, and rarely joined her husband in Augusta. Chamberlain papered over their differences as best he could. He admitted, years later, that she detested his military and political lives in nearly equal measure.[56]

In November 1868, Fannie threatened him with divorce, the culmination of three years of drift and resentment. Possibly Chamberlain's disabilities were part of the trouble. He felt like hell a lot of the time, morose in mood and racked with pain. "There is not much of me left to love. I feel that too well," he had written Fannie plaintively in 1866. His wounds made sexual relations difficult, probably impossible at times. Word reached him that Fannie had complained about their marriage to some of her friends, who in turn had gossiped openly about it. They were saying that Chamberlain had physically abused her—pulled her hair, struck her, beaten her. The allegations sound far-fetched, even taking into account the corroding effects on Chamberlain of three years' experience of unexampled violence. But Fannie evidently repeated the charge to several people, his friends as well as hers.[57]

As a shock tactic, in hopes that the hard realities of life apart might drive the idea of divorce from her mind, Chamberlain proposed a trial separation. Then, reminding her that his political enemies would not hesitate to use the calumnies she had circulated to ruin him, he abruptly dropped his reasonable manner and issued an explicit warning. "You never take my advice, I am aware," he told her. "But if you do not *stop this* at once it will end in *hell*."[58]

No record survives of how Chamberlain and his wife were reconciled. At any rate, they agreed to remain married, if not always together. Chamberlain probably promised that his fourth term as governor would be his last; he had already broken Maine's unofficial three-term rule. Rebuilding the house may also have been part of the agreement. In 1867 he had it moved a few hundred feet up Potter Street to the corner of Maine Street, facing the Bowdoin campus. Four years later, when it looked as though he had returned to Brunswick for good, he carried out the experiment of raising the house eleven feet off the ground and building a new first floor beneath it.[59]

The enterprise transformed the clean-lined little cottage into a twenty-room Victorian manse. Chamberlain added a series of neo-Gothic flourishes inside and out: a grand spiral staircase, a star-studded blue ceiling in the new first-floor drawing room, an arched front doorway, a wrought-iron fence, and tall brick chimneys inset with the Maltese Cross emblem of the Fifth Corps. Whether these experiments in architectural hybridization were aesthetically successful is a matter of taste. The new first floor did provide sufficient space for entertaining. Grant, Sherman, Sheridan, McClellan, and Warren came to call, as did William Pitt Fessenden, James Blaine, and other senior Republican political figures. Longfellow occupied his old rooms for a few days in 1875 during the fiftieth anniversary of his graduation from Bowdoin. Chamberlain no doubt had read Longfellow's translation of the *Divine Comedy*, published in 1865–67.[60]

Rebuilding was costly, probably beyond Chamberlain's means had the governor's salary been his only support. He had invested in several business ventures; in the Maine tradition, he owned shares in a merchant vessel, the *Bombay*, which sailed October 16, 1868, from Philadelphia, bound for San Francisco with a cargo of thirteen hundred tons of coal. Late in 1868, the government awarded him a pension of thirty dollars a month for his Petersburg wound. "Bladder very painful and irritable; whole lower part of abdomen tender and sensitive; large urinal fistula at base of penis; suffers constant pain in both hips," the Pension Bureau's examining physician wrote. The $360 a year sounds like small recompense.[61]

Chamberlain maintained his military contacts, important for a still-ambitious politican. "Our path is strewn with Generals and admirals and old friends galore," twelve-year-old Daisy wrote her brother from Philadelphia in February 1869. Chamberlain commanded the Maine division of the Military Order of the Loyal Legion and delivered his by now well-honed lecture, "The Surrender of General Lee," wherever he could find an audience. But his relations with state Republicans were increasingly strained. He supported Fessenden's Senate vote against Johnson's impeachment in 1868, even though most Maine Republicans, including the powerful Blaine, were strong for conviction.[62]

Though the press of political business caused him to lay aside his Fifth Corps history, war matters continued to claim his attention. Warren, who had begun his long campaign to clear his reputation of Five Forks, wrote to object to Chamberlain's use of the word "halt" in his official report of the White Oak Road operations. In August 1869 he joined other ex-officers on a tour of Gettysburg, part of a long-term project to fix exact positions on the battlefield. On the twenty-sixth, he helped survey the Round Tops.[63]

Chamberlain encouraged his allies to promote his candidacy for the U.S. Senate in 1870, though he declined to campaign vigorously. Diffident about advancing his own interests, he now knew, too, that politics, unlike war, could never stir his soul. In any case, he had shown himself to be a clumsy and sometimes tactless politician, especially when confronted with emotional and divisive social issues such as temperance. The reformers' fervor, their impractical demands, exasperated him. The Republican caucus overwhelmingly chose Lot Morrill over Chamberlain, and the Maine legislature duly sent Morrill on to Washington. Chamberlain's views were at such variance with his party's that the Democrats briefly considered nominating him for governor in 1870. But his friends let the opposition know that such a gesture would embarrass him.[64]

Chamberlain's fourth and last term as governor expired quietly at year's end. For the moment, the future looked blank. With the arrival of spring, he occupied himself with a substantial garden ("my little farm," he called it) and in fitting out his yacht *Wildflower*. Day sails on Casco Bay and an occasional cruise to Portland soothed his troubled spirit. When the Bowdoin trustees offered him the college presidency in the summer of 1871, with an annual salary of $2,600, he accepted at once.[65]

CHAPTER 12

SUBTLE ARTS OF PEACE

———⊰●⊱———

ALEXANDER
RAILROAD CAMPAIGNS, 1871–92

Alexander pictured himself in tarboosh and baggy pants, inspecting the big guns of a Nile fort. The tableau amused him. Recruiting for the Khedive of Egypt, the expatriate former Union general Charles Stone formally offered Alexander the post of chief engineer of the Egyptian army in February 1871. Stone asked for a five-year commitment, with an option for another five years. He promised a salary of seventy Egyptian guineas a month (roughly $350), a house, and forage for four horses. The chief engineer built fortifications and superintended the Khedive's military school. On $350 a month, Aleck could live like a pasha in Cairo; the job sounded challenging, the surroundings exotic.[1]

The free-spending, Europeanizing Khedive, Ismail by name, had gone shares with the French in the Suez Canal, which opened in 1869 and already carried the majority of the seaborne trade between Europe and the East. Nominally a satrap of the Sultan of Turkey, in fact largely independent, Ismail meant to create a modern army to defend the new canal and to carry out forays into neighboring Sudan and Abyssinia. Stone, who, in spite of his equivocal military reputation in America,* had risen to chief of staff in Ismail's army, was one of a number of American ex-officers in Egyptian service, so Alexander would not lack for companionship. He thought over the offer and, in May, sent Stone a letter of acceptance.[2]

---

*Blamed for the Ball's Bluff debacle in October 1861, Stone afterward spent six months in prison on suspicion of treason.

Showing scant enthusiasm for exile, Bettie enlisted Aleck Haskell to try to change her husband's mind. Clinching his argument, Haskell, now president of the Charlotte, Columbia & Augusta Railroad, arranged for the railroad's superintendency to be offered him. The CC&A's lawyer, John H. Rion, actually made the approach, though Alexander doubtless knew his brother-in-law had contrived it. Appropriately enough, in this atmosphere of mercenary negotiation and throne-room patronage, Rion claimed to be an illegitimate son of the last Dauphin of France.[3]

"It was a close call!" Alexander wrote later. He withdrew his acceptance and went to work for the CC&A, the first of eight senior railroad positions he would hold over the next two decades. Restless, never satisfied for long, his roving would be remarkable even by the standards of nineteenth-century America, where the average adult male moved four or five times during his lifetime. "The wandering gentile," his sister Louisa dubbed him.[4]

These were years of extraordinary professional opportunity for Alexander. In August 1872 the University of Georgia offered him the vice-chancellorship. He turned it down and, in October, became president of the newborn Savannah & Memphis Railroad, with headquarters in Opelika, Alabama. In the spring of 1874 he had discussions in New York about a position with the Northern Pacific. In July, Beauregard invited him to go partners in a two-year defense consultancy in the Argentine, at a salary of $5,000 to $7,000 a year. In December, John LeConte offered him the chair of applied mechanics at Berkeley.[5]

In the end, railroads captured Alexander's imagination. With their complexities of operation and masses of workers to be marshaled, they appealed to the soldier and engineer in him. The last decades of the nineteenth century saw a tremendous expansion of the railroad net. Though the southern rail system, ruined by war, had been practically restored by 1870, new construction and consolidation proceeded apace. From 1865 to 1900, total American railroad mileage increased fourfold. Alexander, as a leading member of America's technical and managerial elite, helped make these decades the great age of rail.[6]

The Savannah & Memphis, projected to run from Opelika to Corinth, Mississippi, was hardly one-quarter complete when Alexander took charge. He raised construction capital from the state of Alabama, a generous promoter of railroads, and from larger neighboring lines, building debt as he extended the road. The Panic of 1873, touched off in September when Jay Gould and Company and other major New York banking houses failed, drove the S&M, with scores of other small roads, into default. This was bad timing and bad luck. Four years of hand-to-mouth existence in the Army of Northern Virginia had taught Alexander all too much about the economics of scarcity. Though he managed to guide the cash-starved S&M through the worst of the crisis and the severe depression that followed, he began to contemplate another move.[7]

Through Lawton's intercession, Alexander emerged as the leading candidate for the presidency of the Western Railroad of Alabama. The Western, unprofitable and deeply in debt, defaulted on its bond interest payments and fell into receivership in January 1873. Two years later, Lawton helped arrange its joint purchase, for $3.1 million, by the prosperous Georgia and Central of Georgia railroads. He then convinced William Wadley, president of the Central, to hire Alexander to expand and develop the newly acquired property.[8]

Alexander established Bettie and the children in Montgomery, Alabama, in May 1875, and set himself the task of mastering the intricacies of a new organization. Years later, in an article for *Scribner's Magazine*, he outlined a senior railway executive's multiform responsibilities. He managed a corps of bridge and road gangs, locomotive crews, conductors, ticket collectors, baggagemen, dispatchers, and telegraph operators; oversaw upkeep of the roadbed and track, and of every bridge, trestle, station, water tank, switch, and signal along the line; established schedules for maintenance, repair, or replacement of locomotives and rolling stock; and supervised the purchase of coal, new rails, and crossties. He reviewed detailed reports of train movements, passenger loads, and freight volumes. Burying himself in the details, Alexander renovated the Western and painstakingly built up its earnings.[9]

In Montgomery, a comfortable, modestly prosperous Black Belt provincial capital, the events of Alexander's domestic life unfolded in what began to look like permanent surroundings. A year passed, then another; Bettie allowed herself to dream of a long reprieve from packing for another shift of base. She took pleasure in Bessie's reports from the Academy of the Visitation near Wheeling, West Virginia, where she ranked first in her class in geography, arithmetic, and letter-writing, and second in theory. Sounding like her father at West Point twenty years earlier, Bess vowed to do better. She gave her parents little cause for anxiety, unlike her younger brothers. Eddie developed extravagant tastes. "He doesn't seem to be able to keep money in his pocket, & is unhappy until he spends it all," his mother reported. Willie proved dense about subjects that came easily to his father. "I have been all day working with Willie in his algebra," Alexander reported. "It takes no end of patience & perseverance to get it into his head." Still, he and Willie were close. Alexander would reminisce, late in life, about long walks with the boy along the rail embankment leading out of Montgomery, the two of them kicking companionably at rusted and broken bits of iron littering the wayside.[10]

In theory at least, solutions existed for practically any railroad problem. Bent track could be straightened, locomotives repaired, schedules adjusted, drunks, incompetents, and embezzlers discharged. Such work offered Aleck an escape from the vexed social and political questions that convulsed the South in the Gilded Age. True, railroads were politicized. Government aid, financial speculation, and extortionate rates to carry corn or cotton to market frequently were subjects of fierce political debate. "I have actually heard appeals for free transportation on the grounds that the cars were going anyhow," Alexander once wrote. But unlike some of his friends and family—Aleck Haskell in South Carolina politics, his brother Charlie racking rent out of Fairfield sharecroppers—Alexander never confronted the race question directly.[11]

By 1876, America's centennial year, white rule (Home Rule, in the euphemism of the day) had been largely restored in the Deep South. White politicans—nearly all the successful ones now were Democrats—could campaign for reconciliation rather than resistance. Republican Rutherford B. Hayes took the presidential oath of office in March 1877, even though a Democrat, Samuel Tilden, had won the 1876 popular vote. In return for support from influential Southerners, including Georgia senator John Gordon, Hayes agreed to order federal troops to stand down in Louisiana and South Carolina, where Haskell, as chairman of the state Democratic party, engineered the election of patrician conservative Wade Hampton as governor.[12]

Haskell, a sophisticated political operative, issued conciliatory appeals to blacks, claiming that the planter class of whites, the antebellum leadership, was the freedmen's truest friend. He also directed Democratic county chairmen to restrain their violent followers, instructions only haphazardly obeyed, especially in rural areas. For once, though, whites had no monopoly on violence. Republicans tormented the state's tiny minority of black Democrats. Still, Hampton, one of the state's largest prewar slaveowners and a senior cavalry commander in Lee's army, won a few thousand black votes. As part of the compromise that gained him the disputed office, he pledged to protect the basic rights of blacks. Hampton may have made the promise in good faith. But with the neutralization of the bluecoats, whites knew no restraints. They moved to quell black political aspirations and, eventually, to inflict that most miserable of all Civil War legacies, the system of racial segregation and discrimination known as Jim Crow.[13]

After 1876, southern white leaders could safely redirect their energies to economic enterprise—the building of the New South. "The causes that divided us are gone, and gone forever," Gordon ingratiatingly told an audience of Boston businessmen in May 1878. "The interests which now unite us will unite forever." Gordon's interests, like Alexander's, involved railroading; he had developed a reputation in Congress as a willing accomplice of the railroad powers. Had Alexander been a politician, he might have sounded much like Gordon. In any case, his developing Darwinian outlook, an up-to-date substitute for the deterministic Presbyterianism of his youth, led him to conclude that the outcome of war and reconstruction had been inevitable anyway. "There are two possible theories for this world," he would write, "one of wh is 'chance' & the other is 'Blue Print.' I am a blue printer." His personal blueprint now specified two more job changes, in rapid succession: first to the Georgia Railroad as president in May 1878, then on to one of the largest and most powerful of southern railroads, the Louisville & Nashville, less than two years later.[14]

The first move took the Alexanders to Augusta, where the patriarch had settled in 1872, the second to Louisville, practically a foreign town, distant, chilly, almost northern. They found themselves much alone there. The Alexander girls sailed for an extended grand tour of Europe and the Middle East in the spring of 1881. That fall, Eddie entered Auburn University in Alabama; the young boys, Willie and Leo, were away at boarding school. Aleck and Bettie were homesick in their suite at the Galt House, far from family and friends and the familiar South.[15]

Down in Georgia, the grand epoch in the family's history drew to a close on Easter morning, April 9, 1882, with the death of Adam Leopold Alexander. Using his railroad connections, Aleck reached Augusta in time to be with him at the end. His children buried the patriarch next to his first wife in the family graveyard at Fairfield. Nearly the entire clan gathered at the home place: the Lawtons and the Gilmers, the Hulls, Felix, Charlie, and Hillie and their wives, Aleck and Alice Haskell, Harriet (widowed in 1873), William and Marion Boggs—"more, I sup-

pose," thought Bettie, "than will ever be there again." Boggs, a clergyman, conducted the funeral service, droning on interminably and tiring
everyone out. Afterward, Aleck and Bettie rediscovered Fairfield. "I went
through all the rooms in the house, as I don't suppose I will ever go
there again," Bettie wrote.[16]

Generous to the last, Leopold Alexander left a considerable estate to
be divided among his widow and children. The Augusta house went to
Jane, most of the Fairfield croplands to Charlie, who had been farming
there for a decade. The patriarch willed the mansion itself to all the
children collectively, and cash settlements ranging from $2,500 to
$14,000 to each child individually—an attempt, he explained, "to rectify
as far as I reasonably can the inequalities of fortune arising among them
since the late war." Aleck got $2,500; the ill-favored Hillie, $14,000.[17]

Alexander returned, reluctantly, to Louisville and to his increasingly
burdensome L&N vice-presidency. The L&N's president, Horatio V. Newcomb, had talked him into the job, firing his imagination with his vast
schemes for expansion. Newcomb had recruited Alexander for his Georgia connections, for he had marked both the Georgia and Central of
Georgia roads for acquisition. For the same reason (and at about the
same time), Newcomb induced Gordon to resign his U.S. Senate seat
and accept a $14,000-a-year post with the L&N, part of a complicated
political deal involving the redistribution of public offices and private
preferments.[18]

Alexander's sense of security dissolved when Newcomb, citing ill
health, resigned in the autumn of 1880. The high politics of railroad
finance caused most of the resulting trouble. Alexander disliked and
mistrusted Newcomb's successor, the New York merchant capitalist Chris-
topher Columbus Baldwin. (Baldwin twice ran the blockade during the
war to collect southern debts for his Yankee merchant house—as good
an explanation as any for Alexander's antipathy.) Baldwin extended Newcomb's expansion policies in 1881 and 1882, driving the L&N deeper
into debt. Much of the newly acquired property turned out, on inspection, to be shoddy goods—"track worn out, construction bad, equipment
worse, where there was any," *The Commercial and Financial Chronicle* reported. Baldwin's recklessness stirred dissent among some board members, particularly E. H. Green, another New Yorker, and his allies. L&N
stocks were dropping. Dividends fell from eight percent in 1880 to six
percent in 1881 to three percent in 1882. Alexander backed Green; in

doubt about whether Green's forces could prevail, he began yet another canvass for a job.[19]

"What we will do is *very* uncertain but I feel very much disposed to move *somewhere*," he wrote Bessie, who had reached Constantinople with Lucy by June 1882. Though he sounded fretful, he advised her not to worry, "for every move I have ever made has bettered things." Still, he thought it best to urge frugality on his daughters. The stock market was slumping, he went on, and the $500 he had just sent would have to see them through to the end of July.[20]

When Alexander quit the L&N in early summer, Gilmer, Lawton, and Felix Alexander stepped up their campaign to win the presidency of the Georgia Central for him. He and Gilmer both had joined the Central board in January and already commanded influence there. Alexander decided to leave as little as possible to chance. He traveled to New York in late July to recruit friendly buyers for Central stock. In Savannah, Gilmer negotiated with the elderly, ailing William Wadley, who hoped to pass along the Central presidency to his son-in-law William Raoul. But the growing legion of Alexander stockholders forced Wadley into a compromise that would give Alexander the presidency, with Raoul staying on as vice-president.[21]

Wadley's death, on August 10, deranged Alexander's plans for an orderly transition. When the Central board chose Alexander to succeed him, conflict broke out at once. Raoul evidently believed his father-in-law's death released him from the agreement. He announced he would challenge Alexander at the stockholders' annual meeting in January 1883. Stigmatizing Alexander as the creature of Wall Street speculators, Raoul ran a hard-hitting, effective campaign. Alexander and his allies launched their own drive for votes. It was feeble by comparison. Balloting in record numbers, the stockholders ousted Alexander and replaced him with Raoul.[22]

This deviation from the blueprint caught Aleck unawares. He could afford, however, to be selective about his next employment. His railroad and other investments were lucrative. The North Island enterprises— rice plantations and a ten-boat fishing fleet—paid modestly; he had also acquired and begun to develop South Island, on the other side of the narrow opening of Winyah Bay. This time, though, his job feelers yielded nothing. The Southern Pacific and the Baltimore & Ohio had no place for him. Despite letters of recommendation from Ulysses Grant and Jo-

seph Bradley, Chester A. Arthur,* the latest in the Republican presidential succession, chose another man to fill a vacancy on the Mississippi
River Commission. (Bradley introduced Alexander as "thoroughly reconstructed"—a term, he explained privately, that he used only in a "technical sense, meaning 'reconciled and attached to the old Union.' ")
Alexander put North Island up for sale at $30,000, but found no buyers.[23]

Former Confederates rejoiced in the return of the Democrats to the
White House in 1884. Grover Cleveland did not disappoint prominent
Southerners, who had been shut out of the more gainful government
appointments for a quarter-century. Minor office even came Alexander's
way. In April 1885, at the urging of Union Pacific president Charles
Francis Adams, Jr., Cleveland named him to a government directorship
of the railroad. Adams, a grandson of John Quincy Adams and son of
the wartime minister to England, had fought at Antietam and Gettysburg
and led a black cavalry regiment into Richmond just a few hours after
the Confederate withdrawal. Searching for important postwar work, for
a role for himself, Adams decided to become a railroad expert. In his
studies of railroad economics, he claimed to have discovered a set of
scientific laws that controlled the evolution of railroad development.[24]

Adams opposed government regulation and political meddling, especially by well-meaning reformers; those "sturdy champions of the 'Dear
Peepul,' " he reckoned, ordinarily could be expected to do more harm
than good. He attacked stock gambling and financial predation, most
notably in his *Chapters of Erie and Other Essays* (1871). He argued that
combinations of small lines into large, powerful systems or "pools" were
beneficial, so long as they were honestly managed. From 1869 to 1884,
Adams rose from the Massachusetts Board of Railroad Commissioners to
the Board of Arbitration of the Trunk Line Railroads to the head of the
Union Pacific, the first transcontinental line and one of the most powerful combinations of all.[25]

Adams and Alexander had much in common, beginning with caste
and class, and they evolved a mutually satisfying professional friendship.
Alexander was not the sort of man to hold Adams's youthful abolitionism
against him. They were, after all, members of the brotherhood of those,
north or south, who had fought. In Alexander, Adams recognized a
kindred thinker, unsentimental and clear-sighted, who shared his faith
in scientific principles and his mistrust of high-minded reform.

*An accidental president, Arthur inherited the job upon the assassination of James Garfield. Garfield
was shot in July 1881 and died ten weeks later.

They were in close agreement on most railroad matters. Like Adams, Alexander had scant use for government. He believed the laws of evolutionary economics, Darwinian biological principles applied to the Dismal Science, should be allowed to operate unhindered. Corporate bigness was a good thing—concentrated economic firepower, one might say. It even had a democratic and leveling aspect. "The popular prejudice against corporations is utterly illogical," Alexander wrote. "The corporation is the poor man's opportunity. Without it he could never share in the gains and advantages open to capital in large sums. With it a thousand men, contributing a thousand dollars each, compete on equal terms with the millionaire." Pools, he believed, would rationalize railroad operations, stabilize rates, and assure orderly growth.[26]

Adams had taken over a Union Pacific system vitiated by the financial plundering of Jay Gould and racked by labor strife. In the summer of 1885, in one of his first assignments, Adams sent Alexander on a westward swing to survey the company's labor situation and report to him. In 1877, as a Massachusetts rail commissioner, Adams had used careful fact-finding, public opinion, and patience to help settle a potentially violent Boston & Maine trainmen's strike. The 1870s and 1880s witnessed innumerable murderous clashes, warfare between races as well as economic classes. In September, Alexander found himself investigating an outbreak with elements of both: the massacre of Chinese miners in the Union Pacific coal pits at Rock Springs, Wyoming.[27]

In this incident, armed whites had driven an estimated eight hundred Chinese from the mining camps, shot or roasted a score of them, and burned the immigrant shantytown. U.S. troops were called in to restore order. When the Chinese returned to work, the white miners went out on strike, shutting down the UP mines. Alexander arrived shortly after the riot, toured the stricken area, and, on Adams's behalf, took testimony from survivors.[28]

Most of the Chinese spoke through an interpreter. One, whose name Alexander transliterated as Ah Coon, had a kind of pidgin English. His fractured syntax and queer accent amused Alexander, who of course could not speak Chinese (or, as it happened, any other foreign language). In his usual detached manner, refined on some of the most terrible of Civil War battlefields, he set down Ah Coon's story. When the miners opened fire, he

> ran into a sort of half house & half cellar & hid in hole where he lay
> for several hours while the mob pillaged & burnt all around. At last

two (miners) came in & piled up some boxes to burn the place & one asked the other for a match. Then poor Ah Coon said, 'Oh I feel so belly solly' (very sorry). The other fellow had no match, & when they went for fire Ah Coon & another 'China Boy' broke out & ran. They were fired on & Ah Coon fell & lost a handkerchief in which he had tied up his savings—$2,600 in gold.

Alexander had no answers for Adams. It was not, after all, his kind of problem. Leaving the Chinese, the Europeans, the soldiers, and the railroad managers to sort things out for themselves, he moved on to Utah, Montana (where he descended eight hundred feet into an Anaconda Copper Company mine), and Idaho before returning to North Island in early October.[29]

The Union Pacific appointment left Alexander time to write, an avocation he eventually developed into a third career. He shelved the corps history, a massive task, for a series of lesser projects: railroad screeds, war studies and recollections, articles on the weather, even light verse of ponderous import. In the mid-1870s he amused himself with *Catterel Ratterel (Doggerel)*, a verse parable with a Darwinian motif. Characteristically, his themes were conflict and violent death. The protagonist, a high-minded rat with a passion for Darwin and Herbert Spencer, proposed fitting out his species' feline enemy with bells. Rats would hear the tinkle and hide; cats, denied fresh kills, would lose their claws and fangs and turn into sheep. No longer confined to holes, rats would evolve into large, powerful, and aggressive creatures.

> *Thus, fast acquiring size and strength*
> *We'll eat those mutton cats at length;*
> *And, living on but blood and brains,*
> *As lions do, we'll all have manes*
> *And grow so fierce and carni-veer-ous,*
> *That even men themselves will fear us.*

The learned rat presented his theory to a crowded convention of his kind, to great acclaim. But an unbelled cat turned up uninvited and devoured the philosopher just at the moment of his triumph. Darwin's blueprint remained unaltered.[30]

G. P. Putnam's publishing company eventually brought out Alexander's parable in a handsome little edition, with pen-and-ink illustrations by his daughter Bessie. Putnam's also published his *Railway Practice*

(1887) as part of its Questions of the Day series. Under the *nom de plume* of Jack Hildigo, he contributed articles on natural history to the weekly *Forest and Stream.* From the mid-1870s he produced a steady flow of war pieces. An 1878 letter on Gettysburg in the *Southern Historical Society Papers* rekindled the dispute with J. B. Walton, late of the Washington Artillery, who challenged Alexander's claim of having directed Longstreet's artillery during the battle. Alexander counterattacked, quoting Parson Pendleton to the effect that Longstreet had superseded Walton because he wanted a more capable officer in charge.[31]

When he tried to interest *Century* magazine in an article on railroad theory, the editors pressed him for a piece on Gettysburg instead. The war article, "The Great Charge and Artillery Fight at Gettysburg," eventually appeared in what Alexander called the "Century War Book"—the famous *Battles and Leaders of the Civil War* (1887–88). He also contributed an account of the Knoxville campaign ("Longstreet at Knoxville") to *Battles and Leaders.*[32]

The Gettysburg article occasioned an unlikely correspondence. Alexander made passing mention in the piece of his "faithful little darkey" servant. He was referring to Charley Crowley (for it turned out that Charley had a surname after all). Crowley had enlisted in a U.S. black regiment early in the 1870s and had, at some point, taught himself to read and write. He came across the *Century* article, recognized himself, and, curious about what had become of his wartime master, wrote the Virginia state adjutant general for Alexander's address.[33]

Crowley's army career had been rough going. The old sweats in the 24th Infantry taunted him for having been a Confederate officer's servant. Naturally, he defended himself. As a consequence, he was never free of trouble for long. At some periods he seems to have spent as much time in the guardhouse as on duty. He deserted in February 1888 and was caught and punished. Right away, he thought of Alexander. "Do you think General that you could find a place for me if we are all living when my term of service expires?" He deserted again in December. Writing from a railroad camp outside Fairbanks, Alaska, he asked Alexander to lobby for a pardon and discharge for him.[34]

By then the nomadic Alexanders were in Savannah, home office of the Central of Georgia. Dissentient stockholders had begun scheming to throw Raoul overboard as early as October 1884. Two years later a syndicate of New York financiers, some of whose members were principals in the largest of the southern railway combinations, the Richmond Terminal system, agreed to back Alexander's bid to sink Raoul. The turning point came when Hettie Green, the eccentric financier, wife of E. H. Green (Alexander's onetime colleague on the L&N board) and reputed to be the richest woman in America, agreed to vote her sixty-four hundred shares his way. Alexander won the presidency in January 1887.[35]

Raoul and his supporters again had accused Alexander of fronting for northern financial interests, a charge he found difficult to refute. "His election is considered a victory for the New York capitalists," *The Commercial and Financial Chronicle* reported. By the autumn of 1888 the Richmond Terminal investors who installed Alexander had acquired more than half of the Central's stock. Alexander assured local shareholders they would benefit from the arrangement. He continued to manage the day-to-day affairs of the thirteen-hundred-mile Central system, pursuing his own expansion program without interference, including the construction of a new line into Birmingham to tap traffic in and out of the northern Alabama iron and coal fields. But ultimate financial control lay with the Richmond Terminal.[36]

Borrowing the techniques of Jay Gould and other robber barons, the financiers used the Central to further other schemes and to enrich themselves. The Central's earnings declined in 1888 and 1889. In October 1890, a Wall Street slump drove down Richmond Terminal stock prices and provoked a financial crisis in the holding company. In an attempt to cut operating costs and raise cash, the Terminal's chief executive, John H. Inman, leased the Central to the Georgia Pacific, another Terminal lessee. ("The chain of control has been perfected," the *Chronicle* noted.) Overextension, mismanagement, and accusations of fraud threatened to pull down the rickety Terminal system, and with it the still relatively prosperous Central.[37]

Charles Francis Adams's management theories had failed to account for the buccaneering element of railroad finance. "They were a coarse, realistic, bargaining crowd," Adams wrote of the financiers; and in 1890 Gould and his gang of cutthroats forced him out of the Union Pacific presidency. Alexander likewise underestimated the rapaciousness of the money men. In October 1890, Gould himself turned up on the Richmond Terminal board, a presence that seemed to foreshadow a financial killing for a few speculators and a slow death for the holding company's three operating railroad systems.[38]

Late in 1891, the Terminal sent Alexander's railroad a bill for

$800,000 in unspecified services, and threatened to withhold stockholders' dividends if the Central refused to pay. Alexander sought an itemization of charges and tried to convince the local stockholders it had all been a misunderstanding. Newspapers picked up the story, publicity that probably benefited Alexander. Though the Terminal eventually withdrew the demand, Georgia stockholders believed they had seen the Richmond Terminal's true villainous face at last. Georgia partisans claimed the Terminal intended to ransack the Central. Alexander responded that the financiers had too much at stake for that. "They can only get their money back by developing it," he said—protecting the territory and expanding service.[39]

The stockholders were not mollified. In March 1892, Rowena M. Clarke of Charleston, South Carolina, owner of fifty shares of Central of Georgia, filed suit challenging the lease arrangement and accusing Alexander of mismanaging the railroad. Reviewing the case, the court declared the lease invalid and appointed Alexander as receiver. He seems to have taken the appointment as a vindication. Even so, he resigned the receivership at the end of March, bringing his twenty-one-year career as a railroad baron to an abrupt, unheroic, and unmourned end.[40]

He and Bettie journeyed west over the summer, partly on business (Alexander accepted a short-lived commission on a Columbia River navigation board), but mostly for pleasure. The Steilacoom military grounds had been turned over to the Territory of Washington for an insane asylum; their old house and two others were the only surviving garrison buildings. They wandered about in search of the familiar, a neat, spare, erect, bald gentleman in a salt-and-pepper suit escorting a trim, birdlike lady in white drapery. Aleck led Bettie into the woods beyond the post and stopped to carve their initials into a tree, together with the years 1861 and 1892.[41]

Alexander visited Gettysburg in late April of the following year, two months short of thirty years after the battle. It was his first view of the field since the rain-sodden Fourth of July, 1863. He met broad-shouldered Longstreet there, seventy-two years old now, practically deaf but not at all bashful about using his ear trumpet. Oliver Howard joined the party, too. Aleck had given the pious Lieutenant Howard money for Bible tracts before leaving West Point for the Utah Expedition in 1858. They toured the field and admired the monuments sprouting here and there. Later, Alexander led Longstreet to the edge of the woods on Seminary Ridge where Lee had ridden among the dazed survivors of Pickett's Charge.[42]

CHAMBERLAIN
SOLDIER-PRESIDENT, 1871–83

"It looks as if I could do some good here, and I can stand a great deal of hard work," Chamberlain wrote his mother in September 1871, a few weeks after he took office as Bowdoin's fifth president. In his judgment, the college required a thorough overhaul. His predecessor had added science courses to the curriculum and encouraged the separation of science and theology (the two had long been entwined at Bowdoin), though Paley's *Evidences of Christianity* remained on the list of required reading for seniors. Chamberlain carried the reforms a stage further by establishing a Scientific Department that awarded the bachelor of science degree.[1]

He expanded the study of French and German and gradually introduced the elective system. Women were permitted to audit some courses. Students applauded his decision to move morning chapel back to eight-thirty, after breakfast. "The monastery is not exactly the proper training school for the times," he had said in his inaugural address. He encouraged greater use of music in services in the college chapel, perhaps reasoning that ten dozen bodies in rhythmic sway might generate some warmth in that icy cavern. Within a year, evening prayers were quietly dropped.[2]

Bowdoin had changed, was changing, in other ways. The old guard of long-service faculty had passed from the scene. Alpheus Spring Packard, who had come to Bowdoin in 1819, held the Collins Professorship of Natural and Revealed Religion, but few others of Chamberlain's prewar colleagues remained. William (Chalkboard) Smyth devoted the early postwar years to fund-raising for a Brunswick Civil War memorial. He died in 1868. Timid, reclusive Thomas Upham, whose wife Phoebe had befriended Harriet Beecher Stowe, resigned in 1867, dropped out of public view, and died in 1872. New men arrived: Charles Smith, known as Co-Sine, in mathematics; Henry Johnson, a Dante scholar, in modern languages; and Maj. Joseph P. Sanger, First U.S. Artillery, Bowdoin's first military drillmaster.[3]

Chamberlain considered military training one of his most important innovations. It was one means, short of war, to instill in young men the qualities of discipline and courage he so admired. (A decade or so later it would be argued that college athletics, especially football, were a means to the same end.) Chamberlain told the trustees he had modeled the drill on exercises Plato outlined in his *Republic* for the training of philosopher-kings. In the beginning, students saw drill as a harmless amusement, especially the practice-firing of the four Napoleon guns on loan from the state. The novelty gradually wore off. Critics accused Chamberlain of trying to graft the military values of obedience and subordination onto the college.[4]

An order requiring the purchase of a six-dollar uniform touched off what became known as the "drill rebellion." Comic in some of its aspects, it revealed the authoritarian side of Chamberlain that war service had called into being. Imposing a strict West Point–style honor code, he showed little sympathy for anyone who failed to observe it. "Where a man dealt untruthfully, I regarded him as rotten at heart and good for nothing," he said, seeming to forget that students were not yet men— they were boys still, most of them, working out complicated questions of loyalty and identity. In the event, Chamberlain's handling of the uprising could hardly have been more inept.[5]

The rebellion began in November 1873 with a petition calling for abolition of the military department. Nearly every student signed it—126 of 133. The trustees and overseers declined to act. The issue seemed to die out over the winter, then flared again in the spring. Students called meetings to protest the drill. Discipline broke down. Trainees defied orders and mocked their officers. They dismounted one of the Napoleons and hid the breech blocks of others. Antimilitary slogans were chalked on the chapel walls. When some mutineers were punished, the junior class voted never to drill again. The sophomores and freshmen followed the upper classes into insurgency. Chamberlain reacted by suspending all three classes and sending the students home. He vowed to expel anyone who refused to sign a pledge to obey all the rules and participate in the drill.[6]

With encouragement from the boards and from important Bowdoin alumni, Chamberlain maneuvered himself into an indefensible position. Cyrus Woodman urged him to readmit no student without a written apology and acceptance of a one-year probation. Drills were part of "an important struggle for the national strength and well-being," wrote H. W. Benham, a

Fifth Corps engineer veteran who reminded Chamberlain that the 20th Maine had guarded his pontoons during the retreat from Chancellorsville in 1863. The protesters were "acting in foolishness almost equal to *insanity* to reject this so important instruction," Benham said. Without such training, he went on, lawyers, clergymen, and other natural leaders would find themselves in the ranks of future American armies, with "the drayman or the butcher or worse, as is so often the case, the popular *grog shop keeper*" in command.[7]

The trustees intervened, offering a compromise that amounted to a defeat for Chamberlain. They agreed to make drill voluntary. Most of the suspended students returned ahead of the ten-day deadline, but Chamberlain banished three men permanently and rejected their pleas for clemency, arguing that it would weaken college discipline. "Those expelled for drunkenness and the grossest debauchery can *at least* have been pardoned," George Harriman wrote Chamberlain in a petition for reinstatement. He refused to reconsider. Harriman, though, managed to get in the last word. "You were not victorious in the rebellion," he taunted the president. "You did not suppress the outbreak until the students had gained their point." In the autumn of 1874, only four students signed up for military training. By 1882, it had disappeared from the curriculum entirely.[8]

The affair brought no credit to Chamberlain. He almost certainly felt doubts about his actions, and rightly so; a visiting committee report faulted his handling of the uprising. "The president [must act] in the manner of one doing the duties of his station, because they were duties and not because his station is superior," the committee said. Still, he accepted the criticism without complaint, and turned down an attractive job offer during the summer of 1874—"an honorable position at $6,000 salary," he wrote his mother. He may have felt that to leave Bowdoin so soon after the drill episode would be an admission of defeat. For whatever reason, he chose to remain at his post.[9]

A political future still seemed open to him, though Maine Republicans continued to question his loyalty to the party. A Philadelphia newspaper discussed Chamberlain as a vice-presidential possibility for Horace Greeley, whose breakaway Liberal Republican faction unsuccessfully challenged Grant's 1872 reelection bid. Chamberlain's reputation for honesty, enthusiasm for civil service reform, and conservative views on Reconstruction made him attractive to the Greeley Republicans, though it is difficult to imagine him agreeing to stand against Grant. In any case, Greeley's operatives did not make an approach.[10]

Four years later, the disputed election of Rutherford B. Hayes revived his hopes of office. Chamberlain had a lot of fellow-feeling for Hayes. The nineteenth president had been practically a charter Republican, though not an abolitionist. Thirty-nine years old when war broke out, Hayes had served four hard, unglamorous years as a regimental officer, mostly in West Virginia. Like Chamberlain, he had risen to command a brigade and, briefly, a division. Chamberlain became notorious among Maine Republicans as an administration man—a supporter of Hayes's conciliatory policy toward the white South.[11]

Hayes was right to withdraw the occupation forces, Chamberlain argued; the army had no business enforcing anyone's civil rights. When Chamberlain introduced a resolution praising Hayes at the 1877 Republican state convention, one of James Blaine's allies countered with an amendment that accused the president of betraying the Republican governors of Louisiana and South Carolina. (Democrats regained power in those states as part of the agreement that won Hayes the presidency.) Blaine then negotiated a compromise that made no mention of Hayes but condemned the virtual disenfranchisement of blacks in several southern states.[12]

Chamberlain continued to speak out for Hayes's policy. "We must be considerate in our treatment of those who had convictions about and fought for what they considered to be the doctrine of states' rights," he told a Faneuil Hall audience in November 1877. Though Chamberlain had not toured the Reconstruction South, he could not have been entirely ignorant of conditions there. He and Oliver Howard, who had headed the Freedmen's Bureau after the war, met from time to time. He remained in touch with Adelbert Ames, who had been the carpetbag governor of Mississippi until the Democrats carried out a violent "redemption" of the state in 1876.[13]

Ames conveyed some of his bitter firsthand experience of racial politics to Chamberlain. In Ames's view, white Southerners were waging civil war. "The old rebel here is ripe for anything," Ames wrote him. He thought most Mississippi ex-Confederates hated the Union. Thousands of former slaves fleeing the Redeemed states streamed into Mississippi while Ames still kept a tenuous hold on power. But he could not protect blacks who tried to exercise their political rights.* During the election season of 1874, armed white gangs murdered as many as three hundred

*Nor could Sheridan, commanding occupation forces in Louisiana. The government denied him permission to establish military courts to try White League terrorists as "banditti."

blacks. Supremacists guarding one polling station threatened black voters with a six-pounder cannon. "You can have no idea of the true state of the case here," Ames wrote Chamberlain. "We do hope the north will stand true to the rights of the colored men. Let the Democracy prevail and the negro will rue the day he was made free."[14]

Chamberlain was unmoved. He had, in any case, come to view the war through a prism of moral relativism. He never doubted that the fighting itself had been worthwhile, as a test of manhood and for the bonds it created among the survivors; Chamberlain had fallen in love with war. But he did question whether his cause had been more just than the enemy's. In an 1879 Memorial Day address, he told the story, almost certainly apocryphal, of a Virginia farmer who had lost two sons in the war—one fighting for the Confederacy, the other for the Union. "God only knows which was right," the farmer had etched on the tombstone over his sons' double grave. Fourteen years after Appomattox, Chamberlain found himself close to agreement with the epitaph.[15]

His speech incensed at least one Maine newspaper editor, and probably a fair number of the paper's readers, too. "Gen. Chamberlain plainly says he went into the South, ravaged homes, burned the country and killed the people, and yet is not sure whether or not he was doing right," the Oxford *Democrat* said. "A man who skulked at home, or who fled to a foreign country, is preferable to one who will engage in all the horrors of battle, and then returning, say 'God only knows which was right.' " Honoring one's former enemies was one thing, the *Democrat* seemed to be saying; ambiguities of this kind were quite another.[16]

Prominent Maine Republicans continued to pledge formal allegiance to the ideal of justice for former slaves. Chamberlain's attitude, which found political expression in the Hayes administration's abandonment of southern freedmen, probably cost him his last slight chance of reentering public life. Efforts to arrange for his appointment as minister to England, and later to France, miscarried. Chamberlain partisans argued that Blaine Republicans had blocked his advancement, persecuting him for his political independence. Whatever the cause, by 1879 Chamberlain's prospects were nil. He again caught the attention of the Democrats, still struggling under the Copperhead tag and always in the market for presentable generals. One party operative wrote to say he had heard that Chamberlain planned to support the Democrats' 1880 presidential nominee, Winfield Scott Hancock, another Gettysburg hero. He asked Chamberlain to lend his name to Hancock's campaign.[17]

Even had he wanted to, Chamberlain could not escape the war. As late as 1873, the office of the army Commissary General of Subsistence badgered him for details of a voucher transaction, dating from the autumn of 1862, between the 20th Maine and a Sharpsburg farmer. He lectured widely on the war, a lucrative moonlight avocation. He allowed himself to be caught up in military controversy, too, particularly in the cases of Fitz-John Porter and Gouverneur Warren, both of whom obsessively sought postwar vindication for their wartime actions.[18]

Porter had been accused of disobedience and misconduct in command of the Fifth Corps at Second Bull Run, and cashiered from the service. A tyro officer in camp at Cape Elizabeth in August 1862, Chamberlain could only have known through hearsay of Porter, a McClellan loyalist who had been clamorously critical of McClellan's successor, John Pope. For some reason, Grant had spoken of the matter to Chamberlain, hinting that Porter would be wise to drop his campaign for reinstatement. Porter begged Chamberlain for a full report of the conversation. "I don't care how harsh the reason may be against me—how much it reflects on my honesty, my integrity, or my brains," Porter wrote him. He continued to press his case, and boards of inquiry eventually absolved him. Restored to the army list in 1886, Porter was formally cleared of all wrongdoing the following year.[19]

Warren, who stayed on in the engineer corps after the war, labored just as tirelessly to restore his reputation. He involved Chamberlain closely, bombarding him with requests for precise information about the Five Forks battle. He suggested editing changes to speeches and published recollections to give credibility to his own version of events, or to court or retain allies. "In any allusion to the surrender I would be careful not to slight Genl. H [A. A. Humphreys, commanding the Second Corps] by claiming too much for the Fifth Corps for Genl. H. is ready to fight on our side any time," Warren wrote him, critiquing his Appomattox lecture. Chamberlain, who wholly supported Warren, did his best to oblige.[20]

Some of Warren's friends spun a conspiracy theory around Grant's alleged contempt for the Army of the Potomac and Sheridan's unappeasable appetite for recognition. Carswell McClellan claimed the artillery commander Henry Hunt had told him Five Forks could not have been won without Warren. "He had to be put out of the way that the credit might go elsewhere," McClellan added. Warren had his own uncomplicated view of the case. "Off with his head has been their cry when they have had power," he said of Grant and Sheridan.[21]

Sheridan claimed, in his official report in May 1865, that Warren had failed to exert himself to bring the Fifth Corps up to Five Forks as rapidly as possible, and that "his manner gave me the impression that he wished the sun to go down before dispositions for the attack could be completed." In December 1879, after repeated requests, Hayes granted Warren's petition for a formal inquiry into the charges. Chamberlain testified before the three-officer board in New York City in May 1880. He followed Sheridan, who greeted him cordially as he prepared to take the stand. "We are bound to have the true history of this thing out now," he wrote Fannie nervously. In the end, the board exonerated Warren and concluded that Sheridan had done him an injustice. In November 1881, President Arthur ordered the court's findings and opinion to be published. Warren, only fifty-two years old, died nine months later—"of a broken heart," his friends never ceased to believe.[22]

Chamberlain probably found fighting Five Forks over again in front of a military court preferable to raising money for Bowdoin. For a period in the 1870s, the college was so hard up that the librarian paid for some books and periodicals out of his own pocket. Chamberlain ground out a "development" campaign, that most essential and least appealing of presidential duties, with signal success, adding some $200,000 to the college endowment during his term. He even tried to touch his army friends, Adelbert Ames among them, for donations.[23]

The Bowdoin years saw personal as well as professional gain, loss, and transition. Fannie's father died on Christmas Day 1875. After a difficult beginning, he and Chamberlain had become firm friends; in 1882, Chamberlain donated a memorial window in his memory to the First Parish Church. Joshua Chamberlain, Jr., austere, silent, and Copperhead to the last, died in Brewer in August 1880, six weeks short of his eightieth birthday. Two years earlier, when Chamberlain and his family visited Europe for the first time, he had promised his father a card from Tankerville Castle.* Daisy married Horace Allen, a lawyer from a well-to-do

---

*Chamberlain went to Paris in 1878 as U.S. commissioner at the international exposition of that year. An unremunerative appointment, it was perhaps the best Hayes could do for him.

Boston family long known to the Chamberlains, in April 1881. Wyllys graduated from Bowdoin later that year.[24]

Approaching fifty, Chamberlain retained his formal good looks, despite recurrent, rackingly painful flare-ups of the Petersburg wound. A student in Chamberlain's constitutional law class recalled how intensely he sometimes suffered from it. His still-thick hair had turned nearly all gray, as had the long, drooping mustache he cultivated in the 1870s. Fannie showed more outward evidence of aging. Sallow, nervous, often ill, she consumed quantities of tonics and faddish food cures. Fear of blindness led her to a succession of doctors in search of treatment for her failing eyes.[25]

Daisy's presence relieved the gloom that sometimes threatened to engulf the elder Chamberlains. She and her father were closer than ever during these years; he loved in her the lively, cheerful grace he found lacking in his wife. Daisy reported to Allen in the spring of 1876, when she was twenty, that Chamberlain planned a visit to her in Boston. "We shall have a tear if he comes!" she wrote her future husband. Like his sister, Wyllys had a lively, expressive, and indolent side. ("It has cleared off a good deal," he wrote his grandfather on a breezy April day in 1872, "and I tell you Captain it's a splendid day for kites.") Daisy entered into a comfortable existence with Allen in Boston; her brother never really managed to settle down to sustained work.[26]

In some ways, Tom Chamberlain could be regarded as a casualty of war as much as his elder brother. Sickly, consumptive, lacking Lawrence's inner strength as well as his physical stamina, he could not carry over his army success into peacetime. Tom drank too much (though he evidently held his liquor well), wandered from job to job and place to place, neglected his wife. He worked for a time as a merchant in New York City, then obtained a minor clerkship in a pension office, probably in Washington. He complained about the nature of the work and, inevitably, the salary. "In the army a man stands a chance for promotion—somebody will get killed," he wrote Chamberlain, sounding regretful of the long odds against death on active service in the pension bureau. Characteristically, Tom fixed his ambitions on a port inspector's position that paid three dollars a day "with nothing to do"; failing that, he hoped to try to catch on at the post office.[27]

Political turmoil created one last heroic role for Chamberlain, one he played for all it was worth. The Greenback political excitement came late to Maine, but when it came, it carried the state to the edge of civil war. Greenbackers demanded that the federal government stop pegging the amount of paper currency to the availability of gold and silver. They wanted large issues and unfettered circulation of new greenbacks. Currency became a powerful class issue, creditors favoring hard money, and debtors, especially farmers, soft. Greenbackism dominated the Maine elections of 1878, splitting state voters three ways. Greenback strength denied the Republicans a majority, throwing the contest for governor into the state legislature. Republicans there found dealing with the Greenbackers so distasteful that they agreed to put a Democrat, Alonzo Garcelon, into the statehouse.[28]

The 1879 results were more confusing still. Republicans again won a narrow victory, but this time the Democrats and Greenbackers were allied in a "Fusion" party. Garcelon and his friends in council managed to turn several Republican victories into defeats on technicalities such as an alleged failure to sign or seal election returns in open meetings. At least six Republican legislators lost their seats in this way. In December, Garcelon declared that the Fusionists had won after all.[29]

The Republicans protested that they had been robbed, as they surely had. At Blaine's suggestion, the party organized "indignation" meetings around the state. Democrats countered with rallies of their own. Both sides made warlike speeches. Garcelon sent to the state armory in Bangor for 120 rifles and twenty thousand rounds of ammunition. Leading Republicans urged Garcelon to submit the disputed election to the state supreme court. Garcelon consented. Courts tend to be conservative; Maine's proved no exception. But when the judges ruled the Republicans had won, the Fusionists ignored the verdict.[30]

With massive unrest in prospect, Garcelon summoned Chamberlain. Suspecting the Republicans would try to seize the statehouse when his term expired in early January, the outgoing governor established a First Division of militia and directed Chamberlain to protect state property and institutions until a legally recognized legislature could qualify his successor. Chamberlain came up to Augusta on January 6, 1880, disbanded the guard Garcelon had thrown around the statehouse, and arranged with the railroads to carry troops to the capital in the event of an uprising. To defuse tensions, he returned to the Bangor arsenal the arms Garcelon had ordered.[31]

Acting as though martial law had been declared (a reprise of Southside Virginia, April 1865), Chamberlain padlocked the governor's offices, restricted access to the legislative chambers, and began issuing proclamations. The crisis greatly cheered him, though he sounded surprised and even hurt that the warring factions—especially the Republicans—did not at once hail him as the answer to everyone's problems. "What vexes me," he wrote Fannie, "is that some of our people [Republicans] do not like me to straighten things." Making his headquarters in a small office in the capitol, he passed one nearly sleepless night, then another, awaiting events.[32]

Violence seemed possible, even likely. Chamberlain believed his presence, the force of his personality, offered the surest means of averting it. He continued to appeal to the high court to issue a definitive ruling. Meanwhile, the two rival legislatures met in separate sessions. The Democrats chose an acting governor; Chamberlain declined to recognize him. The Republicans offered the acting governorship to Chamberlain; he rejected that scheme too. "I am determined that Maine shall not become a *South American* state," he wrote Fannie. Blaine pressured him to disband the Fusionist legislature, using force if necessary. He refused.[33]

There were plots, counterplots, and rumors of plots: Chamberlain to be kidnapped; Blaine's house blown up; Blaine shot down in the street. Republicans and Fusionists alike heaped obloquy on Chamberlain, though many old soldiers rallied round. F. B. Ward, late of Company F, 20th Maine Volunteers, who had lost a leg on Little Round Top, offered to raise a company of veterans loyal to him. Chamberlain had no fear for his own safety. At one point during the crisis, he stared down an angry mob threatening him with death. "Killing is no new thing to me," he called out to the crowd from the statehouse rotunda. "I have offered myself to be killed many times." He actually threw open his coat, as though to invite the assassin's thrust. It sounds melodramatic, thus tempting to debunk. The actor Laurence Olivier once spoke of the "pictorial beauty of heroism." He was talking about Shakespeare's *Henry V* and the English archers at Agincourt, but the principle applies here. The gesture caused at least one veteran to speak up for Chamberlain; he calmly threatened to shoot anyone who raised a hand against the general. The mob backed and filled and gradually dispersed.[34]

Was the danger real? These were violent years. There were lots of arms about, and squads of old soldiers on both sides who knew how to use them. The excitement seems to have deprived Chamberlain temporarily of his sense of perspective. "Yesterday was another Round Top, although few know of it," he wrote Fannie. He had learned that night of the plot to abduct him, he told her, and he had "the strange sense again of sleeping inside a picket guard." He renewed his charge of ingratitude, especially on the part of the Republicans. "I wish Blaine and the others would have more confidence in my military ability," he went on. "There are too many men here afraid of their precious pink skins. I shall have to protect them of course, but my main object is to keep the peace & to give the opportunity for the laws to be fairly executed." Tiring of them at last, he ordered Blaine and the others to keep away from the statehouse.[35]

The Supreme Court decided, again, that the Republicans were Maine's duly elected majority party. Meeting on January 17, the Republican legislators chose Daniel F. Davis governor. Chamberlain had his ruling at last. He promptly recognized Davis and, in one last broadside, declared his assignment at an end. Davis locked the Fusion legislators out of the statehouse. There were scattered troubles. Davis called out several militia units, including one with a Gatling gun. The Fusionists began pulling out in ones and twos and making for home. After a day or so, with the new governor firmly in control, Chamberlain returned to Brunswick.[36]

A new college term: more trouble with rowdy sophomores; repeated appeals to wealthy alums; recycled lectures in constitutional law. Chamberlain began to talk of giving up the Bowdoin presidency, and some of the trustees agreed that the time had come. Conflict marked Chamberlain's tenure. "Men meant all too much when they said 'Old Bowdoin,' " he had noted in his inaugural speech, and Old Bowdoin remained stubbornly out of step with what he grandly called "the new Elizabethan Age" of his presidency. His practical, results-oriented schemes threatened Bowdoin's historic liberal-arts mission. Chamberlain tried to turn Bowdoin into an entirely different, not necessarily better, place: a "people's university," in a college historian's words, large, comprehensive, technical and vocational. His major initiative, the scientific department, proved a failure; he had to shut it down for lack of support in 1880. The college dropped his engineering program the following year. Still, he could claim some notable successes. Chamberlain put the college's finances in good order and oversaw permanent gains in science and foreign-language instruction.[37]

But Bowdoin no longer held his interest. He had had his fill of obtuse trustees, feuding faculty, and student outbreaks such as the notorious War of Smith's Mustache in 1882–83. Toward the end of 1881, Chamberlain made his first trip to Florida to investigate business opportunities in that subtropical El Dorado. He became president of the Florida West Coast Improvement Company the following year. Chamberlain expected his syndicate to make lots of money in land speculation, and he thought both he and Fannie would benefit from the soft winter climate. "It would cure Fanny of all her ills," he wrote Sae.[38]

On the return from that first trip, he had left the train at Petersburg and walked the Rives' Salient battlefield. Chamberlain hardly recognized the place. Trees grew thickly upon the slope, bare and sunbaked the day the brigade had charged. The wound that had dropped him to his knees there continued to cause him unrelieved misery. He finally consented, in April 1883, to another attempt at surgical repair, this time under the knife of a Boston surgeon, J. H. Warren. "Dr. says it was as successful an operation as he ever made," Grace (as Daisy now preferred to be called) wrote her mother. Even so, he required a lengthy convalescence. A return trip for aftercare exhausted him. "The Dr. put me to bed & made a sick man of me," he wrote Sae. Warren's doses of opiates and other drugs left him mazed and nauseated. The new incision healed slowly. "The doctor says I shall be better than for twenty years; but I take that at a discount," he went on to Sae, skeptical, obviously, that surgery and medications could ever bring him other than temporary relief.[39]

Chamberlain returned to Maine in early July, rallied, and soon reported himself able to walk half a mile without tiring. Still, poor health could be offered as an excuse to exit Bowdoin. He resigned the presidency at commencement in 1883, leaving office with no regrets. "I want to say to set a caution against your young ambition, that however pleasant and useful the life of a College Professor may be, that of a president is about the most thankless wearing and wasteful life that can be undertaken," Chamberlain wrote his faculty protégé Henry Johnson a few months later.[40]

With this emphatic statement, Chamberlain brought his intimate association with Bowdoin to an end. He could not entirely repress a nagging feeling that he had somehow fallen short. At a picnic once, a woman asked him, just to make conversation, how he happened to be in the war. "I didn't happen," he told her. "When my country called I replied with the best there was in me." Thirty years of life remained to him. Though he could not know it, he had reached the effective close of his public career. He would never be so engaged, useful, or fulfilled again.[41]

CHAPTER 13

MEMORY

—⊷⊶⊷—

ALEXANDER
VIEW FROM A DISTANCE, 1897–1910

ALEXANDER HAD NEVER KNOWN AN-
other job to touch it: a salary of $250 a week in gold, an exotic locale,
unfamiliar birds and beasts to shoot, tropical plants to uproot and ship
home, a gallimaufry of eccentric expatriates to observe, time to spare
for reading, remembering, and assessing. "You can tell Bess that I have
begun to write in her blank books for my recollections of the war & try
to do something every day," Alexander wrote his wife from Greytown
(now San Juan del Norte), Nicaragua, where he landed May 14, 1897,
after a wretched day-sail up the Caribbean coast in a sloop he called *Mal
de Mer*. Alexander carried a U.S. government warrant* to settle a long-
standing Nicaragua–Costa Rica boundary dispute and memories enough
for treble the number of notebooks his daughter had posted to him.[1]

The boundary issues were large; North American interests continued
to view Greytown–Lake Nicaragua–Salinas Bay as a possible route for a
ship canal linking the Caribbean and the Pacific. Both countries sought
the canal, with the revenue, power, and prestige it would bring. Alexander thought either would go to war rather than give it up. Still, the
Nicaraguans and the Costa Ricans had agreed to accept his decisions as
final. Under his general supervision their survey teams began inspecting
the harbor, river, and lagoons that here formed an imprecisely defined
starting point for the international frontier.[2]

*Grover Cleveland appointed Alexander engineer-arbitrator February 6, 1897, a month before he
left office.

Port of entry for American filibuster expeditions in the 1850s, boomtown in the 1880s, Greytown had moldered after the failure of the latest canal venture. A group of abandoned canal company houses, five large dredges rusting away in the Inner Harbor, and a one-car trolley line were evidence of a fleeting prosperity. Of the population of fourteen hundred, most were Jamaicans brought in to dig the canal. They now found subsistence where they could. There were some Carib Indians and Spanish-descended Nicaraguans, and a small, colorful colony of merchants, drummers, and confidence men who made their headquarters at the rum shop and general store of Herbert Bingham, Her Britannic Majesty's consul in Greytown and the unofficial doyen of the expatriate community.[3]

Advised that the boundary survey could take as long as two years, Alexander settled comfortably into two spacious rooms on the second floor of a large, airy cottage opposite the main square. He read *Quo Vadis* and thought it fully as good as *Ben Hur*. After the briefest acquaintance, Bingham's pretty young American wife asked him to read her manuscript novel *Out of This World*. In a letter to Bettie he outlined the story, set in Mexico: "There's a wonderful clairvoyant who finds gold mines, & there are bandits & villains & no end of illegitimate children (one of the heroines is one, the padre has at least one other & one of the villains has *three* already & expects another in a chapter or two) & the biggest heroine of all, who of course is just sixteen, pulls up her dress & shows the biggest hero of all a dagger she carries in her stocking to stick the biggest bandit with, when he comes to abduct her, as he has publicly sworn to do. Now if that is not a pretty good start for an interesting story I don't know what is, & that is only the main thread." He was reading Dumas's *The Three Musketeers* at the same time, he wrote Bettie, and found it not half so exciting.[4]

Alexander surveyed Greytown's human comedy with Olympian detachment, tolerant and amused, and set down the principal characters in letters home with his usual sharp eye for nuance. Howard Pyle, nearing seventy, stranded in Greytown when the canal company failed, held forth at Bingham's bar with stories of fossickers, gamblers, desperadoes, and vigilantes of the Nevada mining days, talking about them, he wrote Bettie, "as I could talk about the classes and the cadets who were with me at West Point." Pyle dyed his whiskers black & dressed like a parson, but his long taper fingers told another story: of greasy marked cards and stacks of gold and silver coin on frayed green baize. Pyle dreamed of a canal revival, with all the opportunity for plunder that implied. "Then," Aleck explained, "he will be in one of the choicest spots on earth for one of his vocation and talents." He claimed to be a Virginian, with family in the Fredericksburg vicinity. As a tease to Bettie, with her innumerable relations, he began referring to Pyle as "your cousin Howard."[5]

The survey occupied only a fraction of his time. The boundary teams submitted the first reports to him June 14, each forty pages long—but in Spanish, so they had to be sent out for translation, occasioning the first of many missed deadlines. Alexander was philosophical. "I am absolutely willing to stay here, on salary, as long as they want or to take one year's salary & return to you," he wrote Bettie. He decided to have the reports printed, too, causing another month's delay.[6]

Aleck gallantly told Mrs. Bingham that her fiction reminded him of H. Rider Haggard's. Flattered (as he had intended her to be), she now confided that she had written a sequel, *The Priest with the Beard*, in which such characters as survived the first book would reappear and others would be restored to life. He reread Wilkie Collins's *The Woman in White*, which he had first encountered nearly forty years ago on the steamer out of Fort Steilacoom. He tried learning a little Spanish, though he complained of too many moods and tenses—"enough to make a cat sick."[7]

He lived for the mails. The ocean steamers called at Limón or Bluefields and transshipped the Greytown post via schooner or the little coastal packets *Rosita* and *Lucy B.* The schooner captain, a Carib named Cacho, had a taste for rum and sailed when it suited him. "I am still straining my wishbone after Polycarpo Cacho," he wrote Bettie during one mailless stretch. "I imagine that he *wants* to come—that he feels the telepathic disturbance set up all over the Caribbean by my longing for my mail & it is only the lack of wind that delays him." He consoled himself by setting down a vivid account of the party Bingham threw to celebrate Victoria's Diamond Jubilee. Champagne, beer, and ginger ale flowed, and a young man extemporized a remarkable imitation of a French horn, accompanying Mrs. Bingham at the piano in a selection from *Il Trovatore*.[8]

Working from memory, he plugged away at his recollections, though slowly at first, bogging down in descriptions of the fighting at First Manassas. "There is much more temptation to detail than there will be after the narrative has gotten used to battles," he explained to Bess. Word came that Frank Huger, who had figured in so many battlefield episodes, had died. He learned, too, from one of the children, that Bettie had been seriously ill. She claimed to have rallied, but he pressed her for assurances that "you are steaming well and on an easy grade." In late September, nearly five months after his arrival in Greytown, he put aside the recollections (he had reached the Seven Days' battles of 1862) to write his first award decision.[9]

Revolution broke out, a feature of life in Nicaragua. There were reports of fighting in Managua and other places. The insurgents were said to have captured the lake steamer *Victoria* and mounted a cannon in her. The governor established an armed picket line outside Greytown. Though tempted, Aleck did not volunteer. "I am getting altogether too much money to risk my carcass," he assured Bettie. "When I was only a Confederate brigadier with but $300 Confederate a month the case was different. I'm two hundred and fifty times as valuable now, & I must be just as many times as careful of myself." He passed the hot, damp evenings out on the piazza and awaited events. The rebels did not come, and in a few days the insurgency collapsed.[10]

The award, issued September 30, established the boundary point of departure at the mouth of the San Juan River. It gave the Nicaraguans most of what they wanted; the Costa Ricans, said Alexander, were gracious in defeat. After a month's holiday, the survey teams were to move inland eighty miles to Castillo and begin marking the land line down to the Pacific. Alexander would remain in Greytown until they called for him. Writing as Jack Hildigo, he turned out an article on reptilian habits ("Do Snakes Care for Their Young?") for *Forest and Stream*. The boundary commissions extended their vacation. "My salary runs on all the same," he wrote home in mid-November. By month's end he had finished his account of the Seven Days.[11]

The evocation of old days and old comradeships moved him deeply. He sent his early work to Bessie. "I'm delighted you like my poor little recollections," he wrote her, "but lots of them bring my eyes full of tears as I write." One night, he dreamed of riding with Robert Lee toward a dawn battle. Taking great care with the siting of the batteries, he had everything in order by sunrise. The firing commenced; "and as Kipling says, 'Then the ugly bullets comes knocking up the dust/And no one loves to face 'em, but every beggar must!' " Alexander woke up abruptly, relieved at first, then vexed. He could not be hurt in a dream battle, and after taking so much trouble with the guns, he resented being denied the satisfaction of firing even a single shot. "That kind of dream makes a first class nightmare," he told Bettie.[12]

Emotions thus aroused would make Alexander's first Greytown April 9—the anniversary of his and Bettie's departure from Steilacoom in 1861 and, of course, of the surrender at Appomattox four years later—more poignant than ever. Thirty-three years after the final collapse, he could look back on events with a feeling of gratitude. "I have lived in the most interesting generation which has ever had its day on this planet," he wrote Bettie. "And of all the happenings of my generation I wd not exchange my lot with any other man's who has lived." From such a distance in time and space, the war years seemed less painful, not so barren of purpose. He exalted them.[13]

The boundary survey went forward in halting steps. At a half-mile a day, with eighty miles of river line and a hundred of land line yet to run, Alexander calculated he would be in Nicaragua for at least another year. Toward the end of February 1898, news reached Greytown that the battleship *Maine* had blown up in Havana Harbor. A few weeks later, another revolution broke out in Nicaragua. Rumor had a column of three thousand men and seventeen guns marching on Managua. After a day or two, the telegraph announced that the uprising had been crushed. At Bingham's, the American expatriates discussed the war excitement back home. Alexander decided to apply for a commission, not as a volunteer but, rather illogically, as a regular. He asked Longstreet to send in an application for a place for him.[14]

The Costa Ricans, meanwhile, had turned bellicose about the boundary and were threatening to demand a new arbitration of the dispute. They pushed troops up to the frontier and looked, so Alexander thought, as though they meant to provoke a war. Then, abruptly, the government in San Jose agreed to accept Alexander's most recent award. The border trouble blew over. Word reached Greytown on April 23 that the United States and Spain were at war. "I suppose it will be fought out mostly at sea," Alexander mused, "for when the Spanish fleet is destroyed that will practically be the end of it." Land forces in Cuba were likely to see a lot more of yellow fever than glory, he thought.* Greytown hummed with rumors of a fleet action in which Spain lost fourteen ironclads sunk, the Americans sixteen! Aleck waited, "like Mi-

---

*Alexander was correct. Only three hundred of the three thousand U.S. fatalities in the Spanish-American War were from combat.

cawber, for anything that might turn up," but the War Department did not seek him out.[15]

Two of his West Point contemporaries, the former Confederate cavalry-men Fitzhugh Lee and Joseph Wheeler, obtained senior commands. "It makes me wonder whether I ought not to have thrown up everything here & gone home months ago & gotten into it somehow," he wrote Bess. He did pull out early in July, returning to the United States on furlough; the fighting ended in August with the Spanish decisively beaten. Someone had written that Bettie had put on weight and gained strength. The report turned out to be false. She looked thin and frail. Bettie evidently had some wasting disease, most likely cancer. Home for nearly five months, Aleck attended her as best he could while he sorted through his business affairs. His income from the Sea Island rice planta-tions and from stock holdings varied, sometimes widely, from year to year, leaving him in a permanent state of financial anxiety. That was why he had sought a regular commission, which "would soon permit me to retire with a salary for life." That was why he decided to return to Nicaragua, despite Bettie's failing health; he could not bring himself to give up the $250 a week stipend.[16]

The Alexanders left South Island in early December for Augusta, where Bettie moved in with their daughter Lucy and her husband, Will Craig. The steamer *Atlas* carried Aleck southward from New York two days before Christmas 1898. The weather was calm and he worked up an appetite, a rarity for him at sea. He ordered goose for Christmas dinner and complained of being served two slices so thin he suspected they had been shaved off a robin. As usual, his keen eye caught every oddity among his fellow passengers. He found the idiosyncrasy of M. Charles Patin, the Belgian consul in Medellín, of particular interest. "It makes him sick—nauseates him—for any body to sit on his *left*," Alexan-der reported. "If his attention is drawn leftwards it makes him sick." His own equilibrium did not survive a rough passage of the Caribbean, during which he fell violently ill.[17]

On land, Alexander stood the tropical climate well. Twice-daily doses of quinine were a prophylactic against malaria. He enjoyed a full and varied diet and weighed, in January 1899, a prosperous 177 pounds. Reaching Greytown on the sixth, he found the teams quarreling over the boundary through Lake Nicaragua. He left them to their own devices and immersed himself in the Gettysburg section of the recollections, alternating shifts at his writing desk with long sessions reading Thackeray and Hume. By early February he had produced sixty pages. "The fighting part [is almost] over & then I'll only have to get back to Virginia & come & pay you that delightful little visit at Bowling Green," he wrote Bettie. Aleck went on to mention a new acquaintance, an acetylene torch salesman named Col. R. F. Mann, late of the 11th Georgia in Charles Field's division.[18]

Counting on the bond of ex-Confederatehood, Mann sought Alexander's help in arranging a monopoly on the import of kerosene into Nicaragua and Costa Rica. Something about Mann, a suspicion, perhaps, of a "scarcity of currency concealed about his person," put Alexander on his guard. He demurred. Mann, who seems to have been something of a B. Traven sort of character, turned out to be penniless. The expatriates in Bluefields had taken up a subscription to send him and his wife as far as Greytown. "If he ever goes on from here it will doubtless be in the same way," Alexander thought. The Central Hotel eventually confronted Mann with a demand for immediate payment of the bill, threatening to turn him out and confiscate his baggage if he refused to settle up. Aleck paid for him, and gave him enough money to see him down the coast as far as Limón.[19]

Word spread of yet another revolt. A *guerrillero* named Reyes cut the telegraph wire and, according to usually unreliable sources, hijacked a lake steamer. "My personal interest in the matter is to know when our mail is to come," Alexander announced. The cruiser HMS *Intrepid* dropped anchor off the Greytown bar on February 16 and flashed the news that Reyes had no designs on all of Nicaragua, but dreamed rather of founding an independent country, encompassing Bluefields and its hinterland, to be called the Republic of Mosquito. "Naturally every man feels a yearning for a Republic of his own—I can feel it myself," Alexander allowed. Still, he thought Reyes ought to try for a better name. "I would call it the Republic of Banana," he wrote Bettie.[20]

Marooned for more than a month without mail during the Reyes rebellion, Alexander grew increasingly anxious about Bettie. "I have a feeling that too much may have happened in such a long time without my knowledge, & there are two bad chances—no news at all or bad news, against one for good news," he wrote her. He had hopes the U.S. gunboat *Marietta* would collect and deliver the mail piling up on the wharf at Bluefields. Meanwhile, he finished the Gettysburg account and moved on to East Tennessee. The survey crawled through the jungle at an aver-

age of a mere five miles a month. A U.S. schooner hove to off the bar
on February 25 and landed six large postal bags. To Aleck's relief, reports from home were favorable. Two days later, word reached Greytown
that Reyes had given up his dream of secession and taken refuge in the
U.S. consulate.[21]

The Century War Books arrived, enabling Alexander to quicken his
writing pace. He finished with East Tennessee in early April and sped
through the winter of 1864 and the Spotsylvania campaign, reaching
the North Anna by June 1. He planned another summer furlough,
but new boundary disagreements seemed likely to delay his leaving.
In early July, one of the Costa Rican commissioners handed him a
long argument, ninety pages of foolscap, in Spanish, French, and
Latin. "I just handed it back to him & told him to translate it & write
it out in English," he told Bettie. By month's end, though, he was
ready to issue his fourth award, the settlement of the lake boundary.
He estimated he would be free to sail for home on the September
30 steamer.[22]

By summer's end, Alexander had advanced the narrative to October
1864 and the battles around Richmond. Equally gratifying, the boundary
teams seemed to have completed the essentials of the survey. The awards
had largely favored the Nicaraguans. They were preparing to celebrate,
even though by now canal odds were long for either country.* The
president, José Zelaya, invited Alexander to Managua for the fete. He
agreed to make the trip before leaving on furlough.[23]

The Nicaraguans gave him a hero's welcome: a twenty-one-gun salute
and four hundred infantry drawn up in an open square, a fifty-piece
band, church bells tolling. They carried him in procession through
streets overlaid with sawdust, American and Nicaraguan flags draped
from the capital's principal buildings. Near his hotel he passed under
an enormous floral arch bearing the inscription "Nicaragua saluda el
General Alexander."[24]

He had an audience with President Zelaya at the palace September
13, and afterward toured a girls' school. He and Zelaya viewed a gaudy
fireworks display from the palace balcony the night of the fourteenth.
On September 15, Nicaraguan Independence Day, there were orations
and bumpers of champagne. Alexander spoke, in English naturally, at
the grand banquet in his honor on the sixteenth. He sat smiling uncom-

*The U.S. Nicaragua Canal Commission recently had converted itself into the Isthmian (Panama)
Canal Commission.

prehendingly as Nicaraguans rose in relays to praise him in Spanish. He set out for Greytown the following morning, arranged his affairs there, and sailed for New York October 14.[25]

Bettie was too ill to meet him. She had deteriorated rapidly and taken to her bed at Lucy's. Far worse than he had been led to expect, she was in constant pain and, Alexander saw at once, close to the end. Friend, companion, wife: Bettie died less than three weeks after his return, on November 20, 1899, aged sixty-three years, in the thirty-ninth year of their marriage. Aleck spent the winter in seclusion on South Island, brooding and sorrowful. Along with regret, he doubtless felt twinges of guilt at having been two thousand miles distant while Bettie passed into the final phase of her illness. Then came a double blow, an incalculable loss, all the more terrible for its unexpectedness. Lucy took to her bed in late April with a severe cold. Pneumonia set in, and within a week she was dead. She was thirty-six years old, the mother of two young children. Thoughtful, reliable, practical Lucy: she had sent him needle and thread in Greytown so he could mend his clothes. He had always imagined Lucy looking after him and Bettie in their dotage. Now she was no more. He fell physically ill with grief.[26]

Lonely and bereft, Alexander went to Bessie in New Orleans, where her husband was teaching history at Tulane. He recuperated there for several weeks before leaving for Nicaragua for the formal settlement of the boundary question. Gradually some of the old *joie de vivre* returned. The Nicaraguans and Costa Ricans met on July 25 in Managua to ratify the treaty. Despite stupefying heat, he noted a large turnout of Prince Albert coats, silk hats, and gloves; following his own dictates of fashion, Aleck wore a black cutaway and carried a palm-leaf fan. He took his seat in the place of honor. The accords were read aloud and signed. A bishop, remote, benign, full of dignity, blessed the proceedings. Later, at cocktail time, someone handed him a large tumbler of neat whiskey. He drank it. At dinner, the Nicaraguans kept up a steady flow of Chateau Yquem, a favorite wine of Aleck's. "I began to feel a sort of feeling in my ankle joints which is my thermometer to tell me when to begin to go slow," he recalled next day, the slipshod sentence suggesting a hangover. He smiled through the speeches, essayed a short one of his own in English, and raised his glass (so he claimed) to every one of the two hundred guests, some more than once.[27]

Alexander returned home for good in mid-August, to South Island first, where he confronted the stack of manuscript books that contained his war recollections. They now struck him as too personal and anecdotal for publication. Over the winter he decided to write another book, incorporating some of the material in the recollections, but primarily a critical and objective analysis of the campaigns. "I want to tell the story *professionally* & to comment *freely* on every professional feature, even though it may seem to reflect on Lee or Jackson or anybody else," he wrote a friend. Here, then, was the genesis of *Military Memoirs of a Confederate.** "I have made a *start*, he went on, "but it is a large job."[28]

It was lonely work. Alexander had as housekeeper/companion during the autumn and winter of 1900–1901 a niece of Bettie's, Mary Mason, a tall, amiable, shortsighted spinster born the same year as his daughter Bessie. Mary, in fact, had been invited to be a bridesmaid at Bessie's wedding in 1886. Longstreet, whose first wife died in 1889, had married a girl of twenty-two eight years later, drawing a burst of Homeric laughter from Alexander. "Longstreet's wedding is very funny," he had said then. "Five years ago I thought he could not live a year." He found no humor at all in his own situation, approaching his marriage to Mary Mason with uncharacteristic solemnity. "All of my children know her & all like her & cordially approve of my marrying her," he informed one of his friends, probably overstating the case. Aleck and Mary were married nevertheless, on October 1, 1901. Alexander was sixty-six, his bride forty. In letters home written on their wedding trip north to Niagara, Montreal, and Quebec, she referred to him as "the General."[29]

Early in the new year, West Point invited Alexander to give an address on the Confederate army at the academy's centennial. It was a signal honor, for Alexander would be the first former Confederate officially recognized there. He spent weeks writing and rehearsing the speech. He kept at the memoirs, too, carrying reference books to the table and reading through meals when Mary was away. He sifted through conflicting accounts, and agonized over the details. "There is no use writing it unless I take time to do it well," he told Mary. In late May, en route to West Point for the June 9 commemoration, he toured Gettysburg with his historian friend Frederic Bancroft, who agreed to advise him on the book.[30]

---

*The recollections, vivid, colorful, fully expressive of Alexander's extraordinary personality, were edited by the historian Gary W. Gallagher and published in 1989 as *Fighting for the Confederacy*.

The speech, titled "The Confederate Veteran," opened with a dozen damp lines of heroic verse not at all in the Alexander manner.* Possibly they were meant to disarm a Southern audience, for he went on to deliver a blunt repudiation of Lost Cause sentimentality. Rather than mourn the result, Alexander said, Southerners should celebrate it. "Whose vision is now so dull," he asked, "that he does not recognize the blessing it is to himself and to his children to live in an undivided country?" The audience several times broke into his speech with bursts of applause; it reached a crescendo, sustained for several minutes, when he mentioned Longstreet, deaf, nearly blind, crippled, who sat only a few feet away from him on the platform.[31]

In 1861 and later, Alexander had justified secession and war by citing the political principle of the sovereignty of the states. He now recognized the hollowness of the idea. The great advances of the nineteenth century—steamships, railroads, the telegraph—made the old, semiautonomous federation of states obsolete. Even as pressures for secession mounted, the process of evolution, inexorably at work under the surface of things, was creating an indivisible nation. War had been necessary to the process, could not have been avoided, and needed no apology. "We didn't go into our cause; we were born into it," Alexander said. "We fought for our homes under men we loved and trusted." But the outcome had been inevitable and right. He finished to prolonged applause. Later, in the receiving line, President Roosevelt enthusiastically pumped his hand. In the immediate aftermath, Alexander had only one critic: Mary Lee. She wrote to reprove him not so much for the content of the speech, but for having delivered it in James Longstreet's presence.[32]

Mary Lee detested Longstreet, judging him guilty of abusing her father's memory. Longstreet had been the Lost Cause's favorite villain during the 1870s and 1880s, but by the turn of the century much of the feeling against him had subsided. Then John Gordon's memoirs, appearing in 1903, rekindled it. Gordon repeated, in extreme form, the old canard that Longstreet's failure to carry out orders had robbed Lee of victory at Gettysburg. Alexander esteemed Longstreet as a soldier and a man. He never wavered in defense of him, in public and in private, for publication and in personal correspondence. "It is true that he obeyed

---

*A sampling: "Once more the light of Jackson's sword / Far flashes through the gloom / There Hampton rides and there once more / The toss of Stuart's plume." Alexander's sister, Mary Cliff, suggested the lines, and he obliged her.

reluctantly at Gettysburg on the 2nd and the 3rd," Alexander wrote Bancroft. "But it must be admitted that his judgement in both matters was sound & he owed it to Lee *to be reluctant*, for failure was inevitable." Longstreet's great mistake came later, in his own memoirs, Aleck thought, particularly the notorious claim that Lee had been off his mental balance at Gettysburg until enough blood had been shed to appease him. "Many an old soldier will *never forgive* Longstreet such a sentiment," he said.[33]

In September 1902 a small blood vessel burst in Alexander's brain, bringing on the first incapacitating illness of his sixty-seven years. Afflicted with dizziness, memory loss, and aphasia, he recovered slowly. That autumn, too, saw the further culling of the once-extensive Alexander clan. The patriarch's youngest, Alice, only fifty-four years old but worn down by the bearing of ten children, died October 29, 1902, following Louisa (1895), Sarah (1897), and Marion (1901). James Hillhouse died December 4, closing out another season of grief for Alexander. As his physical powers gradually returned, he pushed on with the memoirs, reading and writing eighteen hours a day during some stretches. In the spring of 1903, he and Bancroft toured the Petersburg, Fredericksburg, Manassas, and Gettysburg battlefields.[34]

Bancroft became perhaps the closest friend of Alexander's old age. To Bancroft he displayed the full range of his knowledge and interests, practical as well as intellectual. "Didn't you once tell me how to get rid of the bones in fish before or while cooking them? If so, please tell me again. Few persons seem to know," Bancroft wrote him. He even showed him the Perpetual Calendar he had designed and hoped to sell for twenty cents a copy. But they were chiefly preoccupied with the antebellum and war years. Alexander supplied Bancroft with anecdotal material for lectures on slavery and on Confederate soldier life. Bancroft in turn critiqued the memoirs chapter by chapter. "He finds it 'surprisingly lucid concise & comprehensive without being technical,'" Aleck boasted to Bessie. By May 1904 he reported himself ready to open negotiations with a publisher.[35]

As it happened, Alexander did not finish until the spring of 1906. Scribner's published his *Military Memoirs of a Confederate* in April 1907. Aleck claimed, at first, to be appalled by the format. "It had the wide margins & great *big* type & thick paper with uncut edges & every objectionable feature I ever saw in a book down to black binding," he complained to Bessie. Mary Cliff wrote to tease him about the frontispiece, a photograph of a bald, stout, white-mustached, elderly gentleman. "The picture of you isn't very good," she offered, sounding like a true sister. "It looks sad, a look I never connect with you." The book appeared to admiring reviews in the North; in the South the reaction ranged from grudging respect to outright hostility. "I doubt whether our people are yet prepared to have it said that either Lee or Jackson ever made a military mistake," Aleck had remarked a few years before, and events proved his doubt well founded.[36]

Alexander's censures of Jackson's performance during the Seven Days outraged many old Confederates. "The book can do no good whatever, for there is too much criticism in it," the Charleston *News Courier* advised, adding slyly that it was "a pity that [the author's] great capability was not known at the time the war was going on." The New Orleans *Picayune* found Alexander's fault-finding "irritating." He ignored the role of chance in military affairs, the *Picayune* went on, treating battles as though they were mathematical propositions.[37]

Even his friends chaffed him, though gently. "I fear you have given too much to please the Yankee," wrote John Haskell, who went on to challenge Alexander's assertion that all had been for the best. "I have never been able to feel grateful for the good whipping we got in the end," Haskell told him. Another old Confederate noted that the memoirs were perfectly in character with the Alexander he recalled from 1861–65. "I remember being amazed at the freedom of your comments on current events during the war—and how absolutely unbiased you were by your personal feelings," E. W. Haskel wrote.[38]

The absence of bitterness in the *Military Memoirs* impressed historian William E. Dodd, reviewing the book for *The New York Times*. The weekly *Nation* noted, rightly, that Alexander all but ignored social issues and barely touched on the merits of the questions in dispute. Despite this, the *Nation* issued a laudatory verdict: "No preceding book by a Southern soldier surpasses this in good temper, wise discrimination and graphic portrayal." Other reviewers praised Alexander's simple, clear style and, above all, his objectivity. "He is the critic and not the panegyrist," the Louisville *Post* said. "He criticizes alike Confederate friend and Federal foe, the justice for which, in some cases, may be disputed, but the good temper shown must be conceded," E. A. Carman wrote in the *American Historical Review*.[39]

The Confederacy's great military reputations, Alexander announced at the outset, would have to take their chances in a dispassionate analysis—"the criticism of each campaign as one would criticize a game of chess, only to point out the good and bad plays on each side, and the moves which have influenced the result." Joe Johnston and Longstreet shared responsibility for the missed opportunity at Seven Pines, a "phenomenally mismanaged" battle. Jackson's "weak and dilatory performance" cost Lee decisive results at Mechanicsville and Gaines's Mill. Lee erred in invading Pennsylvania, and committed one blunder after another at Gettysburg. "Few battles can furnish examples of worse tactics," Alexander judged. Lee's failure to read Grant's intentions at the outset of the Petersburg campaign denied the Confederacy its last, best chance for a battlefield deadlock and a negotiated peace.[40]

The *Military Memoirs* sold 1,503 copies in the first six months, earning Alexander $901.80 in royalties. He banked the check from Scribner's gratefully. Aleck exaggerated his money difficulties and cried poormouth at the first sign of a downward drift in the stock market. But he also worried, legitimately, about his legacy to the children. Bessie was widowed in August 1907 when her husband fell off a dock at Chautauqua, New York, and drowned; Alexander hoped to leave the widow and her two children financially secure. He sold his Saint Vincent's Island property, eleven thousand undeveloped acres off Apalachicola, Florida, for $50,000 and tried to negotiate the sale of South Island to an 1860 West Pointer named Alex Pennington, whose cavalry brigade had captured Huger's artillery on the retreat to Appomattox.[41]

During 1908 a series of minor strokes undermined Alexander's health. His friends saw, too, that his intellectual powers were in irremediable decline. Mortifyingly, his memory failed him during a speech at a reunion of his old artillery battalion; he now began to avoid such gatherings, in dread that someone might call on him for after-dinner remarks. He confused people, places, and events. "How we pray that the Dear Heavenly Father will deal gently with our declining years," his sister Hattie wrote him from Fairfield, where, no longer able to look after herself, she had gone to live with Charlie Alexander's widow, Rosa.* By October 1908, Aleck could no longer

*Charles Atwood Alexander died January 30, 1907, eight months before the death of the eldest Alexander son, William Felix.

record the daily entry in the South Island Log. Mary took over that duty.[42]

In early December he had another mild attack. It deprived him of the power of coherent speech for several days, and he experienced light-headedness and muddled memory. Mary enlisted Bancroft to help dissuade him from delivering a paper on Grant, promised for the American Historical Association meeting in Richmond at year's end, but he insisted on going. Alexander managed "Grant's Conduct of the Wilderness Campaign" without misadventure. "I got thro my paper with the greatest of ease," he boasted in a letter to Bessie dated January 3, 1909, the day after his return to South Island.[43]

Alexander suffered a more serious stroke on January 10. It left him paralyzed in the right arm and leg. But Mary reported him "remarkably strong and well in every other way." By month's end he felt well enough to sit out on the piazza on fine days. A nurse came down from Johns Hopkins in Baltimore early in February and helped him regain partial use of the crippled parts. An island acquaintance, eighty-five-year-old Ned Green, dropped by for a visit on the mild, springlike afternoon of February 5 and offered his own services as nurse and companion.[44]

With Alexander's approval, Mary decided to accelerate the sale of the South Carolina estates. The Marion, South Carolina, syndicate that had taken a $125,000 option on North and South islands late in 1908 closed the deal February 20, bringing the Alexanders' Sea Island life to a sudden close. By the twenty-third they were en route to Savannah, where they put up temporarily with Leo Alexander, now practicing law there, and his wife. In May, Alexander suffered another stroke, a more severe one this time. Mary took him up to Johns Hopkins for treatment. The doctors could do little for him. Mary tied up such loose ends of his personal and military correspondence as she could, and moved him out to the Blue Ridge for the summer. A friend who came to call described Aleck as "bright & happy" there, like a child.[45]

The Alexanders settled into an apartment on Liberty Street in Savannah in November. Mary attended him through an uneventful winter. Alexander passed the months that remained to him in deep silence. Having said all he needed to say, he endured his voiceless, memoryless condition without complaint. A violent attack of nausea sent him to the sickroom for the last time the night of April 21, 1910. Lapsing into a coma on the twenty-seventh, he died without a struggle at a few minutes past eight-thirty the following evening.[46]

Chamberlain
Requiescat, 1885–1914

Chamberlain's Florida schemes showed early promise. By the autumn of 1885 the orange and banana groves were bearing marketable fruit, and he was pursuing plans for a large tourist hotel in Ocala, negotiating with "one of the most successful of Florida hotel men" to manage it. Another of the recurrent Gulf Coast land booms inclined him to sell off some of the seven thousand acres the syndicate owned around Homosassa, to raise capital for development projects. The work kept him much out of doors. When he felt "queer in the head," as he did sometimes, a quinine pill usually put him right. Homosassa days were hot in late October, the nights comfortably warm and alive with the thrumming of cicadas. "Our enterprises here really are worthy of my best powers," he wrote Fannie. "I feel we are making history, & good history."[1]

Still, outlays were great, returns small. Chamberlain had no real experience of managing large capital ventures. He divided his time between Maine, New York City, and Florida, and so was an absentee developer for much of the year. Wyllys and, for a season, Tom were deputized to look after his interests. Neither proved satisfactory. "The banjo occupies most of my leisure time here," Wyllys wrote home, and he evidently allowed himself plenty of leisure. Then, too, Chamberlain's timing was poor; the golden days of Florida land speculation were yet to come. For whatever reason, the Florida West Coast Improvement Company failed to realize his hopes.[2]

Despite his brave front, doubts about his purpose assailed him. Sae caught echoes of this in one of his letters home. What, she wondered after looking over a copy of the syndicate's circular, was he about in Florida? "It seems to me you might do better with yourself," she wrote bluntly. "There are men not worth so much to the world who can do such things." The gradual decline of the Florida enterprise left him disappointed, though certain still that some good remained for him to accomplish. "Perhaps I have not made all that was possible from my life: but I trust that God has still use for me and has spared me through so many perils and so many years for a blessing somewhere yet to be given or received," he wrote his mother. A job offer from an unspecified northern railroad cheered him ("People here say I can make myself famous in another sphere," he told Grace), but nothing came of it.[3]

He and Fannie formed the habit of spending part of each winter in New York City. By the autumn of 1887 the couple had taken rooms on Fifty-seventh Street near Central Park; they later leased the apartment at 101 West Seventy-fifth Street that became their New York home for a decade. When his health permitted, they joined the wintertime social round. The Chamberlains seemed not to lack for invitations, including one (he could not help mentioning) from "the lady cousins of Lady Randolph Churchill." Chamberlain also had an office downtown, a Wall Street address he found useful for business purposes.[4]

The Brunswick house remained in commission for summer occupancy, and the Chamberlains also stopped for long stretches at Domhegan, the boardinghouse they owned at Simpson's Point on Middle Bay, four miles out of town. Chamberlain renovated the falling-down buildings of the old Israel Simpson shipyard and opened a resort there under the management of one of the shipbuilder's descendants. He and Wyllys put in long days out of doors, haying, fixing up the bathhouse, and cleaning up the beach, occupations that recalled his farm boyhood in Brewer. From Domhegan's refurbished wharf they used to set sail in his ten-ton yacht *Pinafore*, sometimes cruising as far as Portland, twenty miles distant.[5]

Age and infirmity claimed Sarah Chamberlain in 1888. Her firstborn had never ceased to be grateful for her intercessions. "Your prayers for me are always in my heart," Chamberlain wrote her a few months before her death, which occurred on November 5 at home in Brewer. "God has answered them for my good, and will do so still." No prayers, however earnest, could halt the long downward slide of Sally Chamberlain's youngest child. Tom drifted from job to job. He drank too much. He quarreled with friends and business associates. He abandoned his wife on at least one occasion; in the winter of 1886, Delia had been forced to ask her mother-in-law for money to pay her board. Sae stood by Tom to the last, just as their mother would have done. At the end, all the fight had gone out of him. "He told Delia he should not live a month & didn't want to," Sae reported. Tom Chamberlain died of lung and heart ailments, compounded by alcoholism, on August 12, 1896. He was fifty-five years old.[6]

Financial security continued to elude Chamberlain. His name and war record made him an attractive candidate for company directorships, though often such positions were more or less honorary. For a time he headed a New Jersey company that manufactured motors for streetcars. Nothing really took wing. "I am coming to realize better than ever what you have seen so long," Wyllys wrote his mother, "that our man can't be best at *everything*." Wyllys suspected that Chamberlain's associates traded on his name to float a venture, then cut him out as soon as affairs began to prosper. He seemed unable to see it coming. "However," Wyllys went on, "Father stands it very well on the whole, and his reputation is still bright in every way." Wyllys, an inveterate tinkerer with mechanical gadgets, buoyed Fannie with hints that he expected to sell a patent soon for one of his inventions, a development, he suggested, that would assure all their futures.[7]

Without doubt, Chamberlain's persistent health problems diminished his capacity for sustained work. Overexertion, physical or emotional, might bring on an attack, usually without warning. In early December 1886 he saw Fannie off on an extended visit to Grace in Boston, watching forlornly from the bridge above the gallery at Grand Central Station as the train pulled away, clouds of steam rising whitely in the cold air. Depressed and lethargic, he retired to his room to recover his spirits. When he returned to the office, he collapsed at his desk. His body shook with a violent ague, and pain shot through him from hip to hip. He reeled out into the street and found his way to the elevated station. The noisome atmosphere of the car nearly asphyxiated him. He staggered out at the first station stop and discharged his breakfast onto the platform. Home finally, he fell into bed in a state of semiconsciousness, his hands and feet cold as death. New fits of vomiting seized him. Doctors were summoned. They revived him with a footbath of hot water and mustard and diagnosed a severe malarial attack brought on by overstrained nerves. For a few hours he thought death had come for him.[8]

Chamberlain had rightly discounted Dr. Warren's optimistic forecast after the 1883 surgery. In August 1892 a flare-up of what he had begun to call his "war tokens" left him weak and ill for months. His lower abdomen, bladder, and testicles were chronically swollen and sore; the slightest exertion or irritation prostrated him for days. An acute attack in late December disabled him completely for several weeks, a setback that prompted an application in February 1893 for a twenty-dollar-a-month increase in his government pension, to fifty dollars monthly. Despite indisputable medical evidence, the pension bureau turned him down.[9]

He rallied, though this time the respite proved brief. Sharp attacks laid him low in the spring and again at year's end. He had always disliked using painkilling opiates, and he kept off them entirely during this latest bout. "I am getting up, and shall recover rapidly—having no poison in my blood from miserable drugs," he wrote Fannie. Decades of suffering had formed a carapace of stoicism on him, and he could will himself to prodigies of endurance. "When misery passes a certain point it becomes ludicrous," he once wrote Sae. Still, each recurrence left him weaker than before, less able to withstand the next attack.[10]

Chamberlain seems to have been chronically hard up during the later 1890s. When he lobbied the incoming McKinley administration for the post of minister to Turkey in the spring of 1897, he coveted the salary more than the status, such as it was. But with two other Maine men of higher party standing in the running for foreign missions, Chamberlain stood no chance of the appointment. A year later, during the crisis with Spain, he wrote one of Maine's Republican senators to request a field command.* When nothing came of this, he volunteered his services to the state of Maine. After the fighting ended in August, he sought appointment to the peace commission. Again he received a polite rebuff.[11]

His Maine friends refused to accept defeat. When the customs collectorship of Portland became vacant in 1899, Chamberlain and company campaigned hard for this plum, the state's most lucrative patronage office. "He is poor and afflicted and his wife is totally blind," William Whitehouse, a former Maine supreme court justice, wrote in a letter recommending him for the opening. "He keeps up the best appearance he can, and is sensitive and proud, and is the last man to plead, or even admit poverty," Chamberlain's old 20th Maine comrade Ellis Spear wrote Amos Allen, the congressman representing the Portland area. The appointment, Spear went on, would "save his last days from the distress of penury."[12]

Chamberlain leaked word that he "expected a pretty good office" in the Customs Service, even though at least one of his friends had warned him already that the collectorship probably was beyond his reach. The office did go to another man. But in March 1900 a consolation prize,

*Billy Oates, Chamberlain's Little Round Top adversary, commanded a brigade of Alabama volunteers encamped near Harrisburg, Pennsylvania, in the summer of 1898.

the port surveyorship, came Chamberlain's way. This post carried less responsibility and prestige, though the salary, $4,500 a year, was generous for the amount of work required. "A fat berth," the *Portland Press* called it.[13]

Disappointed, Chamberlain likened the surveyorship to "a free bed in the hospital." Still, he was in no position to turn a sinecure down. In fact, the duties were of so purely nominal a character that the Customs Service granted him an extended leave of absence before he had been in office six months. Saying farewell to the now sightless Fannie with a promise "to see things for you," he sailed from New York the first week in November, toured Italy in the late autumn, and spent most of the winter of 1900–1901 in Egypt, making Cairo his base for excursions to the pyramids and a steamer trip up the Nile. He returned to New York in late February relaxed and fit.[14]

The turn of the new century saw a resurgence of interest in Chamberlain's war, fueled in part by the short, decisive, and comparatively painless conflict with Spain two years earlier. He could tap a new market, those born since 1865, for his lectures, articles, and, eventually, the memoir/history he had long intended to write. Chamberlain dusted off his "Surrender of Lee" talk, a hit on the lecture circuit in the 1870s that he had not delivered for twenty years. His "Gettysburg" and "The Dark Side of Civilization" lectures were popular successes too. Rising demand led him to propose a joint lecture tour with John Gordon. Perhaps he had it in mind for the two aging heroes to recreate, on stage, their mutual courtesies at Appomattox. Chamberlain accepted as many invitations to talk of his war experiences or to deliver Memorial Day addresses and other occasional speeches as his health and schedule would permit.[15]

White-haired, his drooping mustache white, too, carrying a cane but somehow giving the impression he had no practical use for it, Chamberlain retained his distinction of appearance and manner far into old age, especially when draped in the dark elegance of a Prince Albert coat, his invariable lecturer's uniform. His rich, strong speaking voice helped create a mood consonant with the elegiac content and grandiloquent form of many of his addresses. The superannuated bluecoats who formed part of every audience rarely failed to respond emotionally to Chamberlain's sonorities, often with tears. This passage from a 1901 Memorial Day address, pitched overtly to the veterans in the crowd, conveys some of the feeling of his oratory:

On each returning Memorial Day your thinning ranks, your feeble step, your greyer faces are tokens that would make me wholly sad, were it not for something undying in your eyes. And you, strong as your hearts are, do not wholly master the feeling that all is declining that made your worth, and the only struggle you can make now is against fast-coming oblivion. You hold together by the power of things you will not forget; though a shadow comes out of the cloud chilling you with the notion that these things and you are doomed to be forgotten.

The overall effect could be potent. An 1881 Bowdoin graduate whose mother had taken him, at age eight, to hear Chamberlain's Gettysburg lecture in New Castle, Maine, remembered leaving the hall spellbound, though utterly unable to recall a single concrete detail about the battle. "I have never forgotten the profound impression his presence and bearing made upon me," he said.[16]

Chamberlain visited the old battlefields again and again, normally by design, and once because he happened to awaken as his Florida-bound train sped past the haunted purlieus of Fredericksburg. "We skirted that field so full of memories of awful scenes & I looked on that slope where in the darkness I buried my dead," he wrote Grace that morning during a stop in Richmond. "Soon we shall come to *Petersburg*—that will be the culmination for me." In July 1888 he joined twenty-five thousand "pilgrims" in observing the twenty-fifth anniversary of Gettysburg. To his surprise and intense gratification, the Society of the Army of the Potomac elected him president that year. "I shall have to do something to prove myself worthy of it," he mused, "but a fellow couldn't get such recognition unless there was something about him to draw men's minds, or hearts." He noted proudly that he had not sought the office; the society chose him over several higher-ranking ex-officers.[17]

Chamberlain returned to Rives' Salient for a second tour in 1903, inspecting the ground with care. There were little hummocks scattered about, he noticed this time, some in the cleared ground of the swale, others on the lower slopes, planted now with peanuts, sweet potatoes, and corn, the soil enriched by blood and old bones. These rounded humps puzzled him at first, until he realized they marked the places where some of the dead of June 18, 1864, had been hastily buried. He could not help marking the contrast with the Pennsylvania battlefield, thickly sown even then with grandiose memorials and monuments. "Some deep places in us are more moved by a forlorn field like this," he said of Petersburg, "than by a glorified one like Gettysburg."[18]

Still, Chamberlain never let pass an opportunity to take part in Gettysburg rites. In the late 1860s he had helped survey the battlefield. Fifteen years later he and Ellis Spear campaigned for a monument in the woods where the 20th Maine had fought. In October 1889 he gave the main address at the dedication of monuments for all the Maine regiments that had been in action at Gettysburg. He accepted, in August 1893, the Congressional Medal of Honor for heroism on Little Round Top. He advised on the preparation of *Maine at Gettysburg* (1896), the written record of the state's involvement in the great battle. He attended the unveiling of the John Reynolds statue in July 1899.[19]

While he refought his war, Fannie battled tenaciously to save her failing eyesight. Chamberlain seems to have thought her an easy target for quackery, but she could hardly be blamed for resisting what, by the late 1890s, looked inevitable to him. "Fanny is blind," he wrote Sae in April 1899, "but *will* stay in charge of this magnetic doctor who does not tell her he cannot help her—if it needs telling." She found a housekeeper and companion in Lillian Edmunds, a distant kinswoman, and Wyllys could always be relied upon for a steady arm when her husband was away.[20]

With the visible world gone dark, Fannie fell into periodic fits of depression. Chamberlain could feel his own strength, physical and mental, ebbing too. After a breakdown in the early summer of 1902, he felt bound to admit "a serious diminution" of his recuperative powers. That, however, did not prevent his contemplating a long cruise in *Pinafore* later in the summer. Fannie had no such consolations. Her husband was sympathetic. "You are so shut up & shut in that the relief of surrounding circumstances cannot come in to lighten a vexation, as it can with us who see the whole compass of things around us," he wrote her in February 1903.[21]

Fannie showed flashes still of the old extravagance. With Miss Edmunds as escort, she ventured down to Portland in August 1903 for a shopping spree the equal of anything in her more vigorous days. She picked out a fine black dress and several silk shirtwaists in black and white. Chamberlain chose a black and white print dress for her. She stopped on the way out to take into her hands an expensive black silk skirt, "elaborately barred and flounced," according to Chamberlain, and felt its rich contours. "Of course," he wrote Grace, "she insisted that she wanted that, too." He reminded Fannie gently that opportunities for wearing such a rich garment were rare now. She agreed, though with reluctance, and left it in the shop.[22]

A fall, a fractured hip: Fannie never fully recovered from the mishap that lamed her during the summer of 1905. Chamberlain glimpsed the end of their forty-eight years together. "I cannot help sending you a most loving greeting, with thanks that we have been so long spared to each other," he wrote her on her eightieth birthday, August 12, 1905. "You have had a useful and honorable & I trust on the whole a happy life. Your husband & children 'rise up & call you blessed.' " Fannie died October 18, 1905, in Brunswick. After the funeral in the First Parish Church, Chamberlain buried her under the tall pines in the cemetery out on the Bath Road.[23]

He returned, alone, to the tapestries, oriental rugs, and Queen Anne furniture of the Brunswick house, and to the war relics, fading with age, dusty in the thin autumn light, that crowded the walls and shelves of the library. Here were a tapestry picture of his war charger, a Confederate battle flag captured at Appomattox, a First Division bugle, Charles Griffin's cap and sword, a flag of the 20th Maine, the base of a shell that had burst near him at Gettysburg. With Fannie's passing, he spent less time in these long-familiar surroundings. These rooms, the star-ceiling chamber, too, began to take on the character of a museum. For several years he lived in a suite at the New Falmouth Hotel in Portland. His favorite picture kept him company there: Sir Galahad, his face suffused with the reflected light of the Holy Grail. Around 1910 he bought a house in Portland, a two-story white clapboard structure, suburban in aspect, at 499 Ocean Avenue.[24]

Miss Edmunds stayed on as housekeeper. She played the piano for him many evenings, and sometimes he sang, favoring the soft, undemanding Hawaiian melodies popular then. Chamberlain lectured when he could, and remained active in veterans' organizations. His military correspondence increased as he prepared to begin his memoir. Friends kept him up to date on the latest controversies. One correspondent sent him a copy of the letter in which J. S. Mosby claimed that Lee, catching sight of Pickett a few days after the shad-bake debacle at Five Forks, turned to an aide and snapped, "Is that man still with this army?" Sally Corbell Pickett, the ringleted general's widow, sent Chamberlain a copy of her apology *Pickett and His Men.*[25]

By 1908 he had begun the account of the Appomattox campaign that his children would publish after his death as *The Passing of the Armies*. It had its origin in the Fifth Corps history he had set out to write in the summer of 1865, "to serve for fireside memories in after years," he put it, and not incidentally to correct the record, as he saw it, as regards Gouverneur Warren. Chamberlain had dropped the corps history twenty years before, despite pressure from colleagues to push on with the job. (William H. Powell published his workmanlike *History of the Fifth Army Corps* in 1896.) The Appomattox project turned out to be far more difficult and painful than he had anticipated. Chamberlain forced himself to re-create, in his imagination, those "horrible scenes, shocking to the senses," of March and April 1865, "burrowing in memory to live again in dreams and haunting visions." Ill health slowed him, too, enfeebling recurrences of the Petersburg trouble in December 1908 and October 1911.[26]

He worked from 1909 on with the assistance of a secretary, Catherine Smith of Brunswick. It was a successful partnership, though the old man could be severe at times. The instructors at secretarial school had taught Mrs. Smith to center a letter on the sheet; Chamberlain scolded her for being wasteful if she set off his correspondence with too much white space. Then, too, her spelling may not have been quite up to his standard, for he gave her a dictionary one year at Christmas. "Remember and Go Forward," Chamberlain wrote on the flyleaf.[27]

"He'd dictate awhile, then fall asleep; then away he'd go again," Mrs. Smith recalled. In fact, the finished book has something of the quality of an oration. *The Passing of the Armies* might perhaps "read" more easily spoken aloud. Its form is Gothic, its content impressionistic, its diction sentimental. There are echoes of Hawthorne's curse of the Pyncheons, and of old professors Smyth and Upham and their anxious visions of a country drowning in blood. "Whoever had misled these men," Chamberlain wrote of the surrendered rebels at Appomattox, "we had not. Whoever had made that quarrel, we had not. It was a remnant of the inherited curse for sin. We had purged it away, with blood-offerings."[28]

At times an air of unreality hangs over Chamberlain's story. Though he describes several sharp fights, there is not much actual blood about, nor much naturalistic description of battle. Death scenes are Victorian set pieces. Expiring officers utter carefully crafted last words. The book lacks the precision and clarity—and thus the expressive power—of the best Civil War memoirs, such as John De Forest's *A Volunteer's Adventures*. There are few traces of humor. High and low, the men around Chamberlain are shadowy figures, except for Sheridan, who bursts with awful vividness out of the memoir's opaque background. Chamberlain is brave beyond all telling, capable of carrying off grand gestures with style and conviction, but solitary, distanced from his fellows and in the thing alone: like Sir Galahad, one supposes, or perhaps the Tankerville knights from whom he claimed descent.

Fifteen years after Appomattox, William T. Sherman gave his a famously uncomplicated definition of war: "Boys, it is all hell," he told a GAR gathering in Columbus, Ohio. "You can bear this warning voice to generations yet to come." Chamberlain, in his book, explicitly challenged Sherman's dictum, in terms that convey the full flavor of his thought and manner:

> Fighting and destruction are terrible; but are sometimes agencies of heavenly rather than hellish powers. In privations and sufferings endured as well as in the strenuous action of battle, some of the highest qualities of manhood are called forth— courage, self-command, sacrifice of self for the sake of something held higher—wherein we take it chivalry finds its value; and on another side fortitude, patience, warmth of comradeship, and in the darkest hours tenderness caring for the wounded and stricken—exhaustless and unceasing as that of the gentlest womanhood. [Sherman] was doubtless speaking of war in its immediate and proximate effects as destruction. He did not mean to imply that its participants are demons.

For Chamberlain, war had been an individual joust, a test of character. "It makes bad men worse," he thought, "and good men better"; knights more noble, knaves more rascally. Chamberlain wrote from intimate acquaintance with Gettysburg, Cold Harbor, Petersburg. But what had he learned from the experience? His memoir would be published in 1915, the year of the gas cloud at Ypres. Hundreds of thousands of men had already been killed and wounded, and the first of the twentieth century's great wars had three years still to run.[29]

He worked fitfully on the memoir. Finding fault with early drafts of some material, he instructed Mrs. Smith to burn a quantity of typed notes and manuscript in the wood furnace at 499 Ocean Avenue. She afterward scattered the ashes in the poppy patch behind the house. Chamberlain could not get along without the salary, so he continued to put in his time at the Customs House. (What did he survey? He left no account of his work there.) He sometimes used the cane these days, but his bearing remained so soldierly, so erect, that even in the ninth decade of his life acquaintances thought him taller than his actual five feet, ten inches.[30]

The Pennsylvania chapter of the Military Order of the Loyal Legion invited Chamberlain to Philadelphia to deliver the principal oration at the centenary observance of Lincoln's birth, February 12, 1909. He planned a return to Gettysburg for July 2 that year. Two months later, he turned out for a reunion of surviving 20th Maine veterans. He went back to Gettysburg again in 1911, and agreed to serve on the committee planning the fiftieth-anniversary commemoration of the battle. In December 1912, *Cosmopolitan* magazine published Chamberlain's "My Story of Fredericksburg." His article "Through Blood and Fire at Gettysburg" appeared in *Hearst's Magazine* the following June. He boasted to Grace of the four-hundred-dollar check the Hearst organization sent him for the Gettysburg piece.[31]

An automobile accident in 1910 left Grace something of an invalid herself, though she lived on until 1937. Wyllys, too, was a continuing source of concern. He had tried law, setting up an office in Ocala, but failed to establish himself. He had read up on electricity, hoping to make a name in that new "science of sciences." Wyllys still puttered about in his workshop, more or less dependent on his father. For a time he had expectations for a clamp hitch he had designed. It could be easily installed with a wrench and screwdriver, his sales letter claimed; no need for a trip to the smithy. Wyllys sold the hitches for $2.50 each—two dollars when purchased in one-dozen lots. "We have plenty of stock on hand," he admitted. Chamberlain generously attributed his son's lack of material success to an inability to market his genius. "Your attention has been absorbed in the inventions in which your brain is so fertile, so that you have not got into the other stratum, or sphere, of making money on it," he wrote him. "That is a 'worldly way' of looking at things, but it has to be regarded." Wyllys never scored a success with any of his inventions. He died in 1928, hoping for a breakthrough gadget right up to the end.[32]

Though not fully recovered from a severe relapse earlier in the year, Chamberlain undertook a final journey to Gettysburg in May 1913 for a meeting of the anniversary committee. Abner Shaw, the 20th Maine surgeon who had helped save his life at Petersburg, accompanied him as escort, friend, and medical adviser. Chamberlain felt strong enough to show a delegation of federal judges over the battlefield. One evening, an hour or so before sunset, he trudged, alone, up the overgrown slope of Little Round Top and sat down among the crags. Nearly fifty years ago, at about the same time, he had ordered the bayonet charge that ended the fighting hereabouts. Now, in his Gothic imagination, the ghosts of the Little Round Top dead rose up around him: Estes and Steele, Noyes and Segeant Buck, Arad P. Linscott. Tom had been here with him. He had sent black-clad John over there, down the reverse slope, to see to the wounded. They were long gone—poor Horace, too, friend of his youth. Only he and Sae were still on their feet. His line would die out, he knew, with the pallid Wyllys. He lingered until the sun dropped below the horizon and the shadows advanced up the hillside, an old man lost in a sepia world of memory.[33]

He survived the trip without damage. Even so, he let Shaw persuade him to forgo a return for the great reunion in July. That was just as well. The intense heat, the excitement, and, in some cases, a surfeit of whiskey played the devil with the frail constitutions of thousands of elderly veterans. There were at least eight deaths and forty-two hundred other casualties, mostly from exhaustion. Chamberlain passed the summer and early autumn in comfort. Then, toward the end of November, he fell seriously ill. Grace came up to Portland to be with him. By year's end the final crisis seemed to be at hand. In early January, to Shaw's surprise, he rallied. "I am passing through deep waters! The Dr. thinks I am going to land once more on this shore," he told Sae in a letter he dictated to Lillian Edmunds. But the agony, he went on, letting his stoic's mask slip, had been unspeakable. The experience had shaken him profoundly. "I am trying to get a little closer to God and to know him better," he wrote Sae. The optimistic Shaw thought some of the nurses could be discharged, though he asked the consulting specialist to stay on a little longer.[34]

But Chamberlain knew. It was, in fact, the end. A violent onset laid him flat abed just when Abner Shaw figured he had beaten the odds yet one more time. Chamberlain died of complications of the Petersburg wound in the forenoon of a bitterly cold February 24, 1914, four months short of fifty years after a musket ball launched from a Confederate rifle pit at Rives' Salient found him as he turned, and whistled through him from hip to hip. The fighting had claimed him at last.[35]

Envoi

Georgia and Maine

April 1910 and February 1914

Mary Alexander set down a final entry in the South Island Log:

> *The strife is o'er, the battle done.*
> *Alleluia!*

She had been with him at the last, Bessie, Leo, Willie, too, though he had recognized no one. The Episcopal funeral services were quiet and spare. Afterward, a small party of Confederate veterans escorted Alexander's casket to the Augusta City Cemetery. Two old soldiers held a Confederate battle flag while the bugler played Taps. He was buried next to Bettie and their daughter Lucy.[1]

If Chamberlain had asked for a simple leave-taking, Grace and Wyllys disregarded his wishes. Four companies of Maine militia, a squad of police, GAR and Loyal Legion detachments, and a band followed the flag-draped hearse from Chamberlain's house down snowy Portland streets to City Hall. Some two thousand people turned out for the memorial service. The Portland municipal organist played funerary pieces by Beethoven and Grieg. The Reverend Jesse M. Hill delivered a eulogy. The inevitable Taps sounded from the gallery. Then the crowd filed out behind the casket to the organ peals of Chopin's Funeral March.[2]

A special train carried the corpse to Brunswick, where a thousand people formed a corridor for the short procession from the Maine Central depot to the First Parish Church. Inside, Miss Sue Winchell sang "Abide with Me" to cello accompaniment. William DeWitt Hyde, the president of Bowdoin, gave the funeral address. After Miss Winchell returned to sing "Nearer My God to Thee," the procession re-formed in the brittle sunlight outside and moved on to Pine Grove Cemetery, beyond the Bowdoin campus. Chamberlain's grave lies alongside his wife's there. The headstone is a three-foot-square block of polished granite. At the last, he extemporized no rhetorical flights of soft-lit Gothic fancy: only his name and the years 1828 and 1914 chiseled into the cold, smooth stone.[3]

Alexander, who at Spotsylvania in 1864 had watched unflinchingly as a wounded Yankee tried to club himself to death, looked ahead to our dismal century. He would not have been out of place in it. Chamberlain cast his glance backward. Only fourteen years after the appearance of *The Passing of the Armies*, the British poet Robert Graves published his memoir of First World War experience, *Good-bye to All That*. There was nothing knightly about Graves's war, nor any "honor answering honor" in the manner of its ending. "Armistice-night hysteria did not touch our camp much," Graves wrote of November 11, 1918. "The news sent me out walking alone along the dyke above the marshes of Rhuddlan (an ancient battlefield, the Flodden of Wales), cursing and sobbing and thinking of the dead."[4]

Claremont, Calif., Norton, Mass., and North Stonington, Conn., 1991–93

NOTES

CHAPTER 1. BEGINNINGS

Chamberlain: The Forest's Edge, 1828–48

1. George T. Little, ed. *Genealogical and Family History of the State of Maine*, vol. 1 (New York, 1909), 132–33.
2. Quotation is from Mildred N. Thayer and Mrs. Edward N. Ames, *Brewer, Orrington, Holden, Eddington: History and Families* (Brewer, Maine, 1962), 168, 53.
   Little, *Genealogical History*, vol. 1, 132–33.
3. Marion J. Smith, *A History of Maine* (Portland, 1949), 309–13.
4. Little, *Genealogical History*, vol. 1, 132–33.
   George S. Wasson, *Sailing Days on the Penobscot* (Salem, Mass., 1932), appendix.
5. Little, *Genealogical History*, vol. 1, 132–33.
6. Thayer and Ames, *Brewer*, 35.
   Little, *Genealogical History*, vol. 1, 132–33.
7. Sarah B. (Sae) Chamberlain to Joshua Lawrence Chamberlain, May 8, 1859, Chamberlain-Adams Family Papers, Schlesinger Library, Radcliffe College, Cambridge, Mass. (hereafter, RC).
   Chamberlain Family Bible, Brewer Public Library, Brewer, Maine.
8. Alice R. Trulock, *In the Hands of Providence: Joshua Lawrence Chamberlain and the American Civil War* (Chapel Hill, N.C., 1992), 30, 404n.
9. Early Church Records, Brewer Congregational Church (1942 typescript copy), Brewer Public Library, Brewer, Maine.
10. Material on Bangor and the lumber trade is drawn from Henry David Thoreau, *The Maine Woods* (New York, 1985 ed.) and Stewart A. Holbrook, "Holy Old Mackinaw," in Ronald F. Banks, ed., *A History of Maine* (Dubuque, Iowa, 1959).

11. Memorandum of Agreement between Joshua Chamberlain, Jr., and A. C. Smith, November 22, 1853, Joshua Lawrence Chamberlain Papers, Hawthorne-Longfellow Library, Bowdoin College, Brunswick, Maine (hereafter, BC).

12. Quotations are from R. G. Wood, *A History of Lumbering in Maine, 1820–61* (Orono, Maine, 1935).

13. Wasson, *Sailing Days*, 25, 30–32.
William H. Rowe, *The Maritime History of Maine* (New York, 1948), 253.

14. Chamberlain Association of America, *Joshua Lawrence Chamberlain: A Sketch* (n.p., 1906), 3.
Brewer *Register*, July 29, 1986, clipping in BC.

15. *Chamberlain: A Sketch*, 5–6.

16. *Chamberlain: A Sketch*, 5–6.
Thayer and Ames, *Brewer*, 251–52.

17. *Chamberlain: A Sketch*, 4.
Typescript of unpublished fragment of memoirs, with notes in Chamberlain's hand (hereafter, Memoirs), BC, 64.

18. Memoirs, 45–46.

19. Memoirs, 45–46.

20. Quotations are from Memoirs, 45–46.

21. *Chamberlain: A Sketch*, 4.

22. Kenneth Roberts, *Trending into Maine* (Boston, 1938), 44.
Thayer and Ames, *Brewer*, 18.
Chamberlain: A Sketch, 4.

23. Material on the Aroostook dispute is drawn from Henry Burrage, "The Aroostook War," in Banks, ed., *A History of Maine*.

24. Quotation is from Edward M. Coffman, *The Old Army* (New York, 1982), 82.

25. Joshua Chamberlain, Jr.'s discharge paper, BC.
Chamberlain: A Sketch, 4–6.
Robert M. Cross, "Joshua Lawrence Chamberlain," unpublished senior thesis, BC, 4.

26. *Chamberlain: A Sketch*, 4–6.
Cross, "Chamberlain," 4.
Joshua Chamberlain, Jr., ledgers, BC.

27. Cross, "Chamberlain," 4.
Early Church Records, Brewer Congregational Church.
Memoirs, 50.

28. Memoirs, 49.

29. Memoirs, 49.
    JLC to Sarah Shepard, February 8, 1847, Chamberlain Family Papers, University of Maine, Orono.
30. Memoirs, 49–50.
31. Memoirs, 49–50.
32. Memoirs, 50.
33. Memoirs, 52–53.

Alexander: The Home Place, 1835–53

1. Sarah Alexander to Adam L. Alexander, August 16, 1835, and November 28, 1835, Alexander-Hillhouse Papers, Southern Historical Collection, University of North Carolina at Chapel Hill (hereafter, AHP).
2. Sarah Alexander to Adam L. Alexander, January 15, 1838, and August 3, 1836, AHP.
    Sarah Alexander to Louisa Alexander, February 3, 1840, AHP.
3. Edward Porter Alexander, *Fighting for the Confederacy: The Personal Recollections of General Edward Porter Alexander*, Gary W. Gallagher, ed. (Chapel Hill, N.C., 1989), 5.
    EPA to Frederic Bancroft, n.d., 1902, Edward Porter Alexander Papers, Southern Historical Collection, University of North Carolina at Chapel Hill (hereafter, AP).
4. Material on the Hillhouse and Alexander family backgrounds is drawn from Eliza A. Bowen, *The Story of Wilkes County, Georgia* (Marietta, Ga., 1950), and Robert M. Willingham, Jr., *We Have This Heritage: The History of Wilkes County, Georgia* (Washington, Ga., 1969).
5. Adam L. Alexander to Sarah Alexander, August 9, 1839, AHP.
6. Sarah Alexander to Louisa Porter, October 8, 1844, AHP.
7. Sarah Alexander to Louisa Alexander, July 11, 1849, AHP.
    Sarah Alexander to Adam L. Alexander, July 25, 1828, AHP.
8. Sarah Alexander to Harriet Alexander, February 19, 1846, AHP.
9. Sarah Alexander to Adam L. Alexander, June 23, 1833, and March 18, 1840, AHP.
10. Adam L. Alexander to Sarah Alexander, December 12, 1827, and August 6, 1839, AHP.
11. EPA to Frederic Bancroft, n.d., 1902, AP.
    Adam L. Alexander to Sarah Alexander, July 5, 1836, AHP.
12. EPA, *Fighting*, 5.

13. Sarah Alexander to Adam L. Alexander, November 5 and 13, 1838, and December 18, 1827, AHP.
   Sarah Alexander to Louisa Alexander, February 1840, AHP.
14. For a portrait of Cynthia Peters, see Marion A. Boggs, ed., *The Alexander Letters* (reprint, Athens, Ga., 1980).
15. Sarah Alexander to Adam L. Alexander, August 27, 1841, AHP.
   Adam L. Alexander to Sarah Alexander, November 24, 1854, AHP.
16. Boggs, *Alexander Letters*, 107.
17. EPA, *Fighting*, 6–7.
   Sarah Alexander to Louisa Alexander, January 1, 1850, AHP.
18. EPA, (hereafter, EPA) to William Felix Alexander, December 31, 1850, AHP.
19. Sarah Alexander to Adam L. Alexander, August 27, 1841, AHP.
20. Sarah Alexander to Louisa Alexander, March 14, 1849, AHP.
   Sarah Alexander to Louisa Alexander, January 1, 1850, AHP.
   Numan V. Bartley, *The Creation of Modern Georgia* (Athens, Ga., 1983).
   Ralph B. Flanders, *Plantation Slavery in Georgia* (Chapel Hill, N.C., 1933), 23.
   EPA to Frederic Bancroft, n.d., 1902, AP.
21. Sarah Alexander to Louisa Alexander, January 1, 1850, AHP.
   Eugene D. Genovese, *The Political Economy of Slavery* (New York, 1965), 143.
22. Boggs, ed., *Alexander Letters*, 129.
23. Sarah Alexander to Adam L. Alexander, January 26, 1848, AHP.
24. Sarah Alexander to Louisa Alexander, February 3, 1840, AHP.
   EPA, *Fighting*, 5–6.
25. Adam L. Alexander to Sarah Alexander, July 5, 1836, AHP.
26. Sarah Alexander to Louisa Alexander, March 28, 1842, and February 5, 1849, AHP.
27. Boggs, ed., *Alexander Letters*, 127–28.
   EPA, *Fighting*, 306.
28. EPA, *Fighting*, 3.
29. The Hester anecdote is told in EPA, *Fighting*, 5–6.
30. EPA, *Fighting*, 4.
31. EPA to William Felix Alexander, December 31, 1850, AHP.

Chamberlain: Brunswick and Bangor, 1848–55

1. Memoirs, 59–60.
   Bowdoin College Catalogue, 1848, BC.
2. Louis C. Hatch, *The History of Bowdoin College* (Portland, Maine, 1927), 2–7.
   Nehemiah Cleaveland and A. S. Packard, *History of Bowdoin College* (Boston, 1882), 4–8.
3. Frank Stearns, *The Life and Genius of Nathaniel Hawthorne* (Boston, 1906), 79.
4. Cleaveland, *Bowdoin*, 131–33.
5. Cleaveland, *Bowdoin*, 120–24, 131–33.
   Hatch, *Bowdoin*, 58–60.
6. Benjamin G. Snow to JLC, March 18, 1848, BC.
   Benjamin Brown Foster, *Down East Diary*, Charles A. Foster, ed. (Orono, Maine, 1975), 313, 316, 336.
7. JLC to "My Dear Pastor," May 5, 1848, BC.
8. This anecdote is drawn from Memoirs, 59–60.
9. Benjamin G. Snow to JLC, March 18, 1848, BC.
   Thayer and Ames, *Brewer.*
   JLC to "My Dear Pastor," May 5, 1848, BC.
10. JLC to "My Dear Pastor," May 5, 1848, BC.
    Benjamin G. Snow to JLC, March 18, 1848, BC.
11. Benjamin G. Snow to JLC, March 18, 1848, BC.
    Memoirs, 55.
12. Memoirs, 61–62.
13. Bowdoin College Catalogue, 1849, BC.
    Memoirs, 65–66.
14. Edward O. Shriver, "Antislavery: Maine and the Nation," in Banks, ed., *History of Maine*, 226.
    Austin Willey, *The History of the Antislavery Cause in State and Nation* (New York, 1969 ed.), 43.
15. Quotation is from Calvin M. Clark, *American Slavery and Maine Congregationalists* (Bangor, Maine, 1940), 159.
    Quotation is from Willey, *Antislavery*, 70.
16. Material on Harriet Beecher Stowe's Brunswick interval is drawn

from Forrest Wilson, *Crusader in Crinoline: The Life of Harriet Beecher Stowe* (Westport, Conn., 1941); Edmund Wilson, *Patriotic Gore: Studies in the Literature of the American Civil War* (Boston, 1984 ed); and Charles E. Stowe and Lyman Beecher Stowe, *Harriet Beecher Stowe: The Story of Her Life* (Boston, 1911).

17. Quotation is from Newman Smyth, *Recollections and Reflections* (New York, 1926), 10.

18. Memoirs, 69.

Foster, *Down East Diary*, 333.

19. Thompson Eldridge Ashby, *History of the First Parish Church in Brunswick, Maine*, Louise R. Helmreich, ed. (Brunswick, Maine, 1969), 157.

Cleaveland, *Bowdoin*, 672.

Trulock, *In the Hands of Providence*, 43.

20. Deborah G. Folsom to Frances C. Adams, February 17, 1853, Joshua L. Chamberlain Collection, Maine Historical Society, Portland (hereafter, MHS).

21. Ashby, *First Parish*, 164, 221.

22. JLC to Frances C. Adams, June 7, 1852, MHS.

23. Quotation is from Ashby, *First Parish*, 235.

24. Dr. George E. Adams diaries, October 2, 1851, First Parish Church, Brunswick, Maine (hereafter, FPC).

25. Adams diaries, December 30, 1851; February 13 and 23, 1852; and July 21, 1852, FPC.

Anna C. Davis to Frances C. Adams, March 10, 1852, MHS.

George E. Adams to Frances C. Adams, July 9, 1852, MHS.

26. JLC to Frances C. Adams, June 7, 1852, MHS.

Memoirs, 69–70.

Bowdoin College Catalogue, 1852, BC.

27. Memoirs, 70–71.

Anna C. Davis to Frances C. Adams, March 10, 1852, MHS.

28. Hatch, *Bowdoin*, 253–55.

Memoirs, 70–71.

Adams diaries, September 1, 1852, FPC.

29. JLC to his parents, August 6, 1852, University of Maine, Orono.

JLC to Francis C. Adams, no date (probably autumn 1852), MHS.

30. JLC to Frances C. Adams, no date (probably autumn 1852), MHS.

Adams diaries, November 25 and December 22, 1852, FPC.

31. JLC to Frances C. Adams, October 31, 1854, RC.
Calvin M. Clark, *History of Bangor Theological Seminary* (Boston, 1916), 150.
32. JLC, journal entry, August 18, 1853, BC.
Memoirs, 50.
Thayer and Ames, *Brewer*, 131.
33. Frances C. Adams to Charlotte Adams, January 10, 1853, MHS.
JLC to Frances C. Adams, March 6, April 14, and July 1, 1853, RC.
34. JLC to Frances C. Adams, March 6, 1853, RC.
JLC to Frances C. Adams, unsigned and undated (probably first part of 1853), RC.
Frances C. Adams to JLC, February 22, 1854, RC.
Frances C. Adams to JLC, December 8, 1861, RC.
35. Frances C. Adams to Charlotte Adams, January 10, 1853, MHS.
36. Clark, *History of Bangor Theological Seminary*, 140.
Deborah Folsom to Frances C. Adams, January 12, 1854, MHS.
37. Deborah Folsom to Frances C. Adams, October 3, 1854, MHS.
Frances C. Adams to JLC, no date (by contents, October 1854), RC.
38. Adams diaries, July 30 and August 11, 1855, FPC.
Memoirs, 71.
George E. Adams to JLC, no date (probably late summer 1855), BC.
Frances C. Adams to JLC, August 12, 1855, RC.
Little, *Genealogical History*, vol. 1, 133.
JLC to Frances C. Adams, July 30, 1854, RC.
39. Adams diaries, December 7, 1855, FPC.

Alexander: West Point, 1853–57

1. Adam L. Alexander to Marion B. Alexander and Alice Y. Alexander, July 11, 1854, AHP.
2. EPA, *Fighting*, 7.
Quotation is from Stephen E. Ambrose, *Duty, Honor, Country: A History of West Point* (Baltimore, 1966), 129.
3. Ambrose, *Duty*, 155–56.
Douglas Southall Freeman, *R. E. Lee: A Biography*, vol. 1 (New York, 1934), 319, 335.
4. Ambrose, *Duty*, 147.
5. U.S. Department of War, "Extracts from the Regulations of the Military Academy," 1853, AP.

O. O. Howard, *Autobiography of Oliver Otis Howard*, vol. 1 (New York, 1907), 48.

6. Ambrose, *Duty*, 148.
7. EPA to Bettie Alexander, May 14, 1897, AP.
   William F. Alexander to Adam L. Alexander, July 23, 1853, AHP.
   EPA, *Fighting*, 298.
   Adam L. Alexander to EPA, July 9, 1853, AP.
8. William F. Alexander to EPA, July 23, 1853, AHP.
9. "Extracts from Regulations," AP.
10. Ambrose, *Duty*, 127, 131.
11. Howard, *Autobiography*, vol. 1, 56.
12. Sarah Alexander to EPA, December 8, 1853, AP.
13. Sarah Alexander to EPA, December 8, 1853, AP.
14. Sarah Alexander to EPA, October 24, 1853, AHP.
    Ambrose, *Duty*, 149–50.
15. Jeremy Gilmer to Adam L. Alexander, October 24, 1853, AHP.
16. Jeremy Gilmer to Adam L. Alexander, October 24, 1853, AHP.
17. Ambrose, *Duty*, 153.
    Howard, *Autobiography*, vol. 1, 51–52.
18. EPA, *Fighting*, 7.
    Sarah Alexander to EPA, January 28, 1854, AHP.
19. Nehemiah Adams, *A South-Side View of Slavery* (Boston, 1854), 10.
20. Adams, *South-Side*, 15, 34, 37, 62.
21. Quotation is from EPA, *Fighting*, 7.
22. Sarah Alexander to Mary Clifford Alexander, February 20, 1853, in Boggs, ed., *Alexander Letters*, 177–78.
23. See Adam L. Alexander's letters for early 1854, AHP.
    Quotation is from Paul Johnson, *The Birth of the Modern* (New York, 1991), 764.
24. Sarah Alexander to Louisa Alexander Gilmer, June 11, 1854, AHP.
25. Adam L. Alexander to Marion B. Alexander, June 15, 1854, AHP.
    Adam L. Alexander to Marion B. Alexander and Alice Y. Alexander, July 11, 1854, AHP.
26. Adam L. Alexander to Marion B. Alexander and Alice Y. Alexander, July 11, 1854, AHP.
    EPA, *Fighting*, 7.
27. EPA to Adam L. Alexander, March 9, 1856, AP.
    Adam L. Alexander to EPA, April 9, 1855, AP.
28. Freeman, *Lee*, vol. 1, 342.

EPA to Adam L. Alexander, April 1, 1855, AHP.

EPA to Adam L. Alexander, April 23, 1855, AHP.

29. EPA, *Fighting*, 8.
30. Adam L. Alexander to EPA, February 20, 1856, AP.
31. EPA to Adam Leopold Alexander, April 23, 1855, AHP.
32. Adam L. Alexander to EPA, December 17, 1855, AP.

    EPA to Adam L. Alexander, May 15, 1856, AP.
33. EPA to Adam L. Alexander, December 25, 1855, AHP.
34. EPA, *Fighting*, 8.

    EPA to Adam L. Alexander, March 9, 1856, AHP.

    Adam L. Alexander to EPA, December 17, 1855, AP.
35. EPA to Adam L. Alexander, February 8, 1856, AHP.

    EPA to James Hillhouse Alexander, May 8, 1856, AHP.
36. EPA to Adam L. Alexander, March 9, 1856, AHP.

    Wilson B. Strong to EPA, January 24, 1907, AP.
37. Howard, *Autobiography*, vol. 1, 93.
38. EPA to James Hillhouse Alexander, May 8, 1856, AHP.
39. Adam L. Alexander to EPA, January 12, 1856, in Boggs, ed., *Alexander Letters*, 193.
40. EPA to Adam L. Alexander, February 8, 1856, AHP.

    EPA to Adam L. Alexander, March 9, 1856, AHP.
41. Marcus Cunliffe, *Soldiers and Civilians: The Martial Spirit in America, 1775–1865* (Boston, 1971), 383.

    EPA to Adam L. Alexander, March 9, 1857, AHP.

    EPA to Adam L. Alexander, January 14, 1857, AHP.
42. EPA to Adam L. Alexander, June 5, 1857, AHP.
43. EPA to Adam L. Alexander, March 9, 1857, AHP.
44. Ambrose, *Duty*, 99–102.
45. EPA to Adam L. Alexander, undated (by contents, June 1857), AHP.

    See Mark M. Boatner III, *The Civil War Dictionary* (New York, 1988 ed.), 616, 811.

    EPA, *Fighting*, 558n.
46. EPA to Adam L. Alexander, undated (by contents, June 1857), AHP.

Chapter 3. Preludes

Chamberlain: Brunswick to the Potomac, 1855–62

1. Bowdoin College Catalogue, 1855, BC.
   George F. Adams to JLC, n.d. (by contents, late summer 1855), BC.
   Deborah Folsom to Frances Chamberlain, October 21, 1856, MHS.
2. George Adams to JLC, n.d. (by contents, summer 1855), BC.
   Circular letter to JLC, November 19, 1855, BC.
   Adams diaries, October 16, 1856, FPC.
   Votes of the Governing Boards, Bowdoin College, 1856, BC.
   Records of the Executive Government of Bowdoin College, 1857, BC.
3. JLC to Frances Chamberlain, May 20, 1857, MHS.
   JLC to Frances Chamberlain, date missing (by contents, May or June 1857), MHS.
4. JLC to Frances Chamberlain, May 20, 1857, MHS.
   Votes of the Governing Boards, Bowdoin College, 1858, BC.
5. Memoirs, 74.
   JLC to Nehemiah Cleaveland, October 14, 1859, BC.
6. George Adams diaries, November 19, 1857, FPC.
   Memoirs, 75.
   Cleaveland, *Bowdoin*, 310–11.
7. JLC to Sarah D. B. Chamberlain, n.d. (by contents, late summer 1859), Joshua Lawrence Chamberlain Papers, Library of Congress, Washington, D.C. (hereafter, LC).
8. JLC to Francis O. J. Smith, September 1, 1859, BC.
   Memoirs, 74–75.
   Votes of the Governing Boards, Bowdoin College, 1860, BC.
9. Ashby, *First Parish Church*, 318.
   Memoirs, 74.
   Ashby, *First Parish Church*, 251–52.
10. Smyth, *Recollections and Reflections*, 39.
11. JLC to Nehemiah Cleaveland, October 14, 1859, BC.
12. JLC to John Chamberlain, November 7, 1855, BC.
    George Adams diaries, September 26, 1860, FPC.
13. JLC to Sarah D. B. Chamberlain, January 31, 1860, BC.
14. JLC to Sarah D. B. Chamberlain, January 31, 1860, BC.
    JLC to Sarah B. (Sae) Chamberlain, February 19, 1860, LC.

15. Hatch, *Bowdoin*, 116–17.

Hudson Strode, *Jefferson Davis: American Patriot, 1808–1861* (New York, 1955), 301–13.

16. Undated draft of an 1866 address titled "Loyalty," BC.

Adams diaries, November 7, 1860, FPC.

17. JLC to Thomas Chamberlain, March 4, 1861, BC.

18. Oliver Wendell Holmes, *The Autocrat of the Breakfast Table* (Boston, 1891), 260–61.

19. Smyth, *Recollections and Reflections*, 43.

Hatch, *Bowdoin*, 117–19.

J. C. Minot and D. F. Snow, eds., *Tales of Bowdoin* (Augusta, Maine, 1901), 268.

20. Howard, *Autobiography*, vol. 1, 123.

Hatch, *Bowdoin*, 117.

21. JLC to Governor Israel Washburn, September 24, 1861, Maine State Archives, Augusta (hereafter, MSA).

Ashby, *First Parish Church*, 249.

Hatch, *Bowdoin*, 117.

Records of the Executive Government, Bowdoin College, 1861, BC.

22. Quotation is from Warren W. Hassler, Jr., *General George B. McClellan: Shield of the Union* (Baton Rouge, La., 1957), 23.

23. Walter S. Poor to JLC, October 13, 1861, LC.

24. Walter S. Poor to JLC, October 13, 1861, LC.

Quotation is from Edward H. Miller, *Salem Is My Dwelling Place: A Life of Nathaniel Hawthorne* (Iowa City, Iowa, 1991), 471.

25. Ralph Waldo Emerson, *Essays & Lectures* (New York, 1983), 60.

"Heroes" quotation is from George M. Frederickson, *The Inner Civil War* (New York, 1965), 30.

Brown quotation is from Len Gougeon, *Virtue's Hero: Emerson, Antislavery and Reform* (Athens, Ga., 1990), 244.

26. Horace Chamberlain to JLC, July 7, 1858, RC.

Frances Chamberlain to JLC, December 8, 1861, RC.

JLC to Sarah B. (Sae) Chamberlain, February 4, 1862, BC.

27. Undated handwritten notes (by contents, mid-1862), BC.

28. Nathaniel Hawthorne, "Chiefly about War-Matters," *The Atlantic Monthly* 10 (July 1862), 48.

29. Memoirs, 76.

30. JLC to Israel Washburn, July 14, 1862, MSA.

31. Memoirs, 76–77.

JLC to Israel Washburn, July 22, 1862, MSA.

George Adams diaries, July 19, 1862, FPC.

Records of the Executive Government, Bowdoin College, 1862, BC.

32. Josiah Drummond to Israel Washburn, July 22, 1862, MSA.

John D. Lincoln to Israel Washburn, July 17, 1862, MSA.

Israel Washburn to JLC, August 8, 1862, LC.

33. *Maine at Gettysburg*, Report of Maine Commissioners (Portland, 1898), 274.

John J. Pullen. *The Twentieth Maine: A Volunteer Regiment in the Civil War* (New York, 1957), 1.

34. Annual Report of the Adjutant General, State of Maine, 1862 (Augusta, Maine), Appendix A (hereafter, Maine AGR).

Maine at Gettysburg, 273–74.

Pullen, *Twentieth Maine*, 13.

35. Ellis Spear, "Historical Sketch" (galley proof), 88, LC.

John M. Brown to JLC, July 26, 1862, LC.

Thomas Chamberlain to JLC, July 21, 1862, RC.

36. *Maine at Gettysburg*, 274.

JLC to Eugene Hale, August 15, 1862, MSA.

Spear quotations are from Pullen, *Twentieth Maine*, 15, 6.

37. Pullen, *Twentieth Maine*, 1–3.

Quotation is from Maine AGR, 1862, 2.

38. William E. S. Whitman and Charles H. True, *Maine in the War for the Union* (Lewiston, Maine, 1865), 491.

Spear, "Historical Sketch," 88.

39. George Adams diaries, September 1, 1862, FPC.

Parish Records, Brewer Congregational Church, Brewer Public Library.

Joshua Chamberlain, Jr., to JLC, n.d. (by contents, early September 1862), RC.

Alexander: West Point to Manassas, 1857–61

1. EPA to Mary Clifford Alexander, December 6, 1857, in Boggs, ed., *Alexander Letters*, 212.

2. EPA to Mary Clifford Alexander, November 11, 1857, in Boggs, ed., *Alexander Letters*, 209.

3. Coffman, *The Old Army*, 59.

4. Coffman, *The Old Army*, 99.

5. Boatner, *Civil War Dictionary*, 862.
   EPA, *Fighting*, 9.
6. Howard, *Autobiography*, vol. 1, 95.
   EPA, *Fighting*, 9.
7. EPA, *Fighting*, 13.
   EPA, Diary of the 1858 Plains Expedition, AP.
8. EPA, *Fighting*, 11–12, 315.
   Edward P. Alexander, *Military Memoirs of a Confederate: A Critical Narrative* (New York, 1907), 3 (hereafter, *Military Memoirs*).
   EPA, Plains diary, AP.
9. EPA, *Fighting*, 11–12.
10. EPA, Plains diary, AP.
    EPA, *Fighting*, 13–14.
    See EPA's 1859 correspondence in the Alexander-Hillhouse Papers for garrison routines and an account of the dispute with Delafield.
    Howard, *Autobiography*, vol. 1, 100.
11. EPA, *Fighting*, 13–14.
    EPA to Adam L. Alexander, September 11, 1859, AHP.
    EPA to Bettie Alexander, May 3, 1899, AP.
12. EPA to Adam L. Alexander, April 24, 1859, AHP.
    Mary Clifford Alexander to EPA, April 23, 1856, AHP.
    EPA, *Fighting*, 14.
13. Adam L. Alexander to EPA, March 16 and April 2, 1857, AP.
    EPA to Adam L. Alexander, May 15, 1856, AHP.
    Adam L. Alexander to Marion B. Alexander, September 14, 1859, AHP.
14. EPA to Mary Clifford Alexander, Nov. 10, 1859, in Boggs, ed., *Alexander Letters*, 216.
    EPA to Adam L. Alexander, March 4, 1860, AHP.
15. EPA, *Fighting*, 147–48.
    EPA to Adam L. Alexander, December 28, 1859, AHP.
16. Sarah Lawton to EPA, March 13, 1860, AP.
    Louisa Porter to EPA, April 13, 1860, AP.
    EPA, *Fighting*, 14.
17. EPA, *Fighting*, 14.
    EPA to Adam L. Alexander, July 22, 1860, AHP.
18. EPA to Adam L. Alexander, September 16, 1860, AHP.
    EPA, *Fighting*, 14–15.
19. EPA to Adam L. Alexander, September 16, 1860, AHP.

20. James M. McPherson, *Battle Cry of Freedom: The Civil War Era* (New York, 1988), 223–24.

EPA, *Fighting*, 16–18.

21. Robert G. Ficken and Charles P. LaWarne, *Washington: A Centennial History* (Seattle, 1988), 22.

22. U.S. War Department, *The War of the Rebellion: A Compilation of the Official Records of the Union and Confederate Armies* (Washington, 1880–1901), vol. 50, part 1, 435–36 (hereafter, OR).

James Morris, *Heaven's Command: An Imperial Progress* (New York, 1980), 368–69.

23. Herbert M. Hart, *Old Forts of the Northwest* (Seattle, 1963), 37.

Edmond S. Meany, *History of the State of Washington* (New York, 1924), 240–54.

Morris, *Heaven's Command*, 368–69.

24. EPA to Adam L. Alexander, July 22, 1860, AHP.

EPA to Adam L. Alexander, October 14, 1860, AHP.

25. EPA to Adam L. Alexander, October 14, 1860, AHP.

EPA, *Fighting*, 20–21.

26. EPA, *Fighting*, 19–20.

27. EPA to Adam L. Alexander, October 14, 1860, AHP.

28. R. M. Willingham, *No Jubilee: The Story of Confederate Wilkes* (Washington, Ga., 1976), 77.

WPA Writers' Program, *The Story of Washington-Wilkes* (Athens, Ga., 1941), 55.

Eliza F. Andrews, *The War-Time Journal of a Georgia Girl*, Spencer B. King, Jr., ed. (Macon, Ga., 1960), 309.

29. Quotations are from Willingham, *No Jubilee*, 72–73.

30. EPA, *Fighting*, 21.

31. EPA, *Fighting*, 21.

EPA, *Military Memoirs*, 4.

Coffman, *The Old Army*, 92.

32. OR, vol. 50, part 1, 456.

EPA, *Fighting*, 21–22.

33. EPA, *Fighting*, 23–24.

34. EPA, *Fighting*, 24

35. EPA, *Fighting*, 24.

36. EPA, *Fighting*, 25, 29.

37. EPA, *Fighting*, 31.

38. EPA, *Fighting*, 33.

39. EPA, *Fighting*, 33–34.
40. EPA, *Fighting*, 35.
41. EPA, *Fighting*, 35–36.
42. EPA to Bettie Alexander, June 2 and 6, 1861, AP.
43. EPA, *Fighting*, 37–38.
    OR, vol. 51, part 2, 150.
    EPA to Bettie Alexander, June 8, 29, and 30, 1861, AP.

CHAPTER 4. APPRENTICESHIP

Alexander: Manassas to Fredericksburg, 1861–62

1. Ellsworth G. Eliot, *West Point in the Confederacy* (New York, 1941), 335.
   EPA, *Fighting*, 38.
2. EPA, *Fighting*, 37.
   Adam L. Alexander to Marion B. Alexander, June 11, 1861, AHP.
3. G. Moxley Sorrel, *Recollections of a Confederate Staff Officer* (Jackson, Tenn., 1958 ed.), 260.
   EPA to Bettie Alexander, July 5, 1861, AP.
   EPA, *Fighting*, 38–39.
4. EPA, *Fighting*, 46.
5. Joseph E. Johnston's report, OR, vol. 2, 474.
   EPA, "The Battle of Bull Run," *Scribner's Magazine* 41 (1907), 84.
6. EPA, "'Battle of Bull Run," 88.
   EPA, *Fighting*, 50.
   EPA, *Military Memoirs*, 30.
7. EPA, *Fighting*, 50.
   EPA, *Military Memoirs*, 31.
8. Quotation is from Sorrel, *Recollections*, 38.
9. EPA, *Fighting*, 52–53.
   Quotation is from EPA, "Battle of Bull Run," 89.
10. EPA, *Fighting*, 54.
    EPA, "Battle of Bull Run," 93.
11. EPA, *Fighting*, 56.
12. EPA, *Fighting*, 55.
13. EPA, *Fighting*, 57.
14. EPA, *Fighting*, 59.
15. EPA to Bettie Alexander, July 27, 1861, AP.

16. Quotation is from William Miller Owen, *In Camp and Battle with the Washington Artillery* (Boston, 1885), 334.

17. First Corps, Army of the Potomac, Special Orders No. 159, July 24, 1861, AP.
EPA, *Fighting*, 62.
EPA, "Confederate Artillery Service," *Southern Historical Society Papers* 11 (January 1883), 104–50 (hereafter, SHSP).
EPA to Adam L. Alexander, September 4, 1861, AHP.
EPA to Bettie Alexander, August 12, 1861, AP.

18. EPA to Bettie Alexander, August 1 and 17, 1861, AP.

19. EPA, *Fighting*, 66–68.
EPA to Bettie Alexander, July 29, 1897, AP.

20. OR, Series 2, vol. 2 (1897), 561, 1317, 1349–50.

21. EPA, *Fighting*, 69.

22. OR, Series 2, vol. 2, 272.
Ishbel Ross, *Rebel Rose: Life of Rose O'Neal Greenhow, Confederate Spy* (New York, 1954), 174, 202.
EPA, *Fighting*, 70.
EPA to Bettie Alexander, June 13, 1862, AP.
Harnett T. Kane, *Spies for the Blue and Gray* (Garden City, N.Y., 1954), 63.

23. EPA to Mary Alexander Hull, December 3, 1861, in Boggs, ed., *Alexander Letters*, 236–37.
EPA to Adam L. Alexander, January 2, 1862, AHP.

24. EPA to Bettie Alexander, December 16, 1861, AP.
EPA to Mary Alexander Hull, January 21, 1862, AP.

25. EPA to Marion Brackett Alexander, January 21, 1862, AP.
T. C. DeLeon, *Four Years in Rebel Capitals* (Mobile, Ala., 1890), 141.

26. William F. Alexander to Adam L. Alexander, January 30, 1862, AHP.
EPA, "Confederate Artillery Service," 109.
EPA to Adam L. Alexander, February 10, 1862, AHP.

27. EPA to Adam L. Alexander, March 7, 1862, AHP.
EPA, *Fighting*, 76.

28. Undated, unsigned letter in EPA's hand (from contents, March 1862), AP.
EPA to Adam L. Alexander, March 20, 1862, AHP.

29. EPA, *Military Memoirs*, 64–66.
EPA to Bettie Alexander, April 28, 1862, AP.

30. EPA, *Fighting*, 73–74.
EPA to Bettie Alexander, April 30, 1862, AP.

31. EPA, *Fighting*, 83–85.
32. EPA, *Fighting*, 74, 91.
33. EPA, *Fighting*, 96, 115.
34. EPA to Adam L. Alexander, July 24, 1862, AP.
35. EPA, *Fighting*, 115.
    EPA to Adam L. Alexander, July 24, 1862, AP.
36. EPA to Adam L. Alexander, July 24, 1862, AP.
37. EPA, *Fighting*, 127.
    War Department order, July 17, 1862, AP.
    EPA to Adam L. Alexander, August 16, 1862, AHP.
38. EPA, *Fighting*, 139–40.
39. EPA, *Fighting*, 143–48.
    EPA, *Military Memoirs*, 242.
40. EPA, *Fighting*, 145, 154.
41. EPA, *Fighting*, 155–56.
    Extracts from EPA's official journal, OR, vol. 19, part 2, 156.
42. EPA, *Fighting*, 158–59.
    Army of Northern Virginia, General Orders No. 130, December 4, 1862, copy in AP.
43. Jennings C. Wise, *The Long Arm of Lee: The History of the Artillery of the Army of Northern Virginia* (New York, 1959 ed.), 299, 73, 141.
    EPA, "Confederate Artillery Service," 99–100.
    EPA, *Fighting*, 105.
44. G. Moxley Sorrel to EPA, November 22, 1862, AP.

Chamberlain: Antietam to Fredericksburg, Autumn 1862

1. Theodore Gerrish, *Army Life: A Private's Reminiscences of the Civil War* (Portland, Maine, 1882), 14–15.
2. Joshua L. Chamberlain, *The Passing of the Armies: An Account of the Final Campaign of the Army of the Potomac Based upon Personal Reminiscences of the Fifth Army Corps* (New York, 1915), 337.
   Spear, "Historical Sketch," 88.
   Maine at Gettysburg, 274.
   Gerrish, *Army Life*, 18.
3. Gerrish, *Army Life*, 18–19.

Quarterly return of ordnance stores, 20th Maine Volunteer Infantry, January 4, 1863, LC.

Maine AGR, 1862, 113.

4. William L. Powell, *The Fifth Army Corps* (New York, 1896), 248.

5. Powell, *Fifth Army Corps*, 304.
   Gerrish, *Army Life*, 24.

6. Gerrish, *Army Life*, 25.
   Pullen, *The Twentieth Maine*, 22.

7. Pullen, *The Twentieth Maine*, 24.
   Boatner, *Civil War Dictionary*, 20.
   Quotation is from Gerrish, *Army Life*, 27.

8. Gerrish, *Army Life*, 27–28.
   Quotations are from Trulock, *In the Hands of Providence*, 68–69.

9. Powell, *Fifth Army Corps*, 272.

10. First quotation is from Shelby Foote, *The Civil War: A Narrative*, vol. 1 (New York, 1958), 688.
    Gerrish, *Army Life*, 33.

11. Powell, *Fifth Army Corps*, 272–73.
    William Marvel, *Burnside* (Chapel Hill, N.C., 1991), 140.

12. Gerrish, *Army Life*, 40.

13. Maine AGR, 1862, 2.
    Pullen, *Twentieth Maine*, 26–27.
    Spear, "Historical Sketch," 89.
    Gerrish, *Army Life*, 38.

14. Powell, *Fifth Army Corps*, 298.
    Gerrish, *Army Life*, 41–42.

15. Powell, *Fifth Army Corps*, 301.
    Quotation is from Gerrish, *Army Life*, 43.
    Maine AGR, 1864 and 1865, 331.

16. Pullen, *Twentieth Maine*, 27.
    Powell, *Fifth Army Corps*, 306.
    Gerrish, *Army Life*, 44–45.

17. Powell, *Fifth Army Corps*, 310.
    Spear, "Historical Sketch," 89.
    Gerrish, *Army Life*, 47–49.
    Maine at Gettysburg, 275.

18. JLC to Frances Chamberlain, October 10, 1862, LC.
    Pullen, *Twentieth Maine*, 37.

19. JLC to Frances Chamberlain, October 10 and 26, 1862, LC.
20. Holmes quotation is from Catherine Drinker Bowen, *Yankee from Olympus* (Boston, 1944), 385.

John W. De Forest, *A Volunteer's Adventures*, edited by James H. Croushore (New Haven, Conn., 1946), 123.

Tom Chamberlain quotation is from Pullen, *Twentieth Maine*, 37.

JLC, *Passing of the Armies*, 20.
21. JLC, "Abraham Lincoln," paper read before the Pennsylvania Commandery, Military Order of the Loyal Legion, February 12, 1909, copy in LC.

Robert G. Carter, *Four Brothers in Blue, or Sunshine and Shadows of the War of the Rebellion: A Story of the Great Civil War from Bull Run to Appomattox* (Austin, Texas, 1978 ed.), 137.

McPherson, *Battle Cry of Freedom*, 559.

Powell, *Fifth Army Corps*, 309.
22. Halleck to McClellan, OR, vol. 19, part 1, 10.

Gerrish, *Army Life*, 49.

Tom Chamberlain quotation is from Pullen, *Twentieth Maine*, 36.

Soldier's quotation is from a newspaper clipping dated October 23, 1862, in JLC Order Book, Pejepscot Historical Society, Brunswick, Maine (hereafter, PHS.)

JLC to Frances Chamberlain, October 26, 1862, LC.
23. JLC to Frances Chamberlain, October 10 and 26, 1862, LC.
24. JLC to Frances Chamberlain, October 26 and November 3, 1862, LC.
25. Powell, *Fifth Army Corps*, 311–13.

JLC to Frances Chamberlain, October 26, 1862, LC.

Gerrish, *Army Life*, 50–51.
26. JLC to Frances Chamberlain, November 3, 1862, LC.
27. JLC to Frances Chamberlain, November 4, 1862, LC.
28. OR, vol. 19, part 1, 88.

JLC to Frances Chamberlain, November 4, 1862, LC.

JLC, *Passing of the Armies*, 27.
29. Marvel, *Burnside*, 161.

Holmes quotation is from Liva Baker, *The Justice from Beacon Hill: The Life and Times of Oliver Wendell Holmes* (New York, 1991), 138.

EPA, *Fighting*, 166.
30. Sorrel, *Recollections*, 123.

OR, vol. 19, part 1, 88.

Gerrish, *Army Life*, 63.

31. JLC to Frances Chamberlain, November 4, 1862, LC.
    Frances Chamberlain to JLC, November 27, 1862, RC.
32. JLC to Frances Chamberlain, November 4, 1862, LC.

CHAPTER 5. BLOOD ON THE PLAIN

Fredericksburg, December 1862

1. OR, vol. 21, 1016.
   EPA to Adam L. Alexander, December 18, 1862, in Boggs, ed., *Alexander Letters*, 243.
   EPA, *Fighting*, 168, 183.
   EPA's official journal, AP.
2. EPA, *Fighting*, 167.
   G. Moxley Sorrel to EPA, November 22, 1862, AP.
   Wise, *Long Arm of Lee*, 371.
3. Sorrel, *Recollections*, 119.
   Wise, *Long Arm of Lee*, 755.
   EPA, *Fighting*, 168.
   Owen, *Washington Artillery*, 177.
4. Wise, *Long Arm of Lee*, 742–43, 747, 755.
   Owen, *Washington Artillery*, 18.
   Dumas Malone, ed., *Dictionary of American Biography* (hereafter, DAB), vol. 14 (New York, 1934), 423–24.
   First quotation is from Sorrel, *Recollections*, 114.
   Second quotation is from Jacob E. Cooke, *Frederic Bancroft: Historian* (Norman, Okla., 1957), 92.
5. EPA, *Fighting*, 160–62.
   Fairfax Downey, *The Guns at Gettysburg* (New York, 1958), 64.
6. EPA, "The Battle of Fredericksburg," SHSP 10 (1882), 384.
   EPA's report, OR, vol. 21, 575.
   EPA, *Fighting*, 169, 171.
7. Sorrel, *Recollections*, 124–25.
   First quotation is from James C. Longstreet, *From Manassas to Appomattox: Memoirs of the Civil War in America* (Bloomington, Ind., 1960 ed.), 298.
   James C. Longstreet, "The Battle of Fredericksburg," in Robert U.

Johnson and Clarence C. Buel, *Battles and Leaders of the Civil War* vol. 3 (New York, 1887–88) (hereafter, B&L), 79.

8. *B&L*, vol. 3, 79.

9. EPA, *Fighting*, 169,186.

10. Ambrose E. Burnside to Henry W. Halleck, December 9, 1862, OR, vol. 21, 64.

 Marvel, *Burnside*, 168–69.

 EPA to Adam L. Alexander, December 18, 1862, in Boggs, ed., *Alexander Letters*, 243.

 EPA, *Military Memoirs*, 289.

 G. Moxley Sorrel to EPA, December 10, 1862, AP.

 Longstreet, *Memoirs*, 301.

11. EPA, *Fighting*, 170.

 Longstreet, *Memoirs*, 306.

 EPA to Adam L. Alexander, December 18, 1862, in Boggs, ed., *Alexander Letters*, 243.

 EPA, *Military Memoirs*, 291.

12. EPA, *Fighting*, 171.

13. EPA, "Battle of Fredericksburg," 387.

 EPA, "Confederate Artillery Service," 104.

14. EPA, *Military Memoirs*, 292–94.

 EPA to Adam L. Alexander, December 18, 1862, in Boggs, ed., *Alexander Letters*, 244.

 EPA's report, OR, vol. 21, 576.

15. EPA, *Military Memoirs*, 296.

 EPA, *Fighting*, 175.

16. EPA, *Fighting*, 175.

 EPA, *Military Memoirs*, 302–303.

 EPA to Adam L. Alexander, December 18, 1862, in Boggs, ed., *Alexander Letters*, 244.

17. EPA, "Battle of Fredericksburg," 449.

 EPA's report, OR, vol. 21, 576.

 Sorrel to EPA, December 13, 1862, AP.

 EPA, *Fighting*, 176.

 EPA, *Military Memoirs*, 302.

18. EPA, *Military Memoirs* 302–303.

 EPA to Adam L. Alexander, December 18, 1862, in Boggs, ed., *Alexander Letters*, 244.

19. Darius N. Couch, "Sumner's 'Right Grand Division,' " in B&L, vol. 3, 113.
    Longstreet, *Memoirs*, 315.
20. EPA, *Military Memoirs*, 305.
    EPA to Adam L. Alexander, December 18, 1862, in Boggs, ed., *Alexander Letters*, 244.
21. EPA, *Military Memoirs*, 306.
22. J. B. Walton to EPA, misdated December 12, 1862, AP.
    EPA, *Fighting*, 177–78.
    Owen, *Washington Artillery*, 191–92.
    EPA's report, OR, vol. 21, 576.
23. EPA, *Fighting*, 179.
    Wise, *Long Arm of Lee*, 396–97.
    EPA's report, OR, vol. 21, 576.
    EPA to Adam L. Alexander, December 18, 1862, in Boggs, ed., *Alexander Letters*, 245.
24. EPA's report, OR, vol. 21, 577.
    Wise, *Long Arm of Lee*, 398.
    EPA, *Fighting*, 180.
25. EPA to Adam L. Alexander, December 18, 1862, in Boggs, ed., *Alexander Letters*, 245.
    EPA, *Fighting*, 181.
26. EPA, *Military Memoirs*, 312.
    EPA, *Fighting*, 185.
27. EPA, *Fighting*, 186.
    EPA's report, OR, vol. 21, 577.
28. EPA, *Fighting*, 187.
29. Carter, *Four Brothers*, 190.
    Powell, *Fifth Army Corps*, 366.
    JLC, "My Story of Fredericksburg," *Cosmopolitan Magazine*, 54 (December 1912), 149.
    OR, vol. 21, 842.
30. JLC, "My Story," 150.
31. Gerrish, *Army Life*, 73–74.
    Charles Griffin's report, OR, vol. 21, 404.
    JLC, "My Story," 151.
32. JLC, "My Story," 153.
33. Powell, *Fifth Army Corps*, 374.
    Joseph Hooker's report, OR, vol. 21, 356.

Griffin's report, OR, vol. 21, 405.

JLC, "My Story," 152.

34. JLC, "My Story," 152.

Unsigned letter (undoubtedly from John M. Brown), *Portland Press*, December 15, 1862, clipping in JLC Order Book, PHS.

Griffin's report, OR, vol. 21, 404–405.

Thomas B. W. Stockton's report, OR, vol. 21, 411.

35. Brown letter, PHS.

Gerrish, *Army Life*, 77–78.

JLC, "My Story," 153.

Unsigned letter (doubtless JLC), *Portland Press*, December 17, 1862, clipping in JLC Order Book, PHS.

Stockton's report, OR, vol. 21, 411.

36. Carter, *Four Brothers*, 196.

37. Rush Hawkins's report, OR, vol. 21, 336.

Erastus Tyler's report, OR, vol. 21, 437.

38. JLC, "My Story," 154.

Carter, *Four Brothers*, 199.

JLC, "Night on the Field of Fredericksburg," in W. C. King and W. P. Derby, eds., *Camp-Fire Sketches and Battle-Field Echoes* (Springfield, Mass., 1888), 128.

39. JLC, "My Story," 154.

JLC letter, PHS.

40. JLC, "My Story," 154.

JLC letter, PHS.

JLC, "Night on the Field," 129.

41. JLC letter, PHS.

JLC, "My Story," 154.

Gerrish, *Army Life*, 78.

42. Carter, *Four Brothers*, 207.

JLC, "My Story," 156.

JLC letter, PHS.

43. JLC letter, PHS.

JLC, "My Story," 156.

JLC, "Night on the Field," 130.

44. JLC, "My Story," 156.

Carter, *Four Brothers*, 201.

Gerrish, *Army Life*, 79.

45. Griffin's report, OR, vol. 21, 405.

JLC, "My Story," 156.

46. JLC, "My Story," 157.

47. JLC, "My Story," 157–58.
Gerrish, *Army Life*, 80.
JLC, "The Last Night at Fredericksburg," in King and Derby, eds., *Camp-Fire Sketches*, 134.

48. Lee quotation is from Foote, *The Civil War*, vol. 2, 45.
JLC, "My Story," 158.

49. JLC, "My Story," 158.

50. Casualty table, OR, vol. 21, 136.
Griffin's report, OR, vol. 21, 405.
Carter, *Four Brothers*, 210.

51. EPA, *Fighting*, 187, 168.
EPA, "The Battle of Fredericksburg," 387–88.

52. Powell, *Fifth Army Corps*, 405.
James Barnes's report, OR, vol. 21, 742–44.
EPA, *Fighting*, 187.

53. EPA, *Fighting*, 188.
Wise, *Long Arm of Lee*, 410.
EPA to Adam L. Alexander, January 18, 1863, AHP.

54. Lincoln to Burnside, December 30, 1862, OR, vol. 21, 900.
Powell, *Fifth Army Corps*, 407.

55. Carter, *Four Brothers*, 225.
Quotation is from D. P. Woodbury to Burnside, January 21, 1863, OR, vol. 21, 990.

56. EPA to Adam L. Alexander, January 18, 1863, AHP.
EPA, *Fighting*, 189.
Carter, *Four Brothers*, 225.

57. Carter, *Four Brothers*, 226–27.
EPA, *Fighting*, 189.
OR, vol. 21, 1004–05.

Chapter 6. Excursion into the Wilderness

Chancellorsville, Spring 1863

1. OR, vol. 25, part 2, 5.
   Foote, *The Civil War*, vol. 2, 239.
   Powell, *Fifth Army Corps*, 418.
   Gerrish, *Army Life*, 84.
2. Powell, *Fifth Army Corps*, 418–19.
   Gerrish, *Army Life*, 84
   Carter, *Four Brothers*, 231.
   Oliver Willcox Norton, *Army Letters, 1861–1865* (Chicago, 1903), 133.
3. Noah Brooks, *Washington in Lincoln's Time*, Herbert Mitgang, ed. (New York, 1958), 56.
   Gerrish, *Army Life*, 84.
   Carter, *Four Brothers*, 205.
4. Little, ed., *Genealogical and Family History*, 134.
   JLC, *Passing of the Armies*, 351.
   Oliver Willcox Norton, *The Attack and Defense of Little Round Top, July 2, 1863* (New York, 1913), 271, 281–85.
5. Norton, *Attack and Defense*, 289, 320.
   Boatner, *Civil War Dictionary*, 695–96.
6. Gerrish, *Army Life*, 69–71.
7. George Adams diaries, February 10 and 17, 1863, FPC.
   JLC to John M. Brown, January 28, 1863, PHS.
   JLC to Governor Abner Coburn, February 26, 1863, MSA.
   OR, vol. 25, part 2, 470.
8. Carter, *Four Brothers*, 235–36, 238, 239–41.
   OR, vol. 25, part 2, 203–204.
9. JLC to Frances Chamberlain, April 24–27, 1863, LC.
   OR, vol. 25, part 2, 239.
   Maine AGR, 1864–65, vol. 1, 331.
   Pullen, *Twentieth Maine*, 74.
10. JLC to Frances Chamberlain, April 24–27, 1863, LC.
    Powell, *Fifth Army Corps*, 428.
    OR, vol. 25, part 2, 262, 269.
11. Stockton's report, OR, vol. 25, part 1, 519.
    JLC to Frances Chamberlain, April 24–27, 1863, LC.
12. Stockton's report, OR, vol. 25, part 1, 519.

S. P. Curtis to "Mr. Purington & wife," June 1, 1863, copy in PHS.
Little, ed., *Genealogical and Family History*, vol. 1, 134.

13. Maine AGR, 1864–65, vol. 1, 331.
JLC to Coburn, May 25, 1863, MSA.
Gerrish, *Army Life*, 89.
OR, vol. 25, part 2, 378.

14. JLC to Coburn, May 25, 1863, MSA.
Maine AGR, 1864–65, vol. 1, 331.
James McQuade's report, OR, vol. 25, part 1, 508–509.
John Sedgwick's report, OR, vol. 25, part 1, 261.

15. Gerrish, *Army Life*, 93.
William Tilton to JLC, n.d. (by contents, autumn 1865), LC.
Maine AGR, 1864–65, vol. 1, 331.
S. P. Curtis to "Mr. Purington & wife," June 1, 1863, copy in PHS.

16. Carter, *Four Brothers*, 271–73.
JLC to Daisy Chamberlain, May 1863, BC.
Eugene A. Nash, *A History of the Forty-fourth Regiment, New York Volunteer Infantry, in the Civil War, 1861–1865* (Chicago, 1911), 133.
Maine AGR, 1864–65, vol. 1, 331.
JLC service records, National Archives, Washington, D.C. (hereafter, NA).

17. JLC to John Chamberlain, May 22, 1863, LC.

18. Maine AGR, 1864–65, vol. 1, 331–32.
JLC to Governor Coburn, May 25, 1863, MSA.
JLC, "Through Blood and Fire at Gettysburg," *Hearst's Magazine* 23 (June 1913), 900.

19. JLC, "Blood and Fire," 900.
Maine AGR, 1864–65, vol. 1, 332.
JLC to Governor Coburn, May 25 and 27, 1863, MSA.

20. Maine AGR, 1864–65, vol. 1, 332.
OR, vol. 25, part 2, 535.
John Chamberlain diary, 1–3, PHS.

21. EPA, *Fighting*, 189.
W. N. Pendleton, *The Memoirs of William Nelson Pendleton*, Susan P. Lee, ed. (Philadelphia, 1893), 256.
Wise, *Long Arm of Lee*, 413–19, 430.
EPA, "Confederate Artillery Service," 102.

22. Army of Northern Virginia, General Orders No. 1, January 1, 1863, copy in AP.
EPA to Adam L. Alexander, April 25, 1863, AHP.

23. EPA, *Fighting*, 189.
   EPA to Adam L. Alexander, April 25, 1863, AHP.
24. War Department order, March 3, 1863, copy in AP.
   EPA to Adam L. Alexander, March 11, 1863, AHP.
   EPA, *Fighting*, 193.
25. EPA to Adam L. Alexander, April 25, 1863, AHP.
   EPA, "Confederate Artillery Service," 105.
   EPA, "Battle of Fredericksburg," 388.
   EPA, *Fighting*, 194.
26. Wise, *Long Arm of Lee*, 429.
   EPA, *Fighting*, 194.
27. EPA, *Fighting*, 195.
   EPA, *Military Memoirs*, 323–25.
28. EPA, *Fighting*, 196.
29. EPA's report, OR, vol. 25, part 1, 821.
   EPA, *Fighting*, 198.
30. EPA, *Fighting*, 199.
31. EPA, *Fighting*, 201.
   EPA, *Military Memoirs*, 330–31.
32. EPA, *Fighting*, 201–203.
   EPA's report, OR, vol. 25, part 1, 821.
   EPA, *Military Memoirs*, 334.
33. EPA, *Fighting*, 203.
   EPA, *Military Memoirs*, 337.
   EPA's report, OR, vol. 25, part 1, 821.
34. J.E.B. Stuart's report, OR, vol. 25, part 1, 887.
   EPA's report, 822–23.
   EPA, *Fighting*, 207–208.
35. EPA, *Fighting*, 208.
36. EPA, *Military Memoirs*, 345.
   Stuart's report, OR, vol. 25, part 1, 888.
   EPA, *Fighting*, 210.
   EPA's report, OR, vol. 25, part 1, 823.
   The Poetical Works of Robert Southey, vol. 6 (Boston, 1860), 102.
37. EPA's report, OR, vol. 25, part 1, 824.
   EPA, *Fighting*, 209–10.
38. EPA's report, OR, vol. 25, part 1, 821.
   EPA, *Fighting*, 213.

39. EPA, *Fighting*, 213.
   OR, vol. 25, part 2, 407–409.
40. EPA's report, OR, vol. 25, part 1, 821.
   Wise, *Long Arm of Lee*, 539.
   Sedgwick's report, OR, vol. 25, part 1, 261.
   EPA, *Fighting*, 214–15.
   EPA, *Military Memoirs*, 358.
41. EPA, *Fighting*, 195.
   EPA, *Military Memoirs*, 319.
42. EPA's report, vol. 25, part 1, 822.
   EPA, *Fighting*, 218.
   EPA to Adam L. Alexander, June 14, 1863, AHP.
43. EPA, *Fighting*, 220–21.
   EPA to Adam L. Alexander, June 14, 1863, AHP.
   EPA's report, OR, vol. 27, part 2, 429.
44. EPA, *Fighting*, 222.
   EPA to Adam L. Alexander, June 14, 1863, AHP.
45. EPA, *Fighting*, 222.
   EPA to Adam L. Alexander, June 14, 1863, AHP.
46. John Chamberlain diary, 1–8, 16, PHS.
   Carter, *Four Brothers*, 276.
   John Chamberlain to Charles Desmond, August 5, 1863, BC.
47. Kate Perkins to JLC, June 1, 1863, RC.
   Sarah (Sae) Chamberlain to Tom Chamberlain, May 26, 1863, RC.
   JLC to "Dear Aunty" (Deborah Folsom), June 15, 1863, LC.
   John Chamberlain diary, 42, PHS.
   Nash, *Forty-fourth New York*, 230.
48. Boatner, *Civil War Dictionary*, 45.
   Carter, *Four Brothers*, 271.
   Powell, *Fifth Army Corps*, 498–99.
   Strong Vincent's report, OR, vol. 27, part 1, 615.
   James Barnes to JLC, December 11, 1865, LC.
49. Vincent's report, OR, vol. 27, part 1, 614.
   John Chamberlain diary, 41–43, PHS.
50. Longstreet's report, OR, vol. 27, part 2, 357.
   EPA's report, OR, vol. 27, part 2, 429.
   EPA, *Fighting*, 223–24.
51. EPA, *Fighting*, 227.

Longstreet's report, OR, vol. 27, part 2, 357–58.

EPA's report, OR, vol. 27, part 2, 429.

52. EPA, *Fighting*, 227–28.

53. EPA, *Fighting*, 229.

54. Nash, *Forty-fourth New York*, 230.

John Chamberlain diary, 47–48, PHS.

Gerrish, *Army Life*, 99.

George Sykes's report, OR, vol. 27, part 1, 592.

55. Longstreet's report, OR, vol. 27, part 2, 358.

EPA, *Fighting*, 229–30.

56. Nash, *Forty-fourth New York*, 143.

Carter, *Four Brothers*, 296–98.

John Chamberlain diary, 48–49, PHS.

JLC, "Blood and Fire," 894–95.

57. Powell, *Fifth Army Corps*, 513.

Gerrish, *Army Life*, 101.

John Chamberlain diary, 50, PHS.

JLC, "Blood and Fire," 896.

58. Powell, *Fifth Army Corps*, 513.

EPA, *Fighting*, 235.

CHAPTER 7. APOTHEOSIS

Gettysburg, July 2–3, 1863

1. Nash, *Forty-fourth New York*, 143.

Powell, *Fifth Army Corps*, 513.

JLC, "Blood and Fire," 896.

2. JLC, "Blood and Fire," 896.

George Meade's report, OR, vol. 27, part 1, 115.

3. Henry J. Hunt, "The Second Day at Gettysburg," in B&L, vol. 3, 296–97.

Nash, *Forty-fourth New York*, 143.

JLC, "Blood and Fire," 897.

John Geary's report, OR, vol. 27, part 1, 825.

4. JLC, "Blood and Fire," 897.

Hunt, "Second Day at Gettysburg," 301.

James Rice's supplementary report, OR, vol. 27, part 1, 621.

5. JLC's report, OR, vol. 27, part 1, 622.
Gerrish, *Army Life*, 105.
JLC, "Blood and Fire," 897–98.
First quotation is from JLC, manuscript fragment (possibly part of a postwar lecture), BC.
Second quotation is from Charles Francis Adams, Jr., *An Autobiography* (Boston, 1916), 135–36.

6. Meade's report, OR, vol. 27, part 1, 116.
Hunt, "Second Day at Gettysburg," 304.
Norton, *Attack and Defense*, 262–63.

7. Hunt, "Second Day at Gettysburg," 304.
Norton, *Attack and Defense*, 262–63.
Meade's report, OR, vol. 27, part 1, 116.

8. Hunt, "Second Day at Gettysburg," 307.
G. K. Warren to Porter Farley, July 13, 1872, quoted in Norton, *Attack and Defense*, 309.

9. Norton, *Attack and Defense*, 38.
G. K. Warren to Porter Farley, July 13, 1872, quoted in Norton, *Attack and Defense*, 309–10.
Hunt, "Second Day at Gettysburg," 305.

10. JLC's report, OR, vol. 27, part 1, 622–23.
JLC, "Blood and Fire," 898.
Maine at Gettysburg, 253.

11. EPA, *Fighting*, 235.
EPA's report, OR, vol. 27, part 2, 429.
EPA to James Longstreet, February 5, 1878, AP.

12. EPA *Fighting*, 235.
EPA to Adam L. Alexander, July 17, 1863, AHP.

13. EPA, *Fighting*, 235, 237.
Douglas Southall Freeman, *Lee's Lieutenants*, vol. 3 (New York, 1946), 115.
First quotation is from Sorrel, *Recollections*, 157.
Longstreet's report, OR, vol. 27, part 2, 358.

14. EPA, *Fighting*, 236–37.
Wise, *Long Arm of Lee*, 636, 642.
Longstreet's report, OR, vol. 27, part 2, 358.
EPA, "Letter," SHSP 4 (1877), 102.
EPA, *Military Memoirs*, 392.
Evander M. Law, "The Struggle for 'Round Top,'" B&L, vol. 3, 320.

15. EPA's report, OR, vol. 27, part 2, 429.
   EPA to Adam L. Alexander, July 17, 1863, AHP.
   EPA, *Fighting*, 239.
   O. B. Taylor's report, OR, vol. 27, part 2, 432.
   Henry Cabell's report, OR, vol. 27, part 2, 375.
16. James A. L. Fremantle, *Three Months in the Southern States* (New York, 1970 reprint), 239.
   John B. Hood, "Letter to James Longstreet," SHSP 4, 149.
   Law, "Struggle for 'Round Top,' " 321.
17. Hood, "Letter to Longstreet," 150.
   Law, "Struggle for 'Round Top,' 322.
18. Law, "Struggle for 'Round Top,' " 322.
19. Law, "Struggle for 'Round Top,' 324.
   EPA, "Confederate Artillery Service," 105.
   EPA, *Fighting*, 240.
   EPA, "The Great Charge and Artillery Fighting at Gettysburg," B&L, vol. 3, 360.
20. EPA, *Fighting*, 240.
   EPA to Adam L. Alexander, July 17, 1863, AHP.
   EPA, "Official Report" (expanded version of the report in OR, dated August 10, 1863), SHSP 4, 236.
21. Sorrel, *Recollections*, 159.
   EPA, *Fighting*, 240.
22. EPA to Adam L. Alexander, July 17, 1863, AHP.
   EPA's pocket diary, AP.
23. JLC, "Blood and Fire," 898.
   Norton, *Attack and Defense*, 263–64.
24. Quotations are from Norton, *Attack and Defense*, 264.
25. JLC, "Blood and Fire," 898.
   Nash, *Forty-fourth New York*, 144.
   Gerrish, *Army Life*, 106.
   Maine at Gettysburg, 253.
26. JLC, "Blood and Fire," 898–99.
   Gerrish, *Army Life*, 106.
27. JLC's report, OR, vol. 27, part 1, 623.
   John Chamberlain diary, 51–52, PHS.
   L. L. Miller to JLC, May 21, 1895, LC.
   JLC, "Blood and Fire," 899.
28. Rice's report, OR, vol. 27, part 1, 616.

JLC, "Blood and Fire," 899.

JLC's report, OR, vol. 27, part 1, 623.

29. JLC, "Blood and Fire," 900.

JLC's report, OR, vol. 27, part 1, 623.

Maine at Gettysburg, 254.

JLC to Governor Coburn, August 27, 1863, MSA.

30. JLC, "Blood and Fire," 900.

G. K. Warren to Porter Farley, July 13, 1872, in Norton, *Attack and Defense,* 309–10.

Foote, *The Civil War,* vol. 2, 503.

31. JLC, "Blood and Fire," 901–902.

JLC's report, OR, vol. 27, part 1, 623.

32. William C. Oates, *The War between the Union and the Confederacy and Its Lost Opportunities* (New York, 1905), 210–12.

Oates, "The Battle on the Right," SHSP 6 (1878), 175.

33. *Maine at Gettysburg,* 255.

JLC, "Blood and Fire," 902.

JLC's report, OR, vol. 27, part 1, 623.

Ellis Spear to JLC, May 22, 1895, LC.

34. Oates, *War between the Union and Confederacy,* 214.

35. Norton, *Attack and Defense,* 260.

Rice's report, OR, vol. 27, part 1, 617.

Augustus P. Martin to JLC, October 21, 1865, LC.

36. Ellis Spear to JLC, July 2, 1882, LC.

JLC's report, OR, vol. 27, part 1, 623–24.

Oates, "Battle on the Right," 176.

Gerrish, *Army Life,* 108.

37. JLC, "Blood and Fire," 903.

G. K. Warren to Porter Farley, December 22, 1877, quoted in Norton, *Attack and Defense,* 328.

38. JLC, "Blood and Fire," 903.

Oates, *War between the Union and Confederacy,* 218–19.

Gerrish, *Army Life,* 109.

JLC's report, OR, vol. 27, part 1, 624.

39. JLC's report, OR, vol. 27, part 1, 624.

Quotation is from JLC, "Blood and Fire," 905.

40. Oates, *War between the Union and Confederacy,* 218.

Oates, "Battle on the Right," 177.

41. JLC, "Blood and Fire," 905.

42. Oates, *War between the Union and Confederacy*, 218.
   JLC's report, OR, vol. 27, part 1, 624.
   Maine at Gettysburg, 262.
43. JLC, "Blood and Fire," 905.
   Oates, *War between the Union and Confederacy*, 219–20.
   JLC's report, OR, vol. 27, part 1, 624.
   Maine at Gettysburg, 257.
44. JLC, "Blood and Fire," 906.
   JLC's report, OR, vol. 27, part 1, 624.
45. Gerrish, *Army Life*, 110.
   Nash, *Forty-fourth New York*, 146.
   JLC's report, OR, vol. 27, part 1, 624.
46. Oates, *War between the Union and Confederacy*, 220.
47. JLC, "Blood and Fire," 908.
   JLC's report, OR, vol. 27, part 1, 625.
   Maine at Gettysburg, 259.
48. JLC's report, OR, vol. 27, part 1, 626.
   John Chamberlain diary, 53–55, PHS.
49. Rice's report, OR, vol. 27, part 1, 618.
   Oates, *War between the Union and Confederacy*, 220.
   OR, vol. 27, part 2, 338–40.
   Oates to Elihu Root, June 2, 1903, LC.
   JLC to Governor Coburn, July 21, 1863, MSA.
   OR, vol. 27, part 1, 178–79.
50. Law, "The Struggle for 'Round Top,'" 326.
   JLC's report, OR, vol. 27, part 1, 625.
   Rice's report, OR, vol. 27, part 1, 619.
51. *Maine at Gettysburg*, 259.
   JLC's field notes, quoted in Spear, "Historical Sketch," 84.
   JLC to Governor Coburn, July 21, 1863, MSA.
   JLC's report, OR, vol. 27, part 1, 625–26.
52. JLC's report, OR, vol. 27, part 1, 626.
   Oates, *War between the Union and Confederacy*, 219.
   Adelbert Ames to JLC, July 3, 1863, PHS.
   JLC to Frances Chamberlain, July 4 and 17, 1863, LC.
53. JLC to Governor Coburn, August 7, 1863, MSA.
   John Chamberlain diary, 71, PHS.
54. JLC to Frances Chamberlain, July 4, 1863, LC.
   JLC's report, OR, vol. 27, part 1, 626.

55. EPA, *Fighting*, 243–44.
56. EPA, *Fighting*, 244.
EPA to Adam L. Alexander, July 17, 1863, AHP.
B. F. Eshleman to EPA, February 5, 1876, AP.
EPA, "The Great Charge," 361.
William Pendleton's report, OR, vol. 27, part 2, 352.
57. EPA, "The Great Charge," 361–62.
Wise, *Long Arm of Lee*, 664.
Owen, *Washington Artillery*, 247.
EPA, *Fighting*, 247.
EPA to Adam L. Alexander, July 17, 1863, AHP.
58. EPA, *Fighting*, 246, 254.
EPA, "Letter," 103.
59. EPA, *Fighting*, 251.
Wise, *Long Arm of Lee*, 666–67.
Owen, *Washington Artillery*, 247.
EPA, *Military Memoirs*, 419.
60. EPA, *Fighting*, 254.
Fremantle, *Three Months in the Southern States*, 275.
61. EPA, *Fighting*, 255.
Longstreet, "Lee's Right Wing at Gettysburg," B&L, vol. 3, 339, 342–43.
62. Original in the Edward Porter Alexander Folder, Miscellaneous Manuscript Collection, LC.
63. EPA, *Fighting*, 254.
EPA, *Military Memoirs*, 421.
64. Handwritten copy of note in AP.
65. Original in Alexander folder, LC.
66. EPA, *Military Memoirs*, 421.
A. R. Wright's report, OR, vol. 27, part 2, 623–24.
EPA, *Fighting*, 255.
67. EPA, *Fighting*, 255.
EPA, "Letter," 105.
68. Sorrel, *Recollections*, 48.
Fremantle, *Three Months in the Southern States*, 247.
EPA, *Fighting*, 255.
Handwritten copy of note in AP.
69. EPA, *Fighting*, 257.
William M. Owen to EPA, January 29, 1878, AP.
70. EPA, "Letter," 106–107.

Henry L. Hunt, "The Third Day at Gettysburg," B&L, vol. 3, 372–73.

George R. Stewart, *Pickett's Charge: A Microhistory of the Final Attack at Gettysburg, July 3, 1863* (Boston, 1959), 135, 159.

EPA, *Fighting*, 258.

Copy of note in AP.

71. EPA, *Fighting*, 249.

EPA to Adam L. Alexander, July 17, 1863, AHP.

72. EPA to Adam L. Alexander, July 17, 1863, AHP.

EPA, *Fighting*, 259.

EPA, "The Great Charge," 364.

Copy of note in AP.

73. Henry Hunt's report, OR, vol. 27, part 1, 240.

John Hazard's report, vol. 27, part 1, 480.

Wise, *Long Arm of Lee*, 679.

Hunt, "Third Day at Gettysburg," 373.

74. EPA, *Fighting*, 261.

EPA to Adam L. Alexander, July 17, 1863, AHP.

75. EPA, *Fighting*, 261.

Longstreet, "Lee's Right Wing," 345.

EPA, "Official Report," 239.

EPA, *Military Memoirs*, 424.

76. EPA, *Fighting*, 262.

EPA, "Letter," 108.

EPA, "Official Report," 239.

EPA to Adam L. Alexander, July 17, 1863, AHP.

77. Longstreet, "Lee's Right Wing," 343.

EPA, *Fighting*, 262.

John Haskell to EPA, September 7, 1901, AP.

78. George Stannard's report, OR, vol. 27, part 1, 350.

EPA, *Fighting*, 264.

Stewart, *Pickett's Charge*, 207.

EPA, *Military Memoirs*, 425.

EPA, "Letter," 108.

79. Stewart, *Pickett's Charge*, 246–47.

EPA, *Fighting*, 265.

EPA, "Letter," 109.

80. EPA, *Fighting*, 266.

Fremantle, *Three Months in the Southern States*, 267–69.
EPA to Adam L. Alexander, July 17, 1863, AHP.

81. EPA, *Fighting*, 266.
EPA to James Longstreet, February 5, 1878, AP.
Wise, *Long Arm of Lee*, 693.
EPA to Adam L. Alexander, July 17,, 1863, AHP.

82. JLC's report, OR, vol. 27, part 1, 626.
JLC manuscript fragment, BC.
JLC to Frances Chamberlain, July 17, 1863, LC.

83. JLC's report, OR, vol. 27, part 1, 626.
JLC, "Blood and Fire," 909.
J. B. Wescott to JLC, February 1896, LC.
John Chamberlain diary, 56–57.

84. JLC's report, OR, vol. 27, part 1, 626.
John Chamberlain diary, 59–62.

85. John Chamberlain diary, 62–70.

86. JLC to Frances Chamberlain, July 21, 1863, LC.
JLC to John Hodsdon, July 11, 1863, MSA.
Atherton Clark's report, OR, vol. 27, part 1, 627.

87. Sorrel to EPA, July 4, 1863, AP.
EPA to Adam L. Alexander, July 17, 1863, AHP.
EPA, *Military Memoirs*, 437.

88. EPA, *Military Memoirs*, 437.
EPA, "The Great Charge," 367.
EPA to Bettie Alexander, July 26, 1863, AP.
EPA, *Fighting*, 267–68.

89. EPA, *Fighting*, 268.
EPA's pocket diary, AP.
EPA to Bettie Alexander, July 26, 1863, AP.

90. EPA, *Fighting*, 270–71.
EPA's pocket diary, AP.

91. EPA, *Fighting*, 272.
EPA to Adam L. Alexander, July 17, 1863, AHP.

92. Powell, *Fifth Army Corps*, 567.
JLC to Frances Chamberlain, September 12, 1863, LC.
EPA to Adam L. Alexander, July 17, 1863, AHP.

Chapter 8. Barren Winter

Alexander: East Tennessee, 1863–64

1. EPA to Adam L. Alexander, July 17, 1863, AP.
   EPA to William Felix Alexander, July 26, 1863, AP.
   OR, vol. 27, part 2, 428–29.
2. EPA, *Fighting*, 268, 273, 285.
   Ella Lonn, *Foreigners in the Confederacy* (Chapel Hill, N.C., 1940), 185.
3. Quotation is from EPA, "Personal Recollections of Knoxville Campaign,"
   typescript, EPA folder, LC (hereafter, "Knoxville").
   EPA, *Fighting*, 285.
   EPA's pocket diary, AP.
4. Longstreet, *Memoirs*, 433–34.
   EPA, *Military Memoirs*, 448.
   Robert C. Black III, *The Railroads of the Confederacy* (Chapel Hill, N.C.,
   1952), 188.
5. Longstreet, *Memoirs*, 436.
   Sorrel, *Recollections*, 181.
   EPA, *Military Memoirs*, 447–49.
   Black, *Railroads*, 191.
   EPA, *Fighting*, 287, 298.
6. EPA, *Military Memoirs*, 449.
   EPA, *Fighting*, 287.
   Mary Clifford Hull to EPA, October 1, 1863, AP.
   EPA to Adam L. Alexander, September 30, 1863, AHP.
7. EPA to Adam L. Alexander, September 30, 1863, AP.
   EPA, *Fighting*, 301–305.
   EPA's pocket diary, AP.
   EPA, "Confederate Artillery Service," 108.
   EPA, "Longstreet at Knoxville," B&L, vol. 3, 746.
8. EPA, *Fighting*, 301.
   Mary Clifford Hull to EPA, October 1, 1863, AP.
9. Longstreet, *Memoirs*, 466.
   EPA, *Fighting*, 305–307.
   Charles M. Blackford, *Letters from Lee's Army*, Susan L. Blackford, ed.
   (New York, 1947), 219, 221.
   James Longstreet to EPA, August 26, 1902, AP.
10. EPA, *Fighting*, 305–306.

EPA, *Military Memoirs*, 480.

Foote, *The Civil War*, vol. 2, 818.

Longstreet's report, OR, vol. 31, part 1, 455.

11. Longstreet's report, OR, vol. 31, part 1, 455.

Longstreet, *Memoirs*, 480–81.

EPA, *Military Memoirs*, 480.

12. Longstreet to EPA, November 3, 1863, AP.

Blackford, *Letters from Lee's Army*, 215.

EPA, *Fighting*, 312–13.

EPA, *Military Memoirs*, 481.

13. Longstreet's report, OR, vol. 31, part 1, 455–56.

EPA, *Fighting*, 315.

14. EPA's pocket diary, AP.

EPA, *Fighting*, 315–16.

Longstreet's report, OR, vol. 31, part 1, 457.

Sorrel, *Recollections*, 202.

EPA's report, OR, vol. 31, part 1, 478.

15. EPA, *Fighting*, 318.

Longstreet's report, OR, vol. 31, part 1, 458.

16. EPA, *Fighting*, 319.

EPA's report, OR, vol. 31, part 1, 478–79.

EPA, "Longstreet at Knoxville," B&L, 3, 747.

17. EPA, *Fighting*, 319–20.

EPA's report, OR, vol. 31, part 1, 479.

Orlando M. Poe, "The Defense of Knoxville," B&L, 3, 737.

18. EPA, *Fighting*, 321.

19. EPA, *Fighting*, 322–23.

Longstreet's report, OR, vol. 31, part 1, 459.

EPA's report, OR, vol. 31, part 1, 479.

20. EPA, *Fighting*, 324.

Longstreet's report, OR, vol. 31, part 1, 460.

EPA's report, OR, vol. 31, part 1, 479.

21. EPA, *Fighting*, 324.

EPA, *Military Memoirs*, 485.

22. EPA, *Fighting*, 325–27.

EPA, *Military Memoirs*, 486–87.

EPA's report, OR, vol. 31, part 1, 479.

23. EPA, "Longstreet at Knoxville," B&L, 3, 748–49.

EPA, *Fighting*, 324, 327–28.

EPA's report, OR, vol. 31, part 1, 479.

Longstreet's report, OR, vol. 31, part 1, 461.

EPA's testimony, OR, vol. 31, part 1, 488.

24. Return of casualties, OR, vol. 31, part 1, 475.

Longstreet's report, OR, vol. 31, part 1, 461.

EPA, *Military Memoirs*, 490.

25. EPA's pocket diary, AP.

Longstreet's report, OR, vol. 31, part 1, 462.

EPA, *Fighting*, 331.

EPA, "Knoxville."

EPA, *Military Memoirs*, 491.

26. Longstreet, *Memoirs*, 520.

EPA, *Fighting*, 332–33.

27. Bell I. Wiley, *Southern Negroes, 1861–1865* (New Haven, Conn., 1938), 25–30, 46.

Clarence L. Mohr, *On the Threshold of Freedom: Masters and Slaves in Civil War Georgia* (Athens, Ga., 1986), 211.

28. Adam L. Alexander to "My Dear Child" (either Alice or Marion Alexander), January 31, 1864, AHP.

EPA, *Fighting*, 334.

29. EPA, *Fighting*, 334–35.

Jeffry D. Wert, *General James Longstreet: The Confederacy's Most Controversial Soldier* (New York, 1993), 360–62.

EPA to Bessie Alexander, March 17, 1864, AHP.

30. Sarah Lawton to Adam L. Alexander, February 29, 1864, AHP.

Owen, *Washington Artillery*, 296.

EPA, *Fighting*, 335.

31. EPA to Bettie Alexander, February 21, 1864, AP.

EPA, *Fighting*, 335.

32. Joseph E. Johnston, *Narrative of Military Operations* (New York, 1874), 288.

Pendleton, *Memoirs*, 310.

EPA, *Fighting*, 335–36.

EPA to Bettie Alexander, February 21, 1864, AP.

33. Johnston, *Narrative*, 288–89.

EPA, *Fighting*, 336.

EPA to Bettie Alexander, February 27 and March 29, 1864, AP.

34. Adam L. Alexander to Marion Alexander, February 21, 1864, AHP.

Copy of War Department order, March 1, 1864, AP.

Owen, *Washington Artillery*, 309.

EPA's pocket diary, AP.

35. Sorrel, *Recollections*, 309.

EPA to Bettie Alexander, March 7 and 17, 1864, AP.

EPA, *Fighting*, 337–38.

36. EPA to Bettie Alexander, March 7 and 17, 1864, AP.

37. EPA to Bettie Alexander, March 23, 1864, AP.

38. EPA to Bettie Alexander, March 23, 1864, AP.

EPA, *Fighting*, 340–42.

39. Longstreet, *Memoirs*, 544–45.

Blackford, *Letters from Lee's Army*, 231.

EPA to Bettie Alexander, March 17 and 29 and April 1, 1864, AP.

EPA, *Fighting*, 342.

EPA's pocket diary, AP.

40. EPA, *Fighting*, 343.

EPA to Bettie Alexander, April 3 and 10, 1864, AP.

41. Sorrel, *Recollections*, 220.

EPA to Bettie Alexander, April 11 and 24, 1864, AP.

EPA's pocket diary, AP.

42. Longstreet, *Memoirs*, 548.

EPA, *Military Memoirs*, 493.

Chamberlain: Virginia, Home, and Washington, 1863–64

1. Powell, *Fifth Army Corps*, 567.

Carter, *Four Brothers*, 337.

2. McPherson, *Battle Cry of Freedom*, 610–11.

Foote, *The Civil War*, vol. 2, 636–37.

Powell, *Fifth Army Corps*, 571.

Quotation is from Carter, *Four Brothers*, 336.

3. JLC to Frances Chamberlain, July 17, 1863, LC.

JLC to Deborah Folsom, June 15, 1863, LC.

4. OR, vol. 27, part 1, 621–22.

Carter, *Four Brothers*, 338.

5. Gerrish, *Army Life*, 121–22.

Carter, *Four Brothers*, 340.

Quotation is from Norton, *Army Letters*, 166.

6. JLC to Governor Coburn, July 21 and August 7, 1863, MSA.

James Rice to JLC, August 11, 1863, LC.

JLC Service Records, NA.

7. George Adams diaries, August 6, 1863, FPC.

JLC Service Records, NA.

James Rice to JLC, August 11, 1863, LC.

8. JLC to Governor Coburn, August 25, 1863, MSA.

JLC Service Records, NA.

Norton, *Army Letters*, 176.

Maine AGR, 1864 and 1865, 332.

9. OR, vol. 29, part 2, 102–103.

Powell, *Fifth Army Corps*, 573n.

10. Gerrish, *Army Life*, 124–28.

Carter, *Four Brothers*, 346–47.

Powell, *Fifth Army Corps*, 571–73.

11. Sarah (Sae) Chamberlain to JLC, September 12, 1863, RC.

JLC to Governor Coburn, September 19, 1863, MSA.

Last quotation is from Carter, *Four Brothers*, 348.

12. JLC to Frances Chamberlain, August 31, 1863, LC.

13. Charles Griffin to Seth Williams, October 7, 1863, MSA.

James Rice to William Pitt Fessenden, September 8, 1863, LC.

Hannibal Hamlin to President Lincoln, October 16, 1863, BC.

14. Maine AGR, 1864 and 1865, 332.

JLC, *Passing of the Armies*, xiv.

Malone, ed., *DAB*, vol. 6, 617–18.

G. K. Warren to JLC, November 12, 1879, LC.

15. OR, vol. 29, part 1, 221.

JLC to Governor Coburn, August 25 and October 28, 1863, MSA.

Charlotte E. McKay, *Stories of Hospital and Camp* (Philadelphia, 1971 reprint), 38.

16. Powell, *Fifth Army Corps*, 575–76.

Carter, *Four Brothers*, 353–54.

17. Gerrish, *Army Life*, 123.

18. McKay, *Stories of Hospital and Camp*, 68–77.

19. Norton, *Army Letters*, 189.

JLC's report, OR, vol. 29, part 1, 581–82.

20. Horatio Wright's report, OR, vol. 29, part 1, 585–86.

JLC's report, OR, vol. 29, part 1, 582.

Norton, *Army Letters*, 291.

Kenner Garrard's report, OR, vol. 29, part 1, 578.

Joseph J. Bartlett's report, OR, vol. 29, part 1, 579.

21. Maine AGR, 1864 and 1865, 332.

JLC's report, OR, vol. 29, part 1, 582.

Wright's report, OR, vol. 29, part 1, 584–85.

22. O. S. Woodward's report, OR, vol. 29, part 1, 583.

Bartlett's report, OR, vol. 29, part 1, 579.

OR, vol. 29, part 1, 576.

23. JLC's report, OR, vol. 29, part 1, 582.

Norton, *Army Letters*, 190.

Carter, *Four Brothers*, 364.

24. Little, ed., *Genealogical and Family History*, vol. 1, 135.

U.S. Surgeon General's Office, *The Medical and Surgical History of the War of the Rebellion*, (Washington, 1870–88), vol. 1, part 3, 77, 89, 120.

25. George W. Adams, *Doctors in Blue: The Medical History of the Union Army in the Civil War* (New York, 1952), 227–28.

Medical and Surgical History, vol. 1, part 3, 184–85.

26. William E. Donnell to Frances Chamberlain, November 16, 1863, LC.

JLC Service Records, NA.

George Adams diaries, November 21, 1863, FPC.

Maine AGR, 1864 and 1865, 333.

Adams, *Doctors in Blue*, 171.

27. Prentiss M. Fogler to JLC, December 21, 1863, LC.

C. C. Hayes to JLC, December 26, 1863, LC.

28. JLC Service Records, NA.

George Adams diaries, January 15 and February 11, 1864, FPC.

Margaret Leech, *Reveille in Washington, 1860–1865* (New York, 1941), 313.

Frances Chamberlain to JLC, March 8, 1866, RC.

29. Frances Chamberlain to Deborah Folsom, with postscript by JLC, April 14, 1864, LC.

Garrick Mallory to JLC, March 18, 1880, LC.

30. JLC to E. D. Townsend, May 9, 1864, copy in PHS.

Frances Chamberlain to Deborah Folsom, n.d. (by contents, early May 1864), LC.

JLC Service Records, NA.

31. Frances Chamberlain to Deborah Folsom, n.d. (by contents, early May 1864), LC.

Little, ed., *Genealogical and Family History*, vol. 1, 135.

CHAPTER 9. THE ENDLESS WAR

Alexander: End Game, May–June 1864

1. EPA, *Fighting*, 349.
   OR, vol. 36, part 2, 947.
2. EPA to Bettie Alexander, April 20 and May 2, 1864, AP.
   EPA, *Military Memoirs*, 496.
3. Pendleton's report, OR, vol. 36, part 1, 1022.
   OR, vol. 36, part 2, 959.
   EPA to Bettie Alexander, May 4, 1864, AP.
   EPA to Adam L. Alexander, May 29, 1864, AP.
   EPA's pocket diary, AP.
4. EPA, *Fighting*, 348–49.
   EPA, *Military Memoirs*, 495.
5. Longstreet's report, OR, vol. 36, part 1, 1055.
   Longstreet, *Memoirs*, 557–59.
   Sorrel, *Recollections*, 229.
   EPA, *Fighting*, 354–56.
6. Longstreet's report, OR, vol. 36, part 1, 1055.
   EPA to Adam L. Alexander, May 29, 1864, AP.
   EPA, *Fighting*, 357.
7. EPA, *Fighting*, 358.
   Longstreet's report, OR, vol. 36, part 1, 1055.
   John Cheves Haskell, *The Haskell Memoirs*, Gilbert E. Govan and
   James W. Livingood, eds. (New York, 1960), 63.
8. EPA to Adam L. Alexander, May 29, 1864, AP.
   EPA, *Fighting*, 359.
   Longstreet, *Memoirs*, 562.
9. Longstreet's report, OR, vol. 36, part 1, 1055.
   EPA, *Fighting*, 359.
   Sorrel, *Recollections*, 232.
   EPA to Adam L. Alexander, May 29, 1864, AP.
10. EPA to Adam L. Alexander, May 29, 1864, AP.
    EPA, *Fighting*, 359.
11. EPA to Adam L. Alexander, May 29, 1864, AP.
    Sorrel, *Recollections*, 233.
    EPA, *Fighting*, 359–61.

12. Longstreet's report, OR, vol. 36, part 1, 1055.
    Longstreet, *Memoirs*, 564–65.
13. Sorrel, *Recollections*, 226.
    EPA, *Fighting*, 363.
    EPA to Bettie Alexander, May 19, 1864, AP.
14. EPA, *Fighting*, 365–66.
    EPA to Adam L. Alexander, May 29, 1864, AP.
    EPA's pocket diary, AP.
    Ulyssess S. Grant, *Personal Memoirs of U.S. Grant* (New York, 1990 ed.), 540.
15. EPA, *Fighting*, 365–66.
    Sorrel, *Recollections*, 242.
16. EPA, *Fighting*, 366.
    EPA to Adam L. Alexander, May 29, 1864, AP.
    Charles A. Dana's dispatches, OR, vol. 36, part 1, 64.
17. EPA to Adam L. Alexander, May 29, 1864, AP.
    EPA, *Fighting*, 369.
    EPA's pocket diary, AP.
18. EPA, *Fighting*, 369–70.
19. Gouverneur K. Warren's journal, OR, vol. 36, part 1, 541.
    EPA, *Military Memoirs*, 511–12.
    EPA, *Fighting*, 369–70
    EPA to Bettie Alexander, May 19, 1864, AP.
20. EPA, *Fighting*, 370–71, 374.
    EPA to Adam L. Alexander, May 29, 1864, AP.
    EPA to Bettie Alexander, May 19, 1864, AP.
21. EPA, *Military Memoirs*, 516.
    EPA, *Fighting*, 372.
    Grant, *Memoirs*, 546.
22. Warren's journal, OR, vol. 36, part 1, 541.
    EPA, *Fighting*, 273.
    EPA, *Military Memoirs*, 515.
    EPA to Adam L. Alexander, May 29, 1864, AP.
23. EPA to Bettie Alexander, May 19, 1864, AP.
    EPA to Adam L. Alexander, May 29, 1864, AP.
    EPA, *Fighting*, 374.
24. Pendleton's report, OR, vol. 36, part 1, 1044.
    EPA, *Fighting*, 374.
    EPA to Adam L. Alexander, May 29, 1864, AP.

25. EPA to Adam L. Alexander, May 29, 1864, AP.
    EPA, *Fighting*, 376.
    Pendleton's report, OR, vol. 36, part 1, 1044.
    Andrew A. Humphreys, *The Virginia Campaigns of '64 and '65: The Army of the Potomac and the Army of the James* (New York, 1883), 95.
26. EPA, *Fighting*, 376–77.
    EPA, *Military Memoirs*, 523.
27. Grant, *Memoirs*, 554.
    EPA, *Military Memoirs*, 522.
28. Horace Porter, *Campaigning with Grant*, (New York, 1897), 107–108.
    Dana's dispatches, OR, vol. 36, part 1, 68.
    EPA, *Military Memoirs*, 523–24.
29. EPA, *Fighting*, 378.
    Humphreys, *The Virginia Campaigns*, 100–101.
    EPA, *Military Memoirs*, 524.
30. EPA, *Military Memoirs*, 526.
    EPA, *Fighting*, 380.
31. EPA, *Fighting*, 380.
    EPA, *Military Memoirs*, 526–27.
    EPA's pocket journal, AP.
    Warren's journal, OR, vol. 36, part 1, 542.
    Grant, *Memoirs*, 557.
32. Blackford, *Letters from Lee's Army*, 245.
    EPA to Bettie Alexander, May 19, 1864, AP.
    EPA, *Fighting*, 382.
    Dana's dispatches, OR, vol. 36, part 1, 73.
33. Humphreys, *The Virginia Campaigns*, 117.
    Grant, *Memoirs*, 560.
    EPA, *Military Memoirs*, 529.
34. EPA to Adam L. Alexander, May 29, 1864, AP.
    EPA, *Fighting*, 387–88.
    EPA's pocket diary, AP.
35. EPA, *Fighting*, 388–90.
    EPA to Bettie Alexander, May 28, 1864, AP.
    EPA, *Military Memoirs*, 531.
36. EPA, *Fighting*, 89–90.
37. Humphreys, *The Virginia Campaigns*, 117.
    EPA, *Fighting*, 390.
    Grant, *Memoirs*, 568–69.

38. Grant, *Memoirs*, 574–75.
   EPA, *Fighting*, 397.
39. EPA to Bettie Alexander, June 10, 1864, AP.
   EPA, *Fighting*, 398–99.
   EPA, *Military Memoirs*, 534–37.
   Humphreys, *The Virginia Campaigns*, 173.
40. EPA, *Military Memoirs*, 536.
   EPA, *Fighting*, 399–400.
41. EPA, *Fighting*, 400–401.
   EPA to Bettie Alexander, June 10, 1864, AP.
   Grant, *Memoirs*, 583.
42. EPA, *Fighting*, 404–406.
   EPA to Bettie Alexander, June 10, 1864, AP.
   Grant, *Memoirs*, 584.
   Joseph Kershaw to G. M. Sorrel, June 3, 1864, copy in AP.
   Haskell, *Memoirs*, 69.
   Humphreys, *The Virginia Campaigns*, 182.
43. Blackford, *Letters from Lee's Army*, 246.
   Foote, *The Civil War*, vol. 3, 299.
   EPA, *Fighting*, 407.
44. EPA, *Fighting*, 410–11.
45. EPA, *Fighting*, 413.
   Blackford, *Letters from Lee's Army*, 252.
46. EPA, *Fighting*, 419–20.
   EPA's pocket diary, AP.
   Grant, *Memoirs*, 594–95.
   EPA, *Military Memoirs*, 549.
   Horace Porter, *Campaigning with Grant*, 195, 198.
47. EPA, *Military Memoirs*, 547.
   Porter, *Campaigning with Grant*, 197.
   EPA, *Fighting*, 421.
   H. J. Marrin to EPA, March 20, 1874, AP.
48. EPA, *Fighting*, 422.
   Grant, *Memoirs*, 600–601.
   Porter, *Campaigning with Grant*, 198.
   P. G. T. Beauregard to EPA, July 18, 1867, AP.
49. OR, vol. 40, part 1, 760–61.
   EPA, *Military Memoirs*, 545–46.
   EPA, *Fighting*, 422, 430–31.

Porter, *Campaigning with Grant*, 198.

EPA's pocket diary, AP.

50. EPA, *Military Memoirs*, 555.

OR, vol. 40, part 1, 761.

EPA, *Fighting*, 432.

Grant, *Memoirs*, 602.

Foote, *The Civil War*, vol. 3, 317.

Chamberlain: Slaughter Pens, May–October 1864

1. Pullen, *Twentieth Maine*, 194–95.

Maine at Gettysburg, 281.

Gerrish, *Army Life*, 170–71.

2. Carter, *Four Brothers*, 397.

Theodore Lyman, *Meade's Headquarters, 1863–1865*, George R. Agazziz, ed. (Boston, 1922), 109.

Gerrish, *Army Life*, 178.

Maine AGR, 1864–65, 333.

JLC, *Passing of the Armies*, 29.

JLC to Governor Samuel Cony, May 18, 1864, MSA.

3. JLC to Governor Cony, May 18, 1864, MSA.

Ellis Spear's report, OR, vol. 36, part 1, 574.

Charles Wainwright, *A Diary of Battle*, Allan Nevins, ed. (New York, 1962), 381.

OR, vol. 36, part 1, 550.

4. JLC, *Passing of the Armies*, 10, 255–56.

5. *JLC: A Sketch*, 15–16.

Pullen, *Twentieth Maine*, 203–204.

OR, vol. 36, part 1, 591–92.

6. Carter, *Four Brothers*, 408.

Wainwright, *Diary of Battle*, 378.

Grant, *Memoirs*, 541, 554.

Dana's dispatches, OR, vol. 36, part 1, 67.

Lyman, *Meade's Headquarters*, 110.

7. Gerrish, *Army Life*, 191.

Warren's journal, OR, vol. 36, part 1, 543.

Carter, *Four Brothers*, 408.

Humphreys, *Virginia Campaigns*, 129.

Grant, *Memoirs*, 569.

8. Warren's journal, OR, vol. 36, part 1, 543.
   Carter, *Four Brothers*, 409–11.
   Wainwright, *Diary of Battle*, 390–91.
9. Humphreys, *Virginia Campaigns*, 167–69.
   Wainwright, *Diary of Battle*, 396.
10. Spear's report, OR, vol. 36, part 1, 574.
    Carter, *Four Brothers*, 418, 424.
    Porter, *Campaigning with Grant*, 174–75.
    JLC, *Passing of the Armies*, 3.
11. JLC's service records, NA.
    OR, vol. 36, part 3, 520, 613, 652, 709.
    JLC to John Chamberlain, December 19, 1864, BC.
    Carter, *Four Brothers*, 428.
12. Maine AGR, 1864–65, 333.
    OR, vol. 40, part 1, 545.
    Horatio Warren to JLC, July 7, 1888, LC.
    Carter, *Four Brothers*, 419–20.
13. JLC, *Passing of the Armies*, 7.
    Lyman, *Meade's Headquarters*, 147.
    Wainwright, *Diary of Battle*, 409.
14. Warren's journal, OR, vol. 40, part 1, 453.
    Lyman, *Meade's Headquarters*, 164.
15. Maine AGR, 1864–65, 333.
    Carter, *Four Brothers*, 435–37.
16. Dana's dispatches, June 13–18, 1864, OR, vol. 40, part 1, 19.
    Grant to Henry W. Halleck, OR, vol. 40, part 2, 115.
    Warren's journal, OR, vol. 40, part 1, 453.
    Lyman, *Meade's Headquarters*, 163.
17. Lyman, *Meade's Headquarters*, 169.
    Dana's dispatches, OR, vol. 40, part 1, 24.
    Humphreys, *Virginia Campaigns*, 222.
18. OR, vol. 40, part 2, 176–79.
19. William Tilton's report, OR, vol. 40, part 1, 457.
    Patrick DeLacy, unpublished memoir, 3, LC (hereafter, "DeLacy ms.").
    JLC "Reminiscences of Petersburg and Appomattox," in Military
    Order of the Loyal Legion of the United States, *War Papers*, vol. 3
    (Portland, Maine, 1908), 171.
20. Maine AGR, 1864–65, 333.
    DeLacy ms., 3, LC.

Little, ed., *Genealogical History*, vol. 1, 136.

Brunswick *Record*, February 5, 1904, clipping in BC.

Horatio Warren to JLC, July 7, 1888, LC.

21. JLC, "Reminiscences of Petersburg and Appomattox," 171.

Maine AGR, 1864–65, 333.

DeLacy ms., 3–4, LC.

22. Charles Wainwright's report, OR, vol. 40, part 1, 482.

Wainwright, *Diary of Battle*, 424.

JLC, "Reminiscences of Petersburg and Appomattox," 171–72.

Lyman, *Meade's Headquarters*, 167.

23. Horatio Warren to JLC, July 7, 1888, LC.

DeLacy ms., 5, LC.

Brunswick *Record*, February 5, 1904, clipping in BC.

24. Maine AGR, 1864–65, 333.

JLC's note, headed "Lines before Petersburg, June 18, 1864," copy in MHS.

25. Horatio Warren to JLC, July 7, 1888, LC.

26. Oliver B. Knowles to JLC, December 15, 1865, LC.

OR, vol. 40, part 2, 187.

27. Horatio Warren to JLC, July 7, 1888, LC.

DeLacy ms., 4, LC.

28. DeLacy ms., 4–5, LC.

Horatio Warren to JLC, July 7, 1888, LC.

29. DeLacy ms., 6–7, LC.

Knowles to JLC, December 15, 1865, LC.

30. Wainwright, *Diary of Battle*, 425.

Warren to JLC, July 7, 1888, LC.

Carter, *Four Brothers*, 440.

Lyman, *Meade's Headquarters*, 170.

31. West Funk to Maine Legislature, n.d. (by contents, 1880), LC.

Maine AGR, 1864–65, 333.

Little, ed., *Genealogical History*, vol. 1, 136.

Patrick DeLacy to JLC, January 15, 1904, LC.

32. Horatio Warren to JLC, July 7, 1888, LC.

Tilton's report, OR, vol. 40, part 1, 457.

33. OR, vol. 40, part 2, 180, 182.

JLC, *Passing of the Armies*, 7.

34. M. L. Richardson to JLC, October 13, 1911, LC.

JLC, *Passing of the Armies*, 350.

OR, vol. 40, part 2, 217.

Little, ed., *Genealogical History*, vol. 1, 136.

Letter fragment, signature missing, September 5, 1910, LC.

35. Patrick DeLacy's account, quoted in Roberts, *Trending into Maine*, 49.

Letter fragment, September 5, 1910, LC.

JLC, *Passing of the Armies*, 352.

Medical and Surgical History, vol. 2, part 2, 363.

36. Little, ed., *Genealogical History*, vol. 1, 136.

Medical and Surgical History, vol. 2, part 2, 363.

JLC to Frances Chamberlain, June 19, 1864, BC.

37. *Medical and Surgical History*, vol. 2, part 2, 363.

Adams diaries, June 19, 1864, FPC.

JLC pension records, NA.

Telegram to John Chamberlain, June 21, 1864, BC.

Sarah (Sae) Chamberlain to JLC, June 23, 1864, RC.

38. Bowen, *Yankee from Olympus*, 185.

Medical and Surgical History, vol. 2, part 2, 363.

39. OR, vol. 40, part 2, 236.

Charles Gillmore to John Hodsdon, July 5, 1864, MSA.

40. John Chamberlain to John Hodsdon, July 22, 1864, MSA.

41. JLC to Samuel Cony, August 31, 1864, MSA.

McPherson, *Battle Cry of Freedom*, 770.

42. George Adams to JLC, September 6, 1864, RC.

43. George Adams to JLC, September 6, 1864, RC.

JLC to Samuel Cony, August 31, 1864, MSA.

44. JLC pension records, NA.

Medical and Surgical History, vol. 2, part 2, 363.

JLC, "Reminiscences of Petersburg and Appomattox," 176.

JLC to Sarah D. B. Chamberlain, n.d., but autumn 1864, BC.

Maine AGR, 1864–65, 334.

George Adams diaries, October 29, 1864, FPC.

CHAPTER 10. THE LAST CAMPAIGN

June 19, 1864–April 12, 1865

1. EPA, *Fighting*, 435.

EPA, *Military Memoirs*, 530.

2. Owen, *Washington Artillery*, 334.

EPA, *Fighting*, 441.

EPA to William Felix Alexander, June 27, 1864, AP.

3. Owen, *Washington Artillery*, 335.

EPA, *Fighting*, 445.

4. EPA to Bettie Alexander, July 1, 1864, AP.

Stephen Winthrop to EPA, October 4, 1874, AP.

EPA, *Fighting*, 446.

5. EPA to Bettie Alexander, July 1, 1864, AP.

EPA, *Fighting*, 445–46.

EPA, *Military Memoirs*, 563–64.

6. EPA's pocket diary, AP.

EPA, *Fighting*, 446, 468, 494.

7. EPA's diary, AP.

EPA to Bettie Alexander, August 14, 1864, AP.

EPA, *Fighting*, 468.

EPA to Bettie Alexander, August 28 and September 1, 1864, AP.

8. EPA to Bettie Alexander, August 28 and September 5, 7, and 15, 1864, AP.

9. EPA to Adam L. Alexander, September 22, 1864, AHP.

10. EPA, *Fighting*, 477–78.

EPA to Bettie Alexander, October 3, 1864, AP.

11. EPA, *Fighting*, 481–82.

12. EPA to Bettie Alexander, October 19 and November 7, 1864, AP.

EPA, *Fighting*, 462.

Howell quotation is from McPherson, *Battle Cry of Freedom*, 835.

John Haskell to EPA, May 7, 1907, AP.

13. EPA, *Fighting*, 491.

EPA to Bettie Alexander, December 25, 1864, AP.

14. EPA to Bettie Alexander, September 25, November 10, 11, 13, and 27, and December 4 and 25, 1864, AP.

15. EPA to Bettie Alexander, November 11 and 27 and December 4 and 25, 1864, AP.

Mary Clifford Hull to Louisa Gilmer, December 7, 1864, in Boggs, ed., *Alexander Letters*, 284.

16. EPA to Bettie Alexander, December 25, 1864, AP.

17. JLC, *Passing of the Armies*, 256–57.

Tom Chamberlain to John Chamberlain, December 18, 1864, BC.

18. Adelbert Ames to JLC, October 18, 1864, LC.

Lyman, *Meade's Headquarters*, 271.

JLC, *Passing of the Armies*, 17.

19. JLC, *Passing of the Armies*, 12.

Wainwright, *Diary of Battle*, 480.

20. Wainwright, *Diary of Battle*, 486.

Griffin's report, OR, vol. 42, part 1, 459.

21. JLC to Sarah (Sae) Chamberlain, December 14, 1864, BC.

Griffin's report, OR, vol. 42, part 1, 459.

Smyth, *Recollections and Reflections*, 59.

22. Smyth, *Recollections and Reflections*, 59.

Lyman, *Meade's Headquarters*, 296.

Wainwright, *Diary of Battle*, 489–90.

23. Wainwright, *Diary of Battle*, 491.

JLC to Sarah (Sae) Chamberlain, December 14, 1864, BC.

Griffin's report, OR, vol. 42, part 1, 460.

24. Tom Chamberlain to Sarah (Sae) Chamberlain, December 13, 1864, BC.

Tom Chamberlain to John Chamberlain, December 18, 1864, BC.

JLC to John Chamberlain, December 19, 1864, BC.

25. Sarah D. B. Chamberlain to JLC, January 1, (no year given; by contents, 1865), RC.

OR, vol. 46, part 2, 193.

George Adams diaries, January 16 and 20, 1865, FPC.

Trulock, *In the Hands of Providence*, 224.

26. EPA to Bettie Alexander, January 3, 1865, AP.

McKay, *Stories of Hospital and Camp*, 121.

27. EPA to Bettie Alexander, January 3, 1865, AP.

EPA, *Fighting*, 487.

28. EPA's pocket diary, AP.

EPA to Bettie Alexander, January 8, 1865, AP.

EPA, *Fighting*, 501.

29. EPA's pocket diary, AP.

EPA, *Fighting*, 505.

James M. McPherson, *Ordeal by Fire: The Civil War and Reconstruction* (New York, 1982), 469–70.

EPA to Bettie Alexander, July 29, 1897, AP.

30. EPA's pocket diary, AP.

EPA, *Fighting*, 505–506.

EPA, *Military Memoirs*, 574.

31. EPA to Bettie Alexander, March 2, 1865, AP.

32. EPA to Bettie Alexander, March 6, 10, 15, and 22, 1865, AP.
EPA, *Fighting*, 508.

33. EPA, *Fighting*, 501.
Sarah Lawton to Adam L. Alexander, March 5, 1865, AHP.
EPA to Bettie Alexander, March 22 and 26, 1865, AP.

34. EPA to Bettie Alexander, March 30 and April 1, 1865, AP.
Richard Harris Barham, *The Ingoldsby Legends*, D. C. Browning, ed.
(New York, 1960), 13.

35. Humphreys, *The Virginia Campaign*, 353.
EPA, *Fighting*, 515–17.

36. EPA to Bettie Alexander, April 3, 1865, AP.
EPA, *Fighting*, 517.
EPA, "Lee at Appomattox," *Century Illustrated Monthly Magazine* 64
(1902), 922.

37. EPA to Bettie Alexander, April 3, 1865, AP.
EPA, *Fighting*, 518.

38. EPA to Bettie Alexander, April 3, 1865, AP.
EPA, *Military Memoirs*, 595.
EPA, *Fighting*, 518–19.

39. EPA to Bettie Alexander, April 3, 1865, AP.
EPA, *Military Memoirs*, 595–96.
EPA, *Fighting*, 519.

40. EPA, *Fighting*, 519.
EPA to Bettie Alexander, April 3, 1865, AP.

41. JLC to Joshua Chamberlain, Jr., February 20, 1865, BC.
JLC to Sarah (Sae) Chamberlain, March 9, 1865, BC.

42. George Adams diaries, February 21, 1865, FPC.
JLC to Sarah (Sae) Chamberlain, March 9, 1865, BC.
Lyman, *Meade's Headquarters*, 316.

43. Grant, *Memoirs*, 695–96.
Humphreys, *The Virginia Campaign*, 325.
JLC, *Passing of the Armies*, 36.

44. Maine AGR, 1864–65, 335.
JLC, *Passing of the Armies*, 43–44.
JLC's report, OR, vol. 46, part 1, 847.

45. JLC, *Passing of the Armies*, 45–46.
JLC's report, OR, vol. 46, part 1, 848.
Wainwright, *Diary of Battle*, 507–508.

46. Maine AGR, 1864–65, 335.
JLC, *Passing of the Armies*, 46–47.

47. JLC, *Passing of the Armies*, 48.

48. JLC, *Passing of the Armies*, 50.
D. F. Wallace to JLC, March 29, 1884, LC.
JLC's report, OR, vol. 46, part 1, 848.

49. JLC, *Passing of the Armies*, 52–54.
Wainwright, *Diary of Battle*, 508.
Humphreys, *The Virginia Campaign*, 325.

50. JLC, *Passing of the Armies*, 56.
Wainwright, *Diary of Battle*, 508–509.
JLC's report, vol. 46, part 1, 848.

51. Maine AGR, 1864–65, 335.
JLC, *Passing of the Armies*, 50.

52. Grant, *Memoirs*, 697–98.
JLC, *Passing of the Armies*, 63–65.

53. Porter, *Campaigning with Grant*, 430.
JLC, *Passing of the Armies*, 66, 71–72.
Lyman, *Meade's Headquarters*, 330–31.
JLC's report, OR, vol. 46, part 1, 849.

54. Porter, *Campaigning with Grant*, 430.
Lyman, *Meade's Headquarters*, 331.
JLC's report, OR, vol. 46, part 1, 849.
Maine AGR, 1864–65, 335.
JLC, *Passing of the Armies*, 72–73.

55. JLC, *Passing of the Armies*, 74–75.
JLC's report, OR, vol. 46, part 1, 849.

56. Lyman, *Meade's Headquarters*, 331–32.
JLC, *Passing of the Armies*, 76–78.
JLC's report, OR, vol. 46, part 1, 849.

57. JLC, *Passing of the Armies*, 82–84.

58. JLC, *Passing of the Armies*, 84.
Porter, *Campaigning with Grant*, 432.

59. JLC, *Passing of the Armies*, 88–91, 98.
Porter, *Campaigning with Grant*, 432.

60. Roy Morris, Jr., *Sheridan: The Life and Wars of Phil Sheridan* (New York, 1992), 247.
JLC, "The Military Operations on the White Oak Road," in Maine Commandery, Military Order of the Loyal Legion of the United

States, *War Papers*, vol. 1 (Portland, 1897), 247.

Porter, *Campaigning with Grant*, 432.

Grant, *Memoirs*, 698.

Romeyn B. Ayres's report, OR, vol. 46, part 1, 869.

61. JLC, *Passing of the Armies*, 103–104.

Alexander Webb to JLC, April 4, 1892, LC.

Porter, *Campaigning with Grant*, 427.

JLC's report, OR, vol. 46, part 1, 849.

62. JLC, *Passing of the Armies*, 103–104.

63. JLC, *Passing of the Armies*, 104, 119–20.

Porter, *Campaigning with Grant*, 435–36.

Grant, *Memoirs*, 701.

64. JLC, *Passing of the Armies*, 122–23.

Porter, *Campaigning with Grant*, 436.

Samuel W. Crawford's report, OR, vol. 46, part 1, 880.

65. Foote, *The Civil War*, vol. 3, 866.

JLC, *Passing of the Armies*, 122–24.

Porter, *Campaigning with Grant*, 436–37.

Humphreys, *The Virginia Campaign*, 360.

66. JLC, *Passing of the Armies*, 127–29.

Porter, *Campaigning with Grant*, 440.

JLC's report, OR, vol. 46, part 1, 851.

67. JLC, *Passing of the Armies*, 130–34.

68. JLC, *Passing of the Armies*, 141.

Humphreys, *The Virginia Campaign*, 353.

Crawford's report, OR, vol. 46, part 1, 881.

Wainwright, *Diary of Battle*, 512.

Thomas Rosser to A. S. Perham, August 29, 1902, copy in LC.

69. JLC, *Passing of the Armies*, 142.

Lyman, *Meade's Headquarters*, 146.

Porter, *Campaigning with Grant*, 440.

John Palmer to A. S. Perham, January 7, 1903, copy in LC.

70. JLC, *Passing of the Armies*, 143.

71. JLC, *Passing of the Armies*, 152–53.

Porter, *Campaigning with Grant*, 441–43.

Grant, *Memoirs*, 702.

Lyman, *Meade's Headquarters*, 334.

72. EPA to Bettie Alexander, April 8, 1865, AP.

EPA, *Fighting*, 519–20.

EPA, "Lee at Appomattox," 923.

73. EPA's pocket diary, AP.

EPA, *Fighting*, 521.

74. EPA, *Fighting*, 522–23.

EPA, *Military Memoirs*, 596.

J. Thompson Brown to EPA, June 3, 1902, AP.

John Haskell to EPA, October 10, 1902, AP.

75. EPA, *Fighting*, 524–25.

76. EPA, *Fighting*, 525, 527.

EPA to Bettie Alexander, April 8, 1865, AP.

EPA, *Military Memoirs*, 603.

Grant, *Memoirs*, 723–24.

77. EPA, *Fighting*, 526–28.

EPA, "Lee at Appomattox," 925.

78. EPA, *Military Memoirs*, 600.

EPA to Bettie Alexander, April 8, 1865, AP.

EPA, *Fighting*, 530.

79. EPA, *Fighting*, 530.

EPA, *Military Memoirs*, 603.

EPA, "Lee at Appomattox," 925.

80. EPA, *Military Memoirs*, 604–605.

EPA, *Fighting*, 530–33.

Charley Crowley to EPA,, December 18, 1887, AP.

EPA, "Lee at Appomattox," 926.

81. EPA, *Fighting*, 534.

EPA, *Military Memoirs*, 606–608.

EPA, "Lee at Appomattox," 927.

EPA to Bettie Alexander, April 9, 1898, AP.

82. W. H. Gibbes to EPA, no date, AP.

John Haskell to EPA, October 10, 1902, AP.

83. Grant, *Memoirs*, 731.

EPA, *Fighting*, 536.

EPA, *Military Memoirs*, 609–10.

EPA to Bettie Alexander, April 9, 1898, AP.

84. EPA, *Fighting*, 538–39.

EPA, *Military Memoirs*, 611–12.

EPA, "Lee at Appomattox," 930.

85. Owen, *Washington Artillery*, 387.
86. JLC to Sarah (Sae) Chamberlain, April 13, 1865, BC.
87. Smith, *Recollections and Reflections*, 69.
    Lyman, *Meade's Headquarters*, 351.
    JLC's report, OR, vol. 46, part 1, 852.
88. JLC, *Passing of the Armies*, 230, 233–35.
    JLC's report, OR, vol. 46, part 1, 852.
    JLC, "The Last Salute of the Army of Northern Virginia," SHSP
    32 (1904), 357.
    JLC Affidavit, for E. W. Whitaker, Portland, Maine, January 2,
    1906, LC.
89. JLC, *Passing of the Armies*, 238–40.
    JLC, "Last Salute," 359.
90. JLC, *Passing of the Armies*, 241.
    JLC, Affidavit for E. W. Whitaker, Portland, Maine, January 2,
    1906, LC.
91. JLC, *Passing of the Armies*, 241–44.
    JLC to E. W. Whitaker, January 9, 1907, LC.
    John B. Gordon, *Reminiscences of the Civil War* (New York, 1903), 442.
    Morris, *Sheridan*, 256.
92. JLC, *Passing of the Armies*, 244.
93. JLC, *Passing of the Armies*, 246–47.
    JLC, "Petersburg and Appomattox," 182.
94. Humphreys, *Virginia Campaign*, 399.
    Wainwright, *Diary*, 523.
    Tom Chamberlain to Sarah (Sae) Chamberlain, April 11, 1865, MHS.
    JLC, *Passing of the Armies*, 247–48.
    JLC to Sarah (Sae) Chamberlain, April 13, 1865, BC.
95. Recommendations and parole in AP.
    EPA, "Lee at Appomattox," 931.
    EPA, *Fighting*, 127, 545.
    Charley Crowley to EPA, December 18, 1887, AP.
96. EPA, "Lee at Appomattox," 931.
    EPA, *Fighting*, 544.
    Porter, *Campaigning with Grant*, 487.
97. EPA, *Military Memoirs*, 613.
    EPA, *Fighting*, 545.
98. George Adams diaries, April 10, 1865, FPC.
    JLC to Sarah (Sae) Chamberlain, April 13, 1865, BC.

99. JLC, *Passing of the Armies*, 255, 258–60.
JLC to Sarah (Sae) Chamberlain, April 13, 1865, BC.
JLC, "Last Salute," 361.
100. JLC, *Passing of the Armies*, 259–61.
Gordon, *Reminiscences*, 444–45.
101. Gerrish, *Army Life*, 261.
JLC, *Passing of the Armies*, 262, 269.
Gordon, *Reminiscences*, 448.
JLC to Sarah (Sae) Chamberlain, April 13, 1865, BC.
102. JLC, *Passing of the Armies*, 274–77.

CHAPTER 11. ANOTHER COUNTRY

Georgia and Maine, 1865–73

1. EPA, *The Confederate Veteran*, address delivered at the centennial of the U.S. Military Academy, June 9, 1902, copy in AP.
2. EPA, *Fighting*, 538, 544–46.
3. EPA's pocket diary, AP.
EPA, *Fighting*, 547.
4. Frederick M. Colston, "Recollections of the Last Months of the Army of Northern Virginia," SHSP, 38 (1910), 13.
EPA, *Fighting*, 549–51.
EPA's pocket diary, AP.
5. EPA to Bettie Alexander, May 4, 1899, AP.
EPA, *Fighting*, 552.
6. EPA, *Fighting*, 552.
Andrews, *War-time Journal*, 212.
7. Bowen, *The Story of Wilkes County*, 144.
8. Andrews, *War-time Journal*, 373.
WPA, *The Story of Washington-Wilkes*, 58–61.
Willingham, *No Jubilee*, 199.
9. Andrews, *War-time Journal*, 303, 345–47, 357, 360.
10. WPA, *The Story of Washington-Wilkes*, 58.
Andrews, *War-time Journal*, 216.
William Reese to EPA, February 26, 1894, AP.
11. William Reese to EPA, February 26, 1894, AP.
Andrews, *War-time Journal*, 269.

EPA to Bettie Alexander, August 6, 1899, AP.

Josiah Gorgas to EPA, September 18, 1865, AP.

12. Willie Mason to EPA, October 12, 1865, AP.

EPA to Bettie Alexander, October 18, 1865, AP.

John F. Stover, *The Railroads of the South, 1865–1900* (Chapel Hill, N.C., 1955), 57.

13. Alexander Lawton to John P. King, September 5, 1865, AP.

Adam L. Alexander to Marion Alexander, September 11, 1865, AHP.

William Pendleton to EPA, October 9, 1865, AP.

Custis Lee to EPA, October 10, 1865, AP.

14. Adam L. Alexander to Marion Alexander, October 1, 1865, AHP.

EPA to Bettie Alexander, October 20, 1865, AP.

15. EPA to Bettie Alexander, October 18 and 20, 1865, AP.

Bettie Alexander to EPA, October 22, 1865, AP.

16. Bettie Alexander to EPA, October 22 and November 26, 1865, AP.

Robert Manson Myers, ed., *The Children of Pride* (New Haven, 1972), 1530.

17. Jeremy Gilmer to EPA, November 4, 1865, AP.

18. Malone, ed., *DAB*, vol. 7.

Eric Foner, *Reconstruction: America's Unfinished Revolution, 1863–1877* (New York, 1988), 400.

Allen W. Trelease, *White Terror: The Ku Klux Klan Conspiracy and Southern Reconstruction* (New York, 1971), 74.

19. William W. Parker to EPA, December 25, 1865, AP.

20. EPA to Bettie Alexander, July 29, 1897, AP.

Foner, *Reconstruction*, 74.

21. Columbia *State*, April 29, 1910, clipping in AP.

Alexander Haskell to EPA, January 9, 1866, AP.

Custis Lee to EPA, February 4, 1866, AP.

22. JLC, *Passing of the Armies*, 277, 280–82.

23. JLC, *Passing of the Armies*, 282.

Little, ed., *Genealogical and Family History*, vol. 1, 137.

24. JLC, *Passing of the Armies*, 283–86.

25. JLC, *Passing of the Armies*, 287–91.

26. JLC, *Passing of the Armies*, 289–90.

Foner, *Reconstruction*, 36.

27. JLC, *Passing of the Armies*, 298–99, 300, 302–307.

Gerrish, *Army Life*, 277.

28. JLC, *Passing of the Armies*, 313–316.
   Gerrish, *Army Life*, 289–90.
29. Gerrish, *Army Life*, 293–94.
   JLC to Sarah (Sae) Chamberlain, June 6, 1865, BC.
   JLC, *Passing of the Armies*, 320–25.
30. Porter, *Campaigning with Grant*, 505–507.
   Gerrish, *Army Life*, 297–98.
   Abner R. Small to JLC, December 22, 1908, MHS.
31. JLC, *Passing of the Armies*, 331–40.
   Porter, *Campaigning with Grant*, 508.
   Maine AGR, 1864–65, 336.
32. JLC, *Passing of the Armies*, 342–45.
   Porter, *Campaigning with Grant*, 508.
33. JLC, *Passing of the Armies*, 375.
   John C. Locke to JLC, April 13, 1865, BC.
   JCL to Sarah (Sae) Chamberlain, June 6, 1865, BC.
34. JLC to Sarah (Sae) Chamberlain, June 6, 1865, BC.
   Sarah (Sae) Chamberlain to JLC, May 7, 1865, RC.
35. Gerrish, *Army Life*, 303.
   JLC, *Passing of the Armies*, 391.
   George Adams diaries, August 2 and 3, 1865, FPC.
   Hatch, *Bowdoin College*, 122.
   Ashby, *First Parish Church*, 250.
36. George Adams diaries, August 15 and 17, 1865, FPC.
   Circular advertising a Fifth Corps history, August 1865, LC.
   William L. Tilden to JLC, September 29, 1865, LC.
37. George Adams diaries, December 3, 1865, FPC.
   George Batchelder to JLC, October 20, 1865, LC.
   Receipt from Tiffany Jewelers, December 5, 1865, BC.
   Frances Chamberlain to JLC, March 9 and 19 and May 1, 1866, RC.
38. George Adams diaries, June 21, 1866, FPC.
   JLC to Frances Chamberlain, April 7, 1866, RC.
   Louis C. Hatch, *Maine: A History* (New York, 1919), 533.
39. Daniel W. Hollis, *The University of South Carolina: College to University*, (Columbia, S.C., 1956), 4–5, 23–24.
40. Francis B. Simkins and Robert H. Woody, *South Carolina during Reconstruction* (Chapel Hill, N.C., 1932), 279.
   Hollis, *University of South Carolina*, 25, 31.

41. Hollis, *University of South Carolina*, 41–42.
    EPA to Mary Clifford Alexander, May 10, 1866, AP.
42. EPA to Mary Clifford Alexander, May 10, 1866, AP.
    J. F. Kershaw to EPA, July 14, 1866, AP.
    James Longstreet to EPA, August 9, 1869, AP.
    Wert, *Longstreet*, 411–13.
43. James Longstreet to EPA, August 9, 1869, AP.
    Copies of printed forms in AP.
44. EPA to George Pickett, June 16, 1866, quoted in Charles Royster,
    The Destructive War (New York, 1991), 157.
    James Longstreet to EPA, February 26, 1866, AP.
    Henry Hull, Jr., to EPA, September 21, 1866, AP.
45. Adam L. Alexander to "My dear child," January 22 and September 3,
    1867, AHP.
    McPherson, *Ordeal by Fire*, 499–501.
    Quotation is from Foner, *Reconstruction*, 276.
46. Foner, *Reconstruction*, 276–78.
47. Foner, *Reconstruction*, 278.
    Hollis, *University of South Carolina*, 45–47.
48. Stephen Winthrop to EPA, June 29, 1868, AP.
    William C. Oates to EPA, August 25, 1868, AP.
49. Trelease, *White Terror*, 74–75.
    Foner, *Reconstruction*, 427–31.
50. Hollis, *University of South Carolina*, 47–50.
    Malone, ed., *DAB*, vol. 16.
    William Kip to EPA, September 23, 1867, AP.
    John LeConte to EPA, July 22, 1868, AP.
    Robert E. Lee to EPA, August 6, 1868.
51. Mary Moody to EPA, May 4, 1868, AP.
    Custis Lee to EPA, November 18, 1867, AP.
    Stephen Winthrop to EPA, January 8 and June 29, 1868, AP.
52. EPA to "Dear Brother," January 9, 1869, AP.
    Hollis, *University of South Carolina*, 50.
    Simkins and Woody, *South Carolina during Reconstruction*, 295.
53. Alfred Godfrey to JLC, November 20, 1866, LC.
    Hatch, *Maine*, 533.
    Second quotation is from Trulock, *In the Hands of Providence*,
    338.
54. Hatch, *Maine*, 534–35, 562.

Evening Post, September 14, 1869, clipping in BC.

Thomas Upham to JLC, September 1867, LC.

55. *Evening Post*, September 14, 1869, clipping in BC.

JLC to Sarah D. B. Chamberlain, January 27, 1869, BC.

Little, ed., *Genealogical and Family History*, vol. 1, 138.

Trulock, *In the Hands of Providence*, 339.

56. Deborah Brastow to Sarah D. B. Chamberlain, August 24, 1867, BC.

Charles Farrington to George Field, August 9, 1870, BC.

JLC to Frances Chamberlain, November 28, 1868, Frost Family Papers, Manuscripts and Archives, Yale University Library, New Haven, Conn. (hereafter, Frost Papers).

Catherine Smith Recollections, Brunswick *Times-Record*, September 7, 1975, clipping in BC.

57. JLC to Frances Chamberlain, March 28, 1866, RC.

JLC to Frances Chamberlain, November 28, 1868, Frost Papers.

58. JLC to Frances Chamberlain, November 20, 1868, Frost Papers.

59. Pejepscot Historical Society, "Museums" (pamphlet).

60. Little, ed., *Genealogical and Family History*, vol. 1, 139.

61. William Rogers to JLC, November 19, 1868, BC.

JLC Pension Records, NA.

62. Grace (Daisy) Chamberlain to "Darling Bill" (Wyllys Chamberlain), February 15, 1869, BC.

For Chamberlain's involvement in veterans' affairs and his lecture engagements, see LC.

Hatch, *Maine*, 537.

63. Gouverneur K. Warren to JLC, December 22, 1865, and August 28, 1866, LC.

JLC–John Batchelder exchanges, LC.

64. JLC to D. L. Lane, August 11, 1870, BC.

Hatch, *Maine*, 563, 567–69.

65. JLC to Grace Chamberlain, April 28, 1871, RC.

Frances Chamberlain to Grace Chamberlain, June 6, 1871, RC.

Hatch, *Bowdoin College*, 129–30.

CHAPTER 12. SUBTLE ARTS OF PEACE

Alexander: Railroad Campaigns, 1871–92

1. P. G. T. Beauregard to EPA, June 17, 1870, AP.
   C. P. Stone to EPA, February 7, 1871, AP.
   William B. Heseltine and Hazel C. Wolf, *The Blue and the Gray on the Nile* (New York, 1961), 260.
2. John Marlowe, *World Ditch: The Making of the Suez Canal* (New York, 1964), 153, 222.
   Morris, *Heaven's Command*, 418–21.
   C. P. Stone to EPA, May 22, 1871, AP.
3. EPA, *Fighting*, 32.
   EPA to Mary Mason Alexander, September 1904, AP.
4. EPA to Mary Mason Alexander, September 1904, AP.
   C. P. Stone to EPA, May 22, 1871, AP.
   Thomas J. Schlereth, *Victorian America: Transformations in Everyday Life, 1876–1915* (New York, 1991), 13.
   Louisa Gilmer to Bettie Alexander, August 24, 1881, AP.
5. William Mitchell to EPA, August 9, 1872, AP.
   Adam L. Alexander to EPA, May 11, 1874, AP.
   P. G. T. Beauregard to EPA, July 2, 1874, AP.
   G. H. Camp to EPA, October 26, 1874, AP.
   John LeConte to EPA, December 8, 1874, AP.
6. Stover, *Railroads of the South*, 59.
7. *The Commercial and Financial Chronicle* (hereafter, *Chronicle*), vol. 14 (January 21, 1872), 124; and vol. 15 (August 17, 1872), 219.
   Maury Klein, *Edward Porter Alexander* (Athens, Ga., 1971), 154.
8. Alexander R. Lawton to EPA, October 24, 1874, and April 10, 1875, AP.
   Stover, *Railroads of the South*, 149.
9. EPA, "Railway Management," *Scribner's Magazine*, 5 (January 1889), 31.
   Klein, *Edward Porter Alexander*, 155.
10. Bessie Alexander to Bettie Alexander, November 3, 1875, AP.
    Bettie Alexander to EPA, September 13, 1880, AP.
    EPA to Bettie Alexander, January 29, 1885, AP.
11. EPA, "Railway Management," 46.
12. C. Vann Woodward, *Reunion and Reaction: The Compromise of 1877 and*

the End of Reconstruction (Boston, 1951), 218–19.

Claude G. Bowers, *The Tragic Era* (Cambridge, Mass., 1929), 515.

13. Hampton M. Jarrell, *Wade Hampton and the Negro: The Road Not Taken* (Columbia, S.C., 1949), 53, 59n, 99.

Simkins and Woody, *South Carolina during Reconstruction*, 547.

Foner, *Reconstruction*, 474–75.

14. Gordon quotation is from Paul H. Buck, *The Road to Reunion, 1865–1900* (Boston, 1937), 105.

Woodward, *Reunion and Reaction*, 124–25.

EPA to Louisa Minis, April 29, 1900, quoted in Klein, *Edward Porter Alexander*, 186.

George Butler to EPA, May 10, 1878, AP.

C. H. Phinizy to EPA, April 25, 1880, AP.

15. EPA to Lucy Alexander, October 3, 1880, AP.

16. Bettie Alexander to Bessie Alexander, April 14, 1882, AP.

17. Abstract of Adam L. Alexander's will, January 30, 1882, AHP.

18. Klein, *Edward Porter Alexander*, 170.

Stover, *Railroads of the South*, 227.

19. *Chronicle*, vol. 31 (October 9, 1880), 382; and vol. 34 (February 25, 1882), 216.

National Cyclopedia of American Biography, vol. 12 (New York, 1904), 94.

Stover, *Railroads of the South*, 228.

Klein, *Edward Porter Alexander*, 174–75.

EPA to Bessie Alexander, June 3, 1882, AP.

20. EPA to Bessie Alexander, June 3, 1882, AP.

21. *Chronicle*, vol. 35 (July 23, 1882), 88.

Jeremy Gilmer to EPA, July 2, 1882, AP.

EPA to Bettie Alexander, July 19, 1882.

22. Klein, *Edward Porter Alexander*, 181–83.

Albert Fink to Alexander R. Lawton, December 13, 1882, AP.

Savannah *Evening Press*, April 28, 1910.

23. C. P. Huntington to EPA, March 14, 1883, AP.

Robert Garretty to EPA, December 12, 1884.

U. S. Grant to Robert Lincoln, May 19, 1883, copy in AP.

Joseph P. Bradley to EPA, May 1883, AP.

EPA to Bettie Alexander, March 13, 1884, and January 29, 1885, AP.

24. Frederickson, *The Inner Civil War*, 206.

Adams, *Autobiography*, 166, 169–71.

25. Frederickson, *The Inner Civil War*, 206–207.
    Adams, *Autobiography*, 176, 193.
26. EPA, "Railway Management," 29, 39–41.
27. EPA to Bettie Alexander, July 17, 1885, AP.
    Adams, *Autobiography*, 174–75.
    Ellis P. Oberholtzer, *A History of the United States since the Civil War* (New York, 1931), 399.
28. Oberholtzer, *History of the United States*, 399.
    EPA to Bettie Alexander, September 25, 1885, AP.
29. EPA to Bettie Alexander, September 19 and 25, 1885, AP.
30. EPA, *Catterel Ratterel (Doggerel)* (New York, 1890).
31. J. B. Walton's letter, SHSP, 5 (1878), 47.
    EPA's letter, SHSP, 5 (1878), 201–203.
32. EPA to Bettie Alexander, August 30, 1886, AP.
33. EPA to Bettie Alexander, August 30, 1886, AP.
    Charley Crowley to EPA, December 18, 1887, and February 19, 1888, AP.
34. Charley Crowley to EPA, February 19 and December 14, 1888, AP.
35. Charles F. Adams to EPA, January 14, 1887, AP.
    Sarah Lawton to EPA, October 28, 1884, AP.
    Chronicle, vol. 43 (November 20, 1886), 607.
    Stover, *Railroads of the South*, 248–49.
36. Stover, *Railroads of the South*, 248–49.
    Chronicle, vol. 44 (January 8, 1887), 59; and vol. 47 (September 8 and October 27, 1888), 274, 486.
    Railroad Gazette, vol. 20 (October 26, 1888), 705.
37. Klein, *Edward Porter Alexander*, 197–98.
    Stover, *Railroads of the South*, 250.
    Chronicle, vol. 53 (March 21, 1891), 462.
38. Frederickson, *The Inner Civil War*, 207.
    Adams, *Autobiography*, 191, 195.
    Klein, *Edward Porter Alexander*, 196–97.
39. *Railroad Gazette*, vol. 24 (January 8, 1892), 33.
    Savannah *Morning News*, December 31, 1891, and January 4, 1892, clippings in AP.
40. Savannah *Evening News*, April 28, 1910.
    Stover, *Railroads of the South*, 251n.
    Chronicle, vol. 54 (March 12 and 26, 1892), 443, 559–60.

41. EPA, *Fighting*, 18.
42. *Weekly News*, May 13, 1893, clipping in AP.

Chamberlain: Soldier-President, 1871–83

1. JLC to Sarah D. B. Chamberlain, September 8, 1871, BC.
   Ernst C. Helmreich, *Religion at Bowdoin College* (Brunswick, Maine, 1981), 108–10.
   Hatch, *Bowdoin College*, 155–58.
2. Helmreich, *Religion at Bowdoin*, 111–12.
   JLC, "The New Education," Bowdoin College inaugural address, July 19, 1872, typescript in BC.
3. Hatch, *Bowdoin College*, 57, 133, 169, 173.
   Cleaveland and Packard, *History of Bowdoin*, 131–33.
4. Hatch, *Bowdoin College*, 134–35.
   Cross, "Joshua Lawrence Chamberlain," 63.
   Frederickson, *The Inner Civil War*, 222.
5. Quotation is from Hatch, *Bowdoin College*, 131.
6. Printed copy of petition, dated November 12, 1873, BC.
   Hatch, *Bowdoin College*, 136–39.
7. Cyrus Woodman to JLC, May 25, 1874, LC.
   H. W. Benham to JLC, June 3, 1874, LC.
8. Hatch, *Bowdoin College*, 142–45, 148.
   Harrison Hume to JLC, March 2, 1875, BC.
   George F. Harriman to JLC, February 8, 1875, BC.
9. JLC to Sarah D. B. Chamberlain, July 4, 1874, BC.
   Hatch, *Bowdoin College*, 144.
10. Selden Connor to JLC, April 25, 1872, LC.
11. Boatner, *Civil War Dictionary*, 389.
    Anson P. Morrill to JLC, August 10, 1877, BC.
12. Hatch, *Maine: A History*, 587
    Stanley P. Hirshson, *Farewell to the Bloody Shirt: Northern Republicans and the Southern Negro, 1877–1893* (Gloucester, Mass., 1968), 37.
13. Copy of JLC's speech, November 1, 1877, LC.
    Malone, ed., *DAB*, Supplement 1, 27–28.
14. Foner, *Reconstruction*, 558–61.
    Adelbert Ames to JLC, January 22, 1875, LC.
15. Oxford *Democrat*, Paris, Maine, June 10, 1879, clipping in LC.

16. Oxford *Democrat*, Paris, Maine, June 10, 1879, clipping in LC.

17. Stephen M. Allen to JLC, April 26, 1876, LC.
Nathaniel P. Banks to Stephen M. Allen, May 8, 1876, LC.
Charles E. Nash to JLC, October 17, 1879, LC.
E. H. Delmar to JLC, September 17, 1880, LC.

18. Commissary General of Subsistence to JLC, July 31, 1873, LC.
Frances Chamberlain to JLC, March 8 and 19, 1866, RC.

19. Fitz-John Porter to JLC, May 23, 1874, LC.
Boatner, *Civil War Dictionary*, 661–62.

20. Gouverneur K. Warren to JLC, December 22, 1865, and November 12, 1879, LC.
Warren to JLC, October 20, 1880, BC.

21. Carswell McClellan to JLC, September 3, 1889, LC.
Gouverneur K. Warren to JLC, November 12, 1879, LC.

22. Sheridan's report, OR, vol. 46, part 1, 1105.
Boatner, *Civil War Dictionary*, 891–92.
JLC to Frances Chamberlain, May 11, 1880, RC.

23. Cross, "Joshua Lawrence Chamberlain," 60.
Helmreich, *Religion at Bowdoin*, 100.
Adelbert Ames to JLC, January 22, 1875, LC.

24. Ashby, *First Parish Church*, 327.
Little, ed., *Genealogical and Family History*, vol. 1, 133, 140.
JLC to Joshua and Sarah D. B. Chamberlain, June 14, 1878, BC.

25. Edgar Oakes Achorn, "General Chamberlain," unpublished manuscript, n.d., copy in BC.
Statement of account, Blanchard Food Cures, New York City, May 13, 1878, BC.
Frances Chamberlain to JLC, March 19, 1866, RC.

26. Grace Chamberlain to Horace Allen, April 15, 1876, BC.
Wyllys Chamberlain to Joshua Chamberlain, Jr., April 14, 1872, BC.

27. Frances Chamberlain to JLC, April 15, 1866, RC.
Sarah (Sae) Farrington to JLC, January 3, 1886, RC.
Thomas Chamberlain to JLC, May 24, 1879, LC.
JLC to Sarah D. B. Chamberlain, June 1 (no year given; by contents, 1879), BC.

28. Hatch, *Maine: A History*, 594.

29. Hatch, *Maine: A History*, 599–602.

30. Hatch, *Maine: A History*, 605–607.

31. Little, ed., *Genealogical and Family History*, vol. 1, 138.
    Hatch, *Maine: A History*, 608–609.
32. JLC to Frances Chamberlain, January 7 and 9, 1880, RC.
33. JLC to Frances Chamberlain, January 9, 1880, RC.
    Hatch, *Maine: A History*, 610–11.
34. Hatch, *Maine: A History*, 611.
    JLC to Frances Chamberlain, January 15, 1880, BC.
    F. B. Ward to JLC, January 15, 1880, LC.
    Chamberlain: A Sketch, 24–25.
35. JLC to Frances Chamberlain, January 15, 1880, BC.
    Hatch, *Maine: A History*, 611.
36. Hatch, *Maine: A History*, 614–15.
37. Cross, "Joshua Lawrence Chamberlain," 70.
    JLC, "The New Education," 2, 9.
    Hatch, *Bowdoin College*, 158–63.
38. Hatch, *Bowdoin College*, 150.
    JLC to Grace Allen, December 23, 1881, and n.d. (by contents, January 1882), BC.
    JLC to Sarah (Sae) Farrington, January 29, 1882, University of Maine, Orono.
39. JLC to Sarah (Sae) Farrington, January 29, 1882, University of Maine, Orono.
    J. H. Warren to JLC, March 2, 1883, Frost Papers.
    Grace Allen to Frances Chamberlain, April 19, 1883, BC.
    JLC to Sarah (Sae) Farrington, July 3, 1883, LC.
40. JLC to Sarah (Sae) Farrington, July 3, 1883, LC.
    Chamberlain: A Sketch, 22.
    JLC to Henry Johnson, February 6, 1884, BC.
41. Lewiston *Journal*, February 27, 1914, clipping in BC.

Chapter 13. Memory

Alexander: View from a Distance, 1897–1910

1. EPA to Bettie Alexander, May 12 and 14, 1897, AP.
   EPA to Mary Clifford Hull, June 10, 1897, in Boggs, ed., *Alexander Letters*, 355.
   U.S. government letter of appointment, February 17, 1897, AP.

2. EPA to Bettie Alexander, May 14 and 20, 1897, AP.

3. EPA to Bettie Alexander, May 14 and 28 and November 21, 1897, and January 21 and March 12, 1898, AP.

4. EPA to Bettie Alexander, May 14 and June 13, 1897, AP.

5. EPA to Bettie Alexander, June 13, 1897, AP.

6. EPA to Bettie Alexander, May 23 and July 4–6, 1897, AP.

7. EPA to Bettie Alexander, July 4–6, 20, and 28, 1897, AP.

8. EPA to Bettie Alexander, June 23 and 28, 1897, AP.

9. EPA to Bessie Alexander Ficklen, July 28, 1897, AP.
EPA to Bettie Alexander, July 13 and September 4, 19, and 24, 1897, AP.

10. EPA to Bettie Alexander, September 24 and 26, 1897, AP.

11. EPA to Bettie Alexander, September 11 and 30 and November 13 and 21, 1897, AP.

12. EPA to Bessie Alexander Ficklen, June 13, 1898, John R. Ficklen Papers, Southern Historical Collection, University of North Carolina at Chapel Hill (hereafter Ficklen Papers).
EPA to Bettie Alexander, November 29, 1897, AP.

13. EPA to Bettie Alexander, April 9, 1898, AP.

14. EPA to Bettie Alexander, January 10, February 14, March 2 and 12, and April 9, 1898, AP.

15. EPA to Bettie Alexander, February 14, April 12 and 23, and May 12 and 15, 1898, AP.

16. EPA to Bessie Ficklen, May 20, 1898, Ficklen Papers.
EPA to Bettie Alexander, April 9, 1898, AP.

17. EPA, South Island Log, microfilm copy in Southern Historical Collection, University of North Carolina, Chapel Hill, 131.
EPA to Bettie Alexander, December 26 and 31, 1898, AP.

18. EPA to Bettie Alexander, January 6, 7, 9, 14, and 19, 1899, AP.

19. EPA to Bettie Alexander, February 2, 7, and 10 and March 1, 1899, AP.

20. EPA to Bettie Alexander, February 7, 9, and 16, 1899, AP.

21. EPA to Bettie Alexander, February 17 and 25 and March 1, 1899, AP.
EPA to Bessie Ficklen, February 17, 1899, AP.

22. EPA to Bettie Alexander, April 7, June 1 and 12, and July 7, 1899, AP.

23. EPA to Bettie Alexander, August 21 and 27 and September 7, 1899, AP.

24. EPA to Bettie Alexander, September 21, 1899, AP.

25. EPA to Bettie Alexander, September 21 and 29, 1899, AP.

26. Augusta *Chronicle*, November 21, 1899, clipping in AP.
EPA to Rosa Alexander, February 23, 1900, AP.
Augusta *Chronicle*, April 29, 1900, clipping in AP.

27. EPA to William J. Craig, May 13, 1900, AP.

EPA to his children, July 24–25, 1900, in Boggs, ed., *Alexander Letters*, 366–70.

28. EPA to William J. Craig, September 26, 1900.

EPA to "My dear Hal," August 20, 1901, AP.

29. EPA to William J. Craig, September 26, 1900, AP.

South Island Log, 141.

EPA to Bettie Alexander, September 19, 1897, AP.

EPA to "My dear Hal," August 11, 1901, AP.

Mary Alexander to Francis Mason, October 10 and 16, 1901, AP.

30. Boggs, ed., *Alexander Letters*, 384.

Mary Alexander to Mary Mason, February 4, 1902, AP.

EPA to Mary Alexander, April 30 and May 12 and 26, 1902, AP.

31. EPA to Mary Alexander, May 8, 1902, AP.

EPA, "The Confederate Veteran."

32. EPA, "The Confederate Veteran."

Mary Alexander to Mary Mason, June 16, 1902, AP.

Unsigned note in EPA's hand, n.d. (by contents, June or July 1902).

33. EPA, review of Helen Longstreet's *Lee and Longstreet at High Tide*, in *American Historical Review* 10 (July 1905), 903–904.

Gordon, *Reminiscences*, 160–61.

Longstreet Memoirs, 384.

EPA to Frederic Bancroft, October 30, 1904, AP.

34. Klein, *Edward Porter Alexander*, 221.

South Island Log, 206.

Frederic Bancroft to EPA, December 4, 1902, AP.

Boggs, ed., *Alexander Letters*, 376.

EPA to Mary Alexander, May 21, 1903, AP.

35. EPA to Mary Alexander, January 7, 1903, AP.

Frederic Bancroft to EPA, May 9, 1904, AP.

EPA to Bessie Ficklen, May 15, 1904, AP.

Frederic Bancroft to Mary Alexander, January 25, 1905, AP.

36. EPA, *Military Memoirs*, 620.

EPA to Bessie Ficklen, December 8, 1906, AP.

Mary Clifford Hull to EPA, April 30, 1907, AP.

Third quotation is from Klein, *Edward Porter Alexander*, 216.

37. Frederick Colston to EPA, May 16, 1907, AP.

Charleston *News Courier*, n.d., clipping in AP.

New Orleans *Picayune*, August 17, 1907, clipping in AP.

38. John Haskell to EPA, May 7, 1907, AP.
    E. W. Haskel to EPA, May 17, 1907, AP.
39. *The New York Times*, September 21, 1907, clipping in AP.
    The Nation 84 (June 13, 1907), 542–44.
    New York Tribune, October 5, 1907, clipping in AP.
    Louisville *Post*, September 20, 1907, clipping in AP.
    American Historical Review, 13 (October 1907), 163.
40. EPA, *Military Memoirs*, vii, 577, 116, 393, 397, 417–18, 547.
41. EPA to Bessie Ficklen, January 25 and October 29, 1908, Ficklen Papers.
    E. A. Alderman to EPA, August 27, 1907, AP.
42. EPA to Mary Alexander, May 28 (no year; by contents, 1908), AP.
    EPA to Mary Alexander, May 4 (no year; doubtless 1908), AP.
    Cooke, *Frederic Bancroft*, 92.
    Harriet Cummings to EPA, July 2 and 22, 1909, AP.
    South Island Log, 307.
43. South Island Log, 307.
    Cooke, *Frederic Bancroft*, 92.
    EPA to Bessie Ficklen, January 3, 1909, Ficklen Papers.
44. South Island Log, 308–309.
45. South Island Log, 310–11.
    EPA to Bessie Ficklen, January 3, 1909, Ficklen Papers.
    William P. Hillhouse to Bessie Ficklen, May 29, 1910, Ficklen Papers.
    M. A. Steele to Mary Alexander, July 9, 1909, AP.
46. South Island Log, 311.
    Walter Adams to Mary Alexander, June 24, 1910, AP.

Chamberlain: Requiescat, 1885–1914

1. JLC to Frances Chamberlain, October 20, 1885, BC.
2. JLC to Frances Chamberlain, October 20, 1885, BC.
   Wyllys Chamberlain to Grace Chamberlain, August 9, 1886, BC.
   Albert Willard to JLC, July 18, 1889. Frost Papers.
   Sarah (Sae) Farrington to JLC, January 3, 1886, RC.
3. Sarah (Sae) Farrington to JLC, January 3, 1886, RC.
   JLC to Sarah D. B. Chamberlain, September 8, 1887, LC.
   JLC to Grace Allen, January 18, 1889, BC.
4. JLC to Grace Allen, February 15, 1887, and n.d. (by contents, autumn 1887), BC.
5. Portland *Press Herald*, November 11, 1960, clipping in BC.

Cross, "Joshua Lawrence Chamberlain," 85–86.

Wyllys Chamberlain to Grace Allen, July 21, 1885, MHS.

6. Little, ed., *Genealogical and Family History*, vol. 1, 133.

Sarah (Sae) Farrington to JLC, January 3, 1886, RC.

JLC to Frances Chamberlain, July 30, 1896, BC.

Albert Willard to JLC, July 18, 1889, Frost Papers.

John H. Jarvis to JLC, September 9, 1889, Frost Papers.

Sarah (Sae) Farrington to JLC, July 30, 1896, Frost Papers.

7. Wyllys Chamberlain to Frances Chamberlain, May 1891, MHS.

8. JLC to Grace Allen, December 13, 1886, BC.

9. Affidavits of Dr. Robert H. Green and Fitz-John Porter, JLC's Pension Records, NA.

JLC affidavit, Pension Records, NA.

10. JLC to Mrs. J. L. Mott, January 28, 1894, BC.

JLC to Frances Chamberlain, January 23, 1894, BC.

JLC to Sarah (Sae) Farrington, March 19, 1885, LC.

11. William P. Frye to JLC, April 5, 1897, and August 20, 1898, LC.

Llewellyn Powers to JLC, April 5, 1898, LC.

12. William P. Whitehouse to JLC, November 20, 1899, BC.

J. P. Baxter to JLC, November 25, 1899, BC.

Ellis Spear to Amos Allen, December 4, 1899, BC.

13. JLC to Sarah (Sae) Farrington, December 24, 1899, BC.

Abner O. Shaw to JLC, December 5, 1899, MHS.

Portland *Press*, clipping in LC.

14. JLC to John T. Richards, December 26, 1899, MHS.

JLC to Secretary of the Treasury, October 22, 1900, MHS.

JLC to Frances Chamberlain, November 6, 1900, BC.

JLC to Sarah (Sae) Farrington, January 5, 1901, LC.

15. JLC to Frank A. Garnsey, January 18, 1899, MHS.

16. Catherine Smith recollections, Brunswick *Times-Record*, September 7, 1975, clipping in BC.

Henry S. Burrage to JLC, June 6, 1908, LC.

Portland *Press*, May 31, 1901, clipping in BC.

Achorn, "General Chamberlain."

17. JLC to Grace Allen, n.d (by contents, February 1887) and July 13, 1888, BC.

18. Brunswick *Record*, February 5, 1904, clipping in BC.

JLC, "Petersburg and Appomattox," 167, 169.

19. Ellis Spear to JLC, July 2, 1882, LC.

Maine at Gettysburg, 249–50.

Record and Pension Office, War Department, August 17, 1893, copy in Frost Papers.

H. C. Merriam to JLC, July 14, 1899.

20. Wyllys Chamberlain to JLC, November 2, 1892, Frost Papers.
JLC to Sarah (Sae) Farrington, December 19, 1894, and April 4, 1899, LC.
JLC to Grace Allen, January 29, 1899, RC.

21. JLC to Frances Chamberlain, July 10, 1902, and February 11, 1903, BC.

22. JLC to Frances Chamberlain, August 3, 1903, RC.

23. Myra Porter to JLC, August 9, 1905, MHS.
JLC to Frances Chamberlain, August 12, 1905, RC.
Brunswick *Record,* October 27, 1905, clipping in BC.

24. Cross, "Joshua Lawrence Chamberlain," 84–85.
Brunswick *Record,* February 20, 1964, clipping in BC.
JLC to Carrie (?), January 27, 1910, BC.

25. Smith recollections, Brunswick *Record,* April 22, 1965, clipping in BC.
John S. Mosby to James Keith, copy from A. S. Perham to JLC, September 1908, BC.
LaSalle Corbell Pickett to JLC, April 25, 1910, BC.

26. Carswell McClellan to JLC, October 6, 1888, LC.
C. W. Meade to JLC, October 18, 1888, LC.
JLC, *Passing of the Armies,* xv, 18.
JLC to Charles Hunt, December 18, 1908, LC.
S. M. Chamberlain to Grace Allen, October 3, 1911, BC.

27. Smith recollections, Brunswick *Record,* April 22, 1965, clipping in BC.
Smith recollections, Brunswick *Times-Record,* September 7, 1975, clipping in BC.

28. Smith recollections, September 7, 1975, clipping in BC.
JLC, *Passing of the Armies,* 271.

29. Sherman quotation is from Royster, *The Destructive War,* 253.
JLC, *Passing of the Armies,* 385–86.

30. Smith recollections, Brunswick *Times-Record,* September 7, 1975, and Brunswick *Record,* April 22, 1965, clipping in BC.

31. JLC to Grace Allen, May 24 and August 28, 1909, May 6, 1911, and February 28, 1913, RC.

32. JLC to Grace Allen, October 13, 1910, RC.
Wyllys Chamberlain to JLC, March 22, 1889, and November 2, 1892, Frost Papers.

Wyllys Chamberlain, sales letter, January 1900, copy in MHS.

JLC to Wyllys Chamberlain, October 18, 1913, MHS.

33. JLC to Grace Allen, February 28, 1913, RC.

JLC to William D. Hyde, May 27, 1913, BC.

JLC, "Through Blood and Fire," 909.

34. *The New York Times*, July 1 and 2, 1913.

Grace Allen to Eleanor Allen, January 15, 1914, RC.

JLC to Sarah (Sae) Farrington, January 20 (no year; by contents, 1914), University of Maine, Orono.

35. Boston *Evening Globe*, February 24, 1914, clipping in BC.

Envoi: Georgia and Maine, April 1910 and February 1914

1. South Island Log, 311.

Savannah *Evening Press*, clipping in AP.

Augusta *Chronicle*, April 30, 1910, clipping in AP.

2. Lewiston *Journal*, February 27, 1914, clipping in BC.

3. Lewiston *Journal*, February 27, 1914, clipping in BC.

4. Robert Graves, *Good-bye to All That* (Garden City, N.Y., 1957), 278.

BIBLIOGRAPHY

Manuscripts

George E. Adams Diaries, First Parish Church, Brunswick, Maine.

Alexander-Hillhouse Papers, Southern Historical Collection, University of North Carolina, Chapel Hill, N.C.

Edward Porter Alexander Papers, Southern Historical Collection, University of North Carolina, Chapel Hill, N.C.

Edward Porter Alexander Folder, Library of Congress, Washington, D.C.

John Chamberlain Diary, Pejepscot Historical Society, Brunswick, Maine.

Joshua Lawrence Chamberlain Papers, Hawthorne-Longfellow Library, Bowdoin College, Brunswick, Maine.

Joshua Lawrence Chamberlain Papers, Library of Congress, Washington, D.C.

Joshua Lawrence Chamberlain Collection, Maine Historical Society, Portland, Maine.

Joshua Lawrence Chamberlain, miscellaneous correspondence, Maine State Archives, Augusta, Maine.

Joshua Lawrence Chamberlain Papers, Raymond H. Fogler Library, University of Maine, Orono, Maine.

Joshua Lawrence Chamberlain Pension Records and Military Service Records, National Archives, Washington, D.C.

Joshua Lawrence Chamberlain Collection and Letterbook, Pejepscot Historical Society, Brunswick, Maine.

Chamberlain-Adams Family Correspondence, Schlesinger Library, Radcliffe College, Cambridge, Mass.

John R. Ficklen Papers, Southern Historical Collection, University of North Carolina, Chapel Hill, N.C.

Frost Family Papers, Manuscripts and Archives, Yale University Library, New Haven, Conn.

Books and Articles

Adams, Charles Francis, Jr. *An Autobiography*. Boston, 1916.

Adams, George W. *Doctors in Blue: The Medical History of the Union Army in the Civil War*. New York, 1952.

Adams, Nehemiah. *A South-Side View of Slavery*. Boston, 1854.

Alexander, Edward Porter. "The Battle of Bull Run." *Scribner's Magazine* 41 (1907).

————. "The Battle of Fredericksburg." *Southern Historical Society Papers* 10 (1882).

————. *Catteral Ratteral (Doggerel)*. New York, 1890.

————. "Causes of Lee's Defeat at Gettysburg." *Southern Historical Society Papers* 4 (1877).

————. "Confederate Artillery Service." *Southern Historical Society Papers* 11 (1883).

————. *Fighting for the Confederacy: The Personal Recollections of General Edward Porter Alexander*. Edited by Gary W. Gallagher. Chapel Hill, N.C., 1989.

————. "Lee at Appomattox." *Century Magazine* 63 (1902).

————. *Military Memoirs of a Confederate*. New York, 1907.

————. "Railway Management." *Scribner's Magazine* 5 (January 1889).

————. *Railway Practice*. New York, 1887.

Ambrose, Stephen E. *Duty, Honor, Country: A History of West Point*. Baltimore, 1966.

Andrews, Eliza F. *The War-time Journal of a Georgia Girl*. Edited by Spencer B. King, Jr. Macon, Ga., 1960.

Annual Reports of the Adjutant General, State of Maine. Augusta, Maine, 1861–66.

Ashby, Thompson Eldridge. *A History of the First Parish Church of Brunswick, Maine*. Brunswick, 1969.

Baker, Liva. *The Justice from Beacon Hill: The Life and Times of Oliver Wendell Holmes*. New York, 1991.

Bartley, Numan V. *The Creation of Modern Georgia*. Athens, Ga., 1983.

Billings, John D. *Hardtack and Coffee*. Boston, 1888.

Black, Robert C. III. *The Railroads of the Confederacy.* Chapel Hill, N.C., 1952.

Blackford, Charles M. *Letters from Lee's Army.* Edited by Susan L. Blackford. New York, 1947.

Boatner, Mark M. III. *The Civil War Dictionary.* Revised edition. New York, 1988.

Boggs, Marion A., ed. *The Alexander Letters.* Reprint. Athens, Ga., 1980.

Bowen, Eliza A. *The Story of Wilkes County, Georgia.* Marietta, Ga., 1969.

Bowers, Claude G. *The Tragic Era.* Cambridge, Mass., 1929.

Boynton, George M. *The Congregational Way.* New York, 1903.

Brooks, Noah. *Washington in Lincoln's Time.* Edited by Herbert Mitgang. New York, 1958.

Buell, Augustus. *The Cannoneer: Recollections of Service in the Army of the Potomac.* Washington, D.C., 1890.

Carter, Robert G. *Four Brothers in Blue, or Sunshine and Shadows of the War of the Rebellion: A Story of the Great War from Bull Run to Appomattox.* Reprint. Austin, Texas, 1978.

Chamberlain Association of America. *Joshua Lawrence Chamberlain: A Sketch.* N.p., 1906.

Chamberlain, Joshua Lawrence. "Five Forks." Maine Commandery, Military Order of the Loyal Legion, *War Papers*, vol. 2. Portland, Maine, 1902.

———. "The Last Salute of the Army of Northern Virginia." *Southern Historical Society Papers* 32 (1904).

———. "My Story of Fredericksburg." *Cosmopolitan Magazine* 54 (1912).

———. *The Passing of the Armies: An Account of the Final Campaign of the Army of the Potomac Based upon Personal Reminiscences of the Fifth Army Corps* New York, 1915.

———. "Reminiscences of Petersburg and Appomattox." In Maine Commandery, Military Order of the Loyal Legion, *War Papers*, vol. 3. Portland, Maine, 1908.

———. "Through Blood and Fire at Gettysburg." *Hearst's Magazine* 23 (1913).

Clark, Calvin M. *American Slavery and Maine Congregationalists.* Bangor, Maine, 1940.

———. *History of Bangor Theological Seminary.* Boston, 1916.

Cleaveland, Nehemiah, and A. S. Packard. *History of Bowdoin College.* Boston, 1882.

Coffman, Edward M. *The Old Army: A Portrait of the American Army in Peacetime, 1784–1898.* New York, 1986.

Cooke, Jacob E. *Frederic Bancroft, Historian.* Norman, Okla., 1957.

Cunliffe, Marcus. *Soldiers and Civilians: The Martial Spirit in America, 1775–1865.* Boston, 1968.

De Forest, John. *A Volunteer's Adventures.* New Haven, 1946.

DeLeon, T. C. *Four Years in Rebel Capitals.* Mobile, Ala., 1890.

Downey, Fairfax. *The Guns at Gettysburg.* New York, 1958.

Eckert, Ralph L. *John Brown Gordon: Soldier, Southerner, American.* Baton Rouge, La., 1989.

Eliot, Ellsworth. *West Point in the Confederacy.* New York, 1941.

Emerson, Ralph Waldo. *Essays & Lectures.* New York, 1983.

Ficken, Robert E., and Charles P. LaWarne. *Washington: A Centennial History.* Seattle, 1988.

Flanders, Ralph B. *Plantation Slavery in Georgia.* Chapel Hill, N.C., 1953.

Foner, Eric. *Reconstruction: America's Unfinished Revolution, 1863–1877.* New York, 1988.

Foote, Shelby. *The Civil War: A Narrative.* 3 vols. New York, 1958–74.

Foster, Benjamin Browne. *Down East Diary.* Edited by Charles H. Foster. Orono, Maine, 1975.

Frederickson, George. *The Inner Civil War.* New York, 1965.

Freeman, Douglas Southall. *R. E. Lee: A Biography.* 4 vols. New York, 1934–36.

———. *Lee's Lieutenants: A Study in Command.* 3 vols. New York, 1942–44.

Fremantle, Arthur J. L. *Three Months in the Southern States.* Reprint. New York, 1970.

Genovese, Eugene. *The Political Economy of Slavery.* New York, 1965.

Gerrish, Theodore. *Army Life: A Private's Reminiscences of the War.* Portland, Maine, 1882.

Gordon, John B. *Reminiscences of the Civil War.* New York, 1903.

Grant, Ulysses S. *Personal Memoirs of U. S. Grant.* New York, 1990.

Green, E. L. *A History of the University of South Carolina.* Columbia, S.C., 1916.

Hall, David, ed. *Witch-hunting in 17th Century New England.* Boston, 1991.

Haskell, John Cheves. *The Haskell Memoirs.* Edited by Gilbert E. Govan and James W. Livingood. New York, 1960.

Hatch, Louis C. *The History of Bowdoin College.* Portland, Maine, 1927.

————. *Maine: A History.* New York, 1919.

Hawthorne, Nathaniel. "Chiefly about War-Matters." *The Atlantic Monthly* 10 (July 1862).

Helmreich, Ernst C. *Religion at Bowdoin College.* Brunswick, Maine, 1981.

Heseltine, William B., and Hazel C. Wolf. *Blue and Gray on the Nile.* New York, 1961.

Hirshson, Stanley P. *Farewell to the Bloody Shirt: Northern Republicans and the Southern Negro, 1877–1893.* Gloucester, Mass., 1968.

Hollis, Daniel W. *The University of South Carolina: College to University.* Columbia, S.C., 1956.

Hood, John B. "Letter to James Longstreet." *Southern Historical Society Papers* 4 (1877).

Howard, Oliver Otis. *Autobiography of Oliver Otis Howard.* 2 vols. New York, 1907.

Humphreys, Andrew A. *The Virginia Campaign of '64 and '65: The Army of the Potomac and the Army of the James.* New York, 1883.

Johnson, Robert U., and Clarence C. Buel. *Battles and Leaders of the Civil War.* 4 vols. Reprint. New York, 1956.

Johnston, Joseph E. *Narrative of Military Operations during the Late War between the States.* New York, 1874.

Kane, Harnett T. *Spies for the Blue and Gray.* Garden City, N.Y., 1954.

Klein, Maury. *Edward Porter Alexander.* Athens, Ga., 1971.

Little, George T., ed. *Genealogical and Family History of the State of Maine.* 4 vols. New York, 1909.

Longstreet, James. *From Manassas to Appomattox: Memoirs of the Civil War in America.* Edited by James I. Robertson, Jr. Bloomington, Ind., 1960.

Lonn, Ella. *Foreigners in the Confederacy.* Chapel Hill, N.C., 1940.

Lyman, Theodore. *Meade's Headquarters, 1863–1865.* Edited by George R. Agassiz. Boston, 1922.

Maine at Gettysburg. Report of the Maine Commissioners. Portland, Maine, 1898.

Marvel, William. *Burnside.* Chapel Hill, N.C., 1991.

McFeely, William. *Grant: A Biography.* New York, 1981.

McKay, Charlotte Elizabeth. *Stories of Hospital and Camp.* Philadelphia, 1876.

McPherson, James M. *Battle Cry of Freedom: The Civil War Era.* New York, 1988.

Miller, Edward H. *Salem Is My Dwelling Place: A Life of Nathaniel Hawthorne.* Iowa City, Iowa, 1991.

Morris, Roy, Jr. *Sheridan: The Life and Wars of General Phil Sheridan.* New York, 1992.

Morrison, James L. *The Best School in the World: West Point, the Pre–Civil War Years, 1833–1866.* Kent, Ohio, 1986.

Munson, Gorham. *Penobscot: Down East Paradise.* Philadelphia, 1959.

Myers, Robert Manson, ed. *Children of Pride.* New Haven, Conn., 1972.

Nash, Eugene A. *A History of the Forty-fourth Regiment, New York Volunteer Infantry, in the Civil War, 1861–1865.* Chicago, 1911.

Norton, Oliver Wilcox. *Army Letters, 1861–1865.* Chicago, 1903.

———. *The Attack and Defense of Little Round Top, July 2, 1863.* New York, 1913.

Oates, William C. "The Battle on the Right." *Southern Historical Society Papers* 6 (1878).

———. *The War between the Union and the Confederacy and Its Lost Opportunities.* New York, 1905.

Owen, William Miller. *In Camp and Battle with the Washington Artillery.* Boston, 1885.

Patterson, Gerard. *Rebels from West Point.* New York, 1987.

Pendleton, William N. *Memoirs of William Nelson Pendleton.* Edited by S. P. Lee. Philadelphia, 1893.

Porter, Horace. *Campaigning with Grant.* New York, 1897.

Powell, William H. *History of the Fifth Army Corps.* New York, 1896.

Pullen, John J. *The Twentieth Maine: A Volunteer Regiment in the Civil War.* Philadelphia, 1957.

Ross, Ishbel. *Rebel Rose: Life of Rose O'Neal Greenhow, Confederate Spy.* New York, 1954.

Royster, Charles. *The Destructive War.* New York, 1991.

Sanger, Donald B., and Thomas R. Hay. *James Longstreet.* Vol. 1, *Soldier.* Gloucester, Mass., 1968.

Schlereth, Thomas J. *Victorian America.* New York, 1991.

Sears, Stephen W. *To the Gates of Richmond: The Peninsular Campaign.* New York, 1992.

Simkins, Francis B., and Robert H. Woody. *South Carolina during Reconstruction.* Chapel Hill, N.C., 1932.

Sorrel, G. Moxley. *Recollections of a Confederate Staff Officer.* Edited by Bell I. Wiley. Jackson, Tenn., 1958.

Stanley, R. H., and George O. Hall, eds. *Eastern Maine and the Rebellion.* Bangor, 1887.

Stewart, George R. *Pickett's Charge: A Microhistory of the Final Attack at Gettysburg, July 3, 1863.* Boston, 1959.

Stover, John. *Railroads of the South, 1865–1900.* Chapel Hill, N.C., 1955.

Stowe, Charles E. *Life of Harriet Beecher Stowe.* Boston, 1889.

Strode, Hudson. *Jefferson Davis: American Patriot, 1808–1861.* New York, 1955.

Thompson, William Y. *Robert Toombs of Georgia.* Baton Rouge, La., 1966.

Thoreau, Henry David. *The Maine Woods.* New York, 1985 ed.

Trelease, Allen W. *White Terror: The Ku Klux Klan Conspiracy and Southern Reconstruction.* New York, 1971.

Trulock, Alice R. *In the Hands of Providence: Joshua Lawrence Chamberlain and the American Civil War.* Chapel Hill, N.C., 1992.

U.S. Surgeon General's Office. *The Medical and Surgical History of the War of the Rebellion.* 3 vols. Washington, D.C., 1870–88.

U.S. War Department. *The War of the Rebellion: Official Records of the Union and Confederate Armies.* 128 vols. Washington, D.C., 1880–1901.

Utley, Robert M. *Frontiersmen in Blue: The United States Army and the Indian, 1848–1865.* New York, 1967.

Wainwright, Charles. *A Diary of Battle.* Edited by Allan Nevins. New York, 1962.

Wasson, George S. *Sailing Days on the Penobscot.* Salem, Mass., 1932.

Wert, Jeffry D. *General James Longstreet: The Confederacy's Most Controversial Soldier.* New York, 1993.

Whitman, William, and Charles H. True. *Maine in the War for the Union.* Lewiston, Maine, 1865.

Wiley, Bell I. *Southern Negroes, 1861–1865.* New Haven, 1938.

Willey, Austin. *The History of the Antislavery Cause in State and Nation.* Reprint, New York, 1969.

Willingham, Robert M., Jr. *No Jubilee: The Story of Confederate Wilkes.* Washington, Ga., 1976.

———. *We Have This Heritage: The History of Wilkes County, Georgia.* Washington, Ga., 1969.

Wilson, Edmund. *Patriotic Gore: Studies in the Literature of the American Civil War.* Boston, 1984.

Wilson, Forrest. *Crusader in Crinoline: The Life of Harriet Beecher Stowe.* Westport, Conn., 1941.

Wise, Jennings C. *The Long Arm of Lee: The History of the Artillery of the Army of Northern Virginia.* Reprint. New York, 1959.

Woodward, C. Vann. *Reunion and Reaction: The Compromise of 1877 and the End of Reconstruction.* Boston, 1966.

WPA Writers Program. *The Story of Washington-Wilkes.* Athens, Ga., 1941.

INDEX